The Teaching Ministry of Congregations

THE TEACHING MINISTRY
OF CONGREGATIONS

Richard Robert Osmer

WESTMINSTER
JOHN KNOX PRESS
LOUISVILLE · KENTUCKY

Scripture quotations from the New Revised Standard Version of the Bible are copyright © 1989 by the Division of Christian Education of the National Council of the Churches of Christ in the U.S.A. and are used by permission.

Excerpt from *Les Misérables* by Alain Boublil and Claude Michel Schänb. Lyrics by Alain Boublil, Herbert Kretzmer, and Jean-Marc Natel. © Alain Boublil Music Ltd. Used by permission.

Book design by Sharon Adams
Cover design by Pam Poll Graphic Design
Cover art: Deep Signal *by Josef Albers/Musee Carnavalet, Paris/Superstock.* © 2005 The Josef *and Anni Albers Foundation/Artists Rights Society (ARS), New York*

First edition
Published by Westminster John Knox Press
Louisville, Kentucky

This book is printed on acid-free paper that meets the American National Standards Institute Z39.48 standard. ∞

PRINTED IN THE UNITED STATES OF AMERICA

05 06 07 08 09 10 11 12 13 14 — 10 9 8 7 6 5 4 3 2 1

Library of Congress Cataloging-in-Publication Data

Osmer, Richard Robert.
    The teaching ministry of congregations / Richard Robert Osmer.— 1st ed.
        p. cm.
    ISBN 0–664–22547–0 (alk. paper)
        1. Christian education. 2 Theology, Practical. 3. Church—Teaching office. I. Title.

BV1471.3.O86 2005
268—dc22

2005042230

To James Fowler
Mentor, Colleague, and Friend

The teaching of the wise is a fountain of life.
Proverbs 13:14

Contents

Acknowledgments

This project would not have been possible without the help of many friends and colleagues. This is especially true of my research on three congregations described in part 2. In each congregation, key people paved my way. I offer special thanks to Joyce Mackickon Walker of Nassau Presbyterian Church; Kyoo-Min Lee, formerly of Somang Presbyterian Church; and Jaco Coetsee and Rodney Tshaka of the Uniting Reformed Church of Stellenbosch. In addition to these people, many others have contributed to my understanding of these congregations: Phil-Eun Lee, Dirk Smit, Hyun-Sook Kim, Shin-Geun Jang, Wallace Alston, Jr., Johan Botha, and David Davis. In addition to these persons, colleagues at Princeton Theological Seminary served as conversation partners as I developed my understanding of the teaching ministry: Kenda Creasy Dean, Gordon Mikoski, Wentzel van Huyssteen, Ross Wagner, and Beverly Roberts Gaventa. Three of my dialogue partners passed away while this book was being written: James Loder, Donald Juel, and Hee-Chun Kang. My appreciation of their contribution is tempered by sadness that I cannot thank them personally. More than they will ever know, students in ED101—An Introduction to Christian Education have helped me develop the perspective offered in this book with their questions and comments.

Doctoral students who have served as preceptors in this course have contributed as well, especially Theresa Latini, Andy Root, Ajit Prasadam, and Jana Strukova. While they were not preceptors for me in this course, Thomas Hastings, Tony Jones, and Jessicah Krey Duckworth have contributed through their thoughtful participation in doctoral seminars. Thanks to all of you!

I have been fortunate to enter the field of practical theology during a period of creative ferment and have learned much from the generation of practical theologians preceding me, through their writings and the International Academy of Practical Theology. Among these colleagues, I want to thank especially Don Browning, Hans van der Ven, Albert Ploeger, Duncan Forrester, Karl Ernst Nipkow, the late Charles Gerkin, Allen and Mary Elizabeth Moore, and Rodney Hunter. One individual deserves special thanks, Friedrich Schweitzer; through our work together on a book project, my understanding of practical theology has been deepened enormously.

Several people must be singled out for the special contribution they made to this book. My editor at Westminster John Knox Press, Stephanie Egnotovitch, offered timely and insightful comments at each step of the way. Special thanks also to Don Parker-Burgard who did an excellent job as copyeditor of this project. Sandra Kunz, a doctoral student at Princeton Theological Seminary, served as my editorial assistant while I was writing a final draft. Without her good judgment and words of encouragement, this project would never have seen the light of day. Janise Matyas Smith, an MDiv student at PTS, read and corrected the final draft as well.

My family has traveled with me as I have written this book, both literally and figuratively. At points, my wife Sally has provided insight on the congregations I was investigating and feedback on my writing. Sarah and Richard, my two children, have passed from adolescence to adulthood while this book was written. Thanks for your understanding and loving support.

Finally, special thanks and appreciation must be offered to James Fowler. My relationship with Jim extends all the way back to Harvard Divinity School, where I was a student in his early classes on faith development theory. Later, at Emory University, he was the director of my dissertation. But he was much more than that; he has been a generous mentor and, later, a colleague and friend. In thanks for all he has given me over the years and to honor his enormous contributions to the field of practical theology, this book is dedicated to him.

Introduction

In 1995, I had the good fortune of viewing a special exhibition in Chicago of the French impressionist Claude Monet. As I wandered from room to room, I was particularly struck by the way Monet treated similar themes in various series, painting repeatedly water lilies, a bridge over a pond, sheaves of wheat in an open field, and the Rouen Cathedral. While the subject matter was similar in each series, it was portrayed in remarkably different ways, reflecting shifts in the time of day or season.

Several years later, I experienced the power of another series in an exhibition of the portraits of Vincent van Gogh. In one of the rooms was a series of self-portraits that van Gogh had painted during the last four years of his life. Each self-portrait was remarkably different in terms of facial structure, facial expression, background, clothing, line, texture, and color.

In their series, Monet and van Gogh invite us to look at a subject and, then, to look again to see something new, as if they are telling us that a single perspective is not enough to capture the fullness of a situation or person. This is particularly evident in van Gogh's self-portraits. In one painting, he appears as a solid, middle-class Dutch businessman, looking away from us with clear eyes, clothed in a stylish coat and hat, and surrounded by a tranquil blue background. In another, he peers out with a slightly tilted, sideways glance, wearing a farmer's clothes, his face set off by a murky gray background. In still another, he appears hatless, his gaze meeting ours and his face offset by short, densely textured brush-strokes of black, dark green, and red—a painting technique also found in *Starry Night*. The background flows into his coat and seems to link him to the sur-rounding cosmos. "I am all of these people," van Gogh seems to say. "If you would understand who I am, you must look and then look again."

Similarly, this book is a series of portraits of congregations. It seeks to portray the teaching ministry of congregations located in different times and places. To understand this ministry in its richness and depth, we must look not once, but several times. No single perspective can capture everything. As you read this book, imagine yourself as traveling through three different rooms of a single exhi-bition. The first room you enter (in part 1) features portraits of Paul's teaching ministry in congregations that were just taking shape as the Jesus movement spread beyond Palestine to the Greco-Roman cities of the first century. In this room, look closely at the congregational portraits emerging from Paul's letters. You are asked to see with fresh eyes the important role teaching played in the building up and edification of these communities. Something important and lasting will emerge from our time in this room, a portrait of three core tasks of the teaching ministry of congregations: catechesis, exhortation, and discernment.

You leave this room and enter a second in part 2. Here you are invited to examine portraits of three contemporary congregations located in different parts of the world: Somang Presbyterian Church of Seoul, Korea; Nassau Presbyterian Church of Princeton, New Jersey; and the Uniting Reformed Church of Stellen-bosch, South Africa. Each of these congregations in its own, unique way has a strong teaching ministry. Like the similar but quite different paintings in Monet's and van Gogh's series, they will help us see different dimensions of this ministry.

You enter a third room in part 3. In a sense, this room is more like an artist's studio than a gallery of completed portraits. Here you are provided with materi-als and implements to create a portrait of your own congregation's teaching min-istry. You become the artist in this room, pulling together the insights that have emerged from your examination of the portraits of other congregations and then plunging into the task of working with the living material of your own particu-lar community. This requires creativity and imagination on your part. It chal-lenges you to step into the artistry of guiding the teaching ministry of your own particular congregation.

It is usually helpful to know something about the encompassing perspective of the exhibition as a whole before you begin to make your way from room to room. The same may be true of the exhibition of this book as well. What is the encompassing perspective that binds together the different portraits emerging in the pages that follow? Throughout this book, I am creating portraits of the teach-ing ministry using methods appropriate to the field of practical theology. Simply put, the methodological commitments guiding my work as a practical theologian are based on the conviction that theology plays a constitutive role in determining what counts as "ministry" and "teaching" in Christian congregations. This represents a departure from the religious education perspective so dominant in the United States and elsewhere for much of the past century, which has largely run its course.

Throughout the past century, many American religious education theorists employed what might be called a generic model of religious education. In this model, religious education was defined in terms of general characteristics that supposedly applied to all religious communities, using the frameworks of philosophy, modern education, and the social sciences. What was lost in this approach was the reality of religious pluralism. Muslim, Buddhist, Jewish, and Christian communities do not view their educational tasks in exactly the same way. In large measure, the nature and purpose of education in these different religious communities are determined on the basis of their distinctive beliefs and practices. Each community's understanding of education emerges from the web of normative commitments that articulate its particular vision of the ultimate purpose of existence and the way of life that best corresponds to this vision. What is this religious community's understanding of the origin, purpose, and final outcome of the world? How are humans to live if they are to align themselves with this picture of ultimate reality?

The answers to these questions vary widely from one religious community to another and shape their understanding of the purpose of teaching and education along very different lines. Some Buddhist communities, for example, do not believe that teaching doctrine is particularly helpful on the path to enlightenment. In contrast, Protestant Christianity historically has viewed the cultivation of deeper understanding of the doctrines of the church as an important part of the teaching ministry. Obviously, a generic, "one size fits all" model of religious education fails to acknowledge these sorts of differences. It also fails to acknowledge the significant differences *within* religious communities over the nature and purpose of religious education, which often reflect internal arguments over the normative shape of their beliefs and practices.

Attempting to avoid the particularity of these sorts of normative claims, and thereby avoid the realities of genuine religious pluralism, is like a con man's shell game. The pea is secretly smuggled under another shell through a sleight of hand. Normative claims were inevitably made in the older, generic model of religious education, but they were smuggled in under the pretense of a generalized philosophical, educational, social scientific, or ethical perspective. It is time to stop being taken in by this shell game. The reality of religious pluralism forces us to acknowledge and justify at the outset our normative convictions. This is the starting point for genuine dialogue across and within different religious communities.

I use a practical theological perspective (defined below) over the course of this book to acknowledge the inherently normative and theological dimension of any attempt to portray the nature and purpose of "religious education" in

Christian communities. Indeed, for the most part, I have dropped the older, generic model's nomenclature altogether, using terms such as "teaching ministry" or "Christian education" to signal the theological basis of my construal of education in and for Christian congregations. In Christian communities, teaching is a form of ministry; ministry is a way of building up congregations for mission; congregations discover their mission within the missions of the triune God. These sorts of convictions and the practices that embody them inform the understanding of the teaching ministry in the chapters that follow. Practical theology acknowledges the importance of such convictions, even as it brings them into conversation with the cultural resources of our contemporary world through interdisciplinary dialogue.

What do I mean by practical theology? Briefly put, *practical theology is that branch of Christian theology that seeks to construct action-guiding theories of Christian praxis in particular social contexts.* In part, it focuses on "how to"—how to teach, preach, raise children, influence society, and so forth. But this "how to" is informed by a strongly developed theory of "why to"—why we ought to practice the Christian way of life in certain ways in light of an interpretation of a particular social context and the normative claims of the Christian community.

Practical theology as a distinct branch of theology emerged in the modern period, largely under the seminal influence of the great German theologian Friedrich Schleiermacher.[1] Yet something like practical theology has always been present in the Christian community, as its leaders and scholars have reflected on the normative shape of Christian praxis and developed models of how it is best conducted. Augustine's theory of preaching in book 4 of *On Christian Doctrine* can certainly be viewed in this way, as can his theory of teaching found in *On Christian Teaching*. Manuals on preaching, leadership, the cure of souls, the moral life, and many other areas of Christian practice appeared throughout the Middle Ages. Indeed, many examples of "proto" practical theology can be found throughout the Christian tradition. But it was not until the modern period that practical theology became a distinct branch of theology. This was prompted by the rise of the modern university, with its more specialized research disciplines, and by the challenge of increasingly differentiated, secular institutions, which forced the church to reflect on the continuing viability of its traditional practices and norms. Henceforth, practical theology was to be a part of the fourfold theological encyclopedia, which also included biblical studies, church history, and dogmatic theology.

The emergence and history of practical theology during the modern period has been traced in greater detail elsewhere, and there is no need to rehearse that story here. Of special importance to the understanding of practical theology informing this book, however, is discussion in this field that began to emerge in the 1960s. Almost from the beginning, this discussion was international in scope, supported initially through a series of consultations involving North American and European scholars, and then through the emergence of the International Academy of Practical Theology and the *International Journal of Practical Theol-*

ogy. Like every field today, this discussion is characterized by a high degree of pluralism. The full range of theological perspectives found in other theological disciplines is found in practical theology as well—from liberation and feminist perspectives to Barthian, evangelical, and charismatic perspectives, with many in between.

Yet within this pluralistic discussion, four distinguishable but mutually influential tasks have emerged as central to practical theology as a field: the descriptive-empirical, the interpretive, the normative, and the pragmatic. Attending to all four of these tasks allows practical theologians to construct action-guiding theories of contemporary Christian praxis. In the epilogue, I explore some of the methodological decisions that lead various practical theologians to carry out these four tasks in quite different ways, helping us make sense of the pluralism of this field.

The *descriptive-empirical* task asks: What is going on? It focuses on the actual state of some form of Christian praxis in a particular social context. It seeks to investigate empirically and to describe as fully and accurately as possible a particular field of experience. Sometimes this sort of empirical research can be taken over from other fields, especially the social sciences. In recent years, however, many practical theologians have come to recognize the importance of carrying out their own empirical research.[2] Social scientists often are uninterested in the questions of greatest importance to contemporary religious communities and sometimes work with reductionistic understandings of religion.

This task is the primary focus of part 2. There I draw on the qualitative research methods of congregational studies to examine three congregations as case studies. While working empirically, I also give attention to the kinds of interests practical theologians bring to this task. In addition to the perspectives of sociology and cultural anthropology that are central to congregational studies, I also interpret each congregation theologically. I develop a "theological discrimen," a central image or theme that attempts to capture in a single synoptic judgment various facets of each congregation's identity, ethos, and mission.[3]

The *interpretive* task asks: Why is this going on? The data of empirical research is not self-interpreting. It must be placed in a more comprehensive framework, offering an explanation of patterns of behavior, attitudes, and ideas. On the surface, it would seem that a sequencing of these tasks necessarily follows: first description, then interpretation. It would be a mistake to view them in this way, however. In recent years, researchers in many fields have come to acknowledge the various ways their interpretive commitments inform their empirical investigation, shaping what they "see." Interpretation interpenetrates description and, in turn, description has the potential of opening up and correcting interpretation. Often the anomalies of empirical research—data not fitting the researcher's expectations—lead to revisions in an interpretive framework. While distinguishable, the descriptive-empirical and interpretive tasks of practical theology stand in a mutually influential relationship.

I undertake this sort of interpretation at a variety of points in this book. First and most obviously, it is present in the discussion of globalization and modernization in the introduction to part 2. In dialogue with the work of Hans van der Ven, I interpret the teaching ministry of contemporary congregations in terms of the changing functions of religion in the contexts of modernity and early globalization. In this part of the book, I also develop other interpretive perspectives on the teaching ministry, what I will call interdisciplinary "frames."

The *normative* task of practical theology asks: What forms *ought* Christian praxis take in this particular social context? It focuses on the construction of theological and ethical norms with which to assess, guide, and reform some dimension of contemporary Christian praxis. Here practical theology looks to the normative sources of the Christian faith. While it is primarily at this point that practical theology will enter into dialogue with disciplines such as Christian biblical studies, dogmatic theology, and Christian ethics, the norms of praxis it constructs are not merely the application of the normative proposals of these fields.

This is the case for two reasons. First, practical theology makes use of different theological forms and patterns in its constructive work. It does not develop doctrines, as in dogmatic theology, or commentaries, as in biblical studies. Rather, it seeks to articulate models of divine and human action that allow Christians to better understand the patterns of God's praxis in the world and to shape the patterns of their lives and communities accordingly.[4] Second, practical theology develops normative perspectives that are closely related to the particular context and practices it has in view. It seeks to develop proposals that can shape a particular form of praxis in a particular historical and/or social context. Norms of praxis in practical theology, thus, are context dependent in a strong sense.

I begin this book by developing a normative perspective on the teaching ministry of congregations. By examining Paul's teaching ministry with his congregations, I construct a theory of the core tasks of the teaching ministry of congregations. I also construct a normative perspective in chapter 8, where I enter into a dialogue with Jürgen Moltmann, developing an account of congregations within the "Theo-drama" of the triune God's creating, redeeming, and glorifying of the world.

The *pragmatic* task of practical theology asks: How might this area of praxis be shaped to more fully embody the normative commitments of the Christian tradition in a particular context of experience? It focuses on the development of action-guiding models and rules of art (open-ended guidelines about how to carry out some form of Christian praxis).[5] The primary focus at this point is on matters of "how to." How might a youth group discussion be structured to support moral reflection and growth? How might families hand on the faith to their children in the midst of their busy lives? What sort of Christian education will equip the members of a congregation to influence the policies of their government? When we pose questions like these, it becomes clear that rules of art are not guidelines that can be applied in a mechanical or rote fashion. They presuppose creativity and good judgment on the part of the practitioner, who must determine a fitting course of action in a particular context of experience. The pragmatic task is the focal point of the final three chapters of this book. There readers will enter what I called above the "artist's studio," exploring models and methods that might prove helpful in guiding the teaching ministries of their own particular congregations.

This then is the encompassing perspective of the gallery you are about to enter. It portrays the teaching ministry in ways that are appropriate to the field of practical theology. So let us begin. Bring your Bibles with you as you enter the first room, for we begin with Christian Scripture and Paul's teaching ministry in congregations.

PART ONE
PAUL'S TEACHING
MINISTRY:
Catechesis, Exhortation, and Discernment

Introduction to Part One

After entering the West Wing of the National Gallery of Art in Washington, DC, my wife and I walked straight ahead to the Rotunda, a beautiful circular area with marble columns surrounding a fountain. We immediately faced a decision. We only had the afternoon to spend in the Gallery. Where should we start and spend most of our time? There was no way to see everything, even briefly. We stood in the rotunda and considered our options.

So too, in this book, as we enter the first room of our gallery, we have decisions to make. Why start with Paul? Why not examine the Gospels' depictions of Jesus' teaching ministry or the shape of the teaching office that emerges in the Pastoral Epistles? Why not investigate the diversity of teaching practices found in ancient Israel? Why settle for one portion of Scripture? The easy answer to these questions would be to say it is simply a matter of personal preference and taste. My wife and I share a love for the French impressionists, so our decision in the rotunda of the National Gallery was not all that difficult. We went straight to the part of the museum where their paintings were located and spent most of our time there. Perhaps the decision to focus on Paul is similarly a matter of personal preference and taste. Through the accidents of scholarly training and upbringing, I have acquired a taste for Paul over the years. Maybe it has something to do with my two years of study at Harvard Divinity School, where my classes in the New Testament were taught entirely by European Lutherans, who are notorious for their preoccupation with the Pauline "canon within the canon." Or perhaps I acquired this taste as a Presbyterian raised in the southern United States, weaned on the Pauline themes of justification by grace through faith and divine election.

No doubt, such subjective factors have entered into the decision to start with Paul. But surely it is not *just* a matter of personal preference and taste? After all, there is no accounting for taste! There are two ways of responding to this issue— one that is short and relatively easy to follow and a second that is a bit more complex. Let's start short and easy.

Paul's letters provide us with the earliest and most direct route into the New Testament's treatment of our topic: the teaching ministry of congregations. Most scholars believe that 1 Thessalonians is the earliest complete writing in the New Testament and that Paul's other letters were written during the earliest decades of the spread of the Jesus movement to the urban centers of the Greco-Roman world. Moreover, Paul's correspondence is addressed directly to congregations. With the exception of Romans, his letters are written for congregations he helped establish and knew intimately. When we study this correspondence closely, we gain insight into the sort of teaching ministry Paul and his coworkers appear to have carried out in these congregations, a ministry they equipped others to continue in their absence.

Yet this leaves us with a second, more complex issue. Isn't it arbitrary to make normative claims about the teaching ministry of congregations on the basis of such a small slice of Scripture? An alternate strategy would be to locate Paul within the New Testament or biblical canon as a whole. But this would not really solve our problem. While helping us to become more aware of the diversity of models of teaching found across the biblical canon, we still would face the task of deciding which of these different models might warrant normative proposals today. Unless one opted for the problematic strategy of synthesis—which seeks to transcend canonical diversity by positing some higher-order, abstract whole that supposedly represents the "biblical" perspective on the teaching ministry— we still face the complex hermeneutical task of weighing some portions of Scripture as more helpful than others.

SITUATED RATIONAL CONVERSATION

In contrast to this sort of synthetic strategy, I am guided by the idea that scholarship of all sorts, including the investigation of Scripture, is best pictured along the lines of a situated rational conversation. The notion of *rational conversation* points to the turn away from a model of rationality grounded in the modern philosophy of consciousness and its picture of reason as an activity in the mind of a solitary individual. It signals the turn toward a communicative model of rationality that pictures reason as a special kind of conversation within a community in which the participants search together for the truth. Sometimes this is viewed along the lines of formal argumentation in which the participants make claims, provide supporting evidence, receive challenges from others in the conversation, and attempt to defend their claims. Sometimes it takes the form of an open, mutual dialogue in which all parties have something to contribute and work together to build shared understanding. Different cultures have developed a wide variety of forms of rational communication to search for the truth.

This is an important part of what I mean by describing rational conversation as *situated*. Different communities and disciplines draw on the resources they have at their disposal in the search for truth. The patterns and forums they use are based on their particular values, the procedures of truth seeking they have devised, and the rhetorical norms of persuasion that are shared in the community. Rationality, thus, is always situated within the particular constellation of resources a community has at its disposal in the search for truth. How does this model of rationality as a situated rational conversation help us with the issue raised above, the seemingly arbitrary nature of the decision to focus on Paul? It helps in four ways.

First, *it encourages us to work with a chastened view of reason.* There is no escaping the fact that our scholarly work is always situated, grounded in the particular resources at our disposal and the particular focus of our work. In other words, the decision to engage Paul as a dialogue partner in the normative task of practical theology is no more or less arbitrary than the decision to use alternative strategies. The fact that it is situated does not mean it is simply a matter of personal preference and taste. I began by offering some of the reasons I believe that Paul is especially helpful in this project's examination of the teaching ministry of congregations. No doubt, other strategies might be used, but they would be equally limited as well. What is necessary is to give good reasons for our choices, not to pretend that we might adopt the one perfect strategy. All scholarship is situated in this sense.

Second, *this model provides us a vantage point on contemporary forms of biblical scholarship that will help us explore Paul's letters.* Pauline studies today is characterized by a high degree of pluralism. If historical criticism was dominant in the recent past, this is certainly no longer the case. Literary, rhetorical, and cultural forms of criticism are now viewed as equally important. This makes the task of entering into a rational conversation with this field more complex. Certain decisions have to be made as to which of these disciplinary perspectives are most helpful in pursuing the primary task of this book and in interpreting particular biblical texts. It is quite common in contemporary biblical studies for well-respected scholars to interpret the same text quite differently, depending on their values, disciplinary perspective, and other factors. Their interpretive judgments are situated in the sense described above, as are my own as I draw on their research. Here again, we should not expect to find the one true "biblical" perspective based on scholarly consensus. Rather, we must give reasons for our interpretive judgments and acknowledge the ways they are grounded in a particular constellation of hermeneutical commitments.

Third, *this helps us conceptualize the nature of cross-disciplinary dialogue in practical theology.* In the introduction, I described this book as an exercise in practical theology in which theology enters into a dialogue with other fields. Rational conversation across disciplinary lines takes place at a number of points in this book. The dialogue with biblical studies in the first part of the book gives way to conversation with the modern social sciences, dogmatic theology, and Christian ethics in the second and third parts. In the epilogue, I describe more fully the range of ways contemporary practical theologians carry out this sort of interdisciplinary conversation. I will argue that in light of the pluralism characterizing virtually all fields today, we will do well to view this as a situated conversation between particular persons and perspectives rather than as an abstract, generalized dialogue between one field and another (e.g., between theology and science). Interdisciplinary conversation in this sense is person- and perspective-specific and, as such, is a situated rational conversation across disciplinary lines.

Fourth, *this model allows us to view Paul as engaged in a situated rational conversation with his congregations.* The fact that Paul presupposes certain beliefs and values—for example, Jesus Christ as the apocalypse of God—does not rule out the inherently rational orientation of his letter writing. He reasons on the basis of his beliefs and values. Moreover, only rarely does he simply assert his apostolic authority; it is more common for him to appeal to the judgment and reasoning of his readers. He makes use of the cultural and religious resources at his disposal to convince his readers of the truth of the gospel and the implications it has for their shared life. What are the resources that Paul uses to carry out this situated rational conversation with his congregations? How does he adapt and transform these cultural and religious resources as he puts them to his own pastoral use? Some of the most important are described below.

THE RESOURCES OF RATIONALITY IN PAUL'S LETTERS

Letter writing. It is commonly accepted by scholars that Paul adopted the standard form of the Greco-Roman letter in composing his letters.[1] This should not be taken for granted. All communication, especially the communication of rational conversation, works within the socially established genres of a community.[2] Paul's adaptation of the genre of the letter is the first move he makes in engaging his predominantly Gentile congregations to join him in reflecting together on the meaning of the gospel for their lives. It allows him to tap into shared expectations, which orient his readers to the overall structure of his argument. When he reworks or varies these expectations, it has the effect of underscoring particular points he is trying to make.

Rhetoric. In recent decades, scholars have given special attention to the influence of Greco-Roman rhetoric on Paul.[3] Paul expected his letters to be read aloud to his congregations in the context of worship (e.g., 1 Thess. 5:27; and Phlm. 2). While I will use the phrase "Paul's readers" throughout this book, you would do well to keep in mind that his letters were probably *heard* before they were *read.* Often they were delivered by one of Paul's coworkers, who read them on Paul's behalf and explained their contents in greater depth. The letters were "stand-ins" for Paul's presence, and their oral delivery by a trusted associate was one of the most important ways Paul maintained his apostolic relationship to congregations in spite of long periods of absence. It is no accident, thus, that Paul seems to craft his letters in ways that take into account the fact that they will be "performed" orally—precisely the focus of rhetoric in antiquity.[4]

Rhetoric was an important art in the ancient world. It focused on teaching free men how to speak persuasively in public life. Serious proponents of this art, such as Isocrates, Cicero, and Quintillian, claimed that true rhetoric is based on the search for truth and goodness. Rhetors were to appeal to the ability of their hearers to reason and make judgments and not merely to "dupe" them into accepting a particular point of view.[5] In Paul's use of various rhetorical strategies in his letters, thus, he was adopting antiquity's most highly developed approach to rational conversation in public forums.

Moral exhortation in popular philosophy. Outside of Christianity, the schools of popular moral philosophy were the only other arena in which the language of conversion was prominent in the Greco-Roman world. They portrayed the acceptance of philosophy as conversion to a new and better way of life.[6] After their conversion, the new disciples of a particular philosophical school were thought to need a "doctor of the soul" to guide them with a combination of encouragement, moral exhortation, and instruction in the philosophical doctrines of the community. This special mentoring was commonly known as *psychagogy* and frequently was offered by way of letters due to the difficulties of travel.

While no standard classification of these letters emerged in antiquity, Stanley Stowers posits a basic distinction between *protreptic* and *paraenetic* letters, based on models found in Isocrates and Aristotle.[7] Protreptic letters challenged the recipient to convert to the philosophical way of life. Paraenetic letters assumed that this conversion has already taken place and focused on two things: (1) encouragement toward the moral ideals of the philosophical school, and (2) dissuasion from habits, attitudes, or courses of action that were viewed as detrimental to the recipient's moral progress. Prominent in these paraenetic letters was the theme of imitation, as writers pointed to their own lives or to the lives of others as examples that might be followed.

These letters varied widely in the degree of censure or praise offered. *Friendly letters* projected a positive tone, offering the mildest form of criticism and urging recipients to continue on the path they were already traveling. *Letters of admonition* warned the recipients of missteps they had taken, attempting to evoke a sense of shame and the need for change. *Letters of rebuke* adopted a harsher tone, calling attention to fundamental flaws in the recipient's character and making use of expressions like "I am amazed!" and "How can you be so foolish!" that were designed to dissuade the recipients from continuing along their current path. *Letters of reproach* offered the harshest form of criticism deemed beneficial, leveling an accusation against an individual who had benefited from the writer's generosity in the past.

Even a general familiarity with the Pauline corpus allows one to recognize the language, tone, and themes of paraenetic letters in contexts where Paul is dealing with matters of moral formation and education (something we will explore in chapter 2). Here again, we find Paul drawing on the resources of his cultural context to carry on a rational conversation with his congregations. Perhaps Paul's Gentile converts were familiar with this tradition of moral exhortation, affording him a convenient language and conceptual framework with which to discuss their postconversion moral life in Christ.

Practices and principles of Scripture interpretation. Paul cites Israel's Scripture close to a hundred times in his undisputed letters. He also frequently alludes to biblical stories and events and makes use of biblical motifs. In his treatment of this material, Paul sometimes draws on practices and principles of Scripture interpretation used by Jewish scholars and by other Christians during this period.[8] It is possible that Paul learned these practices and principles through his education as a Pharisee schooled in the interpretation of the Torah.

Christopher Stanley's careful study of Paul's citation techniques, for example, has shown that his slight alterations of the grammar or wording of biblical texts was a common practice during this period.[9] Likewise, Paul sometimes makes use of the interpretive practice of *gezerah shewa,* based on the principle of analogy, in which similar words or phrases in different passages of Scripture are linked together and used to interpret one another.[10] In addition to these kinds of "midrashic" interpretive practices, scholars also have detected Paul's reliance on a method of interpretation called *pesher,* used widely in the Qumran community. This involves citing a verse of Scripture and then offering an eschatologically oriented interpretation that portrays it as being fulfilled in the community's present situation.[11]

PAUL'S TRANSFORMATION OF THE RESOURCES OF RATIONALITY

This brief sampling of some of the ways Paul draws on the resources of rationality available in his own time and place is by no means exhaustive. But it is sufficient for us to see that Paul is engaged in a process of rational persuasion in his letters and that he makes use of cultural and religious resources close at hand in order to do so. It would be misleading, however, if we were to stop at this point, for Paul transforms and adapts these resources as he puts them to a new and different use. His rhetoric, for example, is not addressed to a political assembly or a court of law. Nor is he making an after-dinner speech. He is addressing congregations he believes have been called into being through the proclamation of the gospel, an announcement of the apocalyptic event of God's salvific action in the death and resurrection of Jesus Christ. He regards this announcement as something new and decisive, as effecting salvation among those who believe and as accompanied by powerful manifestations of God's Spirit. In his letters, he is reminding his readers that they are God's new covenant people and is teaching them how to refashion their identities to better embody their calling, justification, and sanctification in Christ Jesus. It is the unique character of the gospel Paul announces that ultimately gives shape to the epistolary conventions, rhetoric, moral exhortation, and practices of Scripture interpretation he employs in his letters.[12]

In part 1, we explore the purpose and key tasks of Paul's teaching ministry in congregations. While I will draw on scholarly commentaries, I will not work my way systematically through all of Paul's letters in detail. Rather, I will focus in depth on those parts of his corpus throwing light on the key tasks of his teaching ministry. The portraits that emerge are closer to a collage than a representational painting. They place bits and pieces side-by-side to build up a sense of the whole.

Chapter 1

The Purpose of Paul's Teaching Ministry in Congregations

In this chapter, we explore two bodies of material that provide insight into the purpose of Paul's teaching ministry in congregations. The first focuses on the "pattern of teaching" Paul associates with baptism in Romans 6. The second explores his discussion of edification, building up the Christian community in love, found in 1 Corinthians 3–4 and 12–14.

BAPTISM: THE FOUNDATION OF THE TEACHING MINISTRY

Paul did not found the Christian community in Rome, nor had he visited this community when he wrote Romans. In this letter, he is, in effect, proclaiming the gospel to the Roman Christians in written form. It is a gospel in which the righteousness of God is portrayed as revealed and enacted in the death and resurrection of Jesus Christ, a righteousness in which believers participate by virtue of their faith in Christ apart from observance of the law. An important part of Paul's rational conversation with the Romans about these matters is his argument from baptism in Romans 6. In the context of this argument, he makes reference to teaching in verses 17–18: "But thanks be to God that you, having once been slaves of sin, have become obedient from the heart to the form of teaching to which you were entrusted, and that you, having been set free from sin, have become slaves of righteousness." What does Paul mean by "the form of teaching," and what is its relationship to his discussion of baptism? By considering these questions, we gain insight into his understanding of the purpose of the teaching ministry.

The Rhetorical Situation of Romans

We will begin our examination of Romans 6 by attempting to discern the rhetorical situation Paul is addressing in this letter.[1] Both the actual text of Romans and historical accounts of this period throw light on this situation, helping us better understand the various strategies of persuasion that shape Paul's rational conversation with the Roman community. Recall that Paul adapts the standard structure of Greco-Roman letters: opening, body, and conclusion. Since the opening section includes not only an identification of the sender (1:1–6) and recipient (v. 7a) but also a prayer of thanksgiving (vv. 8–15) and summary of the letter's central theme (vv. 16–17), we would expect to find indications of Paul's reasons for writing the letter in these first few verses.

In the opening prayer, Paul expresses his desire to visit the Roman Christians for three reasons: to impart a spiritual gift for mutual strength and encouragement (vv. 11–12), to reap a harvest among the Gentiles of Rome (v. 13), and to proclaim the gospel to them (v. 15). The third reason spills over into Paul's statement of the theme of the letter in verses 16–17, where he describes the gospel as the "power of God for salvation to everyone who has faith, to the Jew first and also to the Greek" and as revealing the righteousness of God "through faith for faith." We receive a clear signal here that much of what follows will deal with the topic of God's righteousness, and a large portion of the body of the letter (1:18–11:36) does indeed focus on God's "rectifying" of sinners as an act of grace that is accepted in faith, which stands at the heart of Paul's understanding of the gospel.[2]

Why would Paul think that he needs to proclaim the gospel to the Roman Christians, for they are Christians already? One reason is that Paul hopes to gain the Roman Christians' support for his future missionary work in Spain (15:23–24). The letter represents an initial presentation of the gospel to lay the groundwork for future cooperation. But something more seems to be at stake in Paul's extensive discussion of righteousness through faith apart from the law. As Brendan Byrne notes, the law functions as a kind of "fall guy" for much of the letter, with Paul arguing repeatedly against any notion of law righteousness.[3] This is not a topic that he develops in all of his letters. The one other letter where it also is treated extensively is Galatians, where Paul confronts Jewish Christian teachers who have successfully persuaded some of the Gentile members of this congregation that they must accept key markers of law observance if they are to become full members of God's people.[4] Paul's response in that letter is to "re-evangelize" the Galatians, as Louis Martyn puts it, reproclaiming the gospel the Galatian Christians had accepted in the past.[5] While there are no indications that these teachers have come to Rome, it is possible that Paul has this conflict in mind when he writes Romans. He is offering the Christians in Rome a kind of preventative medicine that will inoculate them against this potential threat.

The historical circumstances surrounding the Christian community lend plausibility to this line of interpretation. According to the Roman historian Suetonius, the emperor Claudius expelled the Jewish community from Rome around 49 CE because of constant rioting at the instigation of "Chrestus." Many scholars believe Suetonius was referring to strife in the Jewish community caused by Jews who had become followers of Christ.[6] In Acts 18:2, we are told that Paul meets a Jewish Christian couple, Aquila and Priscilla, in Corinth after they have left Rome because of Claudius's edict. With the expulsion of all Jewish converts from Rome, the Christian community would have been composed entirely of Gentiles. They would have been given the opportunity to develop their own leaders and an identity apart from the synagogue. After the lapse of this edict in 54 CE, many Jewish Christians returned to Rome. Aquila and Priscilla did so, as indicated in Romans 16:3. This was a situation with potential for real conflict, with Jewish Christians returning to Rome eager to regain their leadership in the community and to restore a more traditional, Jewish form of Christianity. It is also possible that some of these returning Jewish Christians would have been exposed to the teachings of Paul's opponents in Galatians during their sojourn abroad.

We must tread cautiously in our use of this sort of historical reconstruction. But this scenario does provide a plausible interpretation of the rhetorical situation Paul seems to be addressing throughout the letter. In the face of an alternative understanding of the gospel that portrays righteousness as dependent on some form of law observance, Paul presents his understanding of the gospel as he preaches and teaches it in all of his congregations. It is noteworthy that Paul's presentation does not use the highly charged, polemical rhetoric of Galatians. As Byrne points out, Romans is best characterized as adopting the strategies and tone of *epideictic* rhetoric, which focuses primarily on the celebration of values held in common.[7] This is a wise move on Paul's part, since he is writing to a community that he did not found and does not know firsthand. Thus, he commends his gospel to his readers by presenting it as something they share and can celebrate together. This also allows him to portray alternative interpretations of the gospel as representing a threat to values they hold in common.

This epideictic strategy goes a long way toward explaining the "double address" that many scholars have detected in the first part of Romans. On the one hand, Paul's primary implied audience seems to be Gentile Christians.[8] On the other hand, 1:18–4:25 and brief passages scattered throughout the letter seem to be addressed to a Jewish dialogue partner along the lines of a diatribe. The diatribe is a literary device in which the author creates a conversation with an imaginary dialogue partner, called an interlocutor, who raises objections or draws false conclusions about the argument the author is making.[9] This gives the author the chance to rebut these misconceptions. When addressing the implied audience of Gentile Christians directly, Paul is attempting to persuade his readers to increase their adherence to the beliefs and moral teachings that flow from the gospel they "share" with him. When addressing an imaginary Jewish interlocutor, he is allowing the Gentile Christians to overhear his arguments against law righteousness.

It is helpful to have a sense of the location of chapter 6 within Paul's larger argument in Romans. This can be outlined as follows:[10]

    I.   **Opening** (1:1–17)—Sender, Recipient, Thanksgiving, Theme
   II.   **Body** of the letter
       A. Exposition of the inclusive saving power of the gospel (1:18–11:36)
          1. 1:18–4:24—The inclusion of the Gentiles on the basis of righteousness by faith; a dialogue with a Jewish interlocutor
          2. 5:1–8:39—The sure hope of salvation springing from righteousness by faith
          3. 9:1–11:36—The inclusion of Israel
       B. Summons to live according to the gospel (12:1–15:13)—Paraenetic Material
  III. **Conclusion** (15:14–16:24)—Future plans, Commendations

Part A of the body of the letter offers a lengthy exposition of Paul's understanding of the gospel, dealing with the themes of righteousness and faith. Paul's discussion of baptism in 6:1–14 stands at the very middle of this section and serves as a kind of hinge, linking his discussion of righteousness through faith in the first part of the letter to the paraenetic material taken up in part B.

The Form of Teaching to Which You Were Entrusted

With this background in mind, let us examine Romans 6:17–18 in some detail. It will be helpful if you read all of Romans 6 and keep the text before you. Commentators generally locate these two verses within a passage that begins at verse 15 and runs through verse 23. This, in turn, follows closely on the passage beginning at 6:1 in which Paul reminds his readers of their baptisms. Verses 1 and 15 pose questions along the lines of a diatribe, raising objections to Paul's presentation of the gospel in the first part of the letter. They imply that Paul's emphasis on the gracious nature of God's "rectifying" of human sinners in Jesus Christ apart from their obedience to the law undercuts the motivation for Christians to act morally. Paul rebuts these inferences by setting forth his understanding of the foundation of the Christian moral life.

Throughout Romans 6, Paul uses the metaphor of slavery to describe Christian obedience. We should remember that slavery was a widely established institution with which Paul's readers were familiar. It is likely that some of the Roman

Christians were slaves and that some were free-persons (persons once in slavery who had bought their freedom or been set free by their masters). Paul almost apologizes for his use of this metaphor in verse 19a, and elsewhere he uses the language of freedom to describe the Christian life. But he is aware that the slavery metaphor pictures in vivid terms what it means for Christians to live in obedience to their risen Lord. Indeed, he describes himself as a slave of Jesus Christ in the very first sentence of the letter (*doulos* = "slave"). Harking back to their baptisms, Paul portrays entry into the Christian life as a transfer from one master to another. He uses the literary device of personification to portray sin and death as the old master whom his readers served in their pre-Christian lives. He also personifies righteousness and eternal life, portraying them as the new master now served by those who have transferred their allegiance to Christ.

Paul uses this metaphorical picture to answer the questions raised in verses 1 and 15. *Life under grace is not a life of immorality but a life of obedience. Living under grace involves living out the righteousness that has been given as a free gift by God (v. 23), a life that issues in eternal life.* This is placed in stark contrast to slavery under the dominion of sin, a master who pays his servants the wages of death (v. 23). It would be unthinkable, Paul argues, for those who have transferred their allegiance to the risen Lord to continue to serve this old master.

The pericope we are examining, 6:17–18, is located squarely in this metaphorical complex. Paul gives thanks that the Roman Christians have become obedient from the heart to the pattern of teaching to which they were entrusted. What he means by "obedience from the heart" seems clear, especially if the slavery metaphor is kept in mind. Paul is giving thanks to God that the Roman Christians' obedience of their new Lord is not halfhearted. They do not act with resentment, as if they are being forced to obey. Rather, their obedience is *from the heart*.

But what does Paul mean when he says that they have become obedient "to the form of teaching to which [they] were entrusted"? What does he have in mind? The Greek word translated "form" is *typos*. Elsewhere, it is used by Paul to describe people who embody the pattern of the Christian life and are worthy of imitation (Phil. 3:17; 1 Thess. 1:7). In the context of Paul's argument from baptism beginning in 6:1, it is highly likely that this pattern refers to teaching that explains what it means to be joined to Christ in baptism, teaching they originally received in preparation for their initiation into the church. The term translated "entrusted" is *paradidomi*, which sometimes is translated "handed over," especially in passages where Paul describes Christ as being "handed over" to the powers of sin and death to reconcile the world to God.[11] To gain insight into what Paul means by the image of being handed over to the pattern of baptismal teaching, we must look carefully at what he says about baptism in 6:1–14.

Paul's Argument from Baptism

It is helpful to think of Paul as using baptism in this passage as a paradigm of life in Christ. By *paradigm,* I mean a model that brings into focus a range of disparate ideas and experiences in a concrete image, grounded in a sphere of life with which people are familiar.[12] The first five chapters of Romans are extremely complex, even with the text immediately before you and broken up into verses and sections with subtitles. Imagine the sorts of demands they would place on an audience *listening* to the letter being read in the context of worship or in a small house-church gathering. Paul seems to be aware of the demands he is placing on his hearers, and so he pulls together various strands of his argument in a paradigm with which the Roman Christians are familiar—the practice of baptism! He argues that baptism is a paradigm of (1) incorporation into the redemption of Christ, (2) Christian obedience, and (3) the eschatological nature of life in Christ.

A paradigm of incorporation into the redemption of Christ. One of the most important features of this passage is the way Paul uses baptism to portray Christians' incorporation into Christ's work of redemption. This is brought out in a particularly striking way by Paul's use of verbs beginning with the prefix *sum*, which means "together with." James Dunn's translation captures this nicely:

> So then we were *buried with* him through baptism into death. . . . For if we have become *knit together with* the very likeness of his death, we shall certainly also be *knit together with* the very likeness of his resurrection. Knowing this, that our old nature has been *crucified with* him . . . . But if we have died *with Christ*, we believe that we shall also *live with* him.[13]

"Like" Christ in his death, the Roman Christians were plunged under the baptismal waters, where it was impossible to sustain the breath of life and where the darkness was akin to that of a grave. "Like" Christ in his resurrection, they emerged from the waters to "walk in newness of life" (v. 4) in anticipation of their future transformation. The very pattern of their baptism, thus, points to their participation in the redemption accomplished in Christ's death and resurrection, which grants them righteousness as a free gift.

In effect, Paul tells the Roman Christians: Remember your baptism, for it provides you with a concrete picture of everything I have been saying to this point in the letter—our sinfulness, the failure of the law to free us from sin, the saving significance of the "one man" Jesus Christ, and our participation in his death and resurrection. Paul then relates what God has done in Christ "there and then" to their life in Christ "here and now." As he puts it in verse 11: "So you also must consider yourselves dead to sin and alive to God in Christ Jesus."

A paradigm of Christian obedience. As we have seen, Paul is attempting to counter the charge that his gospel of grace cuts the nerve of the Christian moral life. He does so by "reminding" his readers that baptism not only unites them with God's redemptive work in Christ but also places them under the dominion of the living, risen Lord who is their new master. In his use of baptism as a paradigm of Christian obedience, Paul says in effect: Live out your baptism! You have died to sin and death and risen to righteousness and eternal life. Let this pattern of dying and rising—which lies at the very heart of the gospel—be the pattern of your obedience to Christ.

A paradigm of the eschatological nature of life in Christ. Baptism also is used in chapter 6 as a paradigm of eschatological thinking and living.[14] As numerous scholars have pointed out, Paul appears to follow an intentional pattern in the way he uses verbs in 6:1–11.[15] He uses the perfect tense (an action completed in the past with continuing consequences) to refer to participation in Christ's death and the future tense to refer to participation in Christ's resurrection. Romans 6:5 is representative: "If we *have been* united with him in a death like his, we *will* certainly *be united* with him in a resurrection like his." The participation of the Roman Christians in Christ's death is a present possibility; their participation in his resurrection lies before them.

This is not to say that Christ's resurrection is portrayed as having no impact whatsoever on their present lives. It is portrayed as effecting their present life in 6:4b: "Just as Christ was raised from the dead by the glory of the Father, so we too might walk in newness of life." The idea of God's glory has strong eschatological overtones throughout Paul's writings, including this letter. It refers to the splendor and beauty of God that will be revealed fully when Christ returns. It is closely related to the term Paul uses for "newness" in this passage, *kainos,* the same term he uses elsewhere to refer to new creation of the Spirit, which is a foretaste of the total renewal of creation still to come. In 6:4, "newness of life" is conjoined to *peripateo,* "to walk," a verb that Paul uses to describe a person's moral conduct and that harks back to Israel's Scripture.[16] In the ways Christians conduct their present lives, thus, they can reflect some measure of the glory of the new creation revealed in Jesus' resurrection.

But throughout Paul's discussion of baptism in this section, the accent falls on their *future* participation in Christ's resurrection. Why? Paul is using baptism to teach his Gentile readers how to think and live eschatologically. He is teaching them to take seriously the "not yet" of their life in Christ. Their hope is real, for it is founded on the embodied promise of Christ's resurrection. But it is a hope that will only be fulfilled with Christ's parousia. In effect, Paul is telling the Roman Christians: Remember your baptism. Embrace the elements of struggle in the Christian life as a way of participating in Christ's suffering and death. But live in hope, confident that Christ's resurrection is the firstfruits of the new creation. This is what it means to think and live eschatologically.

Baptismal Catechesis and the Purpose of Paul's Teaching Ministry in Congregations

In Romans 6, Paul reminds his readers of the pattern to which they were "handed over" in their baptisms, a pattern they learned in the teaching that prepared them for initiation into the church. On the basis of our examination of this chapter, we learn three things about the purpose of the teaching ministry of congregations.

1. The teaching ministry seeks to help Christians better understand and participate in God's redemption of the world in Christ Jesus. The Roman Christians are portrayed as incorporated in baptism into God's redemption of the world in Jesus

Christ. Their way of life as a community and as individuals is one of participation in the righteousness they are given as a free gift of grace and have accepted in faith. As we shall see in the following chapter, Paul teaches his congregations the stories of Israel's Scripture and early Christian tradition in order to help them place the events of Christ's redemption in the context of creation and Israel's election as a covenant people. Yet learning Scripture and tradition are not ends in themselves. They are taught so that the members of Paul's congregations might better understand and participate in God's redemption of the world in Christ Jesus. They are to let the pattern of this redemption shape their lives. The teaching ministry serves this purpose.

2. *The teaching ministry seeks to help Christians grow in their relationship with the risen and universal Lord.* The pattern the Roman Christians are taught in preparation for baptism is one of death and resurrection. They have died to sin and risen to new life. Paul interlaces this pattern with the image of transferring allegiance to a new master. They now are to live in the service of their risen Lord, whose reign extends over all of life. This points us toward a dynamic and relational understanding of the purpose of the teaching ministry, to teaching and formational practices that invite us to listen to and heed the voice of the living God and to take seriously the moral claim of God over every dimension of life. As we shall see, this has important implications for our understanding of moral formation and education. Transmitting and studying moral teachings are important, but they are not enough. Such teachings have their proper role within a community that is striving to live in obedience to its living Lord.

3. *The teaching ministry orients the members of the Christian community toward God's promised future for creation.* Paul uses baptism to teach the Roman Christians to think and live eschatologically. The "newness of life" to which they have risen in baptism anticipates God's new creation of the world promised in Christ's resurrection from the dead. As we shall see in the following chapter, an important part of Paul's teaching ministry focuses on helping his predominantly Gentile congregations learn how to view their present lives in light of God's promised future. Discerning the signs of new creation in our midst is an important part of the Christian life. It involves learning how to weigh and judge the many spirits vying for our attention in order to distinguish the guiding light of the Holy Spirit.

EDIFICATION: BUILDING UP THE BODY IN LOVE

We turn now to a very different body of biblical material that can also help us understand the purpose of Paul's teaching ministry in congregations. This material focuses on edification, building up the body of Christ in love. The root of the compound terms commonly translated "edification" in English are *oikos*, meaning "house" or "dwelling," and *domeō*, meaning "to build." The simplest meaning of edification, thus, is "to build up the Christian community, which serves as the dwelling of God's Spirit." Paul uses cognates of *oikos* and *domeō* in many ways throughout his letters, drawing on themes already present in Israel's Scripture, the teachings of Jesus, and the early church.[17] But he develops these themes more extensively than any other writer in the New Testament. Echoing Jeremiah's call narrative, he even describes his own apostleship in terms of "building up and not tearing down" God's new covenant people.[18] Paul offers his most extensive discussion of edification in 1 Corinthians 3–4 and 12–14. Before examining these passages, it may be helpful to consider the rhetorical situation Paul is addressing in this letter and to place this situation in the context of the challenges Paul faced in building up a sense of community in all of his congregations.

The Rhetorical Situation of 1 Corinthians

In 1 Corinthians, Paul is addressing a community being torn apart by factionalism.[19] Leading members of the community view themselves as spiritually advanced and have begun to question Paul's apostolic authority. Different groups profess loyalty to different leaders (3:4), and some even question Paul's understanding of the gospel. It is likely that they find certain features of the apocalyptic framework of his gospel confusing and distasteful. Drawing on cultural categories ready at hand, they reinterpret the gospel in terms of dualisms that portray the spiritual realm as transcending bodily existence.

One of the ways Paul responds to the factionalism and theological confusion of the Christian community in Corinth is by developing the theological framework of edification: the upbuilding of the community in love. The community's *one* Lord, who continues to guide them through the *one* Spirit, is building them up into *one* body in which each part is important and contributes to the common good. In his discussion of edification, Paul provides us with perhaps his most important description of Christian community and the sort of congregational leadership and formation that builds up this kind of community in a church.

Yet it also is important to recognize that the factionalism and disunity of the Corinthians were an extreme form of social tensions and challenges found in Paul's other congregations as well. His congregations were relatively unique in the Hellenistic cities of the first century in terms of their social composition, roles, patterns of power, and other factors. There were no models of community ready at hand that could guide their members in building up a shared life. Three characteristics of Paul's congregations are particularly noteworthy in this regard.

Social diversity. Analysis of the social composition of Paul's congregations suggests that some of his communities appear to have included a fairly wide cross section of Greco-Roman city life.[20] They included slaves, free-persons, artisans, merchants, and persons with enough wealth to serve as patrons of the church, to travel, and to own slaves. While predominantly Gentile, his congregations sometimes included Jewish Christians. This social diversity would have made Paul's congregations one of the few associations in the Hellenistic cities of the first century in which slave and free, rich and poor, men and women gathered together on a regular basis for meaningful face-to-face interaction.

Distinctive roles and social expectations. In the cities where Paul's congregations were located, four different types of communities were well established: the family, voluntary associations (trade groups, eating clubs, etc.), religious groups, and the philosophical and rhetorical schools. While Paul's congregations overlapped each of these groups to some extent, none seems to have served as the primary model of congregational life. Indeed, Paul's communities seem to have developed a somewhat distinctive set of social roles and expectations.[21] By way of illustration, let us see how this is the case with the family. There are many indications in Paul's letters that households served as the primary meeting place of Christian groups.[22] Yet there also are indications that the dominant patterns of family life did not determine the roles established in Paul's congregations.

First, Paul limited the authority of the head of the wealthier households, who served as patrons of congregations by providing them with a place to meet. Normally, the household head would have wielded unquestioned authority in his own home. Yet Paul had no qualms about criticizing the way certain Christian practices were being conducted in a given household, even when these were conducted under the direction of the household head. Second, Paul's communities distributed power in ways that stood in tension with normal household patterns. In Greco-Roman society, the family was viewed as a paradigm of the political order, composed of persons of different rank. Some were fit to rule (free males) and others to serve (women, children, and slaves). Yet Paul's congregations seem to have distributed power in ways that stood in tension with these expectations, basing them not on social hierarchy but on charisma, that is, on the Spirit's free apportionment of gifts and services. Women played prominent leadership roles in Paul's congregations and his missionary work. Moreover, Paul appealed to Philemon to receive back his runaway slave, Onesimus, "no longer as a slave but as more than a slave, a beloved brother" (Phlm. 16). While appealing to Philemon's good will and inviting his free consent in this matter, Paul clearly expected Philemon's Christian convictions to preempt his rights as a household head and slave owner.

Status inconsistency among prominent members. Another feature of Paul's congregations was their attractiveness to individuals who experienced status inconsistency in an unusually intense way.[23] *Status* refers to the evaluation of a person's social position in terms of categories such as political power, occupational prestige, wealth, education, subgroup status, gender, ethnicity, religious affiliation, servitude (slave, free-person, or free-born), and so forth. A person with status inconsistency has high status in some areas but low status in others.

Wayne Meeks argues that there are indications that many of the prominent members of Paul's congregations were characterized by a high degree of status inconsistency.[24] Phoebe, for example, is described by Paul as a *diakonos* of the church in Cenchreae and a benefactor of the Christian mission, including Paul's work. She apparently is a woman of some wealth and independence, having traveled to Rome to deliver Paul's letter and, perhaps, to conduct her own business. These high status roles would have stood in an uneasy relationship with her status as a woman in Greco-Roman society, denying her access to power and influence in public life. Priscilla and Aquila can be similarly characterized. While they are leaders in the early Christian movement and possess sufficient wealth to establish households in several different cities and to support Paul's work, they make their money in the relatively low status occupation of tent making, and are Jews from the eastern provinces living in Rome.

As Meeks notes, modern studies of people characterized by high status inconsistency reveal an especially intense experience of anxiety and cognitive dissonance.[25] Such people must negotiate multiple status shifts as they move through the various roles of their everyday lives. It is not difficult to imagine how this might lead to certain tensions within Paul's congregations, especially around matters of leadership. As we shall see in the next chapter, this may be the case with regard to the Corinthian "wise."

This combination of social diversity, distinctive roles, and high status inconsistency among prominent members helps us understand why Paul must give so much attention to the task of building up a common sense of community in his congregations. While the Corinthian community represents a special case and elicits Paul's most eloquent and richest thinking about these matters, the framework he develops here likely has its roots in his pastoral work as a whole. In his earliest extant letter, 1 Thessalonians, we find Paul already using the language of edification in 5:11: "Therefore encourage one another and build up each other, as indeed you are doing." Likewise in Romans 12:5–8, he uses the images of "one body" and "diverse gifts," which are prominent in his discussion of edification in 1 Corinthians.

Edification in 1 Corinthians 3–4

In 1 Corinthians 3, Paul develops three focal images that lay a theological foundation for his discussion of edification over the course of the letter. Keep these images in mind while pausing at this point to read 1 Corinthians 3–4. In the first image (vv. 6–9), the leaders of the church are compared to servants given the task of planting and tending crops in a field. Paul develops this image to accentuate God's role in the successful growth of the community. The leaders are compared to servants, who have been assigned their specific roles by the owner of the field (vv. 5, 9). Though one plants and the other waters, it is God alone who gives the growth (v. 6). The workers are united in a common purpose (v. 8) and must work together (v. 9) as servants of a common master. Interdependent leadership, thus, is a hallmark of Christian community.

The second image shifts to the metaphor of workers constructing a building. Here too the collaborative nature of leadership in the community is implied, although it is no longer Paul's primary focus. Rather, the accent is now placed on the foundation that has been laid, the care leaders should take to build on this foundation, and the way their work will be judged. Paul compares his role in the community to that of a master builder who has laid the foundation on which others are now building (v. 10), a foundation that is explicitly identified as Jesus Christ (v. 11). The term "foundation" is used five times in this short passage, underscoring the point that the gospel alone is the foundation of the Corinthian community ("no one can lay any foundation other than the one that has been laid," v. 11) and that leaders who have come after him must "choose with care how to build on it" (v. 10). In 3:13–14, Paul introduces several images of God's judgment ("the Day," testing fire, and the apportioning out of a reward), making the point that God alone is capable of judging the "work of each builder" (v. 13). In the fourth chapter of this letter, it becomes clear that some in the Corinthian community are judging Paul, and he warns them that such judgment is properly left to God (4:3–5).

The final image Paul offers is that of the Corinthian community as God's temple. In light of the fact that the temple in Jerusalem was still standing when Paul wrote 1 Corinthians, this is a fairly remarkable claim for Paul to make about the church. The role of the temple as the dwelling place of God is now claimed for the Christian community, including the holiness associated with this sacred space (v. 17b). The Christian community is set apart and serves as the dwelling place of God's Spirit (v. 16). Those in the community who are destroying its unity through their quarreling and factionalism are bringing down God's judgment on themselves (v. 17a).

In 1 Corinthians 4, Paul exhorts the Corinthian Christians on the basis of the three images that he has just offered. As he puts it, "I have applied all this to Apollos and myself for your benefit" (4:6). He explicitly uses language of paraenesis to frame his comments ("admonish," v. 14; and "appeal," v. 16). With withering sarcasm, he contrasts his "weakness" and "foolishness" to the "strength" and "wisdom" of those who view themselves as spiritually advanced. In verses 14–21, he reminds the Corinthians of his special relationship to them. Even if they were to have "ten thousand guardians in Christ," they have only one "father," namely, Paul, who initially brought them to faith (v. 15). He urges them to imitate him (v. 16) and tells them that this is why he sent Timothy in his stead. As his "beloved and faithful child in the Lord," Timothy can serve as a living reminder of Paul's "ways in Christ Jesus, as I teach them everywhere in every church" (v. 17).

As the letter unfolds, Paul will continue to point to his own ministry as an example of the Christian life that the Corinthians are urged to imitate. Already he has placed before them the models of interdependent leadership oriented toward the common good and his own "weakness" and "foolishness." In other parts of the letter, Paul exhorts those who view themselves as spiritually advanced to subordinate their personal "rights" to the needs of the community as a whole, as he does himself. This mutual subordination for the common good is one of the most important ways the Corinthian community is urged to embody the cruciform pattern of its Lord.

Edification in 1 Corinthians 12–14

The theme of mutual subordination in love to build up the common good also is prominent in 1 Corinthians 12–14, the second body of material in 1 Corinthians where Paul gives extensive attention to edification. As Richard Hays points out, these chapters develop an integrated argument about the appropriate use of spiritual gifts in worship, initially introduced in 12:1.[26] Some in the community are placing such emphasis on showy displays of their spirituality in worship (e.g., the gift of tongues) that it is disrupting these gatherings. Paul's response in chapter 14 is to describe the true purpose of spiritual gifts in worship as edification, as building up the community as a whole. First Corinthians 12–14 contains some of the most beautiful writing in the Pauline corpus, and you will be better able to follow my analysis below if you treat yourself to a fresh reading of this material at this point. Take note of the chiastic ABA pattern structuring the three chapters.[27]

A—Spiritual gifts and their abuse introduced in general terms (12:1–31a). In the opening section, Paul offers a general account of the complementary nature of spiritual gifts in the Christian community. He emphasizes the "varieties of gifts" distributed by the "same Spirit" (12:4–11). The latter phrase is used four times in this brief passage, for Paul is emphasizing the common source of the various spiritual gifts that are given for the well-being of the community as a whole. As Paul puts it, "To each is given the manifestation of the Spirit for the common good" (v. 7). He then compares the Corinthian community to a body (vv. 12–26). The moral ideal of the common good and the image of the body were well-established *topoi* in deliberative rhetoric addressing civic strife and factionalism.[28] Paul appropriates and recasts this rhetoric to serve his pastoral purposes. The diversity of gifts and ministries in the Corinthian community, he argues, is by God's design. Just as the parts of the body are interdependent, so too are gifts and ministries of the Christian community. All are called to ministry, not just a few; all are gifted by the Spirit and have something to contribute to the common good. Unity in diversity is the norm.

Throughout this opening section, Paul develops a subtle critique of those in the community who view themselves as spiritually advanced and who lay great emphasis on the gifts of wisdom, knowledge, and tongues. In their spiritual pride, they are dismissive of the contributions of others. Yet Paul locates the gifts in which they take most pride within a more inclusive list, placing tongues and their interpretation *last*. In his analogy of the body, he points out that the "weaker" and "less honorable" members are "indispensible" and clothed "with greater honor" (vv. 22–23).

B—The nature of love (12:31b–13:13). In the second part of his argument, Paul sets forth the norm that lies at the heart of his understanding of edification. This epideictic interlude in praise of love is Paul's antidote to the Corinthians' factionalism and spiritual pride. Paul's message here is clear: Love is the norm that should govern all spiritual gifts. The personification of love in this passage

(13:4–7) and the lyrical language with which it is described have led many to view this as a hymn or poem composed independently of this letter. Yet the verbal and conceptual links of this passage to the rest of the letter make this unlikely.[29]

What does Paul mean by love? In verses 4–7, he personifies love and offers two positive characteristics, followed by a series of terms expressing what love is not. In describing love as "patient" and "kind" (v. 4), Paul points to two aspects of God's covenant love toward Israel: God's forbearance and loving-kindness (cf. Rom. 2:4 and Gal. 5:22, where they also are paired). Of the terms describing what love is not, five are directly related to negative conduct and attitudes of the Corinthians that have already been described in the letter. Paul's message to the Corinthians is clear: Love is the very opposite of the way you are behaving, especially those of you who claim to have the "higher" spiritual gifts.

A—Building up the community in love: the edifying role of spiritual gifts (14:1–40). Paul has now set forth the norm of love that should govern the exercise of spiritual gifts in the community. In chapter 14, he returns to the issue immediately confronting the community that was first mentioned in 12:1: spiritual gifts. An inordinate emphasis on the gift of tongues is disrupting the community's worship. Throughout this chapter, Paul repeatedly portrays edification or the building up of the community in love as the goal and norm of its various spiritual gifts (14:3–5, 12, 26, 40). He contrasts the intelligible speech of prophesy (vv. 3–5, 29–33, 39) and other gifts (vv. 6, 26) that edify the entire congregation to the gift of tongues, which only edifies the individual who praises God in this way (v. 4). He points to his own example. Though he speaks in tongues "more than all of you" (v. 18), he deems this gift as less important than even a small amount of intelligible speech that can "instruct others" (v. 19).

Edification and the Purpose of Paul's Teaching Ministry in Congregations

In the two sections of 1 Corinthians that we have examined, Paul addresses the rhetorical situation of factionalism that is tearing the Corinthian community apart. Yet the task of building up a sense of community was a challenge he faced in all his congregations. As we have seen, his congregations were often composed of a broad cross section of social classes, developed roles at variance with the cultural patterns of their day, and included prominent members who faced the task of negotiating multiple statuses in their everyday lives. In Paul's discussion of edification, we gain insight into the sort of community he hopes these congregations will become. We also gain insight into key features of the sort of congregational formation that builds up this kind of community. We can point to four implications for the teaching ministry.

1. The Holy Spirit is the agent of edification and, thus, of the teaching ministry. Paul places greater emphasis on the Holy Spirit in these passages than in his discussion of baptism in Romans 6. Christ crucified remains important to Paul's portrait of edification. He is the one "foundation" on which the building up of community takes place, and leaders are urged to build on the foundation of the gospel with care. But the Holy Spirit is now portrayed as indwelling Christian communities through the image of the temple and as distributing *charismata,* or spiritual gifts, to all of their members. Indeed, the work of building up the community is first and foremost an activity of the Spirit and only secondarily of human beings. As Paul puts it in 1 Corinthians 3:6–7, it is "God who gives the growth." This has important implications for our understanding of all forms of ministry, including the teaching ministry. As a work of the Spirit, the task of building up the community and its individual members is ultimately not under our control. Paul can plead with and exhort the Corinthian Christians to abandon their factionalism and to treat one another in ways befitting the body of Christ. But there is no guarantee that he will succeed. Indeed, 2 Corinthians portrays this congregation as still dealing with many of the same issues Paul addresses in his first letter. A teaching ministry that trusts the Holy Spirit does not coerce or dominate. It trusts God to give the growth in God's own good time.

2. *The teaching ministry builds up in love, the norm of edification.* In the passages we examined in this section, the ideal of Christian community is portrayed in terms of loving relationships. In 1 Corinthians 13, Paul describes this positively in terms of patience and kindness, drawing on Israel's portrait of God's covenant love as long-suffering and full of loving-kindness. Paul fills out his picture of a loving community by comparing it to a body in which all parts work together for the common good. This is a particularly striking image in light of the socioeconomic diversity and unconventional social roles found in his congregations. The gifts of all are to be acknowledged and put to good use. Indeed, the lesser gifts are to be accorded greatest honor. Unity in diversity is a sign of love, as is the refusal to reduplicate in the church social hierarchies found in the surrounding culture. This rich discussion is a powerful reminder that the teaching ministry must be guided by the norm of love. We might paraphrase Paul in this way: What would be gained if our students learned a thousand Bible verses or could articulate an insightful critique of American society but did not learn to love? Accordingly, we must think of teaching as a form of edification, as building up our students and our congregation in love. This means that the way we treat our students and the sort of relationships we cultivate among them is every bit as important as the teachings we offer them.

3. *The teaching ministry helps Christians recognize and claim their spiritual gifts and to grow in their ministries.* One of the most important implications of Paul's portrait of edification is that *all* members of the Christian community are called to ministry and provided with gifts by the Spirit to carry out their service to God. The teaching ministry has the task of helping the members of a congregation recognize, claim, and exercise their gifts for ministry. Moreover, as members' life circumstances change, altering their sense of what God is calling them to do and be, the congregation's teaching ministry must help them rework their understanding of ministry and vocation. This is a key part of the edification of the community.

4. Leaders teach by example. While all Christians are called to and gifted for ministry, Paul singles out leaders as playing special roles in the community. Two things are striking about his treatment of church leaders in the context of edification. First, church leaders are characterized in terms of the same sort of mutuality and interdependence (1 Cor. 3) that Paul also uses to describe the body as a whole (1 Cor. 12). As such, there is no *qualitative* theological distinction between those who lead and the other members of the congregation. Second, leaders are portrayed as having a special responsibility to teach by example, modeling thinking, attitudes, and behaviors desirable in the entire congregation. Paul is quite aware that leaders can set a negative example every bit as much as a positive one. To counter the spiritual pride of the Corinthian "wise," for instance, he must point to the example of the apostles' "weakness" and "foolishness" embodied in the hardships of their ministry, which reflect the cruciform pattern of Christ (1 Cor. 4:8–13). Likewise, Paul points to his subordination of the gift of tongues in worship to edifying the community through intelligible speech as a model others should imitate (1 Cor. 14:18–19). Leaders teach by example as much as by what they say.

CONCLUSION

In this chapter, we have begun to develop an understanding of the purpose of Paul's teaching ministry in congregations, exploring his portraits of baptism in Romans 6 and edification in 1 Corinthians 3–4 and 12–14. But how does Paul attempt to accomplish this purpose? What does his teaching include? Does he train others to carry on this ministry after he has departed? It is to questions like these that we turn in the following chapter.

Chapter 2

Three Tasks of Paul's Teaching Ministry:

Catechesis, Exhortation, and Discernment

In this chapter, we explore three central tasks of Paul's teaching ministry in congregations. As Paul carries out these tasks, he effects the purposes of the teaching ministry described in the previous chapter. He helps his congregations to better understand and embody their participation in Christ's redemption and to build up one another in love. While it is sometimes possible to focus directly on Paul's explicit comments about this ministry, more often we must work inductively, building on the teaching he seems to presuppose and to practice in his letters. It was not uncommon for Paul to remain with new congregations for a period of time in order to help the gospel take root in these communities. Even after he moved on, Paul viewed himself as standing in a special relationship to the congregations he had established. As their founding apostle, he had an ongoing interest in their well-being, returning for visits when possible, sending coworkers to assist communities in special need, and writing them letters. The way Paul teaches his congregations in the context of these letters provides us with the most important clues about his teaching practices when he was with them.

Over the course of this chapter, I argue that when we look closely at Paul's letters we can identify three core tasks in his teaching ministry: (1) *catechesis,* handing on Israel's Scripture and early Christian tradition; (2) *exhortation*, moral formation and education; and (3) *discernment*, teaching congregations how to understand the circumstances of their everyday life and world in terms of God's promised future for creation. The terms *exhortation* and *discernment* are taken directly from Paul's letters, but he does not often use the term *catechesis*.[1] I have borrowed it from later Christian tradition, where it was used to refer to the instruction offered new converts in preparation for baptism. Etymologically, the core image lying behind catechesis is "to echo" or "answer back." When adult Christians were baptized, they were asked several questions based on the baptismal creed and "answered back" to affirm their acceptance of the pattern of teaching to which they had been entrusted in their baptismal catechesis.

Throughout this chapter, I will use the terms *formation* and *education* to describe Paul's catechesis, exhortation, and discernment. *Formation* has to do with the relationships, practices, narratives, and norms of a community's shared life. It points to those aspects of a congregation's identity and ethos that build up a sense of community among its members as they participate together in a common way of life.[2] In contrast, *education* has to do with those practices that focus directly on teaching and learning. Paul might be viewed as giving attention to the congregation's formation of its members in his discussion of edification. Individual gifts and ministries are to contribute to the "building up" of the community as a whole in love; individuals are formed by their participation in this community. Paul gives attention to education in those parts of his letters where he appears to hark back to teachings offered in the past or offers new teachings to address specific issues before a congregation. We must attend to both formation and education in Paul's teaching ministry if we are to capture its richness and complexity. This has important implications for the teaching ministry of contemporary congregations. We cannot think exclusively in terms of formal education offered in classlike settings. Rather, we also must think in terms of relationships and formational practices that shape people as they participate in a way of life.

CATECHESIS: HANDING ON ISRAEL'S SCRIPTURE AND EARLY CHRISTIAN TRADITION

In the introduction to part 1, I noted that Paul cites Israel's Scripture close to a hundred times in his undisputed letters. To gain a sense of how frequently this occurs, all you have to do is thumb through his letters. Most modern English translations indicate Paul is citing a passage by placing it in quotation marks or marking it off from the rest of the text in a separate paragraph (see Gal. 3–4 for examples of both techniques in the NRSV). Sometimes Paul's citation of Israel's Scripture is accompanied by an extended interpretation of a particular text. But often it involves merely a passing reference. Moreover, he also alludes to Israel's Scripture without citing it directly.[3] In both his citation and allusion, it is almost as if Paul presupposes a working knowledge of Scripture on the part of his readers and expects them to be able to follow his argument.

What are we to make of this expectation of Paul's, especially in light of the fact that he is writing to predominantly Gentile congregations? The most plausible explanation is to assume that Paul and his coworkers spent time teaching their Gentile converts certain portions of Israel's Scripture.[4] These new converts must learn the stories of creation and God's election of Israel as a covenant people to understand the story of Christ. Moreover, they must understand the story of Israel in order to understand themselves as a continuation of this story, as God's new covenant people—called, justified, and sanctified in Christ Jesus. After recalling the story of Israel in the wilderness for the Corinthians, Paul puts it like this: "These things happened to them to serve as an example, and they were written down to instruct us, on whom the ends of the ages have come" (1 Cor. 10:11).

A similar pattern appears in Paul's use of early Christian tradition in his letters. Here too we find him both citing and alluding to material many scholars believe is drawn from preexistent confessional, liturgical, catechetical, and kerygmatic traditions.[5] In Romans 10:9, for example, Paul appears to quote part of an early Christian creed: "If you confess with your lips that Jesus is Lord and believe in your heart that God raised him from the dead, you will be saved." James Dunn groups this sort of creedal material in Paul's letters into six basic categories:

1. Resurrection formulae—God raised him from the dead.
2. "Died for" formulae—Christ died for us.
3. "Handed over" formulae—Jesus was handed over or handed himself over for our sins.
4. Combined formulae—"Christ died and was raised."
5. Confessional formulae—Jesus is Messiah, Jesus is the Son of God, Jesus is Lord.
6. Monotheistic formulae—God is one, the only true and living God.[6]

Paul uses these traditions in a variety of ways. At some points, he pauses to explain the meaning of traditions with which a congregation is familiar in order to bring their practice into line with the beliefs they confess. We will examine an example of this below in Paul's discussion of the tradition of the Lord's Supper in 1 Corinthians 11:23–34. At other points, Paul weaves snatches of tradition almost seamlessly into a passage and does not stop to explain its meaning. In Romans 1:1–6, for example, Paul weaves together his calling as apostle to the Gentiles and what many scholars believe is an early Christian confession (vv. 3–4), grounding his calling in the power of the risen Lord. What are we to make of Paul's varied uses of early Christian tradition and the knowledge he seems to presuppose? Once more, it is plausible to assume that Paul and his coworkers have taught the key elements of early Christian tradition in their catechesis of new converts.

More complicated is the matter of Paul's use of the Jesus tradition. As New

Testament scholars have long noted, Paul does not cite material from Jesus' life with great regularity. His primary interest is in Jesus' death and resurrection, which lie at the heart of his proclamation of the gospel. Scholars are divided, however, about the extent to which Paul alludes to the Jesus tradition in his letters. Some argue that this is very minimal.[7] Others argue that this is considerable.[8] While I incline to the latter position, this point is much less certain and is likely to remain a matter of dissensus among New Testament scholars.

In short, Paul uses Israel's Scripture, early Christian tradition, and perhaps the Jesus tradition in a variety of ways in his letters, ranging from explicit citation and explanation to allusive references woven seamlessly into passages that focus on other matters. These literary practices are best explained if Paul is viewed as assuming a degree of familiarity with this material on the part of his readers. In light of the fact that he is writing primarily to Gentile converts, it is plausible to assume that teaching this material was an important part of his ministry. Indeed, the way Paul draws on this material in his letters is probably best seen as a continuation of teaching practices initially carried out immediately after he established a congregation and remained with it.

If Paul's catechesis of his congregations focused primarily on teaching Israel's Scripture and early Christian tradition, it is important to recognize that Paul interprets this material with a great deal of freedom and creativity. Handing on traditions received from others and Paul's own creative application of this material to the contingent circumstances of his congregations should not be viewed as antithetical. As Leander Keck puts it, "Paul's 'depths' were indeed plumbed as he wrote, but his creativity consisted largely in his capacity to give traditions and traditional material new significance by expounding their implications for the situations he confronted. Paul was a bearer and refractor of multiple traditions and inherited motifs."[9]

In part, Paul's interpretive freedom stems from his overwhelming sense that God did something radically new and different in Jesus Christ. Israel's Scripture points to Christ, but it also must be reinterpreted in light of Christ. Paul also interprets Scripture and tradition with a certain degree of freedom because he believes the Holy Spirit is doing something new and different among his congregations.[10] Walking in the Spirit is not merely a matter of continuing the traditions of the past, but of attending to the signs of new creation in their very midst.

Examples of Paul's Interpretation of Received Traditions

There are four places in the Pauline corpus where Paul makes explicit reference to teachings and traditions he has "handed on" to his congregations:

> As you *learned* from us how you ought to live and to please God . . . , you should do so more and more. For you know what instructions we gave you through the Lord Jesus. (1 Thess. 4:1–2)

> I commend you because you remember me in everything and maintain the *traditions* just as I *handed them on* to you. (1 Cor. 11:2)

> For I *received* from the Lord what I also *handed on* to you, that the Lord Jesus on the night when he was betrayed took a loaf of bread, and when he had given thanks, he broke it and said, "This is my body that is for you. Do this in remembrance of me." In the same way he took the cup also, after supper, saying, "This cup is the new covenant in my blood. Do this, as often as you drink it, in remembrance of me." For as often as you eat this bread and drink the cup, you proclaim the Lord's death until he comes. (1 Cor. 11:23–26)

> For I *handed on* to you as of first importance what I in turn had *received*: that Christ died for our sins in accordance with the scriptures, and that he was buried, and that he was raised on the third day in accordance with the scriptures, and that he appeared to Cephas, then to the twelve. . . . Last of all, as to one untimely born, he appeared also to me. (1 Cor. 15:3–8)

In each of these passages, Paul uses verbs that convey handing on (*paradidōmi*) and receiving (*paralambanō*), which I have italicized. These were technical terms in Judaism during this period that referred to the activity of teaching communal traditions.[11] In three of these passages, Paul makes explicit reference to the fact that he has "handed on" to his readers traditions he had "received" from others.

In 1 Thessalonians 4:1–2, the phrase, "instructions we gave you through the Lord" makes it difficult to know if the moral teachings the congregation has "received" (*paralambanō*, translated "learned") were preexistent paraenetic traditions that Paul has handed on to them or if they were his own moral teaching. It is clear in this passage that Paul offered moral teachings when he first established this congregation. The sort of traditions Paul has in mind in 1 Corinthians 11:2 cannot be determined, but it is noteworthy that Paul commends the Corinthians for following these traditions immediately before he takes up several controversial issues related to worship. In 11:16, he reminds the Corinthians that they are part of a network of congregations that share a common set of practices, something he also mentions in 4:17, 7:17, and 14:33. By reminding them that they are part of a larger movement, he implies that they should not set themselves above the traditions binding this movement together. In 1 Corinthians 11:23–26, Paul recalls the tradition of Jesus' words at his final Passover meal with the disciples. He now interprets this tradition in order to correct certain abuses in the way some of the Corinthians are practicing the supper of the Lord, reflecting the common Greco-Roman practice of apportioning the best food and seats to those of the highest social status.[12] We will explore this passage more fully at a later point in this chapter.

In 1 Corinthians 15, Paul recalls a confession (vv. 3b–5) that he taught them at an earlier time in order to correct certain beliefs about the resurrection of the dead. Apparently, some members of the community find the idea of a bodily resurrection objectionable.[13] Perhaps those in the community who view themselves as "spiritually advanced" find the whole notion of corpses rising to be too crass and embarrassing for their refined tastes. Perhaps the whole idea of the resurrection of the *body* is at odds with their view of salvation as a purely spiritual matter. Paul unfolds the logic of the confession to make two basic points. First, Christ's resurrection from the dead is fundamental to every aspect of Christian belief, for it represents God's triumph over death and is the "first fruits" (v. 20) of the general resurrection and consummation, when God will be "all in all" (15:28). To discard this belief is to discard the very heart of the gospel. Second, their hope in a future resurrection is hope for a transformed body. Salvation is not a spiritualized escape from the body but involves a transformed mode of embodied existence. What is done with the body in the present time matters, a point that underscores Paul's response to ethical misconduct treated at earlier points in this letter.

Two insights emerge from our brief examination of these passages dealing with tradition in Paul's letters. First, in each of these passages, Paul makes explicit reference to the fact that he *handed on* or taught these traditions to his congregations at some point in the past. This makes it highly probable that his practice of citing and alluding to tradition and Israel's Scripture in his letters is a continuation of teaching practices established when he was present with these congregations. Second, Paul does more than merely repeat the traditions taught them at an earlier point. He has *interpreted* this material with a certain amount of freedom, using it to address particular issues that have risen in these congregations. This is especially evident in 1 Corinthians 15. Paul uses what might be described as a circular pattern of teaching and learning. He reminds his readers of traditions they are confessing and practicing already, and then he interprets these very things in order to deepen his readers' understanding (1 Thess. 4) or to encourage them to alter their conduct (1 Cor. 11) or beliefs (1 Cor. 15). This is the same pattern we found him using in Romans 6, where he drew on his readers' prior experience of baptism and baptismal catechesis to pull together his presentation of the gospel in the first part of the letter.

Paul's appeal to tradition and Israel's Scripture, thus, are not designed to elicit unthinking obedience on the part of the members of his congregations. It is one of the ways he carries out a situated rational conversation with his congregations, inviting them to join him in reflecting on the meaning and implications of their life in Christ. We would do well to keep this in mind in our catechesis of contemporary congregations.

Teachers in Paul's Congregations

At several points in his letters, Paul explicitly lists teaching as one of the *charismata* with which the Spirit endows the body of Christ (Rom. 12:6–7; 1 Cor. 12: 6–7; Gal. 6:6). In 1 Corinthians 12:28, he almost goes so far as to describe teachers as a regular ministry of his congregations: "And God has appointed in the church first apostles, second prophets, third teachers. . . ." Nowhere, however, does Paul explicitly describe the tasks that congregational teachers are to carry out. The best we can do is venture educated guesses on the basis of Paul's own teaching practices and the level of knowledge he presupposes in the letters he writes to his congregations.

It is probable that congregational teachers continued the task of handing on Israel's Scripture, early Christian tradition, and perhaps the Jesus tradition after the apostle and his coworkers had departed. The authority of the teacher would, in effect, be the authority of the traditions that he or she handed on.[14] It would make sense for Paul to train a group of teachers to play this role in his congregations and for baptism to be one of the critical points where they would offer catechesis.[15] Our examination of Romans 6 indicates that this pattern was followed across the Christian community and not in Paul's congregations alone, for Paul did not establish the Christian community in Rome.

This does not tell the whole story, however. We have just examined several instances in which Paul moves beyond simply repeating traditions handed on at an earlier point and interprets them to address contingent issues that have emerged in his congregations. In describing teaching as a gift of the Spirit, Paul seems to open the door to this same kind of interpretive activity on the part of congregational teachers. At this point, the teacher's authority is no longer that of the tradition per se but of the Spirit who inspires fresh insight. Presumably, discernment is called for here, just as it is when prophets speak under the inspiration of the Spirit, as called for in 1 Corinthians 14:29 and 1 Thessalonians 5:21. Moreover, in 1 Corinthians 14:26, Paul implies that this sort of interpretive activity is not confined to the designated teachers of the community: "When you come together, each one has a hymn, a *lesson,* a revelation, a tongue, or an interpretation. Let all things be done for building up." Inspired teaching is inherently open to all, for all have access to the same Spirit. While some may be specially trained as teachers, all members potentially can share in the teaching ministry of the congregation through the guiding light of the Holy Spirit.

Catechesis is the first task we have identified in Paul's teaching ministry: handing on and interpreting Israel's Scripture and early Christian tradition. In his catechesis, Paul helps the members of his congregations better understand and embody their redemption in Christ Jesus and new life in the Spirit. He interprets Christ in the context of Israel's stories of creation and her election as a covenant people and helps the members of his congregations refashion their identities as God's new covenant people. He lays an important foundation of beliefs and practices on which he can build at later points when he invites his congregations to reflect with him on how to respond to specific problems they are facing.

EXHORTATION: MORAL FORMATION AND EDUCATION

In this section, we will examine a second task that Paul undertakes in his teaching ministry, focusing on his ministry of exhortation. *Exhortation* is a rather archaic sounding word that is likely to be unfamiliar to many contemporary

Christians. As we look closely at Paul's ministry of exhortation, however, we will begin to discover certain features that are analogous to the teaching ministry of contemporary congregations. *Exhortation brings into focus Paul's approach to the ministry of moral formation and education.* Keying off Paul's use of terms such as *parakaleo* (to encourage, urge, exhort, comfort) and the traditions of moral formation and education prominent in the Greco-Roman world of his day, we gain insight into what this ministry involved.

It is important to avoid the trap of drawing sharp boundaries between Paul's ethical and theological teachings. In the past, scholars have sometimes described this in terms of the distinction between the paraenetic and kerygmatic sections of his letters.[16] One reason to avoid this sort of sharp separation is that Paul's ethics and theology are interwoven in his letters. His exhortation is grounded in his theological concern that his congregations embody a way of life consistent with their election—their calling, justification, and sanctification as God's new covenant people. He often uses language, concepts, and images that weave the ethical and theological sections closely together, and offers mini-exhortations in the midst of "kerygmatic" sections. A second reason is Paul's use of the imitation motif in his exhortation.[17] Paul's portraits of moral exemplars are not to be found in the paraenetic sections of his letters alone. They come in the form of hymns (Philippians), autobiographical statements (Galatians), recollections of his prior relationship with a community (1 Thessalonians), descriptions of his refusal to make use of his apostolic rights (1 Corinthians), and in many other ways. While Paul points to the example of Christ, he also points to himself, his coworkers, the members of congregations, and to congregations as a whole as exemplars that refract the life of Christ in their attitudes and conduct.

Paul's use of the imitation motif is one of his most important strategies of exhortation and for good reason. Identification with exemplars who embody certain aspects of the Christian moral life remains a potent source of moral formation in contemporary congregations. Children imitate their parents; youth identify with older peers and youth group leaders; adult members imitate the formal and informal leaders of their congregations. At their best, moral exemplars serve as "living reminders" of the redemptive pattern of Christ, extending this pattern analogically and metaphorically into the circumstances of their own particular time and place. This sort of mutual upbuilding of the community in love lies at the heart of moral formation as it is understood in this book.

Exhortation in 1 Thessalonians

To gain a better sense of how Paul carried out this second task of the teaching ministry in one congregation, let us examine 1 Thessalonians in detail. Paul's first letter to the Christians in this city is generally considered the earliest complete writing in the New Testament, probably written around 51 CE. The occasion of the letter is a report from Timothy whom Paul had dispatched to the fledgling Thessalonian congregation because it was facing certain difficulties (3:1–7).

While the letter is written by Paul, Silvanus, and Timothy (1:1), using "we" and "apostles" throughout, Paul speaks alone in 2:18 and 3:5, suggesting that his voice is primary.[18]

The letter provides several clues about the rhetorical situation that Paul is addressing in this letter. First, there are several indications that the congregation was predominantly composed of Gentiles.[19] Second, there are no obvious signs of social diversity in this particular community. Abraham Malherbe suggests that Paul probably evangelized while plying his trade as a tent maker in Thessalonika, gathering people in a small apartment behind his shop at the end of the day.[20] If so, this makes it likely that his converts were other manual laborers and the artisans and merchants with whom he came into daily contact. Third, there are indications that the community is experiencing some form of persecution, threat, or distress (1:6; 2:14). While we do not know what this involved, it is clear that Paul is worried that these new Christians will not withstand the pressure they are experiencing. He is overjoyed to hear from Timothy that the congregation has stood firm in the faith and is eager to see him again. He and his coworkers now write this letter in order to further consolidate the sort of exhortation and care they established when founding the community.[21] This is why Paul sent Timothy back to the Thessalonians in the first place—"to strengthen and encourage" them (3:2).

Wayne Meeks and Abraham Malherbe argue that moral formation and care are the *primary* purposes of 1 Thessalonians and that the letter is best understood as modeled on the paraenetic letters exchanged by committed friends and by new converts and mentors in the schools of popular moral philosophy.[22] Many common features of these letters are readily apparent in 1 Thessalonians: reminders of moral precepts and patterns of conduct that the recipients already know and practice, a description of the friendly relations between sender and recipient, the call for imitation of personal models, and discussion of moral commonplaces (the "quiet life," sexual purity, and consolation in the face of death). In Paul's hands, however, these standard features of paraenesis are transformed. Most importantly, exhortation is placed in a theological framework focusing on Paul's theology of election.[23] The members of the community are portrayed as God's elect, who have been chosen by God (1:2) and set apart for sanctification (4:3) and holiness (4:7). Paul, thus, is not merely encouraging the Thessalonians to live a virtuous life. Rather, as he puts it himself in the letter, he is "urging and encouraging you and pleading that you lead a life worthy of God, who calls you into his own kingdom and glory" (2:12). The letter may be outlined as follows:

I.   **Opening**—1:1–9
II. **Body**—1:10–5:22
     A. An account of the apostles' relationship to the community (2:1–3:13)
     B. Clarification of Paul and his coworkers' prior teaching (4:1–5:10)

> C. Guidelines for the community's mutual care and exhortation (5:11–22)
>
> III. **Closing**—5:22–28

As you pause to read this letter, pay attention to Paul's use of the triad: faith, love, and hope.[24] This triad appears at a number of points in the New Testament, leading some scholars to argue that Paul is drawing on a pattern in early Christian tradition used in baptismal catechesis.[25] Whether this is the case or not, it is clear that in 1 Thessalonians faith, love, and hope provide thematic unity to the letter as a whole. They are woven into the various parts of the letter like three leitmotifs in a musical score. This triad makes its first appearance in the thanksgiving of the opening section, the letter's prelude so to speak: "We always give thanks to God for all of you and mention you in our prayers, constantly remembering before our God and Father your work of *faith* and labor of *love* and steadfastness of *hope* in our Lord Jesus Christ" (1:2–3).

Paul explicitly draws his readers' attention to this triad at two points later in the letter, a clear indication its inclusion is intentional. He describes Timothy's report about the community as "the good news of your faith and love," failing to mention their hope (3:6). Throughout the letter, Paul has nothing but praise for the Thessalonians' faith and love. But they are confused about their hope in Christ, something Paul attempts to correct in the second part of the letter. After he has done so, he rejoins hope to faith and love: "But since we belong to the day, let us be sober, and put on the breastplate of faith and love, and for a helmet the hope of salvation" (5:8). While my discussion will follow the three parts of the body of the letter outlined above, I will give special attention to these leitmotifs as they come to the fore.

Moral Formation through Example and Relationship (2:1–3:1)

On the surface, the first part of the letter is a straightforward account of Paul and his coworkers' past and present relationship to the Thessalonians. Paul is explaining why he has not been able to return to them and his hope that he might do so in the near future. A closer reading, however, reveals a moral function. Paul is praising the Thessalonians for their faithfulness and describing the sort of mutuality of care and encouragement among Christians that makes this possible. He also recalls the apostles' tender care for the community, holding it up as an example of the way they are to love one another. What appears to be a simple account of the apostles' past and present relationship to the community, thus, is a model of both faithfulness and love.

The model of faithfulness. In the first part of the body of the letter, Paul lifts up faithfulness in the face of persecution as an important quality of the Christian moral life. He points to his own example in this regard and to the example of the Thessalonians themselves. Paul explicitly links this theme to the imitation motif at two points:

> And you became *imitators* of us and of the Lord, for in spite of persecution you received the word with joy inspired by the Holy Spirit, so that you became an example to all the believers in Macedonia and in Achaia. (1:6–7)

> For you, brothers and sisters, became *imitators* of the churches of God in Christ Jesus that are in Judea, for you suffered the same things from your own compatriots as they did from the Jews, who killed both the Lord Jesus and the prophets, and drove us out. (2:14–15)

In both of these imitation passages Paul praises the Thessalonians for their faithfulness in the face of suffering and persecution. Already they have imitated Paul and his coworkers, the churches of Judea, and their Lord by remaining faithful. In turn, they have become an example for Christians throughout Macedonia and Achaia. As Beverly Gaventa aptly puts it, "The imitators have become the imitated, the evangelized become the evangelists."[26]

It is noteworthy that both of these imitation passages follow closely on Paul's praise of the Thessalonians for accepting the gospel as God's Word and not merely as human teaching (1:5; 2:13). He portrays this Word as still active among them, providing them with the courage to stand firm in spite of human opposition and allowing the word of the Lord to "sound forth" from them (1:8). It is no accident, thus, that Paul describes the apostles' initial visit to Thessalonika in 2:1–4 along these same lines. Though Paul and his coworkers were mistreated in Philippi immediately before arriving in Thessalonika, they still preached the gospel with "courage in our God" in spite of "great opposition" (v. 2). This description is designed to remind the readers of their example of faithfulness, based on their confidence in the gospel as God's Word. Moreover, it is the gospel of Jesus Christ that ultimately is the paradigm of faithfulness they are to imitate. In both of the imitation passages cited above, the Thessalonians' imitation of Paul and the churches of Judea is linked to their imitation of the Lord (1:6), who was killed by the Judeans (2:15; cf. 5:10). A kind of chain runs from imitation of their crucified Lord, to imitation of exemplars of faithfulness near at hand (the apostles and the churches of Judea), to the Thessalonians own role as a living reminder of the Lord's faithfulness for other Christians in their province.

A final dimension of the leitmotif of faith in the first part of this letter is found in 2:17–3:10, which focuses on the congregation's mutual care and encouragement that makes it possible for its members to remain faithful in the face of opposition. Using emotionally charged language, Paul describes himself and his coworkers as "orphaned" from the Thessalonians and as longing with eagerness to see them once again face to face (2:17). When they could "bear it no longer" (3:1), Timothy was sent "to strengthen and encourage you for the sake of your faith, so that no one would be shaken by these persecutions" (3:1–2). Clearly, Paul is worried that without the apostles' support, the Thessalonians will not remain faithful in the face of the persecution they are experiencing. Paul's relief upon receiving Timothy's report almost sounds like that of a concerned parent, as Gaventa points out.[27] Even more remarkable is Paul and his coworkers' response: "For this reason, brothers and sisters, during all our distress and persecution we have been encouraged about you through your faith. For we now live, if you continue to stand firm in the Lord" (3:7–8). Note the clear element of mutuality in this passage. The apostles who offer encouragement are encouraged in turn. In the face of their own difficulties, Paul, Timothy, and Silvanus find their faith strengthened by the faithfulness of the Thessalonians. Care and encouragement run both ways.

A model of love: Paul's tender care of the community. The leitmotif of love also appears in the first part of 1 Thessalonians, although it is not mentioned explicitly after the thanksgiving until 3:6, 12. Here again, it is important to see the moral function of the letter's description of the apostles' past relationship with the Thessalonians. The apostles' tender care of the community is held up as a model for the congregation as a whole, which is exhorted to deepen its relations of mutual love (3:12; 4:9–10). Their care also serves as a model for the leaders of the congregation who offer exhortation and care in the apostles' absence (5:12–16). In 2:5–12, Paul develops two familial images to describe the apostles' care of the community: a wet nurse and a father caring for their children. Both evoke images of loving concern and indicate the sort of family-like relations Paul is attempting to cultivate in the congregation: Just as the apostles lovingly cared for them, they are now to love and care for one another.

In 2:7–8, Paul intensifies the usual image of a wet nurse by portraying her as caring for her *own* children. He makes two points about the prior ministry that he and his coworkers had offered the Thessalonians.[28] First, this ministry involves more than merely handing on a prepackaged bundle of beliefs; it involves the sharing of their very selves. As Paul puts it, "So deeply do we care for you that we are determined to share with you not only the gospel of God but also our own selves, because you have become very dear to us" (2:8). Second, Paul portrays the apostles' ministry as one in which they renounce their own rights (here, the right of financial support pointed to in 2:7, 9) in order not to burden those whom they serve.

Paul then offers the image of a father caring for his children in 2:11: "We dealt with each one of you like a father with his children, *urging* and *encouraging* you and *pleading* that you lead a life worthy of God." As Malherbe notes, Paul is reminding the Thessalonians of the different forms of exhortation and care offered by the apostles while they were with them, signified in the differentiated language of urging, encouraging, and pleading.[29] They paid attention to each one of them and attempted to exhort them in ways that were suited to their personal needs. This too is an example of loving care. As we shall see, Paul commends this same sort of personalized exhortation in his closing instructions to the community.

Moral Education and the Apostles' Prior Teaching (4:1–5:22)

By now, it should be clear why it is not adequate to confine Paul's exhortation to those parts of 1 Thessalonians where he offers explicit moral teaching. In the first part of the letter, what seems to be a simple description of the apostles' relationship with the community actually offers models of faithfulness and loving care. In the second part of the body of the letter, Paul builds on this foundation. Teaching of two sorts is offered: (1) clarification of the apostles' prior moral instruction (4:1–12), and (2) correction of the Thessalonians misunderstandings of Paul's earlier teaching about Christ's parousia, the ground of their hope (4:13–5:10).

Clarification of prior moral teachings (4:1–12). Paul's moral teaching in this section appears to be elicited by questions the Thessalonians have raised during Timothy's recent visit. The passage clearly indicates that moral instruction was offered to the Thessalonian converts by the apostles when they first established the community: ". . . as you learned from us . . . For you know what instructions we gave you" (vv. 1–2); ". . . as we directed you" (v. 11).

The most important theological note sounded in this part of the letter is the sanctification (v. 4) and holiness (v. 7) of the congregation. Like Israel, the congregation is portrayed as set apart by God; therefore, its members' behavior should reflect God's claim upon them. They are to "walk" in a way that is "pleasing" to God (v. 1). In a society that grounds moral appeals in the desire to win honor and glory before one's human peers, Paul's framework represents a striking contrast. Paul reminds his readers of his prior teaching, praising them for the ways they are embodying it already and urging them to do so "more and more" (vv. 1–2, 10).

Of special interest is the way Paul's teaching is directed toward building up a distinct sense of moral identity in the congregation. His teaching on sexual conduct (vv. 3–8) creates a boundary between the community and the surrounding world, as well as reinforcing a sense of discontinuity with their former lives. The Thessalonian Christians are not to act "with lustful passion, like the Gentiles who do not know God" (v. 5). Paul is addressing a predominantly Gentile congregation, and this sort of language reminds them of the break they have made with their former lives and with the conduct of their neighbors. Their new beliefs entail new moral commitments, especially with regard to their sexual conduct. Conversely, Paul's teaching on love (vv. 9–10) is designed to strengthen bonds within the community and between the congregation and Christians in other parts of Macedonia. Paul uses the term for sibling love, *philadelphia*, for the family-like relations he is attempting to cultivate within the community. He also portrays them as "taught by God" in their love for one another.

This love among the Thessalonian Christians, however, does not preclude love toward their non-Christian neighbors, a theme Paul has already introduced in 3:12: "May the Lord make you increase and abound in love for one another and *for all*" (cf. 5:15). While the members of the congregation are to love one another like family members, this love is to extend beyond the community to relations with outsiders. Paul gives greater specificity to how they are to conduct themselves toward "outsiders" by reminding them in 4:11–12 of his prior teaching on this topic, which concludes this part of the letter. They are to "live quietly," "mind their own affairs," and "work with their hands" (vv. 11).[30] These terms draw on a philosophical tradition harking all the way back to Plato, who commended the person who "remains quiet and minds his own affairs." This perspective was sharply criticized by other philosophers, such as Seneca, who argued, "What one avoids, one condemns." Paul seems to strike a middle ground here, articulating a social ethic appropriate to a struggling sect that already has experienced difficulties with its neighbors. When possible, the congregation should avoid social entanglements that might provoke further antagonism. At the same time, he seems to be differentiating the "quiet life" of Christians from the behavior of the Cynics and Epicureans, who were widely criticized for sponging off others and constantly meddling in others' affairs. The Thessalonians are to follow Paul's example (2:7, 9). They are to work with their hands to support themselves (v. 11). In this way, they will not be dependent on others and will win the approval of outsiders (v. 12).

Teaching Christian hope (4:13–5:11). This brings us to the leitmotif of hope, which now comes to the fore. The passage is divided into two parts. The first part deals with a pastoral problem in the community (4:13–18) and the second with the importance of being "watchful" in light of the Lord's imminent return (5:1–11). Paul begins by taking up a theological misunderstanding about the nature of Christian hope, prompted by the death of some in the congregation. What will happen to those who have "fallen asleep" when the Lord returns?[31] It is clear that the apostles have already taught the Thessalonians an eschatological framework to understand Jesus' resurrection, material likely to be new and confusing to a group of Gentiles. In order to reframe their fears about the salvation of those who have died, Paul reminds them of part of a familiar creed: "For since we believe that Jesus died and rose again . . ." (v. 14).[32] He does not go on to explain this with difficult theological or scriptural exposition, as he sometimes does in other letters. Instead, he paints a beautiful word picture of Jesus' parousia, linking his resurrection to his return. The Lord is portrayed as gathering to himself those who have already fallen asleep and those who remain alive. Paul offers this image to console the Thessalonians, not to scare them. He is inviting them to reframe their present experience of grief in light of their hope in God's promised future: ". . . so that you may not grieve as others do who have no hope" (v. 13). Moreover, this hope is to animate their care for one another: "Therefore encourage one another with these words" (v. 18).

Paul continues the discussion of hope in 5:1–10, drawing out the ethical implications of the eschatological framework he has taught them. He urges the Thessalonians to maintain readiness, for "the day of the Lord will come like a thief in the night" (v. 2), perhaps an allusion to the Jesus tradition.[33] As children of the day, Christians are to orient themselves toward the coming day of the Lord (v. 2) and not adopt attitudes and behaviors of the night. In this struggle they are equipped with armor: the breastplate of faith and love and the helmet of hope (v. 8). The allusion here is to Isaiah 59:17, where the armor belongs to God. It is likely that Paul wants his readers to recall the image of Christ's triumphant return he offered them in the previous passage. The armor with which they struggle against sin and evil in the present is given to them by the One who will eradicate these forces in the future.[34]

Mutual exhortation and care in the community (5:11–22). Paul concludes the body of the letter by offering general guidelines about the Thessalonians' care and exhortation of one another:

> Therefore, encourage one another and build up each other, as indeed you are doing. But we appeal to you, brothers and sisters, to respect those who labor among you, and have charge of you in the Lord and admonish you; esteem them very highly in love because of their work. Be at peace among yourselves. And we urge you, beloved, to admonish the idlers, encourage the faint hearted, help the weak, be patient with all of them. (5:11–13)

While verse 11 is often viewed as concluding Paul's discussion of hope in the preceding passage, Malherbe argues it also serves as a transition to his comments on their mutual care and exhortation in 5:12–13.[35] The word translated "encourage" is *parakaleō*, which here has the twofold sense of comforting and exhorting. The word translated "build up" is *oikodomeō*, the sort of edification examined in the previous chapter. Mutual care and moral encouragement are ways of edifying the community in love.

In this passage, Paul gives instructions about two things: (1) how the community is to regard its leaders who continue the ministry of exhortation in the apostles' absence, and (2) the personalized manner of this exhortation and care.[36] He charges the congregation to respect its leaders "in love" (v. 13), creating an explicit verbal link to his earlier discussion of the love and the tender care offered by the apostles. In the same verse, he urges the Thessalonians to be "at peace" with one another, perhaps anticipating that some members will resent their leaders' moral guidance. Paul then shifts to the second concern: the individualized manner of this exhortation and care. Only the "idlers" are to be admonished, perhaps singling out those in the community who are refusing to follow Paul's instructions to support themselves in order to make a positive impression on outsiders (4:11). The other three forms of exhortation are gentler and offered with an eye to the specific needs of the recipients.

In 5:19–22, Paul instructs the Thessalonians to discern the words of the prophets. Since we will examine the way Paul teaches his congregations to carry out discernment in the following section, my comments at this point will be brief. Paul writes: "Do not quench the Spirit. Do not despise the words of the prophets, but test everything; hold fast to what is good; abstain from every form of evil" (5:19–22). As Gaventa notes, the verses hang together, with each subsequent verse explaining the one immediately preceding it.[37] "Do not quench the Spirit" is immediately followed by the admonition not to despise the words of the prophets. Those who disregard prophetic utterance when the community comes together are in danger of "extinguishing the flame" of the Spirit. Paul instructs the Thessalonians to "test" (*dokimazō*) prophetic utterance in order to distinguish good from evil. They are to hold on to what is good and to refrain from what is evil. Here, in his earliest extant letter, Paul takes us to the heart of discernment: seeking the guidance of the Holy Spirit and testing the insights of those who speak under her inspiration in order to distinguish good from evil.

Exhortation in Other Pauline Letters

In 1 Thessalonians, we have an especially nice example of Paul's exhortation of a particular congregation. While it is not possible to examine this second task of Paul's teaching ministry in all of his letters, three features of Paul's moral formation and education in 1 Thessalonians also are prominent elsewhere in the Pauline corpus:

1. Paul's exhortation in a particular letter is grounded in theological themes that are developed throughout the letter as a whole. In 1 Thessalonians, Paul develops exhortation in the context of his theology of election. As a community chosen and set apart for sanctification by God, the Thessalonians are to build up one another in faith, love, and hope. While this theology of election informs Paul's understanding of moral formation and education throughout his various letters, in each epistle he highlights other theological themes that are suitable to the rhetorical situation he is attempting to address in a particular congregation. In Galatians and Romans, for example, extensive attention is given to the theme of justification by grace through faith and not works of the law. In these two letters, he also develops the theme of walking in the Spirit as the basis of the moral life and portrays obedience as rooted in Christians' new life "in" Christ, as we saw in Romans 6. In 2 Corinthians, Paul emphasizes the theme of participation in the suffering of Christ, not only to defend his own ministry but also to provide a model for the Corinthians to imitate. In Philippians, the members of the congregation are portrayed as citizens of a heavenly commonwealth in the face of difficulties they are experiencing with their neighbors. He develops the theme of fellowship, or *koinōnia,* to describe their partnership in his ministry and the importance of unity in the congregation in the face of the crisis they are facing.

Obviously, this discussion barely skims the surface of the theological themes taken up in each of Paul's letters. The important point to keep in mind is that Paul's moral formation and education are grounded in his theology. When you read his letters, you will often be able to see this interconnection if you pay attention to the indicative/imperative structure of Paul's exhortation.[38] By *indicative,* I mean the way Paul describes the Christian life as grounded in God's prior activity in Jesus Christ. This is the basis of their identity as God's people. By *imperative,* I mean the way Paul exhorts Christians to adopt certain patterns of thinking, feeling, and acting in response to God's prior activity and to embody in the shared life of the community their identity as God's people. You also will do well to pay special attention to the introduction of Paul's letters, especially his prayers of thanksgiving and statements of the letter's theme. Typically, Paul provides important clues here about the theological themes he will develop over the course of the letter.

2. Moral exemplars are important in Paul's moral formation and education. Paul begins 1 Thessalonians by giving an account of his past relations with the congregation and his longing to be with them again. We found Paul using this discussion to develop models of faithfulness and love, pointing to his own example, to the example of his coworkers, and to the example of the Thessalonians themselves. Ultimately, these are connected back to the pattern of Christ's own faithfulness and love. Paul points to moral exemplars throughout his letters. It appears to be a key part of his moral formation and education. It is rooted not only in Paul's theology but also in his practice. No doubt his experience of founding and building up congregations led him to realize the shaping power of a living example. If he wanted to introduce his Gentile converts to a new way of life, then he needed to point them to examples of this life with which they could identify. To explore Paul's use of this strategy in other letters, there is no better place for you to begin than passages in which Paul explicitly uses the language of imitation, for example, 1 Corinthians 4:16–17, 11:1; and Philippians. 3:17.

But Paul also develops models of the Christian moral life in many other passages where the term "imitation" does not appear. In 2 Corinthians, for example, he develops the theme of his participation in the sufferings of Christ, a theme introduced initially in the introduction (1:3–11).[39] He offers lists of apostolic hardships (4:7–12; 6:4–10; 11:23–29; 12:10), which depict his own participation in the death of Jesus, allowing it to become visible in his body (4:10). God's power is made evident in the apparent weakness and hardships of his ministry, an example the Corinthian "wise" would do well to imitate.

Similarly, in Galatians 1:11–2:14, Paul offers a kind of "autobiography of reversal," in which he sets forth the exclusivity of the gospel's claim on his life as an example for the Galatians to follow.[40] He embodies the law-free gospel that he preaches and teaches, leaving behind the former works of the law that distinguished him as a Jew. He appeals to the Galatians: "Friends, I beg you, become as I am, for I also have become as you are" (4:12). In the face of Christian teachers who have convinced some of the Gentile members of the congregation to adopt the markers of Jewish identity, Paul urges the Galatians to follow his example and to stand firm in the gospel of grace.

Likewise, Paul appeals to the Philippians to "join in imitating me, and observe those who live according to the example you have in us" (Phil. 3:17). He offers an account of his time in prison and his joy at the way God is using his apparent hardship to further the gospel. The Philippians may soon find themselves confronting this same sort of hardship, and they must put aside their bickering and stand united as a community if they are to face this crisis with joy and confidence like Paul. Philippians also points to the One to whom this chain of imitation and mutual upbuilding ultimately must lead: Christ. At the very heart of this letter is hymnic material that portrays the self-giving love of Christ, "who, though he was in the form of God, did not regard equality with God as something to be exploited, but emptied himself, taking the form of a slave . . . and became obedient to the point of death" (2:6–8).

3. *Paul's explicit moral teachings not only build on and clarify his prior teachings,*

but they also are directed to specific issues that have emerged in different congregations. There are fairly clear bodies of moral teaching in Paul's letters. We saw this in 1 Thessalonians 4:1–12. This sort of moral teaching also can be found in Romans 12:1–15:13, 2 Corinthians 6:14–7:1, Galatians 5:2–6:10, and Philippians 3:12–21. Throughout his letters, Paul also sprinkles in lists of vices (e.g., 2 Cor. 12:20–21; Rom. 1:29–31; Gal. 5:19–21) and virtues (e.g., Gal. 5:22–23; Phil. 4:8). Only rarely does Paul offer general moral teachings (e.g., Rom. 12–14). Typically, his moral teaching addresses specific questions raised by the community or issues that have come to his attention through the reports of others. In 1 Thessalonians, for example, we found him clarifying teaching on Christian hope that had been misunderstood in the community. Most of the time, his moral teachings and lists of vices and virtues have important links to the specific issues with which one of his congregations is struggling.

The highly contextual nature of Paul's moral teachings has given rise to debate among biblical scholars and ethicists about the normative status they are to be afforded.[41] Some scholars view his moral teaching as providing abiding laws and prescriptive rules for the church in all ages.[42] Others see them as having binding force, but only as they are interpreted within their canonical and contemporary contexts.[43] Still others view Paul's moral teachings as embodying universal ethical principles such as love or nonviolence that surpass their particular form in any specific letter.[44] Finally, some scholars shift the focus away from the contents of Paul's moral teaching to the processes of moral discernment by which his congregations determine God's will anew in particular situations. By analogy, they argue, contemporary Christian congregations should focus on learning practices of moral discernment. Within this perspective, some emphasize the congregation's openness to the living God who speaks anew in each and every situation.[45] Others emphasize the *human* processes of discernment, accentuating the role of moral deliberation within an unfolding moral tradition.[46]

There is genuine pluralism, thus, among contemporary scholars about the normative authority of Paul's moral teachings. Regardless of where one comes down on this issue, it should be clear that Paul considered exhortation—moral formation and education—to be a very important part of his teaching ministry. He consistently reminded his congregations of who they are as God's new covenant people and challenged them to embody in their way of life their identity as communities called, justified, and sanctified in Christ Jesus. The importance Paul places on this second task of the teaching ministry has much to teach the contemporary church.

DISCERNMENT: LEARNING TO INTERPRET EVERYDAY LIFE ESCHATOLOGICALLY

In the final part of this chapter, we examine a third task of Paul's teaching ministry, namely, the way he teaches his congregations to engage in discernment. At the heart of Paul's understanding of discernment is learning how to live and think eschatologically, discerning the circumstances of everyday life in the light of God's promised future for creation. We will begin by exploring the relationship between discernment and eschatology and then turn to 1 Corinthians to watch Paul in the process of teaching discernment to one particular Christian community.

Discernment as Bifocal Vision and Interweaving Story Lines

In recent decades, no scholar has done more to underscore the influence of Jewish apocalyptic eschatology on Paul's thinking than J. Louis Martyn, who has developed a metaphor that will be central to my portrait of Paul's understanding of discernment. Throughout his letters, Martyn argues, Paul is attempting to teach his congregations how to view their everyday lives with *bifocal vision*.[47] Martyn's metaphor draws on the common experience of using bifocal eyeglasses, which have two portions: one for seeing things near and another for seeing things far away. In effect, Martyn asserts, Paul is attempting to teach his congregations how to see bifocally, to see simultaneously "*both* the enslaving Old Age and God's invading and liberating new creation."[48]

In unpacking the apocalyptic framework in which the bifocal vision is located, Martyn shifts metaphors from vision to drama.[49] Paul's preaching and teaching of the gospel portray everyday life in terms of an apocalyptic drama in which God is the primary actor. In his description of this drama, Martyn calls attention to the metaphors of war that Paul uses to portray dramatic action. The forces of evil are powerful in human history; they are the "rulers" of the present age and are unwilling to give up their power without a struggle. God's "invasion" of the world in Jesus Christ is a "collision" with these forces, summarized in Paul's "word of the cross." In crucifying Jesus, the forces of sin and death appear to have the upper hand, and God's power looks like weakness. But evil's triumph is illusory, for God has raised Jesus from the dead, validating Christ's suffering love and pointing ahead to his parousia, when the consummation of this warfare will take place. Until this consummation, the Spirit is sent to continue the battle, allowing Christians to resist the power of sin and death in their everyday lives.

To equip his congregations to participate in this apocalyptic drama, Paul teaches them to engage in discernment. They are to test the spirits in order to distinguish between the seductive spirits of the old age and the Spirit of new creation. This requires bifocal vision. First, Paul's congregations must learn to see "things near" as a battle zone, as a scene of conflict between contending forces. Second, they must learn to see "things far," viewing their present struggles with the hope born of God's resurrection of Jesus from the dead and the promise of Christ's parousia.

Building on Martyn's insights, I find it helpful to portray the bifocal vision of discernment in terms of the device of interweaving story lines, nestling one within another to create a multilayered and richly textured whole. This device portrays dramatic action as unfolding on a number of levels simultaneously and is used often in literature and film. One particularly artful example is J. R. R. Tolkien's *The Lord of the Rings,* in which dramatic action unfolds along many narrative axes, gradually coalescing around two primary story lines.[50] One story line follows a band of hobbits, a wizard, several men, an elf, and a dwarf who embark on a quest to cast a special ring of power into Mount Doom, located in the evil empire of Mordor. As the story unfolds, the band is sundered, until at the very end only Frodo, Samwise, and Gollum are present to bring the ring to its fiery destruction. As the story line of the ring bearer unfolds, a second narrative line also is developed, encompassing Gandalf the wizard, elves, a dwarf, and humans, who join together to fight the armies of Mordor head on in Gondor. Although the most powerful forces that contend with Mordor are seemingly narrated by this second story line, it actually is the success of the small and weak hobbits that ultimately leads to Mordor's doom.

The interweaving of story lines captures nicely the narrative elements of dramatic action that frame Paul's understanding of discernment. Within Paul's apocalyptic drama, two story lines are unfolding. One of these story lines focuses on the corporate person, Jesus Christ, the New Adam and firstborn of the new creation. In the events of his death and resurrection, we find the focal point of God's collision with the forces of evil, a collision in which all human beings are represented as Jesus acts on humanity's behalf and in its stead. This story line is yet to be completed, for it awaits Jesus' parousia and the consummation of God's confrontation with evil. A second story line unfolds in Paul's redescription of the everyday lives of his congregations. Repeatedly, he tells these communities that more is at stake than they realize in the petty squabbles and false steps of their life together. They must learn to see the unfolding events of their everyday lives through a new set of lenses.

In this second story line the Spirit is the primary actor, calling together a new people and refashioning their stories to reflect, if only faintly, the dramatic pattern of God's action in Christ. Discernment is especially necessary at those points in this story line when the dramatic action reaches a moment of tension and uncertainty, when some new and further step must be taken but the way ahead is not clear. At such points, the members of the Christian community must use bifocal vision, seeing things far and things near. They must recall the dramatic pattern of the story of Jesus, a story that reaches into the past but also stretches ahead to his future parousia. Simultaneously, they must see the particular, unfolding story in which they are actors as a drama in which the Spirit is at work. How might they follow the Spirit's lead and move ahead in ways that embody God's promised future for creation in their own particular circumstances?

Teaching Discernment to the Christians in Corinth

There is perhaps no clearer example of Paul attempting to teach one of his congregations how to think eschatologically and to use the bifocal vision of discernment than 1 Corinthians. In the discussion of edification in the previous chapter, we caught a glimpse of the factionalism and social tensions of the Corinthian community. It is likely that the spiritual arrogance of one faction was an especially important part of the rhetorical situation Paul is addressing in this letter. At a number of points, Paul appears to quote slogans used by this group, which he then reframes. Wisdom, knowledge, and an exaggerated emphasis on the gift of tongues appear to be prominent features of this group's perspective.

Until recently, it has been common to view the theology of this group as characterized by an "overrealized eschatology." As Richard Hays notes, however, it is Paul who reframes their issues in eschatological terms.[51] It is not that the Corinthian "wise" have an overrealized eschatology; they have *no eschatology at all*. They appear to represent a form of enthusiasm that is "a hybrid of Stoic and Cynic philosophical influences, popular sophistic rhetoric, and charismatic spiritual fervour."[52] It is likely that they see themselves as standing above the conventions of ordinary morality. They are dismissive of life in the body, reflecting a version of the spirit/matter dualism common in Greco-Roman philosophy and widely disseminated in popular culture.[53]

The immediate circumstances prompting the letter are a "report from Chloe's people" (1:11) and a letter from the Corinthians themselves (7:1a). The former described serious conflicts in the community (11:18) and probably also included information about sexual immorality (5:1–8; 6:12–20), legal disputes (6:1–11), abuses of the Lord's Supper (11:17–34), and theological controversy over the resurrection of the dead (15:1–58). The Corinthians' letter probably asked for Paul's judgment on several matters of practice: sex within marriage (7:1b–40), eating meat offered to idols (8:1–11:1), spiritual gifts in worship (12:1–14:40), and the collection for Jerusalem (16:1–4).

In his discussion of these various issues, Paul treats the theme of discernment more extensively than in any of his other letters. He is attempting to teach this community how to use bifocal vision to discern various issues in an eschatological framework. The Greek terms Paul uses to describe discernment in this letter are *dokimazō* and two closely related derivatives of *krinō*: *diakrinō* and *anakrinō*. *Dokimazō* means to examine or put to the test, as well as to accept something or someone as tested or proven. *Krinō* means to judge, separate, or distinguish. It was commonly used in legal contexts to describe the process of assessing evidence or rendering a judgment. *Diakrinō* and *anakrinō* maintain these basic meanings, although the former sometimes is used for "doubt." All of these terms are closely related in the Pauline corpus and, at times, seem to be used interchangeably. There are five places in 1 Corinthians where these terms are prominent: (1) discernment according to the cross (1:10–3:4); (2) self-examination to discern the effects of one's behavior on others at the Lord's Supper (11:28–31); (3) testing the words of the prophets (14:29); (4) church discipline and settling disputes in the community (5:1–6:20); and (5) discernment through debate and discussion in the meat-eating controversy (8:1–11:1).

Discernment according to the Cross (1 Cor. 1:10–3:4)

Paul's discussion of the cross at the beginning of 1 Corinthians provides the theological framework for his portrait of discernment throughout the letter. As various commentators have noted, Paul uses a chiasmic, or criss-cross ABA pattern, of argumentation at a number of points in 1 Corinthians. Fee argues that Paul adopts this chiasmic pattern in 1:10–3:4, using an ABBA pattern.[54]

A—Divisions in the church (1:10–16). Paul introduces the issue of divisions in the church by sharing with the Corinthians that he has received a report from Chloe's people that there is quarreling among them (v. 11). He makes an initial appeal that they be "in agreement" and "united in the same mind and same purpose" (v. 10). He introduces the dominant theological categories that frame his discussion of their quarreling and factionalism, asking if Christ is divided (v. 13) and describing his proclamation as focusing on the cross of Christ (v. 17).

B1—The cross as the apocalypse of God's wisdom and power (1:18–2:5). In this section, Paul reminds his readers of the "message of the cross" 1:18), which he proclaimed" when he was with them (2:1). It is here and here alone that they gain access to God's wisdom and power, which reverse the conventional standards of these things. Paul points to figures of wisdom and power in the world of his readers: philosophers, Torah teachers, and eloquent rhetors (1:20), who have failed to discern God's wisdom and power in the cross. He then introduces a note of reversal. The cross makes foolish the discernment of the wise and makes wise the discernment of the foolish who see in the cross God's hidden ways of salvation now revealed. He asks, "Has not God made foolish the wisdom of the world?" (1:20). He fills out this reversal by pointing to two examples in the Corinthians' own experience: the social composition of their community (1:26–29) and his preaching, which brought them to faith (2:1–5). Look at your own community, Paul tells them. "Not many" were wise, powerful, or from high-status families when they responded to the gospel (1:26). Likewise, his own preaching did not offer "plausible words of wisdom" like professional rhetors but was offered "in fear and in much trembling" (2:3–4).

In between these two examples of eschatological reversal, Paul places a passage that makes a crucial theological point (1:27–31). He weaves together the story line of the corporate person, Christ Jesus, who is their wisdom, righteousness, sanctification, and redemption (v. 30), and the story line of the Corinthian community. God chose the weak and foolish of the world to make it clear that no people have reason to "boast" of their own knowledge or wisdom. Rather, their "boast" rests exclusively on what God has done for them in Jesus Christ.

B2—The Spirit and discernment through the cross (2:6–16). In this passage, Paul reframes the Corinthians' understanding of spiritual wisdom and maturity, especially the perspective of those who view themselves as spiritually advanced and "boast" of their own wisdom and rhetorical power. He then moves to his central point: Knowing God through the message of the cross is only possible through the Holy Spirit. He utilizes a common philosophical principle in verses 10–13: Like is known by like. Just as individuals alone know their own inner thoughts and feelings, so too the Spirit alone has searched the depths of God and knows God's secret wisdom. Only those who have the Spirit can see God's wisdom and power in the cross, for this is "spiritually discerned" (*anakrinō*, v. 14). Paul then generalizes this point: "Those who are spiritual discern [*anakrinō*] all things, and they are themselves subject to no one else's scrutiny [*anakrinō*]" (v. 15). He appears to be engaged in a kind of wordplay here. Those who have the Spirit and discern the unveiling of God's secret wisdom in the cross are in a position to discern what God is doing in the world. Through the Spirit, they discern the world according to the cross, reversing the world's conventional standards of wisdom and power. But the world cannot judge or understand them, for it lacks the Spirit. Paul concludes the section with an inclusio, quoting Isaiah 40:13 to pose a question: Who knows the mind of God? His implied answer is those who have God's Spirit, which gives them access to the "mind of Christ."

A2—The problem of divisions reframed (3:1–4). In these four verses, Paul seems to be responding to criticism that his teaching is not sufficiently advanced for the "wise" in the community. The rhetorical effect of these verses is to reverse these persons' evaluation of their special status. Far from being wise or mature, they are mere "babes" who are still not ready for solid food. Those who are truly mature will embody the pattern of the cross, divesting themselves of the cultural markers of status and power and subordinating their own freedom to the good of the community.

Paul's theology of the cross plays a very important role in 1 Corinthians. Repeatedly, he draws on the paradigm of the cross to portray the Christian life as a reversal of worldly standards of power and wisdom and to criticize behaviors and practices found among the Corinthians.

Discernment and the Lord's Supper (11:28–31)

This passage is part of a larger body of material beginning at 11:17 in which Paul criticizes the Corinthians for the way they are practicing the Lord's Supper in the context of a community fellowship meal. Once again, this block of material appears to follow an ABA pattern.

A—The problem stated (11:17–22). Research into the social composition of the Corinthian community has revealed the likelihood of a broad cross section of contemporary urban society in its membership.[55] This has implications for our interpretation of the problem Paul is addressing. From his comments in verse 21, we can surmise that the common meal, which included the Lord's Supper, was being conducted in a manner that followed the widespread Greco-Roman practice of apportioning the best seats and food to people with the highest social status. Archaeological investigation of the villas of this period, moreover, reveals that dining areas could only hold around ten people, leading us to construct the following possible scenario as lying behind Paul's account: The patron hosting the gathering was inviting the higher status guests into the dining area, where they would recline at table and be served the best food and wine.[56] The poorer members of the community were left outside in the courtyard, where they received the leftovers or ate food they could provide for themselves.

B—The Lord's Supper as a norm (11:23–26). Paul's outrage is apparent. Not only does this conduct exacerbate social tension in the church, but it is also a sin against Christ, whose body and blood are "remembered" and "proclaimed" at this meal. Paul reminds his readers in verses 23–26 of the liturgical traditions that he handed on to them. This tradition focuses on the saving significance of Jesus' death, which inaugurated the new covenant binding the Christian community together. Through his death on humanity's behalf, Jesus has brought into being a new community that is not based on distinctions of social status, gender, and ethnicity. It is a fellowship created by common participation in the salvation offered by the one Savior and Lord.

A—The problem reframed (11:27–34). Paul bids the Corinthians to discern the oneness of the community whenever they participate in the Lord's Supper, recalling the analogy between the one loaf and the oneness of the community already introduced in 10:17.[57] In effect, he applies to the community's life the theme of eschatological reversal in the cross, initially treated in 1:10–3:4. In the way they are conducting the Lord's Supper, the community is perpetuating the world's standards of wisdom and power, giving the greatest places of honor and best food to those with the highest social status. These kinds of distinctions, Paul argues, should have no place in the Christian community. If anything, they should be reversed. It is shameful for the Corinthians to be humiliating those in the community who are poorest and have little to eat.

If this line of interpretation is correct, it helps us understand the confusing and much abused discussion of discernment in verses 27–34. This passage as a whole is knit together by a series of wordplays on judgment and discernment. Verse 27 returns to the problem initially stated in verse 21. Those who perpetuate the world's standards of status and power in the way they practice the Lord's Supper are "answerable for the body and blood." They miss the point of the Supper and "place themselves under the same liability as those responsible for Jesus' death in the first place."[58] In effect, they are putting themselves among those who view the cross as foolishness by treating the poor in the community with disdain. Paul bids them to examine or discern (*dokimazō*) themselves, for if they partake of the Lord's Supper without discerning (*diakrinō*) the "oneness" of body created by Jesus' death, they will bring God's judgment (*krinō*) on themselves.

Testing the Words of the Prophets (14:29)

In 14:29, Paul makes a passing reference to *discernment* of the words of the prophets in the context of material dealing with the orderly regulation of worship. He sketches a picture of a "free-flowing community gathering under the guidance of the Holy Spirit in which 'each one' contributes something to the mix."[59] Prophesy is portrayed as an especially important gift of the Spirit, for the prophet offers inspired insight in the form of intelligible speech. While Paul portrays this gift as highly prized in worship, he insists that it be "weighed" (*diakrinō*), that is, be subject to discernment. The other prophets or, perhaps, the community as a whole must test and judge the value of any particular prophetic utterance.

Practices of Discernment and Congregational Discipline (5:1–6:20)

This material is particularly interesting for our purposes, since it takes up three instances of behavior that Paul believes threaten the moral fabric of the Corinthian community. Throughout this section, Paul addresses the Corinthians as God's new covenant people, set apart in holiness for God's service. He draws on Israel's Scripture, mediated by traditions of Jewish moral teaching and practice, to offer instructions about how the community should respond to the immoral behavior in its midst.[60] Paul is encouraging the Corinthians to take corporate responsibility for these matters and to establish certain practices in which discernment is an important element.

Community exclusionary practices (5:1–13). The first situation addressed by Paul is an instance of gross sexual misconduct in which one of the members of the community is living in a sexual relationship with his stepmother. Paul tells the community that it is to gather in solemn assembly and expel the man from the church. While Paul is hopeful that this action will lead the individual to abandon his misconduct and, thereby, save him (v. 5), his primary concern is with the holiness of the community.

Brian Rosner has called attention to the Deuteronomic background of the exclusionary practice that Paul directs the community to carry out, clearly signaled by his citation of the Deuteronomic exclusionary formula in verse 13: "Drive out the wicked person from among you."[61] This formula is used six times in Deuteronomy to describe Israel's response to gross moral offenses by members of the covenant community. Such violations of covenant norms were seen as the responsibility of Israel as a whole, for they potentially violated the sanctity of the entire community. As in Deuteronomy, the Corinthian community as a whole is portrayed as responsible for the sinful behavior of the incestuous man. Paul is concerned about the effects of this immorality on their common life, signaled by his statement that a "little yeast leavens the whole batch of dough" (v. 6). He also is concerned that the community has not "mourned" (v. 2) the shameful conduct of this man, recalling Israel's sorrow in the face of violations of the covenant— the sort of "godly grief" Paul also describes in 2 Corinthians 7:10.

In a very real sense, Paul discerns this issue for the Corinthian community. While he does not tell its leaders how they are to handle extreme instances of moral misconduct in the future, the clear implication is that they are to develop practices of what the Christian tradition would later call "church discipline" in order to do so. Discernment stands at the heart of such practices. It is noteworthy, moreover, that sexual misconduct is not the only form of immoral behavior condemned by Paul. He also notes the possibility of disciplinary action toward the greedy and violent (v. 13), forms of behavior that have been less apt to come under the scrutiny of Christian discernment than sexual misconduct throughout the centuries.

Lawsuits against believers in 6:1–11. In this passage, Paul addresses another issue that also has to do with the community's responsibility for ordering its common life. Apparently, members of the community are taking one another to court in order to settle disputes. Paul recommends a practice of the diaspora Jewish community: appointing judges to settle disputes "in house."

Bruce Winter's research on civil litigation in the Greco-Roman world of the first century throws light on this passage.[62] According to his research, the court system of the Roman Empire was systematically biased in favor of higher-status and wealthier litigants. This is not surprising, for the judges were members of the privileged classes and would be likely to give preference to their social peers. Thus, the large majority of civil lawsuits were initiated by the wealthy against persons of lesser status and means. It is possible that the Corinthians who were initiating lawsuits against other church members were among the wealthier members of the community and the defendants among the poorer members. As Richard Hays notes, this is consistent with a pattern that appears throughout Paul's Corinthian correspondence in which those with greater status and means treat those of lesser status and means with disdain.[63]

Paul does not pronounce judgment on the guilty parties, as he did in the case of the incestuous man. Rather, he instructs the community in how he would like it to handle such matters. He appeals to the role the saints are to play in the coming eschatological judgment: They are to judge the world and even the angels (vv. 2–3). He then asks, "Can it be that there is no one among you wise enough to decide between one believer and another?" (v. 5). If those initiating the lawsuits are the very upper-class members who are claiming to possess exalted, spiritual wisdom, the note of sarcasm could hardly be more biting. The term translated "decide" here is *diakrinō*, which seems to imply that the judges appointed to handle these sorts of issues are being asked to engage in discernment on the community's behalf.

Paul then models discernment of the issue of lawsuits in terms of the pattern of the cross, recalling the sort of reversal associated with this theme throughout the letter. For the wealthy in the community to initiate such lawsuits at all is already a defeat for them and the community as a whole. In exercising their power and privilege in this way, they are conforming to the power structures of the surrounding world. It would be better for them to be defrauded and wronged than to relate to others in the community in this way. Even worse, by taking advantage of their worldly power and status, they "wrong and defraud" others in the community.

On fleeing sin (6:12–20). In this passage, Paul adopts the rhetorical device of the diatribe in order to carry on an imaginary dialogue with the Corinthian "wise." He appears to quote slogans used by this group to express their attitude toward certain moral matters and then offers his own counterslogans as a kind of rebuttal. Hays outlines this dialogue as follows:[64]

Corinthian Wise	Paul
"All things are lawful for me"	But not all things are beneficial.
"All things are lawful for me"	But I will not be dominated by anything.
"Food is meant for the stomach	The body is meant for the Lord,
and the stomach for food,"	and the Lord for the body
and God will destroy	And God raised
both one and the other."	the Lord and will also raise us by his power.

The first of these goes to the heart of the perspective of the Corinthian "wise," for Paul refers to it again in 10:23. Like certain forms of Greco-Roman philosophy, the "wise" Christian is viewed as being free to do anything he or she chooses in the body, for bodily existence is of no consequence in spiritual matters. Perhaps the man living in incest is an extreme instance of this position. In the current passage, the issue is sexual relations with prostitutes and the claim that such behavior is inconsequential. Indeed, the spiritually "mature" and "wise" believe that they demonstrate their freedom from bodily existence by making use of prostitutes to satisfy their sexual needs, needs that are to be gratified in the same way one satisfies hunger. Hence, they offer the slogan "Food is made for the stomach and the stomach for food" to justify their behavior.

Paul counters this view by weaving together three theological arguments to underscore the importance of bodily existence: (1) God's resurrection of Jesus confers worth and meaning on bodily existence and anticipates the general resurrection of the dead (v. 14); (2) our bodies belong to the Lord to whom we have been united in baptism and whom we now serve (v. 14, 17), for we have been "bought with a price" (v. 20); (3) the body is the temple of the Holy Spirit (v. 19). Under no circumstances are the Corinthians to view sexual relations with prostitutes as a trivial matter. Paul offers two corollaries to these arguments: The Corinthians are to "flee sexual immorality" (v. 16) and to "glorify God in their bodies" (v. 20). In the first, Paul probably has in mind the story of Joseph fleeing Potiphar's wife (Gen. 39:7–23) as this was treated in contemporary Jewish moral teaching.[65] Far from viewing the use of prostitutes as a casual matter, the Corinthians are enjoined to "flee" all such situations, just as Joseph ran away from Potiphar when she attempted to seduce him. The positive corollary of glorifying God in their bodies recalls his portrayal of the body as the temple of the Spirit, rendering their bodily conduct a way of honoring God.

Discernment of a Controversial Social Issue (1 Cor. 8–10)

In 1 Corinthians 8–10, Paul treats a contemporary issue that is causing real disagreement among the Corinthian Christians and the early church generally:

whether it is acceptable for Christians to eat meat that has been sacrificed to one of the pagan gods.[66] It is important to remember that this would have included virtually all meat for sale in the marketplace and would have placed the wealthier members of the Corinthian community in an awkward position when they dined in the homes of friends or in clubs, business groups, and other associations. The Jerusalem Council (Acts 15:1–21) laid down the rule that Gentile Christians were to abstain from "things polluted by idols" (15:29) and "from what has been sacrificed to idols" (21:25). The fact that this remained a controversial issue in the Christian community (see Rev. 2:14, 20) seems to indicate that it was not as settled as the author of Acts implies.

What is striking about Paul's treatment of this issue is the way he gives voice to the various positions that are present in the Corinthian community. He articulates them in terms of the perspectives of the "strong" and the "weak." There is good reason to believe that when Paul refers to the "strong" in this block of material he probably has in mind the same faction of Corinthian "wise" he has been addressing throughout this letter. It is noteworthy that on this issue Paul articulates the perspective of the "strong" sympathetically, even as he corrects it.

Paul also gives voice to the perspective of the "weak" in the community. Apparently, some Corinthian Christians believe that pagan gods continue to have real metaphysical status and power alongside the God in whom they now believe. Any contact with these gods will give them power over a person—eating meat sacrificed to them being a case in point. As Meeks notes, there was a long tradition among Jewish and Greco-Roman writers that satirized the superstitious, religious attitudes of the uneducated.[67] They were often ridiculed as seeing evil spirits everywhere and engaging in superstitious practices to protect themselves from the power of these spirits. Perhaps this is how the "strong" view the position of the "weak." If so, it is important to note that Paul counters this ridicule by articulating the perspective of the "weak" sympathetically as well.

In his treatment of the meat-eating controversy, Paul models for the Corinthians the sort of mutual listening and perspective-taking involved in the communal discernment of controversial social issues. Let us see how he carries this out over the course of these three chapters. As you read this material, keep in mind that Paul's argument follows the chiasmic ABA pattern we have found him using throughout this letter.

A—The perspective of the strong (1 Cor. 8). In this chapter Paul introduces the problem and articulates it from the perspective of the "strong." Many scholars believe that he quotes slogans of the "strong" throughout this chapter (vv. 1b, 4b–c, 8) and then offers his own comments. The "strong" realize that the gods of the pagan temples are not real and, thus, eating meat sacrificed to them poses no danger. It is only threatening to those who are superstitious. Paul adds his own insights to this perspective, linking it to the monotheistic affirmation of Israel's Shema (v. 4) and perhaps part of a Christian confession (v. 5). He then challenges the "strong" to take the perspective of the "weak" in verses 7–13, taking account of the possible effects of their behavior on them. If the "strong" cause other Christians to stumble, then they are harming the very people "for whom Christ died" (v. 11) and are, in effect, engaging in "sin against Christ" (v. 12).

B—1 Corinthians 9. Here Paul seems to digress. His strategy, however, is one that we have seen him use repeatedly. Paul offers himself as an example to be imitated. As an apostle, he has the right to receive financial support from his congregations (9:3–5, 14). But he renounces this right in order not to "put an obstacle in the way of the gospel of Christ" (v. 12). He then sets forth the basic principle that guides his practice: "For though I am free with respect to all, I have made myself a slave to all" (v. 19). This is the norm that should guide the Corinthian "strong." They rightly know that there is no real god but the God revealed in Jesus Christ, granting them freedom with regard to meat sacrificed to idols. But will they use their freedom as Paul does?

A—1 Corinthians 10:1–11:1. In this section, Paul deepens the concerns of the "weak" about eating meat sacrificed to idols by linking their perspective to Israel's Scripture. He describes Israel's wandering in the wilderness in ways that draw out analogies to the Corinthian Christians' experience. Though Israel was "baptized" in Moses and fed with spiritual food, this did not keep it from falling prey to idolatry and practicing sexual immorality. He then exhorts the "strong" to flee idolatry (v. 14). Their affirmation that "an idol has no real existence" (8:4)—an affirmation with which Paul agrees—is now deepened by identifying idols with "demons" (10:19–20). They should not be so smug about their entanglements with such things. Paul also returns to one of their slogans, "All things are lawful" (v. 23), and responds, "But not all things are beneficial" and "not all things build up." He lays down a principle that is similar to his practice, described in the B portion of this chiasmic pattern: "Do not seek your own advantage, but that of the other" (v. 24). He ends with a series of guidelines that allow a certain amount of discretion in how individuals handle this issue. Depending on the scruples of their "conscience" (used five times in vv. 25–29), they may eat meat sacrificed to idols for sale in the marketplace or served in meals offered by others. He ends with an inclusio, reminding his readers one last time of his own example of not seeking his own advantage but that of the many (10:33) and exhorting them to "be imitators of me, as I am of Christ" (11:1).

First Corinthians 8–10 has a great deal to teach the contemporary church about discernment. Paul has stepped right into the middle of a controversial social issue that is the cause of real tension in the Corinthian community. His strategy is to invite his readers to peer over his shoulder as he models for them how they should debate and discuss this issue. Perhaps he hopes that if he teaches them how to discern the meat-eating controversy, they will be better prepared to debate and discuss similar issues in the future. He makes sure that all relevant perspectives are given voice and heard by the other parties in the debate. At times, he deepens these perspectives by drawing on his own knowledge of Israel's Scripture and Christian tradition. He offers a general principle that should guide their treatment of one another, a principle having greater weight because it is embodied in his life and practice. He leaves room for individuals to follow the dictates of their own consciences within the general parameters he sets forth. Contemporary congregations face many controversial social issues today, and their leaders would do well to learn from the way Paul invites the Corinthians to discern the meat-eating controversy in these chapters.

Discernment as a Task of the Teaching Ministry

As we come to the end of this section on discernment, it is important to note that there are other points in Paul's letters where discernment also is treated. Romans 12:1–2, for example, is an especially important passage on moral discernment, framing the paraenesis Paul offers in the latter part of that letter. Likewise, Galatians 6:2–4 treats the self-discernment (self-examination) of leaders who are involved in congregational discipline and exhortation (cf. Gal. 5:13–6:10). Moreover, there are practices closely associated with discernment beyond those treated in this section; prayer is a case in point. But our examination of 1 Corinthians has brought many things into focus, and I highlight four here.

1. Paul teaches and models discernment. Paul wants the Corinthians to learn how to test the spirits, to draw on Scripture to interpret the present, to debate and discuss contentious issues, and to seek the guidance of the Holy Spirit. Discernment is an important part of living and thinking eschatologically.

2. Two frameworks are associated with Paul's understanding of discernment. The first focuses on *bifocal vision,* in which "things near" are viewed as the sphere in which the Spirit is struggling to bring forth new creation amid the counterforces of sin and death, and "things far" are viewed through the lens of God's promised future for creation. The second framework focuses on the *interweaving of story lines* in which the story of God's dealings with the world as narrated in Israel's Scripture and the gospel of Christ are interwoven with the stories and incidents that make up the everyday lives of Paul's congregations. In 1 Corinthians, Paul's interweaving of story lines makes extensive use of his theology of the cross.

3. Paul encourages his congregations to establish certain practices of discernment. These practices were designed to assist the community in making different sorts of judgments—from excluding a member, to settling disputes internally, to determining moral behavior, to handling controversial social issues.

4. Paul leaves room for the free exercise of individual conscience. This is grounded in a commitment to the common good of the congregation and to the principle of love as seeking the good of others.

CONCLUSION

We now have before us three key tasks of Paul's teaching ministry in his congregations: (1) catechesis, handing on and interpreting Scripture and tradition; (2) exhortation, moral formation and education; and (3) discernment, learning to live and think eschatologically, discerning the Spirit's guidance in the circumstances of everyday life within the drama of God's redemption of the world in Christ and his future parousia. In the next part of this book, we will look at three portraits of contemporary congregations as they carry out the tasks of catechesis, exhortation, and discernment. Following Paul's example, we will engage the cultural and intellectual resources of the contemporary world to understand how we might best carry out these tasks today. But also, like Paul, we will adapt and transform these resources as they are brought into dialogue with theology and placed in the service of the teaching ministry of Christian congregations.

PART TWO
FRAMING THE
TEACHING MINISTRY
OF CONGREGATIONS:
Practices, Curriculum, Leadership, and Pilgrimage

Introduction to Part Two

During high school and college, my daughter became a skillful photographer. She has the eye of an artist. Where I see only a dilapidated doorway or clump of rocks, she has the capacity to imagine pictures that are interesting and beautiful. She is particularly gifted in the way she frames the subject matter of her pictures. Over the years, she has purchased a variety of lenses that allow her to frame people and objects in quite different ways. Using a telephoto lens, for example, she sometimes zooms in for sharply focused close-ups with a blurred background; other times, she uses a wide-angle lens to create a panoramic view.

As you enter the second room of this gallery, it will be helpful to keep in mind the way photographers use different lenses to frame their subjects. Over the course of part 2, I use four "lenses" to bring into focus different aspects of the teaching ministry, using what I will call the practices, curriculum, leadership, and pilgrimage *frames*. While the subject matter is the tasks of the teaching ministry emerging from our conversation with Paul—catechesis, exhortation, and discernment—these tasks will be framed quite differently as we examine three case study congregations.

Technically speaking, we will be engaging in both interdisciplinary and multidisciplinary thinking. *Interdisciplinary thinking* is a conversation between two or more fields that results in the construction of a new and richer perspective on a subject matter than is available on the basis of the research and thinking of only one of these fields.[1] In recent decades, many different fields have begun to work in this fashion. Some forms of contemporary cognitive psychology, for example, draw on the research of neuroscience, evolutionary psychology, cultural anthropology, and developmental psychology. Howard Gardner's theory of multiple intelligences is a well-known instance of interdisciplinary work along just these lines.[2] As we saw in part 1, the field of contemporary biblical studies also frequently carries out interdisciplinary work in which the perspectives of rhetoric, history, literary theory, and theology are brought into conversation.

Throughout part 2, I carry out an interdisciplinary conversation in which theology is brought into dialogue with a number of fields. I will refer to the unique perspectives afforded by such interdisciplinary conversation as *frames*.[3] Think of this as analogous to the way an experienced photographer frames her pictures. She selects a particular lens to bring certain features of her subject into focus. But she also varies other factors, such as the f-stop, shutter speed, and type of film. It is the interaction of all these variables that allows her to create a particular picture of her subject.

The same sort of concrete interdisciplinary decisions have gone into the frames that were created to examine the teaching ministry of the case study congregations in part 2. I am not interested in merely an abstract conversation between theology and psychology, for example. Rather, I am interested in bringing a very specific set of theological ideas and perspectives into dialogue with a particular psychologist working in very specific ways to create a frame that brings into focus certain aspects of the teaching ministry. In chapter 4, for example, we examine the teaching ministry of Nassau Presbyterian Church through the curriculum frame. This perspective brings into focus the ways a congregation supports cumulative growth and learning in a systematic, intentional, and sustained fashion. I created this particular frame through an interdisciplinary dialogue between the Reformation's theological emphasis on practices of education in the Christian life and the perspectives on human growth and learning developed by Howard Gardner and James Fowler.

In the epilogue, I describe more fully the transversal model of interdisciplinary conversation informing my work in the following chapters. The important point to grasp at present is that each of the frames developed in these chapters is the result of an interdisciplinary dialogue between theology and other fields. My research on the case study congregations has led me to believe that more than one frame is necessary to bring into focus the different ways catechesis, exhortation, and discernment are actually carried out in these communities. The use of multiple frames is sometimes known as multidisciplinary thinking.[4]

Multidisciplinary thinking marshals the perspectives and analysis of many fields to understand complex, dynamic systems out of the recognition that no single frame or perspective can adequately understand everything going on in such systems. In modern urban planning, for example, multidisciplinary thinking is used to draw on the perspectives of economics, architecture, ecological studies, applied sociology, and population demographics. Similarly, modern education commonly uses the perspectives of psychology, sociology, and ethics in its work. Contemporary genetics, likewise, brings together the frameworks of biology, chemistry, and computer science.

Each of the frames developed in this book is the result of an interdisciplinary conversation. The use of four frames is an exercise in multidisciplinary thinking. All four of these perspectives are necessary if we are to see the ways catechesis, exhortation, and discernment take place in the teaching ministry of congregations. Think of this once more as analogous to photography. The task of framing one picture of a subject by using a particular lens and camera setting is comparable to viewing the teaching ministry through one of the interdisciplinary frames developed in each of the following chapters. Changing the lens several times and varying the f-stop and shutter speed to create quite different pictures of the same subject is comparable to using the multidisciplinary approach of four frames to explore the teaching ministry.

I learned the importance of viewing the teaching ministry of congregations through several lenses from my study of three case study congregations. I did not begin my research with these four frames in mind. As I used the tools of congregational studies to learn more about each congregation's ethos, identity, and mission and attempted to identify the ways teaching and learning take place in each of these quite different communities, it gradually became clear that more than one frame or perspective was necessary.

For example, the congregation I studied in South Africa, the Uniting Reformed Church of Stellenbosch, does not have a particularly strong church school, especially in comparison to the other two congregations. Many of the church's members are semiliterate, and formal classroom teaching is not the most important way that the teaching ministry is carried out in this congregation. When I began to interview its members, however, I quickly realized that they are deeply steeped in the stories of Scripture and have a highly developed sense of their confessional tradition. How did they learn these things? As I discovered more about the history of this congregation, I began to realize that this learning took place as the congregation struggled to come to terms with the adaptive challenges of life under apartheid. The leaders of the congregation played an especially important role in helping its members interpret their experience of oppression with the stories of Scripture and a new confession that rallied their denomination to resist this evil. As I reflected on this insight, I gradually began to develop my understanding of the leadership frame, which I describe in the chapter on this congregation.

Each of the frames treated in the following chapters emerged in a similar way. They grew out of a combination of empirical investigation, reflection on my research, interdisciplinary thinking, and theory construction. What I am presenting here, thus, is the end product of a process that, often, was quite messy and proceeded in fits and starts. In a very real sense, the empirical, interpretive, and normative dimensions of my work as a practical theologian interacted all along the way.

FOUR FRAMES OF THE TEACHING MINISTRY

It is important for the field of Christian education to learn how to work more fully in both an interdisciplinary and multidisciplinary fashion. Why? When one surveys American "religious education" of the past century, one cannot help but be struck by the fact that, too often, its most prominent theorists used a single frame, based on one organizing model, in their writings.[5] Congregations were portrayed as being like schools that offer education in classroom settings. Or congregations were viewed as being like tight-knit small groups, which hand on the faith through the enculturation of face-to-face interaction across the generations. Or congregations were seen as being like activists in a social movement who learn by reflecting on the struggle to change the dominant institutions of society. Intuitively, many pastors and Christian educators have recognized that each of these frames and others like them bring into focus important dimensions of the congregation's teaching ministry. They realize that multiple frames are necessary to capture the various facets of this ministry. Accordingly, in the chapters that follow, I will explore catechesis, exhortation, and discernment through four different frames.

1. The *practices frame* brings into focus the ways a congregation is a community sharing a way of life embodied in its practices, which mediate both traditions of the past and contextual challenges of the present. This frame invites us to think of the teaching ministry in terms of *congregational formation*.

2. The *curriculum frame* brings into focus the ways a congregation is a school that educates its members through practices of education which promote learning in a systematic, intentional, and sustained fashion over the course of the human life cycle. This frame invites us to think of the teaching ministry in terms of *congregational education*.

3. The *leadership frame* brings into focus the ways a congregation is a learning organization that faces adaptive challenges with the potential of altering both its internal life and its relationship to the surrounding social context. It conceptualizes "adaptive work" as a learning process that is promoted by the formal and informal leaders of the congregation. This frame invites us to think of the teaching ministry in terms of *congregational leadership*.

4. The *pilgrimage frame* brings into focus the ways a congregation is composed of individuals at very different points in their faith journeys. It

draws our attention to the importance of developing personalized contexts and relationships that make room for the diverse backgrounds, needs, and interests of individuals in the same congregation. This frame invites us to think of the teaching ministry in terms of *congregational support of individuals* on their unfolding pilgrimages of faith.

I unpack these frames more fully in the following chapters and use each one to explore the teaching ministry in a case study congregation. Each chapter follows a similar format. I begin with a brief discussion of the congregation, developing a "theological discrimen," that is, a focal image that sums up in a single, synoptic judgment the central elements of the ethos, identity, and mission of this particular community.[6] It is an outgrowth of my interviews and observation of the congregation, coordinating the perspectives of congregational studies and theological interpretation. This is followed by an interdisciplinary account of the frame being used to study that congregation's teaching ministry, beginning with a description of the theological perspective informing my understanding of this particular frame and then moving to engage conversation partners from other fields. I then return to the case study congregation and examine its teaching ministry through this particular frame.

THE FOUR FRAMES: AN INTERPRETIVE FRAMEWORK

To better understand why it is important to use multiple frames to understand the teaching ministry, it is helpful to view these frames in terms of the ecclesiological framework developed by the Dutch practical theologian, Johannes van der Ven. In *Ecclesiology in Context*, van der Ven explores the changing functions of the church in the modern world.[7] He identifies four core functions of congregational life: (1) *identity formation,* forming and transforming the Christian identity of the congregation and its individual members; (2) *integration,* incorporating, assimilating, and binding together the individual members of the congregation; (3) *policy formation,* forming goals consistent with the purposes of the congregation; and (4) *management,* developing organizational forms and structures that enable the congregation to pursue its goals. As van der Ven points out, each of these functions has become more challenging in a secular, pluralistic modern world. Christian congregations can no longer take for granted that other social institutions will provide support for these tasks. Indeed, in many cases, other institutions erode the plausibility of Christian beliefs and practices.

I believe that van der Ven's perspective on the challenges facing contemporary congregations has become even more important in the face of globalization. I have written extensively about globalization elsewhere and offer only a brief summary here.[8] I use the term *globalization* as a historical-interpretive category comparable to sociohistorical categories such as modernization and feudalism. Following many other scholars on this topic, I do not think this term should be ceded to politically conservative, free-market advocates. Rather, globalization marks the emergence of new social processes and institutional arrangements that can be contrasted with modernization.

In the West, modernization began to occur in the aftermath of the Reformation and Renaissance. It was characterized by the rise of the modern nation-state and the first impulses toward the creation of national cultural identities, national political and judicial systems, and, eventually, national economies. These early trends were given their distinctive, modern form with the rise of modern science and the industrialization of the economy in the nineteenth and twentieth centuries. Science was both the basis of the technological innovation driving the industrialization of the economy and the key paradigm of modern rationality. As a historical-interpretive framework, thus, modernization focuses on those social processes and institutions closely associated with the emergence of the modern nation-state, the rise of modern science, and the industrialization of the economy, which began during the sixteenth century and continued to unfold through the first half of the twentieth century.

As a historical-interpretive framework, globalization points to a markedly different set of social processes and institutions.[9] It brings into focus the diminishment of the nation-state as the center of cultural, political, and economic activity and the movement away from heavy industry as the driving force of the economy. Three closely related "revolutions" that unfolded in the latter half of the twentieth century have driven globalization to this point: (1) the technological revolution of the electronic media, emerging largely out of the invention of microprocessors for computers but also related to advances in other forms of electronic and satellite communications; (2) the emergence of global systems of various sorts, based on this technological revolution in the media; and (3) the collapse of the Soviet Union and the bipolar structuring of interstate relations that characterized the Cold War, leading to the emergence of new, multipolar forms of political organization and cultural-religious identity.

Obviously, modernization did not stop one day and globalization begin the next. Nation-states are still important centers of cultural, political, and economic activity. Scientific research and technological innovation continue to be important dimensions of contemporary life. But a significant shift has begun to take place, which I believe is best viewed as the early stages of globalization. While it is apparent that the institutional and cultural patterns of modernity are changing, it is unclear at this point what new patterns will emerge.

Particularly helpful is the analytical framework developed by David Held and his colleagues in *Global Transformations* and other writings.[10] They argue that globalization is best conceptualized as a "stretching of social, political, and economic activities across frontiers such that events, decisions and activities in one region of the world can come to have significance for individuals and communities in distant regions of the globe."[11] They point to transregional interconnectedness involving networks and cultural flows across local and national boundaries. These networks and flows are not occasional or random. They are regularized such that there is a detectable *intensification, extension, and speeding up* of interconnectedness, resulting in a deepening enmeshment of the local, regional, and global.

Drawing on this analytical framework, Held and his colleagues argue persuasively that globalization is reshaping the economic, political, and cultural patterns of modernity. They also make the important point that the forces currently driving globalization and the new patterns they are bringing into being are historically contingent. They can be reshaped and engaged critically. One of the purposes of theorizing the processes of globalization is to allow communities to better understand and respond to these forces. Otherwise, these forces simply unfold "behind their backs."

I am aware that much more needs to be said about globalization theory, especially in light of the way it frequently is identified with a neoconservative political agenda. In marked contrast, the perspective I have too briefly developed builds on the thinking of David Held, who stands in the tradition of critical social theory as articulated in the writings of Jürgen Habermas.[12] What I have attempted to offer in these few pages is a glimpse of the interpretive framework that informs my understanding of the teaching ministry of contemporary congregations. As outlined in the book's introduction, this is the second task of practical theological reflection.

I conclude by placing van der Ven's understanding of the challenges facing contemporary congregations in the context of globalization theory. If anything, these challenges have become more complex and urgent in this new social context. Consider the challenge of identity formation. In light of the global media, increased travel, and the migration of populations to cities within and across national borders, young people today face the daunting task of constructing a meaningful sense of identity in the face of many different cultural "others." They are quite aware that the values and beliefs of their own cultural communities are only one option in our multicultural world. In the face of this sort of intensification and extension of the experience of cultural pluralism, religious communities face a significant challenge in building up and transforming the individual and corporate identities of their members.

The same is true of the other challenges van der Ven identifies. Religious switching, interreligious marriages, and migration make it more difficult than ever to integrate people into religious communities in ways that bind them together and, simultaneously, acknowledge their diverse backgrounds, needs, and interests. Likewise, many communities around the world are caught up in changes so rapid and large that they seem beyond local residents' control. In such circumstances, congregational leaders face the daunting task of helping their churches understand and respond to these adaptive challenges in ways that are consistent with their values and beliefs.

With slight modifications, it is possible to relate the frames developed in the following chapters to van der Ven's framework. Each of the core functions he identifies represents an important vector of growth and learning in contemporary congregations, as summarized below. I group together policy formation and management because I believe that the concept of learning organizations comprehends both tasks. Moreover, I associate two frames with the function of identity formation, for I view this as taking place both through practices of congregational formation and through the education of the congregational curriculum.

Functions of Congregations and Frames of the Teaching Ministry

Identity Formation

Function: building up and transforming individual and corporate Christian identities

Frames: Practices

Curriculum

Learning the Christian way of life through participation in the shared practices of the congregation

Growth over time toward post-conventional forms of Christian identity through practices of study

Integration

Function: incorporating and binding together the members of the community in ways that acknowledge their diverse backgrounds, interests, needs, and gifts

Frame: Pilgrimage

Building communities that support the unique spiritual pilgrimages of their individual members and that challenge their members to rework their understanding of their vocations—their calling to partnership with God—over the course of their lives in the context of Christian community

Policy and Management

Function: Setting goals in light of the mission of the congregation and developing organizational forms and roles by which to work toward these goals

Frame: Leadership

Building congregations that are learning organizations in which leaders help members respond to the adaptive challenges of their own time and place

Chapter 3

Three Case Study Congregations

In this chapter, I begin to share the results of several years of research on three case study congregations: Somang Presbyterian Church of Korea, Nassau Presbyterian Church of the United States, and the Uniting Reformed Church of Stellenbosch, South Africa (hereafter referred to as URC Stellenbosch). In my research on these congregations, I used a combination of different methods, including interviews of ten children, ten youth, and ten adults in each congregation, videotaping, interviews of church leaders, and participant observation.[1]

Over the course of this project I have become increasingly aware that congregations are not static. They are communities in motion. Since I completed my research on Somang, Rev. Sun Hee Kwak—the senior minister of the congregation for its entire history—has announced his retirement. How the congregation handles this transition will have enormous implications for its future, and the recent history of this sort of transition in the megachurches of Korea reveals many potential problems. Nassau's new pastor, David Davis, had been at the congregation for only two months when I began this research. In many ways, my research reflects the ethos of the congregation prior to his arrival, still largely shaped by his predecessor, Wallace Alston, Jr. Even as I complete my research, signs of change are already visible. Over the past decade, URC Stellenbosch has entered a new social context with the arrival of free, democratic elections in 1994, marking the end of apartheid. Its response to the challenges of this new context are part of the story I will tell. But it also is clear to me that its adaptation to this context is still unfolding and that the younger generation is likely to challenge it to renegotiate its identity even further in the near future. What I offer in the following chapters, thus, are photographs of three congregations taken at a particular moment in time. To give you some idea of where these congregations have come from and the social and historical contexts that have shaped them, I provide a brief account of each congregation's story in this chapter.

SOMANG PRESBYTERIAN CHURCH OF SEOUL, KOREA

Somang's Story: An Introduction

Somang Presbyterian Church began as a prayer group with eleven members in the apartment of Min-Chul You on August 24, 1977.[2] In twenty-four years, Somang grew into a congregation of 43,978 registered members. It is one of the so-called megachurches of Korea, although it is by no means the largest.

In October 1977, Rev. Sun Hee Kwak was invited to become the minister of this community and the congregation affiliated with the Presbyterian Church of Korea. Rev. Kwak had served as the pastor of the First Presbyterian Church of Incheon for sixteen years before studying at Fuller Theological Seminary in the United States, where he received a doctorate in missiology in 1976. Upon his return to Korea, Rev. Kwak served as the president of Soong-Eui Women's College, and as he began his work in this fledgling house church he received no salary. Min-Chul You's apartment complex was located in the Apkujong Dong area of Seoul, south of the Han River. During the late 1970s, no large businesses were located in this part of Seoul. Nor were there many churches in this area. This all changed very quickly, as Apkujong Dong became an important residential area for the new business and professional class that emerged as Korea modernized. At present, it is one of the most desirable residential areas in Seoul.

From the outset, the congregation grew rapidly, which Min-Chul You attributes to Rev. Kwak's outstanding preaching. Within nine months of its founding, the church relocated to the third floor of a nearby business complex to accommodate the overflow crowds. In 1981 it built a worship center in Kangnam, located in the same part of Seoul, where the church remains.

During this early period, the church faced two crises that were to play an important role in shaping its identity. One focuses on the request of an elder who was a well-known and powerful politician in the Korean government. When he was appointed to a new position in the Blue House (comparable to the American White House), he approached Rev. Kwak about having the church host a special celebration in his honor. After prayerful deliberation, Rev. Kwak reached the conclusion that this was not appropriate. The elder was furious and attempted to rally opposition to Rev. Kwak in the church. For a time, there were pro-Kwak and anti-Kwak factions in the congregation. When it became clear that the large majority of the congregation supported their pastor, this elder left the church, taking approximately fifty members with him.

A second incident took place around 1987 when Rev. Kwak proposed an expansion of the original worship space and church complex. Several lay leaders actively opposed this proposal and began to campaign against the idea. As the conflict unfolded, a key member of this oppositional group accepted a bribe from one of the construction companies who wanted the church's business if it went ahead with the expansion. Word leaked out that this had taken place, causing much consternation in the congregation. Eventually, this person and some of his supporters came to Rev. Kwak, apologized to him personally, and wrote a letter of apology to the congregation as a whole, admitting their wrongdoing. They eventually left the congregation. This second crisis seems to have elicited more sadness than outrage. In an attempt to bring closure, many members of the church gathered for an all-night prayer vigil. They then gave themselves to the task of raising money for the building program, which included a mission and education complex, an office building, and a retreat center.

These two incidents shaped the identity of the congregation in several ways. First, the congregation developed a strong sense of unity. In its members' minds, a basic tenet was now established: No one person, regardless of how rich or famous he or she might be, is more important than the church as a whole. No special elite in the church would be given inordinate power and influence over its affairs. Second, these two events enhanced Rev. Kwak's charisma in the congregation. He was viewed as a leader who stands by his principles and is unwilling to be pushed around. Prior to the second incident, a kind of division of labor between the pastor and elders was present in the congregation. The pastor preached and provided pastoral care; the elders made all important decisions in the congregation. After this incident, the decision-making process became more hierarchical and centered around Rev. Kwak. Although Westerners might be inclined to interpret this negatively, it is important to place this style of decision making in context. Many Korean churches are torn apart by power struggles between the minister and elders. Since these two early incidents, Somang has been almost completely free of such conflicts.

The birth and meteoric growth of this congregation overlapped the most intense period of modernization in Korean history. The 1960s saw the beginning of a turbulent period of industrialization, urbanization, and democratization in Korean society. It has been common for the Western media to portray this period of Korean history in terms of either the imagery of the Cold War (i.e., Korea as the flashpoint in Asia of the conflict between democracy and communism) or as a showcase example of the "Asian economic miracle" (i.e., Korea as embodying the way a country can become a successful player in the global marketplace). A closer look, however, reveals a period filled with government and business corruption, massive social dislocation, labor unrest, and a slow, painful journey toward democracy.

Somang's growth during this period raises certain questions, especially from the perspective of Western social scientific theory. As social scientists have documented repeatedly in the United States and Western Europe, an increase in education and personal prosperity is inversely related to church affiliation.[3] When these factors are combined with urbanization—with its greater anonymity and pluralism—the most common result is an increase in religious disaffiliation.[4] What is remarkable about Somang's rapid growth during this period was its ability to appeal to some of the most highly educated members of the Korean population, many of whom were the beneficiaries of Korea's economic development. These are trends that fly in the face of Western church demographics. Moreover, Somang has learned how to inculcate a service orientation among the very people competing most successfully in the global economy, fostering an anti-elitist attitude among its nation's cultural elite.

The key to understanding Somang's success as a congregation lies in paying attention to the distinctive matrix of congregational practices it has established over the course of its short history. These are clearly articulated in Rev. Kwak's theology of ministry and are readily apparent to observers. These practices form a vital matrix for Christian identity formation in a cultural context that offers few of the traditional Western supports for Christian identity. Moreover, these practices have preserved and creatively transformed many elements of Korean culture, especially Confucian elements. In a time of rapid modernization and globalization, this "creative conservation" of local culture may prove to be one of the most important tasks brought into focus by our examination of this congregation through the practices frame.

Somang against the Backdrop of Recent Korean History

Strategically located on a peninsula between China and Japan, Korea has a lengthy history of cultural influence and political intrusion from neighboring powers.[5] Because of these intrusions, it developed something of an attitude of distrust toward foreigners and was commonly known as the Hermit Kingdom. The end of this isolation and the beginning of modern Korean history began with the signing of its first international treaty in 1876 with Japan, which forced Korea to give Japanese citizens legal rights in the country and opened up several Korean ports to international commerce. This was followed by a new level of competition for influence in Korea between China, Russia, and Japan. Japan's victories in the first Sino-Japanese War (1894–1895) and the Russo-Japanese War (1904–1905), resulted in Japan's annexation of Korea in 1910. Japan's colonial rule of Korea had the tacit blessing of the other two Pacific powers of this period, England and the United States. Indeed, Theodore Roosevelt brokered the peace treaty ending the Russo-Japanese War in 1905 (for which he won the Nobel Peace Prize), which, in effect, made Japan the colonial lord of Korea.

Japanese colonial rule was brutal, and it still leaves a bitter taste in the mouths of most Koreans. Japan imposed a centralized police-state on the Korean people and attempted to strip away the population's cultural and historical identity. Through their control of the educational system, the Japanese overlords attempted to force Koreans to speak Japanese, adopt Japanese names, and accept a pro-Japanese interpretation of their history. They turned the imperial palace into a zoo and replaced many historic sites with "modern" Japanese-style structures.

According to historian Won Kyu Lee, the Japanese conquest of Korea left many Koreans deeply disillusioned with Confucianism and the aristocratic feudalism of the old Korea.[6] The leadership and solidarity displayed by many church leaders in the face of Japanese imperialism gave the church new credibility and led to the first period of church growth in the country. Sixteen of the thirty-three intellectuals who petitioned for Korea's independence in what came to be known as the March 1 Protest were Christians. In response to this petition, at least half a million Koreans took part in demonstrations, with many Christians at the forefront. The Japanese army arrested 45,000 and killed 7,500, including a group of protesters who were locked in a church that was burned to the ground.[7] Throughout this period, churches served as sanctuaries for protestors and contributed to the leadership of the nationalist and prodemocracy forces.

During World War II, Koreans were drafted into the Japanese army as foot soldiers or were forced to serve as laborers outside of Korea. In 1941, 1.4 million Koreans were in Japan alone, with 770,000 serving as laborers.[8] Workers in the Japanese mines had twelve-hour shifts, and women miners (between 60 and 70 percent of the workforce) were forced to work bare-breasted to "prevent" them from stealing. The Japanese conscripted over 100,000 Korean women to serve as "comfort women" for Japanese soldiers, a role that was little more than a form of sexual slavery.

At the end of World War II, Korea was forcibly divided along the thirty-eighth parallel, with Soviet troops initially occupying the north and American troops the south. An occupying American army and its military leaders supported the establishment of a conservative group of leaders in the south, under the leadership of Syngman Rhee, whose primary credential was his professed hatred of the communist north. Organized guerrilla warfare began in the south as early as 1948, and border fighting escalated throughout 1949. A full-scale civil war broke out in 1950, drawing in troops from the United States and China. When the Korean War finally ended on July 27, 1953, the original division of the country along the thirty-eighth parallel remained. But the cities and the economies of the north and south were in ruins. A sad legacy of autocratic rule was firmly reestablished in both countries, creating tensions and problems that remain with Korea to the present.

The postwar period saw the beginning of the modernization of South Korea's economy and educational system and a shift in the population from the countryside to urban centers. By 1989, 42 percent of South Korea's population lived in or near Seoul. The *chaebol*—gigantic, octopus-like corporations that dominate much of Korea's economy—also emerged during this period, especially during the 1960s and 70s. Their growth was often marked by the close—many would say corrupt—collusion of government and business. Between 1973 and 1978, Korea's GNP grew an average of 11 percent per year. Between 1985 and 1988, it grew by more than 12 percent. Foreign investment rose significantly.

This rapid economic growth came at enormous cost to the Korean population. Working conditions were often harsh, and labor unions were ruthlessly suppressed by business and government. While Korea ostensibly has been holding democratic elections since the end of World War II, in reality its political life has been characterized by a series of coups, the suppression of dissent, and the jailing of political opposition. Supplied and trained by the United States, the Korean CIA played a particularly unsavory role, not dissimilar to the security police in apartheid South Africa.

Throughout this period of social dislocation and political instability, many individual Christians and Korean churches, once more, played a role in supporting the forces of democratization. A Korean version of liberation theology, *Minjung* theology, emerged, and Protestant leaders such as Hyong-gyu Park, a Presbyterian minister, were prominent in the struggle for civil rights. It was not until 1987, however, that mass demonstrations by students, workers, religious groups, labor unions, and many ordinary Koreans led to the fall of the government. This ushered in a period of political reform and the first genuinely democratic elections in the country's history. In the decade that followed, steps were taken to expose the political corruption of the past and to establish Korea's fragile democracy on a firmer foundation.

It was precisely during this period of turmoil and transition that the Christian church saw its most rapid growth in Korean society. In the early 1960s, there were only 5,011 Protestant churches in South Korea, with 623,072 registered members. By the early 1990s, there were seven times as many Protestant congregations and eighteen times as many members of churches.[9] The Roman Catholic Church grew significantly as well. By the end of this period of church growth, Christians represented around 25 percent of the population. Korean sociologists such as Young Shin Park point out that the social dislocation and turmoil of modernization created a widespread sense of uncertainty and anxiety to which the churches were able to provide a meaningful response.[10]

Much of this church growth took place among the middle class, which expanded rapidly during this period and was highly invested in governmental reforms and economic growth. Will the churches and their middle-class members continue to contribute to the building of democratic public life and the extension of Korea's new economic prosperity to other segments of the population? This question is especially important for a congregation such as Somang Presbyterian Church, which has been able to attract many of the highly educated, successful members of the Korean middle class.

THE UNITING REFORMED CHURCH
OF STELLENBOSCH, SOUTH AFRICA

URC Stellenbosch's Story: An Introduction

The Uniting Reformed Church of Stellenbosch, South Africa, is a "coloured" congregation. My use of this term is based on the 1996 census of South Africa, which divides the population into white, black African (having roots in central Africa), coloured, and Indian (from India), categories widely used by contemporary South Africans in their everyday language, although with increasing debate. The coloured population is a result of the intermarriage of the Khoi and San peoples (the native peoples of the Cape before central Africans and Europeans arrived) with slaves brought by the Europeans from other parts of Africa, Indonesia, Malaysia, and elsewhere.[11]

The Uniting Reformed Church (URC) denomination to which this congregation belongs emerged out of the struggle against apartheid. It was founded in April 1994, a few days before the free elections that brought the "new" South Africa into being. It marked the union of the Dutch Reformed Mission Church (DRMC), founded in 1881 by missionaries of the white Dutch Reformed Church (DRC) for the coloured population, and the Dutch Reformed Church in Africa, established by missionaries of the DRC for the black African population. The term "uniting" was intentionally adopted in hopes that this unification would subsequently include the white and Indian branches of the Dutch Reformed family.

URC Stellenbosch, thus, was originally a part of the Dutch Reformed Mission Church, established for the coloured population. The congregation was founded in 1905 by the "mother church" of the DRC in Stellenbosch. The founding pastor was a white missionary, Rev. Latsky, who was the first of a series of white pastors that has continued to the present. When Rev. Latsky retired in 1946, the congregation had four hundred members, was financially independent, and had its own church building near downtown Stellenbosch. The older members of the church remember him fondly as the "founding father" and as shaping the congregation along the lines of the "warmhearted" Reformed piety of a missionary church. They describe the church as a "very good place for young people," with a youth choir, Youth Brigade, Sunday school, and catechism classes on the Heidelberg Catechism. The church also sponsored a day school, providing general education for the children of the coloured population. Throughout this period, church members worked as laborers in the wine and tobacco industries, held blue-collar jobs at Stellenbosch University, and were domestics for private families.

Rev. Latsky was succeeded by Rev. G. C. Oosthuizen, who stayed for only four years. While he was pastor, the National Party swept into power, inaugurating an aggressive policy of "separate development"—the literal meaning of the term *apartheid*. He was followed in 1952 by L. G. van der Werken, who continued the programs and warmhearted piety of his predecessors. Under his leadership, the congregation purchased land in the Idas Valley suburb on the outskirts of Stellenbosch and began to establish a mission church in that area. This missionary orientation has consistently been a part of the ethos of the congregation. Over the years, it has established three congregations in the Stellenbosch area: Vlottenburg, Koelenhof, and Kylemore. As it turned out, however, the land purchased in the Idas Valley suburb was to play a quite different role in the life of the congregation.

When van der Werken departed in 1959, he was succeeded by Rev. P. H. Müller, who served as pastor from 1960 to 1975. During this period, the apartheid policies of the Nationalist government intruded directly into the life of the congregation in a variety of ways. For example, the confirmation services of many coloured and black churches of the Stellenbosch area had grown so large that they had begun to use the town hall. Without warning, the government banned all use of this facility by "nonwhites," but diabolically made certain exceptions to this policy, allowing some congregations (including URC Stellenbosch) to use the town hall for confirmation. This strategy was designed to create friction within and between the black and coloured communities—and it succeeded.

In 1970, the long-time coloured neighborhood of the congregation was declared a "whites only" area. The entire coloured population was forced to move to new areas designated by the municipal government. Many were relocated to Cloetesville and Idas Valley. Cloetesville was little more than a farming area on the outskirts of town. There were few houses, no schools, no churches, and no social supports of any kind. Especially devastating for the church was the forced sale of its original church building to the government, which then sold it to a white Baptist community. To this day, the older members of the church look back at this event with great sadness. As one put it, "The white government described itself as Christian, but they said, 'You're not my color, so you can't stay with us.' Today the whites are trying to regain our trust. We don't hate. Being a Christian means a lot to us. They laugh and smile, and we truly say, 'We forgive you and love you.' But it is hard to forget, very hard to forget."

During this period of relocation, it was difficult to maintain even a semblance of congregational life. Part of the congregation continued to worship in the old church building until 1976. They suffered the indignity of being forced to lease the very space they once had owned. Others began to worship in an old hall located in Cloetesville. Still others joined forces with the mission church the original congregation had established in Idas Valley. This was the beginning of the "two-headed" congregation that characterizes URC Stellenbosch to the present. While it considers itself to be *one* church and has *one* pastor, it is composed of two worshiping communities located in different parts of Stellenbosch.

In my interviews with church members, two somewhat different perspectives emerged as people looked back at this period. Some believe that the church council was far too quiet about what was going on in the community during this period and wonder why their white pastor did not provide them with the sort of leadership needed to link their faith to "the cry for justice burning in the hearts of the people," as one member put it. They articulate a sense of shame that the congregation sometimes received preferential treatment by the white powers-that-be. But other church members offer a different perspective on this period, portraying church leaders as forced to make difficult and compromising decisions to keep the congregation alive. They recall Rev. Müller's work in paving the way for the new church building that eventually was built in Cloetesville and recall times when the congregation was unable to pay his salary. They also recall the enormous burden he shouldered in attempting to sustain pastoral care, Christian education, and worship for church members now located in two separate areas.

The decision-making process about the architectural design of the new church building in Cloetesville is in many ways a paradigm of the overall turmoil of this period for the congregation. The original sanctuary was quite traditional, with a steeple and bell tower. The design proposed for the new building attempted to balance two concerns: (1) to create a space with a fellowship hall, offices, class-rooms, and kitchen area that could serve the surrounding community, and (2) to create a modern sanctuary that marked a break with the past—a sanctuary without a steeple, bell tower, or stained glass windows. While there was unanimity about the former, the latter sparked great controversy. It was as if this proposed design became a symbol of the anger and grief many felt over the loss of their former place of worship. In the end, the modern design was accepted, although the pews of the old building were moved into the new sanctuary to retain some sense of continuity with the past.

With the church building almost finished, Rev. Müller resigned and was succeeded by Rev. A. S. van Dyk in 1976, who remained its pastor until 1980. The financial strain from the building program forced Rev. van Dyk to become a lecturer in biblical studies at the University of Western Cape, and he did not serve as a full-time pastor. It also compelled the church's leadership to take steps that many considered distasteful. At one point, the church treasurer began depositing the income of the congregation into his own personal account in order to prevent the bank from automatically deducting payments to service the loan for the new building. This was the only way some money could be set aside for the minister's salary. When the church council became aware of what was going on, a heated debate over the ethics of this practice ensued.

In June 1976, the first year of van Dyk's ministry, the Soweto uprising occurred. Black students took to the streets to protest the government's policy of requiring all high school subjects to be taught in Afrikaans. Within a short period of time, the protest spread across the country. Many schools closed because of student boycotts. Some were burned down. When the government reacted by sending riot police into the townships and arresting or banning protesters, the violence only escalated. Soweto became a symbol of a new level of resistance to apartheid.

Cloetesville schools were boycotted and shut down. Rock throwing encounters between coloured youth and riot police were daily occurrences right outside the new church building. It was sometimes unsafe for the congregation's white pastor to drive into Cloetesville to carry out his responsibilities. Church members remember coloured youth being arrested by the police on trumped-up charges and adults losing their jobs because they were accused of associating with protesters. During this period, the son of a prominent family of the church was killed by riot police.

Rev. van Dyk was outspoken in his criticism of apartheid, a risky stance for a white pastor. While the members of the congregation felt a profound sense of pain and anger, their inherited missionary theology had not equipped them to think theologically about the social events that were unfolding around them. Learning to make sense of these events in terms of their faith would be the focal point of the teaching ministry of the congregation in the coming years, involving a significant reworking of the congregation's sense of identity and mission.

In 1980, Rev. van Dyk left the congregation to serve the national church in Zimbabwe and was replaced by Johan Botha, who had worked in the coloured community as a volunteer while a student at the University of Stellenbosch. Botha's leadership proved to be a watershed in the life of the congregation, even though he was its full-time pastor for only eighteen months. Members recall Botha as an excellent preacher, administrator, and financial advisor, laying the organizational foundation on which the current pastor has built.

Rev. Botha's most important contribution, however, lay in helping the church make the transition from its older missionary piety to a new theological perspective that addressed more directly the political events and circumstances of life under apartheid. In the words of one of the church leaders during that period, "Johan Botha was the one who took us from a phase of religious childhood to religious adulthood in our thinking." In the years immediately preceding Rev. Botha's tenure, the Synod of the Dutch Reformed Mission Church adopted a public declaration condemning apartheid as a heresy and calling for a visible demonstration of church unity in the form of a new denomination that would bring together all branches of the Reformed churches. This was the first step toward the creation of the Uniting Reformed Church of South Africa. In chapter 6, we will take a closer look at the way Rev. Botha drew on this denominational process to lead the congregation through its own learning process, which ultimately was to alter its identity and mission.

After eighteen months, Rev. Botha became the general secretary for public witness of the Uniting Reformed Church, and in 1982 was succeeded by Jaco Coetsee, the present pastor. It is clear to me that Rev. Coetsee is loved and respected by the members of both Cloetesville and Idas Valley branches of this congregation. Under his leadership, the Idas Valley congregation has purchased a new building for its worship services. Both branches of the congregation have continued to grow. He also organized the congregation into a decentralized system of wards or house churches and has taken a leadership role in rallying Stellenbosch's pastors to join together in responding to the massive social problems that continue to plague this area. In chapter 6, we will focus especially on the many ways he has interwoven teaching into his leadership of the congregation.

URC Stellenbosch against the Backdrop of Recent South African History

The mosaic of contemporary South Africa began to take shape approximately two thousand years ago when various tribes of cattle herders from central Africa migrated to the south, where the Khoi and San peoples were already living.[12] These tribes were diverse and had their own cultural traditions and languages. The European migration began in 1652 when the Dutch East India Company established a trading colony at the Cape. The Dutch were soon followed by French and German Protestants and, in the early nineteenth century, by the English. European traders were primarily responsible for the wave of Asian migration that began around 1860, as they brought slaves and indentured workers from European colonies in southeastern Asia to the colonies in southern Africa, many of whom became farm laborers. Some Indian merchants came freely and established their own businesses.

Dutch colonial rule lasted from 1652 to 1795 and was briefly reestablished between 1803 and 1806. In 1795, Britain conquered the Cape colony as part of a general campaign to establish worldwide control of trade by sea. British rule created many difficulties for the Afrikaner population, descendants of the Dutch colonists. After 1830, several waves of Afrikaner settlers, commonly known as the Voortrekkers, moved to the interior to escape British rule. This brought them directly into conflict with the black African tribes living in this area. Especially bloody was their conflict with the Zulu kingdom, which under the innovative military leadership of King Shaka had expanded and consolidated Zulu control over much of the interior of the country.

Three independent Afrikaner republics eventually were established as a result of the Voortrekkers' migration. With the discovery of diamonds in the interior in the 1860s and gold in the 1880s, the British government sought to extend its control over these republics. This resulted in the Anglo-Boer War of 1899 to 1902, which involved over 200,000 British troops. In order to combat the guerrilla tactics of the Afrikaner forces in the countryside, the English commander ordered all Afrikaner women and children removed from their farms and placed in concentration camps, the first such camps in the twentieth century. Over 26,000 people died in these camps, more than double the total number of soldiers who died on both sides. Though the British established a unified South Africa in 1910, the Anglo-Boer War set in motion a chain of events that would sweep the National Party and its apartheid policies into government several decades later.

The war left many Afrikaners impoverished. This was intensified by a severe drought across southern Africa in 1929, which coincided with the worldwide economic depression. Within one generation, the social profile of the Afrikaner community changed markedly, as displaced landowners migrated to the cities in search of work as laborers. A 1932 report funded by the Carnegie Corporation found over 300,000 Afrikaners living below the poverty level. As the economic gap between these new "poor whites" and the black African and coloured population diminished, the ideology of Afrikaner nationalism and apartheid began to have great appeal in this increasingly defensive community. These ideas were supported by local Afrikaner theologies, which justified "separate development" through appeals to Scripture and Reformed theological themes.

Taking full advantage of these conditions, the National Party swept into office in 1948 and began to promote an aggressive program of apartheid. The term *apartheid* literally means "apartness" and "separateness" and commonly refers to policies of separate development and total segregation of the races promoted by the South African government between 1948 and 1994. But make no mistake. The foundations of apartheid had already been laid under British colonial rule. Laws that took the land from the black and coloured majority, denied these groups the right to vote, and controlled labor in a discriminatory fashion were already firmly in place by the 1940s. The National Party built on this foundation. During the 1950s alone, almost a hundred apartheid laws were adopted. The Population Registration Act of 1950, for example, classified all people in terms of race. New laws mandated the segregation of business areas, public facilities, educational institutions, and residential zones. They prohibited interracial social contact and denied all nonwhites the right to participate in the electoral process. During the 1960s, this policy was renamed "separate development" in the face of international criticism of apartheid, even as the government escalated its use of police and security forces to enforce its discriminatory policies and quell protest.

Resistance to these policies took a variety of forms—political, social, military, and ecclesiastical—which have been described in some detail by Nelson Mandela, Desmond Tutu, John de Gruchy, and others.[13] The "long walk to freedom," to borrow Nelson Mandela's phrase, was marked by decades of social and political turmoil, including armed struggle. Leaders of the African National Congress and other political groups were imprisoned. Many ordinary people who were protesting the policies of the government were jailed, tortured, or killed outright. The awful nature of the government's repression has only come to light recently in the harrowing accounts of the Truth and Reconciliation Commission.[14]

The church's role during the apartheid era was mixed. Throughout this period, the South African government received theological justification for the policy of separate development by theologians affiliated with the white Dutch Reformed Church. Some of these theologians were members of the theological faculty of the University of Stellenbosch. Many leading politicians were members of the DRC. Some scholars argue that the policies of apartheid also received passive support from the members of the white, English-speaking churches as well. South African theologian Dirk Smit, who is a member of URC Stellenbosch, provides a helpful summary of the role of neo-Calvinism in the justification of apartheid and the policy of separate development:

The emphasis on pluriformity in creation, stressed by the Reformed theologian in the Netherlands, Abraham Kuyper, played a major role in the theology of apartheid. The idea was that God intended and loved this pluriformity in the created order and that it should therefore be preserved. Humankind was created as pluriform as the rest of creation. The two biblical pericopes of the division of people at Babel (Genesis 11) and Paul's speech about the borders between people (Acts 17:26) were interpreted in this fashion and they played a crucial role in providing biblical sanction to the apartheid ideology. . . . Each race now had a God-given responsibility to maintain its identity. Each "people" was "chosen" for a specific "calling."[15]

In the face of this sort of theological justification of apartheid, ecumenical bodies and denominations both within and beyond South Africa began to pressure the white denominations to change their policies during the 1970s and 80s. Under the leadership of Beyers Naudé, founder of the Christian Institute of Southern Africa, many began to call for a Confessing Church movement comparable to the one that appeared in Germany under the Nazis.[16] The World Alliance of Reformed Churches, the World Council of Churches, and the Dutch Reformed Missionary Church came to the conclusion that theological justification of apartheid was a heresy and that a *status confessionis*—the confrontation of the church with a novel and partial interpretation of the gospel that threatens its very identity and witness—existed in the Christian community of South Africa.[17]

Especially important to the story of URC Stellenbosch were the actions of the Dutch Reformed Missionary Church. The denomination followed its declaration of a *status confessionis* with the creation of a confessional statement that came to be known as the Confession of Belhar.[18] This became an important rallying point in its call for all branches of the Reformed family to unite in order to send a powerful signal to the rest of society that the largest Christian body in South Africa would no longer collude with the apartheid policies of the government. While the black Dutch Reformed Church in Africa joined the DRMC in forming a new denomination, the white DRC and the Indian Reformed Church of South Africa chose not to participate. Johan Botha, Dirk Smit, and others affiliated with URC Stellenbosch were deeply involved in these events. We will explore this period in chapter 6, giving special attention to the ways leaders moved the congregation through a learning process that resulted in a profound shift in its theological identity and sense of mission.

NASSAU PRESBYTERIAN CHURCH OF PRINCETON, NEW JERSEY, U.S.A.

Nassau's Story: An Introduction

Nassau Presbyterian Church of Princeton, New Jersey, U.S.A., came into being in 1973 through the unification of First Presbyterian Church and St. Andrews Presbyterian Church (formerly Second Presbyterian). The roots of First Church stretch all the way back to the 1750s when Presbyterian services were first held at the College of New Jersey, later renamed Princeton University. Given the rich documentation of the history of Nassau Presbyterian, I develop my account of its story primarily in terms of its teaching ministry.[19] Also, I give primary attention to the American social context from the 1960s forward. This decade is generally viewed as the starting point of a major restructuring of American religion.[20] Hence, I depart slightly from the format used in my accounts of the first two congregations. I tell Nassau's story up to the 1960s, then depart to offer a brief discussion of important trends characterizing American religion since the 1960s, and conclude by picking up Nassau's story line.

From the colonial period to the Civil War. In the 1750s, Princeton was a small village of thirty to forty houses, a way station on the coach line between New York City and Philadelphia. The first building of First Presbyterian Church was completed in 1764, but a board of trustees and session were not formed until the 1780s. The congregation installed its first full-time pastor, Samuel Snowden, in 1795.

Church records indicate that Rev. Snowden established a pattern of catechetical instruction common to most Presbyterian churches during this era. This included a "system of private Instruction and visitation in families, with catechising in private houses, in the different quarters of the Congregation, and accompanying it with a Lecture in each place, suitable to the occasion."[21] This pattern of Christian education emerged from the Reformation of the sixteenth century and was brought to the American colonies by the Puritans and other immigrants from Europe.[22] The teaching ministry largely focused around three pivotal activities: (1) the baptism of infants, which included the promise by parents to instruct their children in the home; (2) instruction of children in the Westminster Shorter Catechism by parents and the pastor or elders during home visitation; and (3) special catechism classes for young people when they reached the "age of discretion," culminating in their examination prior to admission to the Lord's Supper. This emphasis on the teaching of the catechism remained in force in the congregation through the Civil War era. The fourth pastor of the church, George Woodhull (1820–1832), organized this system of catechetical instruction more fully, dividing the congregation into four geographical districts, with the pastor and two of the elders responsible for different areas.

Over the course of the nineteenth century, the congregation established a second form of Christian education, the Sunday school and, briefly, a third, a Presbyterian parochial school. In the United States, the Sunday school movement was a lay-led, parachurch organization that ran parallel to the denominations.[23] It established "sabbath schools" throughout the country and produced study material with a strong evangelical flavor. A Sabbath School Association was formed in Princeton in 1815, and by 1818 a Sunday school was affiliated with First Church. The congregation constructed a new session building in 1831 to house the Sunday school. This building also came to be used by the Free School for the Borough of Princeton. This school offered both general and Christian education, setting the stage for the congregation's participation in the Presbyterian Church's brief experiment with parochial schools.

In 1848, First Church's session voted to take under its care three Presbyterian parochial schools—one for young boys and girls, a second for older boys, and a third for older girls. Lewis Joseph Sherrill, author of the definitive history of Presbyterian parochial schools, describes the regulations for these schools, drafted by the pastor and an elder in consultation with the faculty of Princeton Theological Seminary, as "the classic instance of the elaboration of the Presbyterian parochial idea."[24] Teachers were to be members of First Church, and the pastor and an elder were to inspect the school monthly. The entire session was to be present at the school's semi-annual examinations. All books were to be approved by the session, and every child old enough to read was to be provided with a Bible, the Westminster Shorter Catechism, and a hymnal. Young children were initially to be instructed in a simple children's catechism and then to begin memorizing the Westminster Shorter Catechism at the rate of four questions per week. The school day was to begin and end with prayer. While tuition was charged, the regulations stated that the session reserved the right to admit "indigent scholars" to the schools tuition free.[25] Even after public education was reorganized in Princeton in the 1850s—with First Church's pastor, James Macdonald, a member of the new school board—the Female Benevolent Society kept these parochial schools going for a number of years.

A final part of the congregation's story during this period is its role in the rancorous fight between New School and Old School Presbyterianism. During the 1820s, Charles Finney, a Presbyterian minister, had come into national prominence through the success of his revival campaigns in upstate New York, giving rise to a movement known as New School Presbyterianism. Old School Presbyterians considered Finney's "scare tactics" inappropriate on theological grounds, as an attempt to convert people through human manipulation instead of trusting the Holy Spirit to call the elect in God's own good time. By 1831, half of the congregations in the New Brunswick Presbytery (First Church's presbytery) were identified with this revivalistic movement.[26]

College students and members of First Church, under the leadership of a seminary student sympathetic to Finney-style revivalism, pressured the pastor and session to allow the church building to be used for a protracted revival meeting. When the session refused this request, this group circulated a petition of protest and began holding services in the building housing the Sunday school. In 1832, the session received a request from twenty-three persons for help "in forming & organizing a Second Presbyterian Church in this Borough."[27] Although the session denied this request, it led to the resignation of the pastor a week later. Apparently, the desire to form a new church more congenial to New School beliefs and practices continued to simmer beneath the surface of the congregation, because on December 23, 1847, a decade later, the session granted a second petition by eleven church members to withdraw and form the Second Presbyterian Church of Princeton. Over the course of this protracted struggle, the finances and church membership of First Church suffered. Between 1835 and 1849, the church had a net loss of 144 members.

While First Church and Second Church eventually established cordial relations, they projected different profiles from the beginning. First Church was closely connected to the university and seminary, and its membership included long-time residents of the community, including the "old money" of Princeton. Its theology was solidly Old School. Second Church was more open to the new currents of revivalism and proved more effective in attracting the laborers who migrated to Princeton to work in a brick factory and pottery. At a later point, many of the local shop owners were to join Second Church. It came to be viewed as the town church—less academic, friendlier, and more family oriented. Princeton now had two Presbyterian congregations with different identities.

From the Civil War period to the 1960s. The final decades of the nineteenth century were a time of rapid industrialization throughout the United States, especially in the Northeast. During this period, the volume of industrial production, the number of workers employed in industry, and the number of manufacturing plants in the United States all doubled. In 1860, agriculture represented 50 percent of the total national wealth; in 1900, it represented only 20 percent. Throughout this period of rapid social change, Princeton largely remained a university town surrounded by farmland. While train lines now provided access to New York City and Philadelphia, the major institutions of the community remained the university and seminary, which put Princeton on the map nationally.

While First Church and Second Church both cultivated ties to these institutions, they were much stronger in First Church. This is reflected in the contrasting patterns of leadership in the two churches. Between 1896 and 1951, every minister of First Church was both a graduate of Princeton University and a graduate of Princeton Theological Seminary.[28] Two of its ministers were called directly from the faculty of the seminary, and its interim ministers were all seminary professors. Moreover, it was not uncommon for half of the members of the session to be affiliated in some capacity with Princeton University. Many university students attended worship on Sunday morning, since the university still required students to attend church at least two Sundays a month. In marked contrast, the minister of Second Church who stands out during this same period, William Tucker (1940–1957), was born and educated in the South and is remembered as embodying the warmhearted, storytelling oratory of southern Presbyterian preaching. Following his departure, Second Church began to struggle.

It is noteworthy that the various histories of First Church, put together at the request of the session, consistently draw attention to their pastor's role in the community, presbytery, and national church. Robert Cawley's comments on James Macdonald, pastor during the Civil War period, are typical: "He exemplified what the First Church of Princeton has always been proud of—the pastor in the community's service."[29] This accent on leadership beyond the congregation has remained an important part of the congregation's ethos to the present.

The first pastor of First Church in the twentieth century who was not a graduate of both the university and seminary was John Bodo, who served the church between 1951 and 1959. A native of Budapest and graduate of Union Theological Seminary in New York, Rev. Bodo did have some Princeton pedigree, having received his Th.D. from the seminary in 1942. His pastoral style was more confrontational, and he pressed the congregation as a whole to become more involved in social action. While he was pastor, First Church elected its first women elders to the session, and the session began to take a stand on controversial social issues. In 1957, for example, the session distributed copies of a Covenant for Open Occupancy to the members of the congregation, a pledge to support an end to housing discrimination in Princeton.

Rev. Bodo's leadership also had an important impact on Christian education at First Church. Reflecting a trend that was widespread during the first half of the twentieth century, First Church's Sunday school gradually become the focal point of its teaching ministry, marginalizing the study of the catechism and catalyzing two building projects.[30] When Rev. Bodo arrived, Jane Mackay, the wife of the president of the seminary, had been the superintendent of the Sunday school for many years. She was a staunch supporter of the Uniform Lesson Plan and its emphasis on memorization of Bible verses. When Rev. Bodo insisted that the congregation begin to use the new denominational curriculum, Christian Faith and Life (edited by his former professor at Union, James Smart), Mrs. Mackay resigned. As I noted earlier, the Sunday school movement from the very beginning was primarily a lay movement. It should be no surprise then that this attempt to "modernize" the church school at the insistence of the pastor led to the Sunday school's decline at First Church. Almost a decade would pass before new signs of creativity in the congregation's teaching ministry appeared and, only then, under new pastoral leadership.

The Restructuring of American Religion since the 1960s

Many historians and social scientists point to the 1960s as a watershed in American history. Changes in the major institutions of American society and the emergence of various social movements were to have a lasting impact on American life. These resulted in a restructuring of American religion, with important implications for mainline Protestant churches such as First and Second Presbyterian. Three changes stand out.

First, the major institutions of American society became more clearly differentiated from religion, with important implications for higher education. During the first half of the twentieth century, colleges and universities had already begun to pull away from denominations and church benefactors as major sources of funding, resulting in a blurring of their religious profile. Following World War II, an influx of new money from state and federal governments intensified this trend. This was motivated in part by the space race and the military build-up of the Cold War. This further diminished the mainline churches' influence in the academy, a trend impacting directly university congregations like First Church.

Second, the United States began to move toward a postindustrial economy, altering certain long-standing patterns of work and family. It became far less likely for either management or workers to remain with one company in one place for the entirety of their adult lives. This had the effect of destabilizing congregational membership.[31]

Third, various social movements emerging during this period reshaped long-standing patterns of moral meaning that had given definition to Americans' lives (e.g., the civil rights movement, the antiwar movement, the women's movement, and the counterculture).[32] These various social movements called into question ideals such as the Puritan work ethic and the life trajectory with which it was associated in the middle class: high achievement in school, entry into a stable career by the male breadwinner, and establishment of long-term family commitments, with the wife in charge of the domestic sphere. For the first time in American history, women began to enroll in large numbers in institutions of higher education and to pursue their own careers. Reacting to these cultural trends, evangelical Protestantism emerged as both a cultural and political force in the 1970s. Groups such as the Moral Majority began to use highly sophisticated political tactics to support candidates who held their views on hot-button issues such as abortion, school prayer, and homosexual rights.

In short, the 1960s and 70s were decades of tremendous ferment in American life. They would reshape American religion along four lines.

1. Moral and religious pluralism became more prominent. Between 1952 and 1985, Protestantism declined from 67 percent of the total population to 57 percent, with shifts within Protestantism marked by the decline of the membership of the historic mainline denominations and gains among conservative Protestant groups.[33] During this same period, Roman Catholicism grew from 25 percent to 28 percent of the population. Other religions grew from 1 percent to 4 percent, and the unaffiliated sector of the population from 2 percent to 9 percent. Throughout this period, polling data consistently revealed greater interdenominational and interfaith tolerance among all religious groups, including increased acceptance of people who do not belong to any religious community.[34]

2. An "individual-expressive" style of religious affiliation was established. This style, also described as the "new voluntarism,"[35] is characterized by two elements: (1) the diminished importance of denominational identity in determining religious affiliation; and (2) greater emphasis on the personal dimensions of religiosity, the perceived "fit" between a religious community and the felt needs of individuals and families. Together these trends led to the increased prevalence of religious "switching," the movement from one religious group to another.

3. Religion became polarized by clashes between conservatives and liberals. Largely this was an outgrowth, first, of the involvement of many pastors in the civil rights and antiwar movements and, somewhat later, the rise of the New Religious Right. As Robert Wuthnow points out, the rise of "special purpose" groups with specific moral and political agendas became a prominent feature of denominational life during this period.[36]

4. Congregations, not denominations, became the key factor in religious affiliation and involvement. Recent empirical research on congregations by Nancy Tatom Ammerman, Penny Edgell Becker, Stephen Warner, and others have drawn attention to the increased importance of the local "cultures" and programs of congregations—in contrast to denominational cultures and programs—in an era when religious switching and the individual-expressive mode of affiliation have become more important.[37] In a pluralistic social context that affords individuals great freedom in affiliating (or not) with a particular religious community, the life and program of local congregations have become critical to people's decisions to join them and remain involved.

Nassau's Story Continued: From the 1960s to the Present

During this period, each of the four trends identified above had an impact on First Church and Second Church (which changed its name to St. Andrews Presbyterian Church in 1965) By far, the most important impact was the merger of the two congregations in 1973. The session of First Church formally proposed the merger in 1973, and within one hundred days it was ratified by both congregations. One-third of the membership of each congregation, however, voted against the merger. In spite of this opposition, the existing charters of the congregations were dissolved and a new church formed, Nassau Presbyterian. Wallace Alston, Jr. was called to serve as the first pastor of this church in 1973. Initially, the facilities of both churches were retained, and worship services were held weekly in both sanctuaries. After five years, the St. Andrews property was sold for $400,000 and a mission fund established.

It is perhaps more than a little symbolic that Rev. Alston was the first pastor of First Church in the twentieth century without a degree from Princeton University or the seminary. In many ways, he was destined to chart a new course for a new church, although I believe strong elements of continuity between First Church and Nassau can be detected. Fresh from the struggle of the civil rights movement in the southern Presbyterian church, Rev. Alston continued First Church's strong commitment to leadership in the service of the community and national church. Moreover, he continued the tradition of intellectually demanding preaching, long important to this academically oriented university church.

One of the most significant changes Rev. Alston made was forging these two congregations into something genuinely new: a high quality, program-oriented church directed by a specialized, professional staff. It is not that First Church and St. Andrews had not hired assistant pastors and seminary students in the past. What I am pointing to is something different: the hiring of a professional staff with specialized responsibilities for developing a program in specific areas of the congregation's life. The first full-time choir director and organist, Kenneth Kelley, was hired in 1979. This was followed by the hiring of a director of the choir program for children and youth in 1982 (initially part-time, but full-time as of 1989), a full-time director of Christian education in 1989, and a full-time youth minister in 1991.

The development of a specialized, professional staff cannot be directly attributed to growth in the congregation, since Nassau had a net loss of 899 members between the merger of the congregations in 1973 and the year 2000. What are we to make of this shift if it is not responsive to growth in membership? Probably it is best viewed as a response to changes taking place in the broader Princeton community, which reflect the four trends described in the previous section.

In the 1970s and 1980s, Princeton was transformed from a university town surrounded by farmland into a part of the megalopolis stretching from New York City to Philadelphia. It now was populated by professionals with no long-term roots in the Princeton community and no ties to the university and seminary, both of which had long dominated the ethos of the town. The religious profile of Princeton shifted as well. A vibrant Jewish community built a new center near downtown Princeton, and new Protestant churches were established both in and around Princeton, including several evangelical congregations.

Clearly, Nassau now found itself in a very different social context, characterized by religious pluralism and a growing population of professionals with a cosmopolitan orientation who had moved to Princeton from other parts of the country, worked in New York, Philadelphia, or along the Route 1 corridor, shopped outside of Princeton in new malls and shopping centers, and sent their children to many different schools. Many of Nassau's potential new members had no long-term ties to the area and faced future relocation. The congregation's turnover rate increased markedly during this period.

Nassau adapted to this new social context in a variety of ways, resisting these trends at some points and accommodating them at others. While many congregations, for example, have incorporated various media, role-play sermons, and contemporary praise music in their worship, Nassau has retained its more formal, Reformed style of worship. It also has continued traditions of intellectually demanding preaching and leadership beyond the congregation. Nassau's most important accommodation to its new social context has been to evolve a program-oriented style of congregational life and leadership. It has attracted new professionals moving into the Princeton area because of the excellence of its Christian education and music programs, as well as the aesthetic and intellectual depth of its worship. It has developed outstanding youth groups. This program orientation makes it possible for members who work, shop, and often live outside of Princeton to participate in the church in clearly demarcated segments that fit into their busy and widely dispersed schedules. In chapter 5, we will explore these issues more fully, giving special attention to the ways they have shaped the congregation's curriculum of Christian education.

You now have had a first glimpse at three case study congregations. Our task in the chapters that follow is to explore the teaching ministry of these congregations in greater depth through the practices, curriculum, leadership, and pilgrimage frames.

Chapter 4

Somang Presbyterian Church of Seoul, Korea:

The Practices of a Congregation Living under the Word

As I walked down the side aisle of this spacious, modern sanctuary, I was struck by the many people who were already there and the many more quietly streaming into the pews. They were gathering for Dawn Prayer at Somang Presbyterian Church, which begins at 5:30 a.m. Monday through Saturday. Approximately two thousand people gather every morning to take part in this practice. As people found a place to sit, many closed their eyes and appeared to pray silently. They were coming together to begin the day in the context of worship, gathered around the Word in the company of other believers.

As a bell chimed, Rev. Kwak, the senior minister, rose from his seat at the front of the church and greeted those who had gathered. He invited the congregation to join him in a hymn unaccompanied by the organ, and then offered a prayer on the congregation's behalf. This extemporaneous prayer was quite long by American standards, about twelve minutes. Rev. Kwak then directed the congregation to join him in reading aloud a passage of Scripture. In Somang's practice of Dawn Prayer, the congregation systematically works its way through the Bible, starting with Genesis and moving through Revelation. The passage read aloud on this day was from Ezekiel. Following the communal reading of Scripture, Rev.

Kwak offered a short expository sermon on the passage. The congregation then prayed together the Lord's Prayer. The lights were dimmed, Rev. Kwak sat down, and the individuals gathered in the sanctuary began to pray, both silently and aloud. After five to ten minutes, people quietly started to leave the sanctuary, one by one.

SOMANG PRESBYTERIAN CHURCH:
A COMMUNITY OF PRACTICES

As I attended Dawn Prayer over the course of my time with this congregation, I was struck by the shaping power of this practice on both the individuals who are regular participants and the congregation as a whole. Prayer and the study of Scripture are baselines of the congregation's life. Morning by morning, two thousand members gather in the context of worship to place the work of the coming day before God and to listen expectantly for God's Word to them before they scatter to different parts of Seoul.

As I noted in chapter 3, Somang grew from a small prayer group to a church of 43,978 registered members in only twenty-four years. To care for this large congregation, Somang has eighteen associate ministers who have specialized responsibilities in specific areas of the congregation's life (e.g., ministries for children, youth, or university students; pastoral counseling). Each associate also provides oversight for members who live in a specific geographical area. They conduct funerals, special worship services, and Bible studies for the three thousand people of their "ministry zone," as well as offer pastoral care.

There can be no question that one of the keys to the phenomenal growth of this congregation is the leadership and preaching-teaching ministry of Rev. Kwak, the only senior minister this congregation has ever had. One does not have to observe Somang for very long to realize that Rev. Kwak is invested with charisma by the congregation in the sense described by sociologist Max Weber, that is, he is viewed as endowed with special gifts, wisdom, and spiritual authority.[1] Focusing on Rev. Kwak alone, however, would cause us to miss the vitality of congregational practices that serve as a powerful source of identity formation and transformation in ways that surpass the influence of any one person. These practices link the members of this congregation to Christian traditions of the past and also teach them how to embody the Christian story within their own cultural context. In this chapter, we examine Somang's teaching ministry through the practices frame. This particular congregation is an especially interesting case study, for it raises four questions about the shaping power of congregational practices in identity formation.

1. Somang is located in a cultural context that offers few of the supports for Christian identity formation found in most Western countries. Christians represent only 25 percent of the Korean population, and religions such as Buddhism and Shamanism have a longer history in Korea. Approximately 65 percent of

Somang's members are new Christians who joined the congregation with little prior knowledge of Christianity.[2] *How is it possible for a congregation in a pluralistic context to shape the identities of its members?*

2. Somang does not seem to fit the secularization thesis that has dominated Western sociology in the past century. It came into existence and grew rapidly during the most intense period of modernization in Korean history and attracted highly educated, upwardly mobile members of Korean society. *Why has Somang grown so rapidly during a period of modernization?*

3. Somang represents a particularly interesting example of how local culture and Christian tradition interact. A Korean scholar I interviewed characterized this congregation as "a brilliant combination of Calvinism and Confucianism," pointing to the congregation's cultivation of Reformed piety and, simultaneously, the building on and reshaping of certain dimensions of its Confucian cultural heritage. In the face of globalization, which is eroding local cultural traditions around the world and recasting all relationships in terms of the models of the marketplace, this sort of creative conservation of cultural and religious identities may prove to be one of the most important tasks facing Christian congregations in the future. *How does Somang conserve local cultural traditions while creatively transforming them?*

4. Somang is a particularly interesting case study of the ways theology and practice can interact in a congregation. Somang's identity-shaping practices are grounded in the theology of ministry articulated by Rev. Kwak at the very outset of his leadership of this congregation. In many ways, Somang's practices embody this theology, and this theology provides principles that guide the congregation's praxis. *How does Somang bring theology and practice into this sort of mutually influential relationship?*

The answers to these four question can only be discovered if we focus our attention on the matrix of practices found at Somang. Our task is to explore these practices as sources of Christian identity formation and of catechesis, exhortation, and discernment.

A Theological Discrimen: A Church Living under the Word

Over the course of my research on this congregation, a theological discrimen emerged that helped me pull together in a single focal image many aspects of this congregation's ethos, identity, and sense of mission: *Somang is a church living under the Word.* I have shared this focal image with a variety of leaders and members of the congregation, and they have said that it rings true to their understanding and experience of the congregation. Somang is a congregation that emphasizes the Reformed tradition's threefold understanding of the Word of God: (1) It is strongly *christocentric*, placing special emphasis on an eschatological understanding of Christ; (2) it emphasizes the *Bible* as mediating the Word to the contemporary church; and (3) it holds up the present *proclamation* of the Word through preaching and teaching as the heart and soul of congregational life. This emphasis on the Word does not lead Somang to fall prey to a narrow biblicism. Biblicism is an approach to Scripture interpretation that construes the Bible as a kind of rule book of timeless moral and religious truths, whose "literal" words can be applied with no attention to their original context or to the contemporary context. In marked contrast, preaching and teaching at Somang emphasize the contextuality of biblical interpretation. This is a congregation that takes the Bible very seriously but not literally.

In my interviews of adults, this attitude toward Scripture was particularly evident when I asked them to characterize themselves and Somang in terms of the categories "liberal" and "conservative" and to explain what these terms mean to them.[3] All but one of the adults described themselves and the church as *both* liberal and conservative. As one person put it, "This church is special. It doesn't have too many rules and leaves people free without coercion by the minister. It doesn't have an annual revival meeting; it doesn't put pressure on you to give money; there are no rules about smoking and drinking. All of this is voluntary. At the same time, it depends on Bible teaching to help the people understand how they are to live. So I guess it's both liberal and conservative." Many of the adults and youth shared that they study the Bible regularly in Bible studies, cell groups, Dawn Prayer, and personal devotions.

Two theological motifs receive special attention in Rev. Kwak's theology of ministry and are important elements in the congregation's understanding of what it means to live as a congregation under the Word: eschatology and joy. Eschatology was given special attention in the thesis Rev. Kwak wrote for his doctorate of missiology, subsequently published as the book *Eschatology and Christian Mission*.[4] He draws on the theology of the *missio Dei* to criticize the world-negating pietism and premillenialism that some of the early missionaries bequeathed to the Korean church and the way many Korean Christians syncretize biblical eschatology with the "eschatologies" of Buddhism, Shamanism, and Confucianism found in Korean popular culture.[5] According to the biblical witness, he argues, the church is to serve as a provisional sign of God's coming kingdom; its hope in God's promised future does not lead to other-worldly escapism but gives Christians a new ethical framework with which to interpret and act in *this* world. I was surprised how frequently the theme of eschatology emerged in adult interviews.

Closely related to Rev. Kwak's treatment of eschatology is the motif of joy in the Christian life, a theme that also appeared repeatedly in my interviews. *All* of the adults I interviewed pointed to this as one of the distinguishing characteristics of their church. As one put it, "In many Korean churches, the minister puts a lot of pressure on the people. You have lots of do's and don'ts. The minister tries to keep them at church all day. Many Christians go around with sour faces and feel burdened. That is not what goes on here. Rev. Kwak always encourages us to be happy Christians." Korean scholars familiar with this congregation describe Rev. Kwak's emphasis on joy as especially important in light of the widespread experience of *han* by many Koreans. Literally, *han* means "wounded heart" and points to the unconscious residue of past wounds and the experience of present suffering that prevent many Koreans from enjoying their lives in the present. These scholars note that Rev. Kwak's emphasis on joy helps Somang's members to heal memories and enjoy their present lives. The Christian life is experienced as freeing and providing release, not as weighing them down with one more set of obligations.

Somang, thus, may be interpreted theologically as a church living under the Word that gives special attention to eschatology and joy in the Christian life. As we shall see in the last part of this chapter, Somang teaches its members how to embody this understanding of the Christian way of life by inviting them to participate in a matrix of practices. Before turning to this task, I explain in the following section what I mean by the practices frame, a frame that emerges from an interdisciplinary conversation between theology and the theory of multiple intelligences developed by Howard Gardner.

THE PRACTICES FRAME

To a large degree, recent discussion of practices has been sparked by Alasdair MacIntyre, Stanley Hauerwas, and others working primarily in a neo-Aristotelian framework.[6] While there is much to commend this perspective, my use of the concept of practices is critical of neo-Aristotelianism along two lines. First, if the concept of practices is to be used by practical theologians with integrity, then both the concept and conceptual framework of neo-Aristotelianism must be more thoroughly transformed in light of Christian theology than has been the case to the present. (At a later point in this section, I explore the way Reinhard Hütter carries this out in *Suffering Divine Things*.[7]) Second, I do not follow the social theory commonly associated with neo-Aristotelianism, which portrays moral and religious communities as self-enclosed and with little positive interaction with their social contexts. In contrast, the social theory adopted in this book views moral and religious communities along the lines of "open systems" that both shape and are shaped by other social and natural systems in their environments.[8] I have noted the creative interaction of Confucian culture and Christian tradition at Somang, which we will continue to explore. Changes in the external environment shape the internal life of congregations and vice versa, as the influence of Somang and other congregations on Korean society demonstrates. From this we see that practices must be viewed against both the traditions they bear and the ways they are responsive to their social contexts.

Practices in Theological Perspective

With these two important qualifications in mind, I believe there is much to be learned from the recent discussion of practices. Drawing on this discussion, I define *religious practices* as follows: *Religious practices are socially shared, tradition-bearing activities that embody an interpretation of the ultimate context of existence and have sufficient depth to forge a common sense of identity among the members of a community and to shape the character of individual participants.* In this defini-tion, four characteristics of religious practices are central:

1. Tradition bearing. Practices are not made up on the spot; they have the char-acter of patterned routines with certain roles that are shared by those who par-ticipate in a religious community on a regular basis. Sometimes they embody local traditions, but they often partake of traditions that unite a religious com-munity with communities of the past and with a broader religious community in the present. One reason religious practices have depth is that they transmit the spiritual legacy of many generations, often built up over many centuries.

2. Socially shared activities building up a common sense of identity. Religious practices focus primarily on the activities of the community qua community, not the actions of individual members. Through their joint participation in these activities, the adherents of a religious community learn to play certain roles, fol-low certain patterns, and make use of certain cognitive scripts, which are held in common and create a common sense of identity.

3. Character shaping. Character points to those habits of thought, feeling, and action that give shape, texture, and motivation to the individual self. It is more enduring than the segmented roles and scripts adopted by individuals as they move from one sphere of life to another, for it has to do with long-lasting pat-terns and dispositions of the self. Religious practices have the potential to form and transform the character of those who participate in them.

4. Embody an interpretation of the ultimate context of existence. This is the most important mark of *religious* practices, and it distinguishes them from the prac-tices of other forms of social life. Thus, I will give it more extended discussion. Theologians and philosophers of religion have used a variety of terms to describe the ultimate context of existence.[9] My understanding follows the lead of H. Richard Niebuhr as interpreted by James Fowler.[10] Niebuhr portrays human meaning-making and action as shaped by people's interpretation of the field of forces impinging on them at any given time. Implicit in all such interpretive activity, he argues, is an interpretation of the ultimate context of existence, the "context of contexts" that impinges upon and ultimately determines the condi-tions, direction, and outcome of our immediate and particular contexts. Reli-gious communities bring to expression in an explicit and focused way this ultimate context, resituating the patterns of everyday life in a larger field of forces. In our examination of Paul, for example, we found him framing everyday life within the horizon of a cosmic, apocalyptic drama.

In *The Meaning of Revelation*, Niebuhr draws special attention to the role of narrative in religious communities' interpretation of the ultimate context of exis-tence.[11] Narratives, he argues, play a special role in personal and social life, for they have the capacity to unfold identity through time. They allow persons and communities to answer the three questions of individual and corporate identity: Who are we? Where have we come from? Where are we going? Narratives are unique in their capacity to hold together present, past, and future. Niebuhr goes on to describe revelation as having the effect of refiguring the story by which individuals and communities construct their personal and corporate identities, placing their particular stories within the context of an interpretation of the ultimate context of existence. This potentially allows them to recover repressed dimensions of their past, to interpret their present life in a wider field of actors and forces, and to open up new possibilities for their future.

The most important characteristic of a religious practice is the way it teaches its participants to construe their everyday lives in terms of an interpretation of the ultimate context of existence and to align their lives accordingly. In the explicitly Christian framework developed in this book, this is described in terms of the praxis of the triune God, a framework offered in chapter 8. Acknowledging the theological dimension of Christian practices necessitates a further step in our dialogue with neo-Aristotelianism in which we ask what sorts of changes must be made to this philosophical framework when it is engaged by Christian theology.

No one has stated more clearly what is at stake in this interdisciplinary dialogue in recent years than Reinhart Hütter in *Suffering Divine Things*. Hütter examines the larger conceptual framework of Aristotle, the ur-source of much of the contemporary discussion of practices. To summarize his rich discussion, I briefly describe the key terms he examines:[12]

- *Pathos.* This is "suffering" in the sense of undergoing or incurring, as opposed to acting or doing. Pathos focuses on the way a person is determined and constituted by an "other" or the accidents of history. The accent is on "receiving" and being influenced by this "other," in relation to which one is relatively passive.
- *Poiesis.* Aristotle limits this to the work of artisans and artists, whose goal is the creation of a "product" of some sort. Along with praxis and *theoria, poiesis* is a comprehensive form of life that serves as a counterpoint to pathos.
- *Praxis.* Like *poiesis,* this is a comprehensive form of life in which human beings initiate activity and are not merely determined pathicly. In Aristotle, praxis focuses on the cooperative activity of free citizens of the polis, whose goal is the creation of a happy life and not merely a product.
- *Practices.* These are discrete, socially shared forms of action within the praxis of the polis that generate certain particular goods.

Following his discussion of the basic meaning of these terms in Aristotle and the later philosophical tradition, Hütter then transforms these concepts by redescribing them in terms of Luther's theology:[13]

- *Poiesis.* The church is the *poiesis* of the Holy Spirit, the creation of its work in calling this community into being, transforming it toward the likeness of Christ, bringing it into communion with the triune God, and drawing it into the history of the end time.

- *Pathos.* The pathic nature of the Christian life is basic, for it centers on the receptivity of faith in which it receives the gift of God's salvation in Christ. It is God's action, not the church's action, which constitutes human beings as forgiven sinners and as new creations. Human beings cannot create these identities. They can only receive them as free gifts.
- *Praxis.* The life of faith is a comprehensive way of life characterizing the church, the *vita passiva*, in which the word of grace is received anew each day through the activity of the Holy Spirit.
- *Practices.* The Holy Spirit works through the "mediate forms" of church life, its core and auxiliary practices, to communicate the gospel and transform persons toward the likeness of Christ.

Notice that Hütter has redefined and reordered the conceptual meaning of each of Aristotle's basic terms. *Poiesis* is no longer a lesser category, describing the activity of artisans and artists; it now describes the activity of the Spirit in bringing persons and communities into communion with God's free gift of grace. The praxis, or way of life of congregations, is portrayed as responsive to the Spirit's *poiesis*, and the discrete practices of the congregation, moreover, have their home within this praxis. In short, Hütter transforms the entire conceptual framework of neo-Aristotelianism as he redescribes its most important categories in terms of Luther's theology.

Hütter also provides a theological description of *core practices* of congregations. Drawing on Luther's portrait of the seven marks of the church, he describes them as: (1) the preaching of the Word of God, (2) baptism, (3) the Lord's Supper, (4) the office of the keys in church discipline, (5) ordination and church offices, (6) public prayer, praise, thanksgiving, instruction, and (7) discipleship in suffering.[14] These core practices are the means by which the Holy Spirit carries out her *poiesis* and are essential to the church's very *esse,* or being, as God's people. They are to be distinguished from the *auxiliary practices* of congregations, which are concerned with its *bene esse,* or well-being.[15] While auxiliary practices can be altered or abandoned from era to era and from church to church, the core practices of congregations are constitutive of their being as the church. If they are missing or distorted, then the church's identity and mission are at risk.

Other theologians have developed accounts of the core practices of congregations that are based on different theological frameworks. John Howard Yoder, for example, describes the core practices of the church as: (1) binding and loosing, (2) the sharing of goods, (3) the formation of a new humanity in baptism that eradicates social distinctions, (4) the identification and nurture of the spiritual gifts of the congregation, and (5) governance through discernment.[16] Yoder's account rests on his commitment to the Anabaptist theological tradition. Using the term "discipline" in ways that are similar to practices, Quaker writer Richard Foster describes (1) inward disciplines: meditation, prayer, fasting, study; (2) outward disciplines: simplicity, solitude, submission, service; and (3) corporate disciplines: confession, worship, guidance, celebration.[17] I will develop my own normative account of congregational practices in chapter 8 in dialogue with the dogmatic theologian Jürgen Moltmann.

In the remainder of this book, I follow Hütter's distinction between praxis and practices: *Praxis is the comprehensive way of life of a congregation; practices are the discrete, socially shared forms of action that embody this praxis.* I alter slightly Hütter's terminology of *core* and *auxiliary* practices, for *auxiliary* too easily leaves the impression that these practices are unimportant. Instead, I will use the term *mediating practices* to describe practices that are context dependent in a strong sense.[18] Mediating practices typically are local or regional, but this does not make them unimportant. Indeed, I believe that a sign of creativity and vitality in a congregation is the presence of dynamic mediating practices. Later we will examine Somang's practices of anonymous giving and the recycling of leaders, examples of mediating practices as I use this term. Both practices have been developed to respond to certain issues that often are problematic in Korean churches, but they do this in ways that embody important dimensions of the Christian way of life.

In practical theology, an additional set of categories must be added to this distinction between core and mediating practices, what I will call *identity-shaping* and *peripheral* practices. This second set of categories plays an especially important role in the empirical investigation of a congregation and is used to determine the relative importance of a practice to a congregation's identity and mission on the basis of four criteria: (1) the centrality of a practice to the overall ethos of a congregation; (2) acknowledgment of a practice's importance in public statements of the congregation's identity and mission; (3) the extent of congregational participation in a practice as seen in numbers; and (4) expenditures of financial and staff resources to support a particular practice.

I use the paired categories of core and mediating practices primarily to carry out the normative task of practical theology. They enable us to evaluate the relative adequacy of the matrix of practices of a particular congregation in light of a normative theological framework, such as those developed by Hütter, Yoder, and Foster. Determining the identity-shaping and peripheral practices of a congregation is primarily a descriptive-empirical task of practical theology and is the central focus of the last part of this chapter.

Interdisciplinary Dialogue Partner: Howard Gardner

Howard Gardner is best known for his theory of multiple intelligences, in which intelligence is not a single monolithic phenomenon. Gardner argues that the human mind/brain is composed of eight relatively distinct forms of human cognition: linguistic, spatial, logical-mathematical, bodily-kinesthetic, musical, intrapersonal, interpersonal, and naturalist. He is considering the category of existential intelligence.[19] In *Frames of Mind*, Gardner defines intelligence as "the ability to solve problems, or to create products, that are valued within one or more cultural settings."[20] This relatively simple definition looks in two directions simultaneously: (1) the bio-psychological potentials of the individual; and (2) cultural amplifications of these potentials in different contexts.

Intelligence as a differentiated set of *bio-psychological potentials* points to distinct information-processing mechanisms located in different parts of the brain, which are responsive to different kinds of information, have distinct developmental histories, and are subject to different kinds of dysfunction. Differences between individuals, in part, are due to the fact that people tend to be stronger in some of these intelligences than others. Some are gifted musically or athletically; others are gifted linguistically in oral or reading tasks; still others have strength in logical-mathematical intelligence or in carrying out tasks requiring strength in fine motor skills.

Cultural amplifications point to the ways these bio-psychological potentials are shaped by the social contexts with which they interact. Intelligence and context go hand in hand. Intelligence can only be understood and fairly assessed in relation to the adult roles and products that are valued in particular cultural settings. Gardner commonly describes these roles and products as "endstates"—the blend of knowledge and skills that are viewed as important in a particular domain, discipline, or a culture as a whole.

One of the most important influences on Gardner's thinking about the relationship between bio-psychological potentials and cultural amplifications is David Feldman's nonuniversal theory of development.[21] Feldman portrays human development along the lines of a continuum. At one end are those universal forms of development such as perspective taking (the ability to construct other persons' and groups' perspectives) that can be found across all cultures. Most forms of development do not fall at this end of the continuum, however, because they have to do with growth in knowledge and skills that are specific to a particular culture, domain, or discipline. Most people growing up in the United States, for example, develop a certain level of linguistic competence in English, but not everyone develops competencies in specific domains such as repairing cars, sewing clothing, or sailing boats. In relation to each of these activities, developmental sequences can be identified as people acquire greater understanding and skill appropriate to the roles of novice, apprentice, and master of the domain. Development in most areas of life, thus, is nonuniversal. It must be viewed as relative to the endstates (the valued roles and products) of a particular sphere of life and the particular blend of intelligences (in Gardner's sense) that are necessary for competent and creative functioning in these different spheres.

Gardner's depiction of intelligence in terms of both bio-psychological potentials and cultural amplifications deepens our understanding of religious practices in four important ways.

1. It helps us to recognize that intelligence is nurtured and developed in many spheres of life beyond classrooms, including the practices of a religious community. The development of intelligence should not be viewed exclusively in terms of formal education. Rather, intelligence also develops in domains that cultivate knowledge and skills that are important to valued roles and products of a particular community. The practices of a religious community are one of many domains where this sort of amplification of intelligence can occur. They embody a community's way of life, mediating the endstates or roles and products that are valued by that community.

2. It broadens our understanding of human development. Under the influence of Jean Piaget, religious educators have often viewed development in terms of an invariant and universal sequence of stages. Gardner and Feldman help us to realize that we must also view development in relation to specific domains, disciplines, and practices. Growth toward greater competence and maturity in these areas is developmental but not universal. Learning the Christian way of life by participating in the practices of a congregation promotes development by allowing people to gradually build up the knowledge and skills appropriate to the roles and products valued by this community, such as worshiping God, offering forgiveness, carrying out acts of compassion, and sharing one's burdens with trusted others.

3. It helps us understand a practice can have formative power on diverse people. One of the most important insights to emerge in Gardner's work is the fact that as early as childhood, it is possible to identify different preferences and strengths in individuals' cognitive profiles. Some are strong in music, others in language skills or in visualizing pictures that they will paint. Practices are such potent sources of formation because they often draw on and engage a wide range of intelligences, affording meaningful participation by people with markedly different cognitive profiles. Worship, for example, often engages linguistic, musical, logical, interpersonal, intrapersonal, spatial, and bodily-kinesthetic forms of intelligence.

4. It helps us recognize the importance of mentoring relationships in promoting growth. Gardner has given special attention to apprentice models of growth and development in which people acquire valued knowledge and skills by entering into mentoring relationships with more experienced practitioners of a particular domain. Artists, artisans, doctors, and mechanics commonly learn in this way. This sort of apprenticeship and mentoring has occurred in a wide variety of ways in the Christian tradition—in confirmation, spiritual direction, care giving, and clergy formation. Such relationships play a key role in introducing people to the practices of the Christian life and in helping them appropriate these practices more deeply over time.

Focus Questions of the Practices Frame

This theological reflection on the neo-Aristotelian discussion of practices and interdisciplinary dialogue with Gardner's theory of multiple intelligences bring into focus several important questions that can be used to guide a researcher or congregational leader in examining the practices of a congregation.

1. What are the identity-shaping and peripheral practices of the congregation and how might they be evaluated in terms of the core and auxiliary practices projected by a normative theological framework? A congregation's praxis—its comprehensive way of life—represents its most important interpretation of what it means to live as God's people. If core practices are missing or severely distorted, then the members of the congregation are not really learning what a life of discipleship entails. This question invites us to move in two directions simultaneously: to empirical examination of actual practices of a congregation and to normative assessment of their adequacy. In this chapter we focus primarily on the former.

2. *Do the leaders of the congregation articulate publicly the theological vision of the church's identity and mission that is reflected in the actual practices of the congregation? Does this vision point to hoped-for changes in the future?* These questions draw attention to the learning that takes place when a community both "teaches what it practices" and "practices what it teaches." Teachings important to Christian identity and mission have their greatest power—they ring most true—when they are already embodied in the community's shared life. These questions also invite us to look for ways the congregation draws on its theological vision to form a critical perspective on its present life, helping it spot areas that need to be reformed.

3. *What sort of catechesis, exhortation, and discernment take place through the practices of a congregation?* In our examination of Somang's Dawn Prayer, we saw an example of catechesis (working through the Bible systematically) embedded within a practice focusing primarily on worship. The practices frame broadens our understanding of the teaching ministry beyond formal education and invites us to look for ways catechesis, exhortation, or discernment are woven into the practices of the congregation—or might be.

4. *In what ways do the practices of a congregation appeal to the varied forms of intelligence that people possess?* This question invites us to recognize the important ways congregations draw on and cultivate the multiple intelligences of their members outside of formal contexts of teaching and learning.

In our exploration of the matrix of Somang's practices in the remainder of this chapter, I begin with a summary of what I believe are the identity-shaping and peripheral practices of the congregation (question 1). I then describe these practices in detail, linking them to their public articulation in Rev. Kwak's theology of ministry (question 2) and the ways catechesis, exhortation, and discernment are cultivated through a particular practice (question 3). In my descriptions, I also draw attention to the blends of intelligence cultivated (question 4).

SOMANG PRESBYTERIAN VIEWED THROUGH THE PRACTICES FRAME

Overview of Identity-Shaping and Peripheral Practices

Let us begin with an overview of what I believe are the identity-shaping and peripheral practices of Somang Presbyterian Church, based on the criteria developed above.

Identity-Shaping Practices

The practice of Sunday morning worship. Somang offers five services for adults every Sunday morning, as well as special worship services for children, youth, university students, and young adults. The adult services in particular are characterized by solemn reverence and simplicity and focus primarily on the preached Word.

The practice of Dawn Prayer. At 5:30 a.m., Monday through Saturday, members of the congregation gather for a service of worship. This service focuses primarily on prayer and the study of Scripture, working systematically from Genesis to Revelation.

Practices of Scripture interpretation. This cluster of practices focuses primarily on the preaching ministries of the senior minister and associates and the large number of Bible studies conducted throughout the week. Most of the associate ministers offer Bible studies for those who are a part of their "ministry zone," which are open to other members of the congregation. The congregation also supports a large number of small groups, which focus on Bible study and personal sharing.

The practice of Sabbath keeping. The congregation discourages carrying out church business on Sunday. Its leaders also encourage church members not to become involved in more than one church activity, such as teaching or the choir, that takes place on Sunday, and not to work at their secular jobs. Sunday is to be a day of rest. Following church, families are urged to spend time together in recreational activities that support the bonds of family life.

Practices of anonymous service and giving. This cluster of practices is quite diverse and includes the many service activities that small groups carry out on behalf of the congregation, as well as the major initiatives sponsored by the congregation as a whole. All service and financial contributions are anonymous. The congregation does not give special recognition to individuals or groups who carry out especially noteworthy service or give large monetary gifts or endowments to the church.

The practice of educating and recycling leaders. Somang builds community among its members through their participation in classes, committees, outreach projects, and cell groups. The leaders of these groups are quite important. Many participate in leadership education before they take up their responsibilities. Typically, their leadership is confined to a definite period of time (often two years). Leaders of especially important committees or groups are encouraged to serve in less prominent positions when they step down: working in the nursery, providing support for the kitchen staff, or teaching in the church school. Leaders are "recycled" in this way to build servant leaders and to prevent elites from forming in the church.

Peripheral Practices

Practices of the "domestic church." The "domestic church" is the church in the home. In my interviews of children and youth, very few pointed to significant times of worship, prayer, or Bible study in their home. While the congregation provides some support for the "domestic church," teaching parents how to successfully integrate this into family life does not appear to be a major ministry priority.

Practices that democratize church leadership. The democratization of church leadership and the "dethroning" of elites in the congregation are explicitly lifted up by the theology articulated by Rev. Kwak. My observation of the congregation leads me to believe that teaching members democratic methods of decision making receives far less attention than one might expect in a congregation composed of such highly educated and competent members.

This brief overview helps us begin to see the distinctiveness of Somang's matrix of practices. While practices of Sunday morning worship, Scripture interpretation, and Sabbath keeping are familiar to all Christians, the practices of anonymous service and giving, Dawn Prayer, and the recycling of leaders are likely to be unfamiliar and are good examples of the local and regional nature of mediating practices. We now look at these practices in greater detail in order to better understand why they are such a potent source of identity formation in Somang. This also gives me the opportunity to indicate some of the ways they embody the theology of ministry articulated in the writings of Rev. Kwak and his son Joseph, who was an associate pastor of the congregation when I carried out my research.

Identity-Shaping Practices in Greater Depth

Sunday Morning Worship

In the writings of Rev. Kwak and his son about worship and in my interviews of them, they place great emphasis on the importance of establishing "pious worship" at Somang.[22] "Piety" and its cognates have a long and honorable history in the theology of the Reformed tradition, harking back to Calvin's definition in the *Institutes of the Christian Religion*: "that reverence joined with love of God which the knowledge of his benefits induces."[23] For Calvin and the Reformed tradition generally, a Reformed aesthetic of "pious worship" includes three elements: (1) a clearing away of distractions that might draw the attention of worshipers away from God's address through the preached Word—with a strong preference for the oral and musical over visual, tactile, and olfactory; (2) a blending together of architecture, music, and a simple liturgy to foster an atmosphere of reverence and to draw the attention of the worshipers to the living Word of proclamation; and (3) simplicity in the flow of the service, the prayers offered, and the ideas of the sermon. Sunday worship at Somang embodies all three of these elements in a particularly striking way, mediating the worship traditions of Reformed Protestantism to the contemporary Korean context.

Clearing Away Distractions and a Preference for the Oral and Musical

Given the large size of this congregation, the church offers five different Sunday worship services. In addition to these services, Somang also offers age-level worship services, followed by church school—timed to allow children to participate in these activities while their parents attend the adult service. Parents with infants have a special room where they can watch the adult service on a closed-circuit monitor while they keep their infants with them; toddlers and preschoolers participate in simple worship activities in their own gathering place; university students have their own service on Saturday afternoon.

Obviously, for pragmatic reasons the church must offer many different worship services. It would be impossible for the central sanctuary, which seats 3,500, to hold everyone. But there are two theological reasons for age-level worship services.[24] First, the adult service should be free of the distractions that children inevitably create. Not only should parents be free to focus their attention exclusively on worshiping God, but even more importantly, the atmosphere should be one of solemn reverence. The worshipers are entering into the presence of the Holy God, and this is not to be taken lightly. Second, worship's purpose is to allow people to encounter God's Word in terms they can understand. This has important implications for the way worship is conducted in the various age-level services. Those who lead these services make a conscious effort to address issues of relevance to the age group and to use age-appropriate language. The youth and college students I interviewed were quite positive in their evaluation of the preaching of their respective worship services, especially the moral issues addressed in this setting.

The Architecture, Music, and Simple Liturgy Work Together to Foster an Atmosphere of Reverent Expectation

The exterior and interior architecture of Somang's sanctuary are quite modern. Looking at the central entrance to the sanctuary at a distance, your attention is drawn to a large tower on the left. The tower, shaped like an arrow with the point in the ground and a cross on the top, is described by Rev. Kwak as representing God's arrow of the Word as it has been "shot" into the midst of humanity. When you enter the sanctuary, your attention is immediately drawn to the altar, resting on an elevated area at the front. It is in the shape of an open scroll and is approximately twenty feet long. On the front of the altar are words from the Lord's Prayer and on the ends of the altar top are verses from Genesis and Revelation. The lectern where Rev. Kwak preaches and conducts the service is directly behind this altar. Centered behind the lectern is a large panel of clouded glass that stretches from the floor to the ceiling. Approximately three-quarters of the way up this panel is a large cross.

If the "arrow tower" creates a sense of downward, vertical movement outside, the altar-lectern area carries this sense of verticality into the sanctuary itself. The visual message seems to be that God's Word will enter this space through the preaching and praying of the worship leader, who serves as a conduit of God's address to the congregation. This Word is closely linked to the explication and application of Scripture, dramatically represented by the large, scroll-shaped altar.

This interpretation of the visual message of the architecture receives further support from the relative lack of importance ascribed to the choir, one of the most surprising findings to emerge in my interviews. The five choirs that participate in each of Somang's worship services are outstanding, and most congregations would be exceptionally proud if they had even one choir as good as any of Somang's five. Yet the choirs were not mentioned *even once* when the adults and youth I interviewed described what this church does well! As I puzzled over this finding with several choir members, one of them offered this insight: "We work hard to make wonderful music. But we are just a part of the background of the worship service. Our task is to prepare the congregation for Rev. Kwak's preaching. That's what people come here for." While music is important to the aesthetic of Somang's worship, it is viewed as preparing the way for the proclamation of the Word.

There is a striking contrast between the music of the adult service and that of the youth, university, and young adult services. The latter all use contemporary music with a beat. One of the youth services I observed included a dance performance by several university students that would have been right at home on MTV! In my interviews of youth, virtually all articulated a very strong preference for the more expressive music of their own service over that in the adult service.

Simplicity in the Flow of the Service, the Prayers, and the Ideas of the Sermon

The adult service is elegant in its simplicity. It is conducted entirely by Rev. Kwak, except for an elder who offers a prayer. It follows the basic pattern established when the church was founded. There are no announcements during the service; the language of the sermon and liturgy is simple and direct; all prayers are extemporaneous and use everyday language.

Summary Reflection

How do catechesis, exhortation, and discernment take place through this practice? It is tempting to point to different parts of the service to answer this question. Scripture is interpreted and "handed on" through preaching and the singing of the choir and congregation. Discernment is modeled as biblical meanings are related creatively to the contemporary context and as a life of prayer is modeled in the language and attitudes of the worship leader. Moral issues are addressed in the sermons, including the services for young people. All these things are true. Yet it is not primarily at the level of the individual parts of the service that worship is best construed as a source of identity formation at Somang. Rather, it is the way the parts "add up" to an aesthetic whole, projecting a distinctive ethos and cultivating a particular set of tastes. Sunday by Sunday, Somang's members build up the mental habits and dispositions of a Reformed piety. They learn to come before God with reverence and awe; they acquire the expectation that God will speak to their lives and world through their pastor's preaching; they learn the habit of joining others in praising God in song and bringing the concerns of their lives and world before God in prayer. If we were to think of catechesis, exhortation, and discernment exclusively in terms of formal education, we would miss the ways that worship cultivates a fundamental set of attitudes toward the Bible, the moral life, and the ongoing discernment of God's will.

Taking account of the aesthetic whole of Somang's worship also throws light on the ways this particular practice cultivates the different intelligences described in Gardner's theory. Linguistic, musical, interpersonal, spatial, and intrapersonal intelligence are all addressed in one way or another. Yet *a clear preference for the spoken word suffuses the whole*. From the verticality of the architecture, to the subordinate role of the choir, to the centrality of preaching and praying, the practice of Sunday morning worship cultivates the expectation that the congregation will be addressed by the one Word of God, Jesus Christ, through the mediate words of proclamation. In a real sense, the congregation is being schooled in a set of theological understandings: This is what it means to live as a congregation under the Word, and this is the sort of piety appropriate to this way of life. This theological message is mediated by the whole ensemble of worship, which cultivates a particular blend of intelligences to teach theology at the ground level.

Routinizing Prayer and Bible Study through Dawn Prayer

Although Dawn Prayer is practiced in many Korean churches and is an excellent example of a mediating practice, I believe it is important to the particular ethos of Somang as a church under the Word for two reasons. First, Dawn Prayer establishes Bible study and prayer as important dimensions of the piety of the congregation as a whole. Elders, Kwonsas (women leaders), and the leaders of cell groups and many other groups participate in this practice on a regular basis, and their example appears to influence others. All but one of the youth interviewed told me that they pray on a regular basis, and half said they learned to pray from their mothers or grandmothers (not one from a father!), whom they described as participating regularly in Dawn Prayer at some point.

Second, Dawn Prayer serves as a venue by which new Christians receive an elementary introduction to the Bible and learn how to pray, which is especially important for Somang because so many of its members were not raised in Christian families and received no Christian education as children. One of the adult interviewees described the significance this way:

> When I first became a Christian and joined this church, I had never really prayed before. I thought of prayer as being like magic. In the village where I grew up, we used to have special ceremonies every year asking the spirits to give our family prosperity in the coming year. I think this is how I thought of prayer. But I remember one of Rev. Kwak's sermons in Dawn Prayer when he told us to think of prayer as like tuning in a radio signal from far away. We learn how to listen for God's voice and to follow it. It is not a matter of magic but of learning to bend our own will to God's. This is why Dawn Prayer is so important to me. This is how I want to start each day.

It is not difficult to see the importance of the practice of Dawn Prayer for catechesis and discernment. It "routinizes" Bible study and prayer in the lives of the two thousand people who participate in this practice every day and the many more who listen on the radio or follow online. In ways that are similar to the adult catechumenate of the ancient church, a significant portion of the congregation gathers at the beginning of the day for the "handing on" and "receiving" of Christian Scripture and for prayer. Like the catechumenate, moreover, this practice "schools" participants through a process of formation in which cognitive meanings, personal insight, interpersonal examples, music, and bodily postures are woven together in an integrated whole, shaping habits and dispositions.

Practices of Scripture Interpretation

This cluster of practices takes us to the heart of catechesis at Somang. In Dawn Prayer, the congregation works its way through the Bible in a systematic fashion. Preaching that relates the Bible to contemporary life is the hallmark of Sunday morning worship in all age-level services. The study of Scripture is also at the heart of Somang's curriculum, the formal educational offerings of the church. These include Sunday school classes, cell groups, and Bible studies during the week. In the year 2000, the congregation had 750 teachers leading classes for 6,500 students. All church school teachers participate in a year-long program *before* they begin to teach. This provides them with a basic introduction to theology, the Bible, developmental psychology, and different teaching methods. The leaders of small group Bible studies for university students, likewise, participate in an ongoing seminar that examines the text discussed in their group that week.

In short, Scripture interpretation stands at the very center of practices of worship, study, and personal devotions. Setting the tone for this diverse cluster of practices is Rev. Kwak's treatment of Scripture in preaching and teaching. It is noteworthy that *every* youth and adult I interviewed responded to the question "What brings this congregation together?" by pointing first to Rev. Kwak's preaching. Similarly, in response to a question posed to adults—"What does this congregation do well?"—*all* mentioned Rev. Kwak's preaching, portraying it as setting the tone for preaching and teaching throughout the entire congregation.

How can we characterize Rev. Kwak's style of preaching? For my research purposes, it is fortunate that three volumes of his sermons have been translated into English and that the congregation provides simultaneous English translation of his sermons in Sunday worship. Moreover, several Korean scholars have studied his preaching style.[25] Building on their insights and adding my own observations, I would identify the following core characteristics: (1) creative interpretation of Scripture; (2) insightful, contextually sensitive address of contemporary issues; (3) the creation of analogies between Scripture and everyday life in examples, illustrations, and stories; (4) reliance on the themes of classical Reformed theology in the background, not the foreground, of his sermons; and (5) appeals to both the mind and the heart, while eschewing moral harangues and emotionalism. Many of these same characteristics occur in the preaching and teaching of the associate pastors and lay teachers.

Westerners are apt to feel uncomfortable with such emphasis on the influence of the preaching-teaching ministry of one person in such a large congregation. I remind them of what I noted earlier, that Rev. Kwak is invested with charisma by the members of this community. He is both the founding father of the church and its spiritual mother—a trusted guide, teacher, and healer. It should not be surprising to find his approach to Scripture interpretation as setting the tone for the rest of the congregation. When I prompted intellectuals who are members of this congregation to reflect with me on the source of Rev. Kwak's charisma as a preacher and teacher, they pointed to three things: (1) his ability to relate the Bible to the everyday life; (2) the perception that he practices what he preaches in a lifestyle of frugality, modesty, and integrity; and (3) the widespread perception that he takes great delight in his preaching and teaching. These same intellectuals also pointed to an important cultural dynamic that leads many Korean Christians to invest their pastors with this sort of charisma: Confucianism's positive valorization of relationships of dependency and mutual obligation. "We" takes precedence over "I" and is characterized by networks of mutual obligation between parent and child, teacher and student, and minister and congregation.

There are conflicting views among Korean intellectuals about the desirability of the continuing influence of Confucianism in modern Korean society. Some scholars believe that modernization has led the younger generation, the academic community, and the business community to reject what they identify as the "group-think," hierarchicalism, and dependency that Confucianism fosters. Only the churches, they argue, continue to hold on to these elements of Confucian culture. In contrast, others see a more positive role for the network of mutual obligations that Confucian culture fosters. They argue that dependency can be creative and life giving. One pastoral theologian I interviewed pointed out that dependence on the preaching and teaching ministry of a charismatic leader like Rev. Kwak can actually strengthen critical capacities of the ego in other areas of life. After all, he pointed out, do not strong attachment relationships during infancy lead to inner security and independence in later childhood? Does not "regression in the service of the ego" often serve as the seedbed of artistic creativity? In a highly stressful, competitive urban environment, he noted, it is appropriate for Christians to be temporarily dependent on their spiritual leaders, especially in worship.

Needless to say, these are complex issues. I raise them to caution Western readers not to project their own set of cultural values onto their understanding of this congregation. Such Western values may include the following: autonomy (the freedom to criticize all authority and form one's own rational judgments), an individualized identity (the self as "I" not "we"), and a distantiated posture toward the world (especially the objectification of nature epitomized by modern science).[26] This cluster of values is uncomfortable with notions of creative dependency, binding mutual obligations, and group identity. Yet it may well be that the relationship of Somang's membership to the preaching and teaching of its spiritual leader is one of the ways it is preserving and reshaping local culture in the face of the acids of globalization.

The Practice of Sabbath Keeping

As noted in my initial summary of this practice, Somang discourages its members from carrying out church and secular work on Sundays and encourages them to make this a time to renew the bonds of family life. I think we can best understand the formative power of this practice by viewing it against the backdrop of contemporary Korean society. A byproduct of Korea's rapid modernization has been an increase in the pace of life. The shift from a rural to an urban way of life and the demands of successful participation in a global economic system place great pressure on all age levels. The practice of Sabbath keeping is a source of moral formation at Somang in which Calvinism and Confucianism, once again, interact in a mutually transformative fashion. The Sabbath is established as a day of rest. Yet Sabbath keeping is not taught in terms of a rigid moral code of proscribed activities; rather, it builds on and transforms certain elements of Confucian culture.[27]

On the one hand, it places limits on the strong achievement orientation of Korean society; success at work should not be the center of one's Christian identity. On the other hand, it builds on a cluster of familial moral obligations that are an important part of Korea's Confucian heritage. The Sabbath is to be a day when families spend time together, especially in outdoor activities such as hiking and walking in parks. In the Kwaks' theology of ministry, they explicitly describe the Sabbath as a time to establish family harmony and closeness. In the face of globalization's relentless "marketization" of all spheres and relationships, Somang's emphasis on the renewal of familial relationships in the context of Sabbath keeping represents an important alternative. Here again, we find the congregation helping its members renegotiate their cultural identities in the context of a tradition-bearing Christian practice.

Practices of Anonymous Service and Giving

Somang views itself as a missionary church called by God's Word to serve the world. This is readily apparent in the many outreach activities its members pursue, the spirit of volunteerism that permeates the church, and its enormous financial expenditures on major projects beyond the congregation. Standing at the heart of this diverse cluster of practices is the virtue of *anonymity* in serving and giving. Rev. Kwak lifts up this virtue in both his theological writings and his preaching and teaching, portraying it in terms of biblical and Reformed themes of self-sacrifice and self-denial. While these themes have fallen into disrepute in some forms of Western theology, Somang and its leaders unabashedly hold them up as positive moral and spiritual ideals. Christians are to place their lives and resources at God's disposal, and when they do so, they will experience a "mysterious inner joy" that is a mark of spiritual maturity.[28]

Concretely, this moral ideal issues in certain practical guidelines. The church never gives publicity or certificates to individuals who carry out some especially noteworthy service, either in the church or the community. It does not publish the names of individuals who give large monetary gifts to the church. Rather, it encourages all service and giving to be carried out without the desire for public recognition.

The fruits of this approach are amazing. In the year 2000, the total amount of money received by the church was 164 million dollars, excluding money given for special projects. Thirty-five percent of this money was spent on running the church and 65 percent on outreach. In 2001, the outreach portion went up to 68 percent. The projects supported by the congregation are numerous. Somang has offered extensive help to North Korea, the place of Rev. Kwak's birth, providing rice plants and grain during times of famine, building hospitals and orphanages, and, recently, committing itself to the construction of a university of science and technology. It has already built Yanbian University of Science and Technology in mainline China. Graduates of this university have the opportunity to continue their studies in Seoul, and the church built and supports the Somang Dormitory, which houses them while they are in Korea. The church supports the Somang Mission House for Workers, providing a meeting place for Christian workers from other countries who currently are living in Seoul. It built, staffs, and supports financially a facility for the homeless, providing temporary housing and the chance for its residents to participate in various rehabilitation programs. It built and supports Bethesda, a facility for those with severe learning and physical disabilities. The church provides Bethesda's residents with a comprehensive program of counseling, medical care, physical therapy, vocational training, and a weekly worship service designed for the members of this population. The church currently supports twenty-four overseas missionaries.

This financial support of outreach is matched by the spirit of volunteerism permeating the congregation. As I observed the Christian education program, I was struck by the teacher-student ratio. No class had more than ten students for every teacher. In the Preschool 2 class (kindergarten age), there were fifty children and twenty-five adults. In the Nursery 2 (toddlers) class, there were around forty children and twenty-five teachers. This meant that all students were greeted as they entered the room. Adults gave them hugs, helped them place their shoes in shoe bins, and sat with children who needed special attention. This spirit of volunteerism extends beyond the church. Somang's leaders encourage members to cluster in small groups of people who share a common interest, profession, or special skill. For example, the congregation has groups for doctors who volunteer their services in medical missions, as well as for professors, bankers, building contractors, businessmen, educators, and so forth. Altogether, there are around five hundred such groups in the church.

Obviously, the many practices of serving and giving found across the congregation are a powerful source of moral formation. They challenge this congregation of successful and highly educated people to look beyond their own needs to the needs of the world. Many of the adults interviewed explicitly used the language of "joy" or "happiness" to describe what they get out of this sort of service. One shared the following story:

> After I joined Somang and got to know more people, I began to notice that there is a spirit of happiness in this church. I asked one of my new friends about this. She's older than I am and has been coming to this church for a long time. She told me, "We are happy because we don't think about ourselves all the time. We learn to think about other people." She invited me to go with her cell group's work with poor people. Every so often, they gather coats and other clothing, and they take them to a mission house where homeless people are being fed. . . . So I went with her cell group. We spent all day there. We worked in the kitchen; we served food and talked to the people there and got to know them a little bit. We helped them find coats and clothing that fit them. At the end of the day, we came back to the home of one of the women and had tea together. We talked about our experience and we prayed together for the people we had met. . . . You know, at the end of that day I felt happy. I felt I was doing what God wanted me to do. . . . Later I talked to my own cell group about this. We are all young mothers, and most of us are new to the church. We decided that we would start doing this together. The first time we did it, we went with my friend's group.

I doubt that the leaders of the congregation are even aware of the service of this particular cell group. They probably are unaware that this young woman and her cell group were mentored by a group of older women who helped them catch the vision of anonymous self-giving. Yet it is at this level—the level of informal, mentoring relationships—that a service orientation takes root and is modeled across Somang's life.

Practices of Educating and Recycling Church Leaders

One of the most interesting facets of Somang's ethos is the way it nurtures and recycles the leaders of the church. This is best described in terms of a guiding principle—characterized by Joseph Kwak as "decorticating the nobility of the congregation"—which issues in certain concrete practices.[29] The somewhat awkward term "decorticating" comes from an early draft of Joseph Kwak's book on Somang. He later changed it to "dethroning." While decorticating is uncommon in everyday English, it captures nicely what the practices of recycling leaders is all about. It means to strip away the outer layer of a plant, tree, or fruit. The purpose of "stripping away" markers of worldly and ecclesial status is to encourage those who hold positions of leadership and responsibility "not to consider themselves as being elevated to a higher status or standing."[30]

There are contextual issues that make this principle important in Korea, according to the Kwaks. The spiritual elitism of Buddhism and the bureaucratic hierarchicalism of Confucianism often creep into the Korean church. Those who have special spiritual experiences or hold high-status offices in the church (e.g., elders) are often viewed as the "nobles" of the congregation. This sometimes results in divisive conflicts between the minister and elders or between different factions in the congregation. Somang experienced this sort of conflict early in its life, as I noted in chapter 3. Since then, the congregation has attempted to avoid these conflicts by taking the principle "no nobles in the congregation" very seriously.

Accordingly, this principle shapes the congregation's leadership practices in the following ways. The church does not follow the custom of designating certain seats for the elders. It eschews special prayer meetings and discipleship programs that might give rise to a spiritual elite, and it tells its members that attendance at Dawn Prayer is not to be viewed in this way. To counter the common custom of allocating the best burial sites in a church cemetery to leading members, Somang encourages the practice of cremation and the mingling of the ashes at its retreat center.

In general, church members serve in positions of leadership for two-year terms. They then step down and are strongly encouraged not to make any attempt to influence the person taking their place. In some areas, the church goes to considerable lengths to educate those who are about to hold a new position of leadership in the church, making sure that anyone—regardless of background—can serve in this capacity. We have seen, for example, the extensive preparation and support the church offers teachers. Moreover, members are encouraged to offer leadership in different areas of the congregation's life. Those who hold positions of importance and status in the church are urged to provide leadership in areas that might be considered less important.[31] I observed men and women with high-powered careers during the week working in the nursery and youth church school, and serving as the secretary of a church committee.

In a congregation that is filled with people of considerable wealth, worldly status, and power, leadership practices that "strip away" these markers in the church through certain leadership practices represents a worthy goal. How successful they are in achieving this goal is difficult for me to evaluate on the basis of my research. It may well be that an invisible spiritual or political elite is present. When I pressed adult interviewees about this, however, they vigorously contended that this is not the case.

Peripheral Practices in Greater Depth

Obviously, in a congregation as large as Somang, there are many peripheral practices, practices that are present in the congregation but are not central to its identity or mission. Here I will describe only two such practices. These are held up in the theology of ministry articulated by the Kwaks but do not appear to be well-established in Somang.

Practices of the Domestic Church

Direct observation of the family life of members of Somang was not a part of my research. Thus, I am relying on what I discovered in my interviews of children, youth, and adults. Rev. Kwak lifts up the "domestic church" as an important ideal for all Christian families—establishing the church in the home.[32] Parents are encouraged to take their role as teacher seriously, helping their children learn how to pray, studying the Bible with them, and "showing by example how to live in the shadow of God."[33]

Support of the practices of the domestic church is not absent altogether from Somang. The congregation offers a variety of educational programs to strengthen new marriages. It requires all couples married by its pastors to receive premarital counseling and to take part in a special class. It offers a newly wedded couple's class and a married couple's Bible study. It also sets certain guidelines for parents. In our discussion of Sabbath keeping, for example, we found the congregation encouraging parents to reclaim Sunday as a time to renew family relations. Somang also encourages parents not to become overinvested in the church: "It is wrong when married Christians spend and invest so much time at church at the expense of caring for their families. . . . God not only exists in our churches, but He also exists in our households."[34]

In spite of these examples of support for the "domestic church," I did not find a great deal of evidence that the congregation places the same sort of priority on this ministry as on those identity-shaping practices described above. In my interviews of children, youth, and adults, little mention was made of the family as a setting where prayer, Bible study, or worship are practiced. Moreover, there are few signs that the congregation sponsors a vital ministry for families with young children and youth beyond the programs noted above. There are many congregations in the United States with family ministries more central to their identity and mission. Programmatic initiatives such as parenting classes, family retreats, and marriage education classes reflect an ethos in which building strong relationships in the home is a major priority.

Perhaps even more significant, I found little evidence that Somang is really engaging the problems and possibilities of what might be called the emerging, postmodern family form.[35] In this chapter, I have pointed to many instances in which the congregation is both conserving and transforming elements of Korean culture by resituating them in a Reformed theological framework and ethos. Surely one of the most important challenges to traditional Korean culture today is the changing role of women, with important implications for family life. Increasingly, Korean women are graduating from universities and pursuing their own careers. This represents a direct challenge to the sharp delineation of gender roles found in Confucian culture, in which women lose their familial identity when they marry, and find themselves in a subordinate position to both their husband and mother-in-law.

Many younger couples are no longer satisfied with these traditional patterns of family life. Some are attempting to share the tasks of child rearing and earning a living more equally, which often places them at odds with the expectations of their parents and grandparents. I found little evidence that Somang is helping young couples struggle with these kinds of issues. At present, establishing the "domestic church" in the new, more egalitarian context of Korea remains on the periphery of its life.

Practicing Democracy in the Congregation

In my brief overview of recent Korean history in the previous chapter, I pointed to the long road Korea has traveled toward democracy. Social scientists who have studied the recent wave of democratization around the world make an observation that is germane to our investigation of Somang.[36] They point out that it is not enough to establish democratic political institutions, for equally important is the emergence of a democratic *civil society*. This is the network of associations "between" the public and private spheres that teach the virtues and practices of democratic life, such as fair and open debate, tolerance of diversity, and the capacity to handle conflict with civility. Historians, sociologists, and theologians have drawn attention to the important contribution of Christian congregations and other religious communities in both establishing and supporting a vibrant civil society.

My observation of Somang has led me to the conclusion that this congregation does far less than it might in contributing to the formation of a viable democratic civil society in contemporary Korea. While its membership includes many highly educated and prominent members of Korean society, the practices and virtues of democracy are peripheral to Somang's identity and mission. I make this observation in spite of the fact that "demonstrating democratic administration" is one of the principles the Kwaks lift up in their theology of ministry.[37] Practices of democratic governance are not absent altogether, however. All church committees, for example, make decisions through democratic voting procedures. Moreover, elders are elected through a process with the trappings of a political campaign.

Yet there are a number of indications that practices of democratic governance are peripheral at Somang. In the year 2001, only two of Somang's seventy-nine elders were women. While there are many *Kwonsas* ("senior mothers" not on the session) in the congregation and women clearly play a very important role in the work and service of the congregation, they are not represented in its ruling body. Moreover, a Korean scholar who has studied the congregation reports that meetings of the session last on average only twenty minutes, with minimal discussion of key decisions.[38] Typically, they simply confirm decisions already made by the ordained leadership.

My interviews add further support to this impression. A comparison of the response to an interview question asked of the youth and adults of all three case study congregations is revealing. The question was part of a sequence dealing with discernment: "Some Christians think that church leaders best discern God's will for the congregation when people have the chance to debate and discuss issues openly and honestly. Sometimes this means they disagree with one another. Does this sort of debate and discussion take place in this congregation? If so, where does it occur? Do you think that this is an important form of discernment?" Not a single youth or adult of Somang viewed debate and discussion as something that presently takes place at Somang, although half of the youth thought it ought to. In marked contrast, every single youth and adult in the other two case study congregations viewed debate and discussion positively and could point to specific contexts and instances where it was practiced in their congregation's life. As this contrast began to emerge, I started probing the Somang interviewees more deeply on this issue and later asked several intellectuals who are members of the congregation to reflect with me on what I was finding. They pointed to two factors that might have led to this sort of response: the high incidence of conflict in Korean congregations—something Somang wants to avoid—and the trust the congregation has in Rev. Kwak's leadership. As one person put it: "We learn how to debate issues in the university and deal with conflict all of the time in our everyday lives. We want the church to be a place that is peaceful, and we have great confidence in Rev. Kwak's wisdom."

These are important contextual factors, but I cannot help but wonder if Somang is doing less than it might in teaching its members the practices and virtues of democracy. In a society that only recently established democratic political institutions, placing the practices of democratic governance on the periphery of the congregation's life fails to actualize the church's potential contribution to building a strong democratic civil society. It also fails to "hand on" the Reformed tradition's long-standing commitment to the common good and its suspicion of centralized authority. Surely this also is an area that is worthy of "creative conservation."

CONCLUSION

We have now looked closely at a picture of Somang Presbyterian Church of Seoul, Korea. What we have seen has been shaped by the practices frame, focusing on the ways this congregation engages in catechesis, exhortation, and discernment through the varied practices of its shared life. If I had used one of the other lenses developed in later chapters of this book, my picture would have looked quite different. Moreover, I focused primarily on the descriptive-empirical task of practical theology in creating this picture, staying away from normative evaluation for the most part. Only in my descriptions of the peripheral practices of the congregation did I begin to shade over into this sort of assessment.

We turn now to the very different congregational picture of Nassau Presbyterian Church, examining this congregation through the curriculum frame.

Chapter 5

Nassau Presbyterian Church, Princeton, New Jersey

The Curriculum of a Congregation Living in Hope

In 1986, on the occasion of the celebration of the 150th anniversary of the present building of Nassau Presbyterian Church,* the senior minister, Wallace Alston, Jr., preached a sermon that focused on the motto of the church seal, still found on several plaques in the church building: *Speremus Meliora*, "We hope for better things."[1] He began by reminding the congregation that circumstances were not so bright when the motto was originally adopted in 1786, several years after the Revolutionary War. The country's economy was in disarray, and its fledgling government had yet to solidify. Locally, the congregation had paid a heavy price for the war. The original church building had been occupied by the armies of both sides and its pews used as firewood for a makeshift fireplace inside the sanctuary. Local homes had been plundered and destroyed. It was precisely at this moment that fifty-two members of the congregation adopted a motto that gave expression to their belief that God is sovereign and could take hold of the nation and the congregation, allowing them to move into the future with hope.

---

*In Chapter 3, I described the merger of First Church and St. Andrews (formerly Second Presbyterian) to create Nassau, which is located in the former's historic building.

113

Dr. Alston then briefly rehearsed several key events in the life of the congregation, including one that reveals the darker side of its history—the separation of African Americans from the congregation in the 1830s. When First Church's second building was destroyed by fire in 1835, African Americans who had long worshiped at First Church began to worship apart. They eventually petitioned the session to be dismissed from the congregation and allowed to form their own church—a request that was granted. While little is known of the circumstances that led to this division, Dr. Alston read a portion of a letter by James Alexander, a member of the congregation, written to a friend in 1837:

> We have a new and handsome edifice. While it was building the negroes worshipped apart, in a little place of their own. The majority of the pewholders wish them to remain as a separate congregation. . . . I am clear that in a church of Jesus Christ, there is neither black nor white. . . . Yet I think the blacks very unwise in insisting on such a privilege now . . . . [I]n consequence of the abolition movements, the prejudice of the lower classes of whites against the blacks has become exorbitant and inhuman.[2]

Dr. Alston then came to the climax of the sermon:

> For those of us who gather in this building Sunday in and Sunday out, that building is a monument to God's judgment on our past and on our present. As the prophet Nathan said to David long ago, "Thou art the man," so that sanctuary says to this, "Thou art the church." And it calls us to repentance before Almighty God and our neighbor. So it is providential, I think, that our 150th anniversary coincides with the first Sunday in Advent, when we gather each year at the Lord's Table. For Advent is a time when hope makes sense and when we dare to hope for better things—not because of what we believe about ourselves but because of the faithfulness of this God in whom we trust.

He concluded by pointing the congregation to the hope that should animate it today, a hope that might yet allow it to be an instrument of racial reconciliation in the Princeton community and the world.

Though preached many years ago, this sermon and the motto to which it points capture the identity and mission of present-day Nassau Presbyterian Church: *Speremus Meliora*—"We hope for better things." It serves as my theological discrimen of this congregation. It is no accident that on the occasion of an anniversary celebration—when congregations are most likely to feature those parts of their past that are bright and positive—Dr. Alston would confront the congregation with the darker side of its history and point ahead in hope to the role it might yet play as an agent of reconciliation. Few American congregations can hark back to a church motto over two hundred years old, and fewer still without becoming trapped in the past. How Nassau manages to maintain this future-oriented sense of identity and mission through its teaching ministry lies at the heart of this chapter.

SPEREMUS MELIORA:
A THEOLOGICAL DISCRIMEN OF NASSAU PRESBYTERIAN

Nassau's Ethos

Over the course of my investigation of Nassau, four characteristics emerged as central to its ethos: (1) a strong orientation toward leadership beyond the local church, (2) a culture of thinking, (3) an expectation of excellence in all forms of ministry, and (4) ambivalence toward community within the congregation. Each of these characteristics is linked to the theological discrimen identified above.

Leadership beyond the Local Church

Located on the edge of Princeton University and within several blocks of Princeton Theological Seminary and Westminster Choir College, Nassau is rich in human resources. Professors, administrators, and students from all of these institutions are participants in Nassau and regularly provide leadership. Just as important, the congregation has attracted many members beyond these three institutions who are highly educated, have careers as professionals or in management, and are active in voluntary organizations beyond the church. In the brief overview of Nassau's history offered in chapter 3, we saw that leadership beyond the local church had long been prized in First Church, one of the congregations out of which Nassau was formed. It is a part of the way it tells its story and sings the praises of its ministers. Nassau continues to view itself as called to leadership beyond the congregation—in the denomination, presbytery, the Princeton community, and American society. It seeks to address contemporary issues in the hope of contributing to a better future.

This self-perception is borne out in a wide variety of ways. Nassau's members include authors of widely used church school curriculums and music, drafters of mission statements and catechisms sponsored by the denomination, a former moderator of the General Assembly, a former president of the World Alliance of Reformed Churches, two recent moderators of the New Brunswick Presbytery, and the current chair of its Committee on Ministry. Nassau provides leadership in the Princeton area through a variety of programs and organizations it helped found and continues to support, such as the Trenton Children's Chorus (a multiracial choir), the Crisis Ministry of Princeton and Trenton, and the Trenton After-School Program for low-income children. The list could go on.

One of the most telling findings to emerge from my interviews of adult members (none of whom are affiliated with the seminary or choir college) is the importance they ascribe to public virtues. When asked to describe some of the qualities of their ideal of the Christian moral life, the interviewees most frequently lifted up: (1) a commitment to social justice, (2) leadership in the area of human rights, (3) tolerance toward those who are different, and (4) courage in the face of opposition. While they also pointed to numerous personal virtues—fairness, honesty, thoughtfulness, joy, and a readiness to forgive—none was named by even half of those interviewed. There was a strong preference for the sort of virtues we would associate with leadership in the public domain.

A Culture of Thinking

A second characteristic of the ethos of this congregation is the way it encourages its members to think. In virtually every facet of the congregation—from committees to sermons to the educational program to the youth group—its members are encouraged to ask questions and to explore them in a context of faith. Here again, we gain insight into its orientation toward the future. In spite of its strong commitment to the Reformed tradition, the congregation is not interested in merely handing on the pat answers of the past. As the brochure on youth ministry puts it, "We offer time for the youth of this community to reflect on their faith and lives and put their faith into action" and "We offer a home, a time, a place for the youth to gain perspective on the world around them."

The high value the congregation places on a thinking faith was apparent in my interviews of adults and youth. In response to the question "How does this congregation help you grow as a Christian?" I received comments like the following: "It uses the intellectual resources of the seminary and university really well. Sometimes in a discussion I'll hear someone give their opinion and I'll think, 'Wow, that's really good! I never would have come up with that.'" All of the adults I interviewed believed debate and discussion to be "important" or "very important" in the congregation's ability to discern God's will and believed them to be regularly practiced in Nassau's committees and educational program. These interviews also revealed the venues seen as important to a thinking faith. Nine out of ten adults pointed to adult education and preaching, and five to church committees and service opportunities. Two characteristics of adult education repeatedly came to the fore: the diversity of topics in the adult church school and the intellectually challenging ways these topics are treated.

An Expectation of Excellence in All Forms of Ministry

A third dimension of Nassau's ethos is the expectation of excellence in the sense of a superior performance. Speakers in adult education often are world-class scholars; committees are run by professionals, therapists, corporate managers, and college-educated volunteers; the professional staff is expected to be not merely good but *very* good. While there can be little doubt that this reflects the strong achievement-orientation of Nassau's members and its location on the edge of an Ivy League university, this commitment to excellence in the ministries of the congregation also reflects its unwillingness to rest on its laurels, to be satisfied with what it has already accomplished; it looks ahead to what it might yet be.

A good example of Nassau's commitment to excellence is its music program. All of the adults I interviewed identified the music program as something Nassau does particularly well, and five of ten children identified the choir as their favorite church activity. In his writings on theology and aesthetics, Frank Burch Brown uses the phrase "excellence in taste" to describe a "cultivated aesthetic imagination" that is discriminating and unsatisfied with a steady diet of religious kitsch.[3] This captures nicely what the music program of Nassau attempts to cultivate. It does so, first, through the music of Sunday morning worship; second, through the extensive teaching and rehearsal of its choir programs; and third, through special musical performances, which in recent years have included Igor Stravinsky's *Symphony of Psalms,* Robert Ray's *Gospel Mass,* and a commissioned piece by jazz pianist Dave Brubeck, based on poetry by Langston Hughes.

Nassau's Ambivalence toward Community

In my interviews and observation of Nassau, one issue consistently emerged as a problem area: the quality of fellowship or sense of community within the congregation. If ambivalence is the condition of holding opposing feelings simultaneously, then I think this captures nicely Nassau's attitude toward fellowship or community. There are two, equally strong sides to Nassau's ambivalence.

One side focuses on the importance ascribed to community in the public discourse of the congregation. The congregation's promotional literature makes extensive use of the language of community, describing the church as "an inclusive community inviting all people to come in and be fed." A "hospitality bag" is offered to visitors, which includes a message from the deacons: "We are so glad you have come to worship with us this morning. . . . We hope to get to know you!" Moreover, my adult and youth interviewees appear to view this language of community as more than empty rhetoric. All reported that they had friends in the congregation. Among the adults this ranged from 33 to 100 percent of their total friendships. The youth were effusive in their praise of the peer relations of the youth group.

The other side has to do with an equally strong feeling that it is important to respect the privacy of church members and hesitation about making fellowship a major priority in the congregation. As one person put it, "One of the things I like most about this church is that it lets you find your own way. There's not a lot of pressure to join this group or that. You can stay far or get close. It's pretty much up to you." My impression is that this comment expresses a pervasive dimension of Nassau's ethos. Its formal worship, short-term series in adult education, and relatively few small groups do not make it easy to find fellowship in this congregation. Moreover, the rate of turnover in the congregation has increased in recent decades, a result of the influx of professionals and corporate managers settling in the Princeton area. As one long-time member put it, "It's become easier to remain aloof at Nassau. . . . Life in this part of New Jersey has become a lot more hectic. People just don't have the time to get involved."

With the arrival of a new pastor, Rev. David Davis, and two new members of the church staff, Nassau may be in the early stages of a transition in this area— something noted by several adults I interviewed. Yet Penny Becker's research in *Congregations in Conflict* describes congregations like Nassau—with a strong

commitment to leadership beyond the church and to their own theological tradition—as likely to be ambivalent about community precisely because they do
not want to become too inward.[4] If this is the case, then altering this ambivalence
will take a change in Nassau's model of "church," which is not likely to occur
quickly or easily.

Congregational Culture and Educational Curriculum

In the following section, we turn to the curriculum frame, which brings into
focus the educational program of a congregation. Before doing so, however, I
want to pause briefly and reflect on why it is important to take account of Nassau's identity and ethos in a chapter that focuses on the educational curriculum.
During the latter part of the twentieth century, an important debate emerged in
American Christian education between those who advocated a *faith enculturation* approach to Christian education (e.g., C. Ellis Nelson, John Westerhoff) and
those who argued for a *critical* approach (e.g., Thomas Groome) or *transformational* approach (e.g., James Loder).[5] Proponents of the latter two perspectives
argued strongly against those who portrayed Christian education primarily as a
matter of socializing people in the preexistent norms of the congregation. They
contended that Christian education ought to help people become aware of these
norms and to reconstruct them (Groome) or to open people to the transforming
power of the Word and Spirit beyond mere socialization (Loder).

My research on Nassau and the other two case study congregations leads me
to believe that viewing this debate as a simple either/or is not adequate. It does
not take into account the wide variety of possible relationships between enculturation and education in religious communities. A congregation's culture can
support critical reflection in education, or it can impede it. Its practices can
involve people in forms of action which raise important issues that, subsequently,
are taken up in education, or they can draw people into deadening cycles of con-
ventionality. In studying congregations, thus, we must give a careful, nuanced
description of the actual relationship between enculturation and education in
each particular case.

Our brief examination of Nassau's identity and ethos makes this point quite
vividly. This congregation prizes leadership beyond the local church and a culture of thinking. These dimensions of Nassau's identity and ethos are communicated to its members in a variety of ways, from sermons to mission trips to
committee meetings. Its members are encouraged to ask hard questions and not
to settle for pat answers; they are urged to view the church as contributing to the
common good and not merely as meeting members' needs. In a very real sense,
Nassau enculturates its members into these norms, and its educational program
builds on them. There is a positive, symbiotic relationship between congregational culture and educational curriculum, that is, they are mutually enhancing.
Yet this is not always the case, and in the final part of this chapter, I share the
story of one instance in which Nassau's educational program stood in a critical

relationship to its culture, resulting in certain changes to this culture. I also return to the issue of Nassau's ambivalence toward community, an element of its ethos that education might engage more critically.

THE CURRICULUM FRAME: PRACTICES OF EDUCATION IN THE CONGREGATION

The curriculum frame brings into focus the ways a congregation is like a school with a systematic, intentional, and sustained course of study. It helps us look at how a particular community helps its members grow and develop through an organized program of education, gradually deepening their understanding of Scripture and tradition, their moral capacities, and their ability to engage in various forms of discernment. Of the four frames developed in part 2, the curriculum frame focuses our attention on practices of education most commonly associated with the teaching ministry, such as the church school, Bible studies, confirmation, and discipleship groups. These are settings in which formal teaching and learning take place, at the heart of a congregation's program of education.

The curriculum frame invites us to step back from individual practices of education and look at the big picture. Think of this in terms of the way a wide-angle lens affords a panoramic view. When we look at all of the educational offerings of a congregation in one large, panoramic view, we are able to see four kinds of things. First, we are able to develop a picture of the *subjects* covered in the congregational curriculum and those that are left out. Second, we can see the *teaching methods* most commonly used in the curriculum, which allow students to engage the subject matter in some ways and not others. Third, we are able to develop a picture of the *educational pathways* of the congregational curriculum, the ways it supports certain lines of development and cumulative learning as people pass from childhood to adolescence to young adulthood to parenthood and so forth. We will explore this concept more fully at a later point. Fourth, we can develop a picture of the *people who are participating* in the educational program of the congregation. It is significant if many children and adolescents participate in the educational program but virtually no adults do. It tells us something if very few new members are choosing to join church school classes started many years ago and primarily have long-term members as participants.

There are many good reasons for the leaders of congregations to grapple with the "big picture" questions that the curriculum frame brings into focus. Some of the most important of these are theological. The Protestant Reformers of the sixteenth century made educational practices such as catechetical instruction, Bible study, and catechetical preaching a hallmark of the reform movement and established schools in which Christian education was a part of the general curriculum. Why did they place so much emphasis on education?

Theological Perspective: The Reformers' Theology of Education

To Martin Luther, John Calvin, Martin Bucer, Philip Melancthon, and the other early Reformers, study in the Christian life was a form of obedience to the Word of God. They saw it as an all-important way of deepening both the congregation's and the individual's understanding of the knowledge of God given to faith. Scripture's account of God's self-communication in Christ was viewed as the all-important source of knowledge of God, as was the ongoing teaching and preaching of the church, which focused on the exposition of the Bible. In their writings, four theological reasons for the importance of Christian education can be identified.[6]

1. Christian education allows Christians to move beyond an *implicit faith*— a simple, trusting acceptance of the doctrinal and moral teachings offered by the authorities of the church—to an *explicit faith* in which individuals understand and accept the faith for themselves. Nowhere is this attitude more clearly seen than in the Reformers' commitment to the translation of the Bible into the vernacular, which allowed ordinary Christians to study Scripture themselves. It also is found in their commitment to practices of catechetical instruction in the home and congregation, which gave all young people the opportunity prior to their admission to the Lord's Supper to understand the faith into which they had been baptized as infants. Many congregations in the reform movement also taught a longer and more complex catechism to adults in catechetical preaching and during home visitation.

2. Christian education is necessary if the congregation is to serve as the *priesthood of all believers*. Sharing in Christ's ministry is not the special privilege of the clergy or church hierarchy. It is the task of the congregation and its individual members. All are "priests," called to ministry and gifted by the Spirit. Christian education is a part of the edification of the congregation, building up the body of Christ and equipping its members for ministry.

3. Christian education equips individuals to pursue their various roles and responsibilities in different spheres of life as an *expression of their vocations*. The world is the theater of God's glory, and individual Christians are to serve and glorify God as workers, citizens, parents, and neighbors. Christian education is needed if Christians are to understand the roles and responsibilities of everyday life in the context of faith. This is one of the reasons the Reformers established schools and universities. A higher level of education not only created more knowledgeable citizens, parents, and workers, but it also equipped people to view their worldly responsibilities as vocations.

4. Christian education supports the freedom of *individual conscience*. The church's role is not that of a moral watchdog, prescribing the "Christian" position on every area of life. Rather, through practices of education, the congregation lays a foundation that prepares individuals to make use of their own moral judgment in everyday life. In the generations following the Reformers, this was given special attention in the "cases of conscience" literature.[7]

It is no accident that this theological rationale seems to echo certain themes we discovered in our examination of Paul in part 1. A recovery of Pauline theology was an important part of the reform movement, even as the Reformers also reworked Paul's theology to address their own historical and social context. I find this theological rationale for Christian education persuasive, and it lies at the heart of my theological understanding of the curriculum frame. Yet my own constructive proposal modifies the Reformers' perspective in three ways, which take account of our present intellectual and historical context.

1. While following the Reformers in giving Scripture a central role in the congregational curriculum, I believe that we must develop a more complex account of the relationship between the knowledge of God given to faith and Scripture. Obviously, the Reformers lived before the rise of post-Enlightenment, biblical scholarship, which has made us more aware of both the diversity within Scripture and the cultural and historical distance between its "worlds" and our own. Today we are less apt to think of knowledge of God found in Scripture as "plain" or "clear," as did the Reformers. Rather, we have learned to view it as emerging out of a hermeneutical process, a process of interpretation that yields new understanding. Understanding emerges out of the interplay of the horizon shaped by our contemporary lifeworlds and the horizon projected by various biblical texts. It takes the form not of timeless truths but of insights that are subject to counterreadings by others and to new understanding emerging out of future interpretation.

2. We must move beyond the model of education that informed the Reformers' understanding of the teaching ministry. This model was based on the recovery of the classical humanistic tradition of education by leading figures in the Renaissance. A canon of classic texts was placed at the very center of the curriculum, providing the authoritative models of grammar, genre, writing, and speaking that students were to imitate and internalize.[8] Modern educational theory later rightly criticized this model of education, calling attention to the active role of the learner in the construction of knowledge and the unfolding developmental capacities of children and youth described by the social sciences. It shifted the curriculum away from a closed canon to education based on the modern disciplines, which pursue knowledge through an ongoing process of inquiry. In the following section, I enter into a dialogue with Howard Gardner to construct a model of the congregational curriculum informed by the contemporary social sciences and educational theory.

3. Contemporary Christian education must take account of the pluralism of public life and our globalizing, multicultural world. While the Reformers paid attention to the Christian life beyond the congregation in the themes of vocation and individual conscience, they did so in ways that assumed the "established church" pattern of early modern Europe. Church and state were to cooperate in a specific geographical region, and congregations were able to assume the support of state-sponsored Christian education. Today our societies are pluralistic in ways that are quite different than the "established church" pattern of the past,

and they pose a new challenge: How can religious communities ground their members in the beliefs and practices of their own religious traditions while also preparing them for dialogue with cultural and religious "others"? We must rethink early Protestantism's understanding of the congregation's relationship to public life and the practices of education supporting this relationship. Later I enter into a dialogue with James Fowler to explore the idea of postconventional Christian identity and some of the ways this might be cultivated through the congregational curriculum. This is a religious identity that forms a critical perspective on one's own beliefs and values and is capable of entering into a dialogue with cultural and religious "others."

Interdisciplinary Dialogue Partner: Howard Gardner

In chapter 3 I began a conversation with Howard Gardner, examining some of the ways his theory of multiple intelligences deepens our understanding of the formative power of religious practices. As we turn now to his writings on education, three concepts that emerged in this earlier discussion continue to be important:

- *Intelligence* encompasses two dimensions: (1) the diverse bio-psychological potentials of the mind/brain, which are the biological basis of Gardner's theory of multiple intelligences, and (2) the cultural amplifications of these intelligences in different social contexts, practices, domains, and disciplines.
- *Development* is primarily nonuniversal and context dependent. It is conceptualized in terms of growth in the knowledge, attitudes, and skills that are necessary to function well in a particular area of life or society as a whole.
- *Endstates* are the roles, activities, and products that are valued in a particular domain, discipline, or culture, such as the ability to use problem-solving reason along the lines of the experimental sciences, or to sing the great social epics of an oral culture. I believe it is helpful if congregations think of endstates in terms of the Christian way of life and the roles, practices, and products that embody this life. Various branches of the Christian tradition portray this way of life quite differently, and congregations within the same denominational tradition do so as well. For this reason, I believe it is best to think of the curriculum locally, at the level of the congregation. Each particular congregation, thus, must determine the endstates it values and seeks to cultivate through the curriculum.

As Gardner has pointed out, his theory of multiple intelligences does not, by itself, constitute a theory of education; it can be used in a variety of models of the educational curriculum. Indeed, Gardner has explored some of the ways schools located in different societies educate the human intelligences along quite diverse lines.[9] Much depends on the endstates they value and the teaching methods they deem most effective.

In his writings on education, thus, Gardner has worked along two lines simultaneously. He has developed a set of *formal categories* that can be used to examine the curriculum of any school, and he has developed his own *normative theory of education* that describes the sort of curriculum he would like contemporary schools to adopt. Since the latter is designed for schools offering general education, it is less helpful in thinking about the curriculum of a congregation. Most congregations today do not teach their members how to read and write or introduce them to the arts and sciences. The endstates of congregational education are different, focusing, for example, on the knowledge, attitudes, and skills of Christian discipleship. The formal categories Gardner develops, however, are quite helpful in reflecting on the "big picture" questions of the congregational curriculum. Building on the concepts reviewed above, four categories lie at the heart of the curriculum frame.

1. *Educational pathways* are lines of development and cumulative learning that are supported by the curriculum over time. At the broadest level, this category brings into focus the growth and cumulative learning that takes place as people move from one phase of the curriculum to another, passing from childhood to adolescence to young adulthood, to parenthood, and so forth. Since everything cannot be learned all at once, the curriculum must sequence the subjects covered. Some Bible stories are covered in some classes and other stories in other classes. As people move from one phase of the curriculum to another, they travel a path that allows them to accumulate different forms of biblical knowledge and to learn different ways of interpreting this material.

Yet the idea of an educational pathway can also be used in a more limited way. It is rare for people today to grow up and remain in the same congregation their entire lives. Thus, it is important to identify more specific and limited educational pathways that the curriculum offers to particular age levels or groups of people. In some congregations, for example, the practice of confirmation sets up a pathway for young people to travel over an extended period of time. Likewise, some congregations set up a specific pathway for new Christians or new parents, or they project pathways for adults along the lines of a Christian academy, with introductory and advanced courses. Still others offer pathways into specialized congregational roles such as caregiver, catechist, or lay preacher.

2. *Developmental readiness* focuses on the individual's psychological readiness to acquire certain kinds of knowledge, attitudes, and skills. While Gardner encourages us to think beyond the sequence of cognitive stages formulated by Jean Piaget, he is sensitive to the ways biological and psychological maturation affect peoples' readiness to learn. The different forms of intelligence he has identified have their own developmental trajectories with different critical periods and lines of maturation. Moreover, he is quite explicit about not throwing out "the Piagetian baby with the bath water."[10] Piaget's framework remains helpful

in discerning the readiness of people to use certain types of reasoning and to engage materials with different levels of cognitive complexity. Recent research on postformal reasoning, moreover, has added to our understanding of cognitive development across adulthood.[11] Likewise, Daniel Goleman's work on emotional intelligence has helped educators become aware of the role of emotional readiness in learning, as well as the ways the emotions can be "schooled" in educational settings.[12] In part, the sequencing of the subject matter in the congregational curriculum takes account of the developmental readiness of children, youth, and adults to engage certain kinds of material.

3. *Teaching approaches* takes us beyond *what* is taught to *how* it is taught. Education is not merely a matter of transmitting knowledge. It structures the ways students engage the subject through different teaching methods. The same book of the Bible, for example, can be taught using the lecture or discussion methods. The discussion method can follow a question outline composed by the teacher in advance or work inductively by building on student insights. The curriculum frame brings into focus the teaching approaches used most frequently in different classes in order to better understand how people engage the subject matter in these settings. It makes a difference if all adult classes, for example, use the lecture method and none use participatory methods that allow for discussion or imaginative methods drawing on the arts. Adult education is apt to focus entirely on the mastery of knowledge and less on helping people build connections to their everyday lives.

In his theory of education, Gardner develops an approach to teaching that builds on his account of multiple intelligences, sometimes called *multimodal teaching*.[13] This teaching approach is important not only in general education but also in Christian education. Simply put, the core notions of a subject are taught using a variety of methods and learning activities that engage the different forms of intelligence Gardner has identified. Rather than teaching a subject matter solely by speaking and reading (linguistic) or reasoning (logical-mathematical), the teacher uses learning activities that allow students to engage it in other ways—for example, song (musical), role play and examples (interpersonal), journaling (intrapersonal), or artistic expression (spatial and bodily-kinesthetic). Students are viewed as having diverse intellectual profiles with different blends of strength and weakness. By presenting the core notions of a subject in a variety of ways, multimodal teaching increases the likelihood that all students will have a chance to learn. It also enhances their understanding, stretching them beyond one way of engaging the subject (e.g., in abstract ideas) and helping them to grasp it in other ways (e.g., using interpersonal intelligence to relate it to personal relationships or spatial intelligence to help them "see" patterns and images).

4. *Phases of the curriculum* builds on and draws together the concepts presented above. In light of the developmental readiness of students and a sequencing of the subject matter, this category divides up the educational pathway of the curriculum into distinct periods of learning. Think of phases as the different parts of the journey people take as they travel along the pathway of the curriculum.

Building on Gardner's insights and adding my own, I identify three phases of the curriculum for children and adolescents.[14] I then turn to the work of James Fowler to identify two further phases for adults.

Preschool Phase: The Natural Learner

The "natural learner" of the preschool years largely develops outside of formal contexts of education. During this period, children acquire basic symbolic competence in many areas. Language is unquestionably the most important of the competencies acquired during this period, allowing children to build a basic understanding of the meaning (semantic), appropriate rules (grammar), and use (pragmatics) of their native language. What is remarkable is the way most children acquire linguistic competence naturally, through their everyday interactions with adults and peers.

Along with language, children also begin to form cognitive schemas and categories that allow them to sort their experience into patterns. One of the most important of these schemas is called *prototypes*, which is the basis of a child's ability to form categories. In classical philosophy, categories were viewed as based on linguistic definitions. In contrast, prototype theory argues that children form categories on the basis of paradigmatic instances of a category. For example, they construct the category of birds as small, flying creatures with beaks and wings on the basis of prototypes with which they are familiar, such as robins or blue jays. Only then do they expand this category to include nonprototypical members such as chickens and ostriches.

Two other cognitive schemas that emerge during this period also are important: *action scripts* and *narrative scripts*. The former is the schema of a sequence of actions that occur in situations a child encounters frequently. When going into a restaurant, for example, an action script might lead us to expect something like the following sequence of events: Wait to be seated; read menu; give order to waiter; eat food; pay bill; leave restaurant. Over time, children gradually complexify simple action scripts in order to accommodate variation—for example, the different action sequences associated with eating at McDonalds or a fancy restaurant. Simple story scripts appropriate to preschool children draw on a common narrative schema that appears to be constant across all cultures, in spite of marked differences in content. These scripts begin by introducing the setting of the story, including its central characters. They then unfold a simple plot of one or more episodes in which characters and actions are portrayed in terms of binary opposites such as good/evil, lost/found, large/small; the plot culminates in a clear ending. This schema is found in fairy tales and folk stories around the world.

Three important implications for the congregational curriculum flow from this description of the "natural learner." First, since the most important growth and learning of the natural learner takes place outside of settings such as the church school, the congregational curriculum must give special attention to parent education. The family is potentially one of the most important venues of Christian education during this period. In the home, children can begin to learn elementary action scripts for activities such as prayer, helping others, and sharing. If parents read their children simple, age-appropriate Bible stories, then they lay a foundation for their children's understanding of God and the church. But most important, if parents communicate their love for God in the way they relate to their children, then their children can build their initial prototypes of God, Jesus, and the church on the basis of their experience of loving others who care for them. Special classes that target the parents of preschool children, thus, are a key part of the congregational curriculum.

A second implication follows. The more the church school is like a loving family in its approach to preschoolers, the more effective it will be in communicating the gracious God revealed in Jesus Christ. Just as parents' relationships with their children are very important, so too are the relationships of teachers with preschool children. The most important learning of this period is not fostered by formal teaching. It emerges naturally in the context of relationships and experiences and allows children to begin constructing their initial prototypes of God, Jesus, and the church. While there is a place for age-appropriate learning activities, these are secondary in importance.

Finally, the church must take very seriously the images of God and the Christian life that are formed during the preschool years. In his research, Gardner has found that by the end of this period children have begun to build lasting models of the physical and social world—what he calls "intuitive theories of the unschooled mind."[15] These intuitive theories continue to play a powerful role throughout life and, often, are highly resistant to formal education. It is not uncommon, for example, for adolescents and adults to use simple "prototypes" (called "stereotypes" in the social domain) to understand whole classes of people (e.g., all Asians are hardworking, orderly, and quiet). They also use simple narrative scripts to reduce complex social events to binary schemas of good guys and bad guys along the lines of folk stories and fairy tales. This is true in religion as well. Prototypes and images of God, simple stories of good versus evil, and elementary models of prayer and other practices formed during childhood continue to influence adults. The preschool years, thus, are more important than is often recognized, and congregations would do well to consider carefully the kind of support they offer parents of preschoolers and the sorts of experiences they offer children at the church.

Primary Phase: Cultivating Literacy

In most societies, schooling involves some form of formal instruction. In literate cultures, it focuses initially on learning the notational systems a particular culture has developed to preserve its heritage and to carry out adult roles and tasks later in life. With this in mind, Gardner describes the curriculum of the primary school years as focusing on education in the basic literacies of a particular society. He does not provide, however, an extensive description of what he means by literacy, leading me to supplement his thinking with my own insights and those of others.[16] As used here, literacy includes three dimensions.

1. *Elementary facility in the most important notational systems of a society.* This includes the ability to read, write, and perform simple mathematical operations, as well as learn less obvious notational systems like musical notes.

2. *A concept of cultural literacy that corresponds to the nonuniversal, context-dependent theory of development Gardner employs across his writings.* Cultural literacy points to the acquisition of the basic knowledge, attitudes, and skills that are needed to function with a minimum level of competence in a particular area of life. Cultural literacy in baseball, for example, involves learning the basic vocabulary and rules of the game, as well as the action skills involved in hitting, catching, throwing, and so forth. One can be culturally literate in some areas and illiterate in other areas. Many American boys are culturally literate in baseball, basketball, and football, but are illiterate in soccer, sailing, and rugby.

3. *A concept of understanding.* This is the ability to use the knowledge, attitudes, and skills of a particular domain or discipline in a flexible fashion in the face of relatively novel situations. Understanding is the ability to generalize knowledge, attitudes, and skills beyond the original context in which they are learned. It requires more than rote learning. It is the ability to use math skills learned at school to count one's change when buying candy at a store. Understanding in this sense becomes more complex as people move through the phases of a curriculum.

Today most congregations are not responsible for teaching young people reading, writing, and arithmetic, so the first dimension of literacy identified above plays little role in a congregational curriculum. But the second and third dimensions of literacy are quite important. They expand our understanding of what it means to cultivate biblical, theological, and moral literacy and to help children acquire elementary literacy in the practices of discernment.

Consider biblical literacy. Often this is taken to mean that a person has acquired a great deal of Bible knowledge. The idea of cultural literacy helps us to see why this is too narrow. Biblical literacy is not a matter of learning many, disembodied Bible "facts," but of acquiring elementary facility in the sorts of knowledge, attitudes, and skills that will allow Christians to participate competently and intelligently in practices of Scripture interpretation at later points in their lives. It prepares Christians to listen with a discerning ear to the way a Bible passage is handled in a sermon, to interpret a biblical text with integrity in a small group Bible study, or to integrate Scripture into one's personal prayer life. These endstates of Scripture interpretation will only emerge much later in life. But they are unlikely to emerge at all unless the congregational curriculum cultivates biblical literacy during childhood, helping children build up a basic stock of Bible knowledge, introducing them to the elementary skills of Bible interpretation, and modeling attitudes that encourage them to turn to the Bible as a source of guidance. No one starts out an expert when first learning a game, but there is no chance that he or she will ever become an expert without first learning to play.

The analogy of learning to play a game can take us one step further in understanding what is involved in cultivating literacy. There is a very fine line between learning to play a game and actually beginning to play. Consider basketball. In practice, a good coach teaches children the fundamentals of dribbling, passing, and shooting. Skills are broken down into their component parts. The fundamentals of shooting, for example, include keeping your eye on the basket, your elbow in, and following through. Through practice and repetition, these skills become habits. But there is no substitute for actually playing. The goal is to use what you have learned in practice in actual game situations. Cultivating biblical, theological, moral, and discernment literacy is something like this. It involves learning the component skills and knowledge in practice and beginning to actually use these things to live as a Christian.

John Dewey provides a helpful way of thinking about these issues. Education, he said, is more than preparation for future life; it is the first steps in actually beginning to participate in that life. For this reason, he believed that the classroom should be a "democracy in miniature," meaning that the classroom itself should be a place where democracy is already practiced and experienced. I think it is helpful to think of classes and groups of the congregational curriculum along these same lines, that is, as "communities of faith in miniature." Children are not simply preparing to be the church; they *are* the church in this particular setting. They acquire literacy and understanding in various facets of the Christian way of life when their class prays together, cares for one another, and learns together, embodying certain aspects of the community of faith within the class itself.

Secondary Phase: Teaching Disciplines

Some of Gardner's most important recent thinking about education has focused on secondary education.[17] Here attention shifts from the basic literacies to the disciplined forms of inquiry a society has developed to explore matters of truth, goodness, and beauty. Hence, much of what Gardner has to say about this phase of the curriculum centers on the modern disciplines. He conceptualizes understanding in the disciplines as passing through four stages, centering around disciplinary knowledge, methods, and purposes: (1) *naive*, students use the intuitive knowledge formed earlier in life in which disciplined forms of inquiry play no role; (2) *novice*, students begin to acquire an introductory understanding of the elementary knowledge and methods of a discipline but have little real understanding of the criteria that justifies their use in a particular field; they remain dependent on external authorities such as a teacher or expert to authorize particular knowledge and methods; (3) *apprentice*, students are now grounded in disciplinary knowledge, methods, and skills, informed by a sense of the purpose of a discipline; they use disciplinary knowledge and methods flexibly; and (4) *master*, students now use disciplinary knowledge and skills in a creative and critical fashion; they are aware that competing frameworks are available within a discipline and that reasons must be given to justify the adoption of a particular perspective.[18]

While congregations do not teach the modern academic disciplines any more than they teach reading and writing, they do teach disciplines of the Christian life that the church has evolved across the centuries and is continuing to create. These disciplines also involve specialized knowledge, a variety of methods, and a guiding purpose. Just as adolescents possess the developmental readiness to learn the disciplines of biology, art criticism, and physics, they also are ready to begin learning more disciplined approaches to the Christian life, moving through levels analogous to naive, novice, apprentice, and master.

Many Lutheran congregations, for example, continue to teach Luther's Small Catechism in confirmation. At its best, this is not simply a matter of memorizing answers but of learning to think theologically. The assumption is that adolescents can now use abstract reasoning and are ready to reach at least an apprentice level of theological understanding. By learning the basic beliefs of their own tradition, they take an important step forward in understanding what it means to claim their baptismal identity and to live out their baptism in their everyday lives. They also take an important step toward becoming a mature member of a community that thinks in terms of the theological categories of a particular tradition.

Or consider prayer. Many adult Christians are best characterized as holding a naive understanding of prayer, viewing it as asking God to meet their needs in times of crisis. Perhaps, they were never given the opportunity by their congregations to explore prayer as a rich and complex discipline. But some congregations do provide this opportunity, beginning with their youth. On retreats, they introduce young people to the rich tradition of prayer and invite them to try out different ways of praying; they teach a theology of prayer in the church school or confirmation class; they include times of prayer on mission retreats and in small groups; they help individuals develop a personal prayer life by offering them spiritual direction or encouraging them to covenant with prayer partners; youth leaders are encouraged to pray for one another and for others in the group.

Young people are capable of learning these disciplined approaches, but are they willing? Recall the analogy of learning to play a game that I offered to think about literacy. Many people learn to play at least one sport during childhood, but far fewer go on to play this sport in high school. A much higher level of commitment is required. The same sort of motivation and commitment is required to learn more disciplined approaches to the Christian life. Adolescents are unlikely to make this commitment unless they are surrounded by peers and trusted adults who communicate in word and example that these disciplines are life giving and a pathway to Christian maturity. Building a sense of community and solid relationships among youth, thus, is a critical element of education in this phase of the curriculum. Not only are these relationships a source of motivation, but they also serve as the basis of peer norms with which young people identify during this part of their lives.

The Adult Phases of the Curriculum:
James Fowler and Postconventional Christian Identity

To this point, Gardner has written relatively little about education beyond secondary schools. Thus, I will turn to a second dialogue partner, James Fowler, for help in conceptualizing the adult phases of the curriculum. Fowler's theory of faith development has made an important contribution to religious education for over twenty-five years, and it is not my purpose here to offer a critical evaluation of his theory, something I and many others have done elsewhere.[19] I am interested in entering into a dialogue with his portrait of adult faith stages, for they provide us with a picture of the sort of postconventional Christian identity that the congregational curriculum ought to support in our globalizing, multicultural world.

On the surface, Fowler's theory appears to be much narrower than Gardner's, for it stands in the structural developmental tradition of psychology based on the theory of Jean Piaget. As we have seen, Gardner argues that Piaget's understanding of cognitive development focuses on only one form of intelligence, the logical-mathematical. While I largely agree with this assessment, I think it would be a mistake to view Fowler's work along the same lines. His focus is the self engaged in meaning making, especially its construction of an interpretation of the ultimate context of existence. This sort of meaning making involves the human imagination and is much broader than cognition as conceptualized by Piaget.[20] Indeed, I would argue that Fowler's framework offers a more adequate account than Gardner's theory along two lines and, as such, is a good example of the importance of engaging more than one dialogue partner in practical theology's interdisciplinary work.

First, Fowler provides a more adequate account of the self than Gardner. Recent research on the brain has led some scholars to argue that a sense of self is central to every act of knowing.[21] They point out that models of the brain like Gardner's—which portray the intelligences as localized in different parts of the brain—do not adequately take account of the integrative centers of the brain that are closely associated with a sense of self. In contrast, the self engaged in meaning making lies at the heart of Fowler's theory. Second, Fowler looks extensively at the domains of morality and religion, which are treated relatively superficially in Gardner's work. Indeed, Fowler portrays faith—the activity of composing an interpretation of the ultimate context of existence—as a *human universal* and explores the important role of religious communities in supporting this activity.

The relationship between Fowler's stages and the phases of the congregational curriculum can be summarized as follows:

The Preschool Phase	*Intuitive projective faith*—the composition of images of God and the world in relation to the divine
The Primary Phase	*Mythic literal faith*—the composition of narratives of God and God's people
The Secondary Phase	*Synthetic conventional faith*—the composition of beliefs and values informed by the conventional norms of the congregation and significant others
The Critical Phase	*Individuative reflective faith*—the composition of a

| | critically examined and self-chosen system of beliefs and values |
| *The Postcritical Phase* | *Conjunctive faith*—the composition of multiple perspectives on faith and morality and the ability to dialogue with perspectives different from one's own |

As noted above, I am particularly interested in drawing on Fowler's adult stages of faith, for they help us understand the sort of education that supports postconventional Christian identity. The concept of postconventionality has been used by psychologists, philosophers, and theologians to describe the development of a critical perspective on the conventional norms that are a part of a particular community's way of life and the capacity to understand and appreciate the perspectives of other communities and groups.[22] Within the various theories of postconventionality that have been widely discussed in recent years, Fowler's theory is unique.[23] Most of these theories portray development toward postconventionality along modernist lines, as the movement "beyond" our particularized cultural and religious identities to forms of autonomy that all human beings potentially share. In contrast, Fowler draws on Paul Ricoeur to describe a postcritical role for symbols, appropriated in a second naiveté. This leads him to portray postconventionality as the appropriation of the symbolic depths of a particular tradition in ways that both relativize this tradition and provide a basis from which to engage perspectives quite different from this tradition. I will describe this more fully below. On the basis of Fowler's theory, two phases of the adult curriculum can be projected.

The Critical Phase: Individuative Reflective Faith

Individuative reflective faith is the first postconventional stage of adult faith described in Fowler's theory. In this stage, individuals stand back from the values and beliefs formed during childhood and adolescence and reflect critically on the traditions in which they were raised, often exploring other perspectives on life's ultimate meaning and purpose. This allows them to compose a system of values and beliefs that is their own. They may choose to reaffirm the tradition in which they were raised or adopt values and beliefs that are quite different than those learned earlier in life. In either case, the "work" of this stage is forming a faith stance that is *individuated*, one that is critically examined and self-chosen. During the critical phase of the curriculum, Christian education supports the work of faith individuation in three ways.

1. Opportunities to think critically and systematically. Values and beliefs are taught as comprehensive systems of thought and action that can be compared and contrasted with other such systems. Suppose a young adult raised as a Lutheran was catechized in Luther's Small Catechism in confirmation. She now is given the opportunity to reflect on Lutheran theology more systematically, exploring different strands of this tradition and comparing it with the theological perspectives of other Christian traditions and of other religions. This sort of education also includes critical questions that might be posed to her own tradition (e.g., Lutheran quietism, individualism, and bifurcation of life into two kingdoms). Reflecting critically on her own faith tradition provides her with the capacity to make choices: what she accepts and what she rejects in her own faith stance.

2. *Principled moral reasoning.* Overarching ethical principles such as love and justice are taught that transcend the conventional morality of a particular society or cultural group. Adults are given the opportunity to use these principles to test the adequacy of moral actions and public policies, supporting maturity in the moral judgments of individual conscience and the capacity to offer good reasons for one's actions.

3. *Self-exploration.* Classes and groups are offered that allow adults to reflect on their biographies to promote greater insight about the trajectory of their life to the present and the norms into which they were socialized. The goal is to support greater choice and agency in forming beliefs and values that are truly their own.

Postcritical Phase: Conjunctive Faith

In Fowler's theory, the conjunctive stage of faith assumes the individuation of the previous stage and places these self-chosen beliefs and values at risk by seeking out perspectives that are different from those held by the individual. This stage is characterized by a newfound epistemological humility along two axes.

First, the systemic orientation of the previous stage is now seen as limited. This rests on an awareness of the limitations of any system of thought in grasping the fullness of truth, goodness, and beauty. It affirms the need for multisystemic thinking, for a variety of perspectives. Second, the methods and procedures of rationality are viewed as limited ways of gaining access to truth, goodness, and beauty. Fowler explains what this means in terms of Ricoeur's understanding of a second naiveté, highlighting the role of symbols in mediating a postcritical stance in the construction of meaning.[24] Symbols are no longer viewed as reducible to their rational meanings but as multivalent and transrational, that is, as possessing the capacity to evoke insights, intimations of wholeness, and glimpses of transcendence that defy reductive, rational explanations. In this stage, people thus develop the capacity to draw on the symbolic depths of their own religious tradition in ways that open them to the perspectives of other individuals and groups. During the postcritical phase of the curriculum, Christian education can support the multisystemic and dialogical stance of conjunctive faith in three ways.

1. *Teaching multisystemic thinking.* Awareness that no single system of thought captures all aspects of truth, goodness, and beauty is cultivated by approaching subjects from a variety of perspectives. For example, the doctrines of creation and the *imago Dei* are approached differently in Christian theology and in evolutionary science and cultural anthropology. Learning to draw on a variety of such perspectives in matters of faith is affirmed and encouraged.

2. Cultivating encounters with cultural and religious "others." These sorts of encounters are a part of our everyday lives today, but what is being pointed to here is something different. It is intentional exposure to persons and perspectives that challenge the assumptions and norms of the adult participants. This can be done through interracial, interreligious, and ecumenical dialogue. It can take the form of immersing people in forms of service or mission that literally take them out of their everyday world and expose them to people whose life circumstances are quite different than their own. Reflection on the ways their understanding has been challenged by these experiences is crucial.

3. A dialogical approach to moral reasoning and decision making. Adults are taught the procedures, reasoning strategies, attitudes, and skills of moral dialogue. This sort of "discourse ethic" affirms the importance of engaging all sides of the issue, offering moral reasons for one's position, and affirming the moral worth of those with whom one disagrees. Participants are given the chance to formulate their own stance on an issue, with no expectation that the group will reach consensus.

Focus Questions of the Curriculum Frame

We now have before us the categories and concepts of the curriculum frame. How might the leaders of a congregation's educational program draw on this theoretical perspective to develop a picture of the curriculum of their own congregation? The following focus questions outline a process that might be used.

1. What classes or groups are identified when an inventory is made of the congregation's curriculum and what subjects are covered and teaching approaches used in each of these settings? Developing the "big picture" of a congregation's curriculum is not easy, especially in large churches with many groups and classes. The best way to begin is by taking an "inventory" of each phase of the curriculum, simply noting the classes and groups in which Christian education is offered to children, youth, and adults. You can then identify the subjects covered and the teaching approaches most commonly used in each of these settings.

2. When you look closely at each phase of the curriculum, what subjects receive primary attention? Do students have the chance to engage these subjects in developmentally appropriate ways? Here you are asked to broaden your perspective from particular classes and to look at an entire phase of the curriculum. Drawing on Gardner and Fowler, I have offered a framework that might be used to reflect on each phase, which I link to the categories of catechesis, exhortation, and discernment when I carry out this activity. During the primary phase, for example, this involves looking for the ways the curriculum cultivates biblical, theological, moral, and discernment literacy. This reflective exercise allows you to develop a sense of what is actually going on in each phase and to assess relative strengths and weaknesses.

3. What educational pathways does the curriculum offer that allow people to build knowledge, attitudes, values, and skills in a cumulative fashion over time? The next task is to stand back and look at the curriculum as whole. As people move from childhood to adolescence to adulthood, does the curriculum take them anywhere?

Is cumulative growth and learning supported as people move from one phase of the curriculum to another? Consider also pathways for specific groups such as confirmands, new members, people nearing retirement, or new parents. What sort of pathways might groups of people travel over an extended period of time?

4. *What endstates inform the curriculum and how are they related to the congregation's identity and ethos?* This question asks you to identify the endstates of the curriculum—the roles, activities, and products that are valued by the congregation and influence what the curriculum is educating people toward. It then asks about the relationship between these endstates and the identity and ethos of the congregation as a whole. This is important because the education of the curriculum can be related to the ethos of the congregation in a variety of ways. Ideally, the curriculum builds on and deepens the ethos of the congregation. But this is not always the case. Sometimes education in the curriculum must attempt to change certain facets of the congregation's way of life.

NASSAU'S CURRICULUM

In the remainder of this chapter, I examine Nassau Presbyterian Church through the curriculum frame. While space constraints make it impossible to pursue each of the focus questions in depth for every phase of the curriculum, I offer an extended example of the ways these questions can be used to examine a congregational curriculum.

An Inventory of Nassau's Curriculum

The Primary Phase of the Curriculum

- *Church school*—stories of the Bible as found in the *Covenant People* curriculum; use of multimodal teaching methods along the lines of multiple intelligence theory (including music, storytelling, discussion, crafts, and a wide variety of learning activities); some emphasis on practices of the Christian life; fifth and sixth grades have an overview of the Old and New Testaments, using a curriculum written by leaders of the congregation
- *Choir program*—explanation of the biblical and theological meaning of musical pieces in the context of rehearsal; performance as a form of ministry
- *Vacation Bible school*—thematic focus on the Bible using the *Storyteller* curriculum; multimodal teaching

The Secondary Phase of the Curriculum

- *Church school*—middle school classes focus on essential elements of the Christian tradition such as the Lord's Prayer and Ten Commandments;

senior high class studies books of the Bible in depth; discussion method prominent, with some multimodal teaching

- *Youth groups*—middle school group (grades 6–8) on Wednesday evenings; senior high group (grades 9–12) on Sunday evenings; group-building activities common in both groups; a range of faith and ethical issues covered in each group, using a wide variety of interactive teaching methods; more emphasis on discussion in the senior high group
- *Youth choir program*—explanation of the biblical and theological meaning of musical pieces in the context of rehearsal; performance as a form of ministry
- *Confirmation*—ninth graders; Wednesday evenings over the course of the year; focus on the Apostles' Creed; learning centers and small group discussion prominent
- *Mission trips*—a special thematic focus for each trip; service-learning model of education focusing on action and reflection, both during and after the trip

The Postconventional Phases of the Curriculum

- *Church school*—ongoing series in four areas: (1) Bible, (2) history and theology, (3) faith and family issues, and (4) contemporary social and ethical issues; frequent use of outside resource people; lecture, followed by discussion, is dominant teaching approach, though some series are intentionally designed for greater interaction
- *New members classes*—four hours on worship, church membership, history and polity of the Presbyterian Church, and finding your way into Nassau's program; lecture and discussion
- *Leadership education*—education for deacons, elders, and teachers; provides a theological and biblical understanding of their roles and teaches specific skills needed to carry them out; officer training retreats have focused on discussion of a book
- *Event of the month*—bus trips to places of interest in proximity to Princeton, such as the Cloisters, the Civil War battleground of Gettysburg, and the Metropolitan Opera; includes a presentation by a scholar as part of the trip and sometimes special classes prior to the trip
- *Adult choir program*—explanation of the biblical and theological meaning of musical pieces in the context of rehearsal; performance as a form of ministry
- *Weekday ad hoc small groups*—includes groups such as the Women's Prayer and Spirituality Group, the Theological Book Group, the Women's Early Bird Bible Study, the Men's Breakfast Group, and others; prominent use of discussion method
- *Extended trips*—study trips lasting several weeks; in 2000, for example,

this trip was "A Reformation Pilgrimage" to Europe, accompanied by a seminary professor

Intergenerational Classes in the Curriculum

- *Family fellowship*—monthly fellowship gatherings, which sometimes include an educational component; interactive teaching, often using learning centers
- *Worship education*—designed for families of first-grade children; one session for all parents of young children, focusing on the history and theological meaning of the Lord's Supper and its role in worship; followed by a joint session of parents and children
- *Preaching*—occasionally, sermons have an explicit teaching focus; for example, Rev. Davis interpreted to the congregation Stravinsky's *Symphony of Psalms*, which was then performed by the adult choir in the context of worship
- *Art exhibits*—periodic art exhibitions in conference room, open to all ages
- *Nassau at six*—occurs seven to eight months of the year; primarily a concert performance; sometimes includes a minilecture designed to place the pieces in context

Fall Classes in the Adult Church School—1997–2000

1997: Jerusalem: Three Faiths, Three Millennia; New Jersey Elections: Two Views; The Meaning of Money; Parenting for Faith; Children's Sexuality for Parents; Hope for Global Future; Hallelujah: Handel's *Messiah*; Caring at Christmas; Advent: Love, Joy, Peace, and Hope; Christmas Carols Unplugged

1998: Paul's Letter to the Romans; Genesis for Princeton's Young Adults; Introduction to the New Testament; Stories of Jacob and Joseph; Suffering and Jeremiah; Central Americans among Us; Consumer Rites; Langston Hughes; Sacred Spaces; Jazz; Surviving Parenting Teenagers; The Great Ends of the Church; An Alternative Christmas; Advent and Birth Stories in Matthew

1999: Jihad, Just War, Holy War; Living Life on Purpose with a Purpose; Helping Children Use Their Bibles; Supporting Bible Teaching in Grades 5 and 6; An Exploration of Sibling Relationships; Conversation with Congressman Holt; Prospects for Protestantism; *Aida*; Ellen Reasonover: The Rest of the Story; Needle Exchange Programs: Do They Work?; Y2Xmas; Paul's Letter to the Romans; Exodus to Judges for Young Adults

2000: The Gospel according to John; The Gospel according to Matthew; What Presbyterians Can Do Better; Ancient History between Abraham and Christ; The Role of Women in Early Christianity; Capital Punishment; Ethical Aspects of Clinical Trials; Theologies of Nonviolence; Helping Children Read Their Bibles; *Turandot*; Teaching Your Children about Money; The Discipline of Simplicity; The Body Project; Gospel of John (short version)

The Primary Phase of the Curriculum

Helen Wise is the lead teacher of the third and fourth grade class and is generally considered a master teacher in Nassau's church school. A particularly gifted storyteller, she uses this method frequently in her teaching, along with a variety of other creative teaching methods. She embodies multimodal teaching, using a wide range of learning activities to engage a variety of intelligences. If my interviews of Nassau's children are any indication, they learn a great deal in her class, and many consider it their most important point of connection to the congregation. It provides us with a striking example of the way a church class can serve as a "community of faith in miniature."

Since the class includes both third and fourth grades—ranging between thirty-five and sixty students—Mrs. Wise divides it into "tribes." Each tribe has its own adult "tribe leader," whom Mrs. Wise reminds at the beginning of every year that their most important job is "to serve as a pastor to their children." When I observed her class, these adults arrived early and set out materials on round tables scattered around the spacious room, the gathering points of the tribes. As children arrived, each was greeted by name and informal conversation began to take place. The first activity was to tally the points the tribe had accumulated that week—for being present; for bringing an offering, a Bible, and their copy of *The Storybook Bible*; and for reading Bible stories during the past week. When a tribe accumulates five hundred points, it is rewarded with a special "POBS party" (present, offering, Bible, storybook).

Mrs. Wise got the tribes' attention by striking a chord on the piano, which was used to signal a shift from one activity to another throughout the class. She called for a "gathering" of the tribes at the front of the room for a discussion of prayer. She began by naming different types of prayer (adoration, confession, thanksgiving, intercession, and supplication) and invited the children to share their understanding of the meaning of these terms. There was a lot of participation by the children. Mrs. Wise called on each child by name and seemed to have a sense of whom to affirm, tease, or challenge to think more deeply. Over the course of the discussion, she made the point that Christians pray to God in different ways and that God answers their prayers in different ways.

The tribes returned to their tables, where they cut out a magazine picture that reminded them of something they have prayed about, pasted it on a piece of construction paper, and wrote a phrase or sentence that expressed the meaning of the picture. They then rotated as tribes from one table to another and were asked to talk about a different dimension of prayer at each table. At one point, the tribes had a chance to pray together. The class ended with a litany in which each child read aloud the phrase he or she had written down and the class responded in unison. Mrs. Wise then called one of the girls who had finished reading all of *The Storybook Bible* to the front of the class. Mrs. Wise read a special letter that she had written in the front of the girl's copy, which lifted up her special gifts in an affirming way. This ritual happens whenever a child has completed reading this book.

While this particular session was more discussion-oriented than others I observed, it included pictures, personal examples, and practical advice about prayer. I was also struck by the amount of sharing by both children and adults. The adults obviously had thought about prayer in advance and were comfortable sharing their own experiences of prayer. They were good listeners and asked questions that built on the children's insights. I came away with the impression that the class is a place where the children are affirmed and have fun, where they pray and learn together. Most classes include a time when the tribes pass around a bean bag with a smiley face on one side and a sad face on the other, sharing a good or bad experience from the past week.

The importance of viewing each of the classes and groups of the congregation as a community of faith in miniature is something I learned from my observation of this class. It was particularly brought home to me by the way Mrs. Wise handled her own experience of tragedy while I was studying Nassau. During this year, Mrs. Wise's son, Andrew (age 24), was diagnosed with an unusual and particularly aggressive form of cancer. He had just entered young adulthood and was still living at home. Many of the children of her class knew him well from church and as a lifeguard at the neighborhood pool. His illness was diagnosed in September and he died in the middle of December.

Throughout this very difficult period, Mrs. Wise shared her grief and her faith with the class. I talked to some of the children and adult tribe-leaders about this, and all of them shared how deeply they had been affected by this experience. As one adult put it, "She showed us how to deal with this sort of loss as a person of faith. She's a great one to affirm the kids. But now she was inviting them into her pain and asking for their prayers and support. She shared with them how some weeks her time with them on Sunday morning was her one little glimmer of happiness. It was incredibly meaningful to all of us." Mrs. Wise speaks of all that she "received" from the class during this period. Many of the children went to her home for "calling hours" right after Andrew's death; others sang in the children's choir that took part in his memorial service; they prayed for her and wrote her letters. Adults can receive comfort and support from children, and children can learn some of their most important lessons about faith when adults are "real" with them. But this will only occur if a class is more than a place to learn information and is a community of mutual care and sharing in which the faith already is being practiced.

This brief description of Mrs. Wise's class is our initial entry point into the primary phase of Nassau's curriculum. While no other class is quite like this one, my observation of other classes and venues such as vacation church school leads me to believe her class provides a window onto the primary curriculum as a whole. Two characteristics are especially pervasive. First, like Mrs. Wise, many other teachers use a variety of creative and interactive teaching methods. Their teaching is multimodal in Gardner's sense. This is a priority of teacher education at Nassau, and it appears to be having an effect. Second, the attention Mrs. Wise gives to building relationships with the children and cultivating a sense of community in her class also is common across this phase of the curriculum. Teachers take time to get to know the children in their class and often interweave serious study with group-building activities, times of sharing, working together on helping projects, and praying together.

At the end of the previous section, I offered several focus questions that might guide you in reflecting on your congregation's curriculum. The second question asks about each phase of the curriculum as a distinct unit. The goal is to determine the subjects covered in this phase and the ways students are encouraged to engage this material. Drawing on Gardner's framework and the categories of catechesis, exhortation, and discernment, I will examine the primary phase of Nassau's curriculum along these lines.

Catechesis. The church school for children uses *Covenant People*, a curriculum created by the denominational board of the Presbyterian Church. It focuses primarily on Bible stories but also includes the option of studying questions from the new Presbyterian catechisms and learning certain practices of the Christian life. Overall, Nassau's teachers appear to focus primarily on teaching the Bible. Moreover, the congregation frequently offers classes for parents of this age group to encourage Bible reading in the home. Fifth and sixth graders engage in a survey of the Old and New Testaments, knitting together the individual stories they have learned across this phase of the curriculum into a comprehensive narrative. Attention to Christian tradition primarily takes place in choir rehearsal and the worship education classes for first graders and their families.

While teacher education does not provide teachers an explicit method of Bible interpretation that might guide their teaching, my observation leads me to believe that most classes include the following elements: (1) Children's questions and interests vis-à-vis a particular passage are taken seriously, (2) the text is presented in a creative fashion to engage a variety of intelligences, and (3) children are invited to respond to the passage in ways that make connections to their everyday lives. In my interviews of children, they were able to recall a number of Bible stories with relative ease. They also demonstrated understanding of these stories, revealing an age-appropriate ability to link them to everyday life. Overall, I view the cultivation of biblical literacy as a strength of the primary phase of Nassau's curriculum, with less explicit attention given to theological literacy.

Exhortation (moral education). During this phase of Nassau's curriculum, moral knowledge is cultivated primarily through teaching Bible stories with biblical characters portrayed as moral exemplars. Children are asked to construct concrete analogies that connect the moral dimensions of these stories to their everyday lives, through concrete reasoning, artistic expression, role play, and other learning activities. Moral action is encouraged through helping projects and through the cooperative learning approaches used in some classes, which emphasize sharing and teamwork. In some classes, moreover, the children have learned how to accommodate students with special needs.

All of these are important ways that moral literacy is cultivated in this phase of the curriculum. Overall, however, Nassau undertakes moral education indirectly during childhood, largely out of a fear of moralism, an attitude closely related to the ethos of the congregation. While church school teachers sometimes cultivate the empathetic capacities of their students, they do not intentionally introduce a language of the moral emotions in their teaching. Nor do they offer children a clear set of moral guidelines that can guide their everyday lives, guidelines that are reinforced as children move from one grade to another.

Discernment. Fostering literacy in practices of discernment such as prayer, sharing among Christian friends, and debate/discussion varies widely from class to class. In Helen Wise's class, I saw a teacher who has woven these practices into the rhythm of her class. Other teachers also appear to teach the building blocks of discernment through debate and discussion by encouraging children to ask questions and by affirming the importance of listening to different perspectives on the subject matter. Likewise, many teachers also cultivate the habit of bringing the concerns of children's everyday lives into the class in structured times of sharing and prayer—creating the expectation that sharing among friends is a part of Christian community. As far as I can tell, however, these activities are not cultivated in a systematic and intentional manner from grade to grade, as part of a curricular plan to foster literacy in the practices of discernment across this phase of the curriculum.

The Secondary Phase of the Curriculum

During this phase of the curriculum, Nassau offers Christian education in five different venues: church school, youth groups, youth choir program, confirmation, and mission trips. The subject matter and teaching approaches vary considerably from one venue to another, for each setting introduces the youth of Nassau to a somewhat different way of practicing the Christian life in a more disciplined fashion. I will describe the moral discussion of a Sunday evening youth group as our entry point into the secondary phase, and then point briefly to disciplined approaches to the Christian life learned in other settings.

Twice a month, the Sunday evening youth group for senior highs discusses a contemporary moral issue. These topics are chosen by the youth cabinet and adult leaders on their fall planning retreat. In recent years, these topics have included issues such as homosexuality, capital punishment, dreams, drugs and addiction, and body image. Almost every year, the group has at least one discussion on relationships and sex, the topic of the session I observed.

When the group had gathered, Rev. Lisa Nichols Hickman, the youth pastor, welcomed the members and asked them to get into groups of two or three to share the highs and lows of the week. She then called the groups together and told them the topic of the evening was sex and relationships. She handed out sheets to every youth with biblical passages and quotations from contemporary authors that dealt with some aspect of this topic. Youth were asked to read this sheet silently. They then broke into small groups of six to eight and were provided with a sheet of questions to guide their discussion. While adult advisors participated in these groups, they did not lead the discussion or dominate, simply raising questions and offering occasional insights. The youth seemed to be used to this sort of nonintrusive participation by the advisors and quickly began to deal with the questions on their discussion guide. Moreover, there seemed to be a high degree of trust in the group, for they seemed to be pretty honest about what they thought even with an observer like me looking on. Some argued that it is all right to be sexually active as long as you love the other person and are in a committed relationship. Others argued back that they think the Bible teaches that sex before marriage is not what God wants.

When the small groups gathered back together, each group shared two of the most important insights of its discussion. Rev. Nichols Hickman then spontaneously built on these insights, leading a discussion designed to help the group to think more deeply about issues that had emerged. At times, she encouraged the youth to listen more closely to each other or referred them back to the handout to introduce biblical and moral themes. She asked follow-up questions that invited the group to build on one another's insights. The meeting ended with a brief worship service led by the youth cabinet.

I interviewed several former members of the youth group who are now in college and asked them what they thought about these discussions. They were uniformly positive, pointing to three things that they have especially come to value. First, the leaders did not "preach" at them, but gave them the chance to explore what they thought and to hear what their friends thought without adults telling them what they ought to think. Second, it was safe to express any point of view and to disagree with other members of the group. They trusted the adult leaders to keep their comments in confidence. They also liked having the chance to argue about these issues with other members of the group, though this had been intimidating when they first started going to the youth group. Third, they really appreciated Rev. Nichols Hickman's ability to lead this sort of discussion. As one college student put it, "She really knows how to ask just the right questions, and she taught us how to listen to each other. She's a whole lot better at leading a discussion than some of my professors are!"

One way of thinking about what is going on in these sessions is to view them as teaching Nassau's youth a disciplined way of taking part in a moral conversation. This involves gradually learning certain skills of thinking and communication that center around the following: (1) There is more than one side to every issue, even when you are talking about the moral teachings of the Bible; it is important to listen to other viewpoints; (2) disagreement and debate are good things, but they have to be carried out with mutual respect; (3) when you express your own point of view, you need to be prepared to give reasons to support it; (4) confidentiality is the basis of trust, so what is shared in the group must stay in the group; and (5) reaching a consensus is less important than coming to an informed point of view that is truly your own. It is no accident that Nassau would make a "disciplined" approach to this sort of moral conversation an important part of its moral education with youth; it reflects its commitment to a culture of thinking.

Rev. Nichols Hickman is quite gifted in leading this sort of discussion, but there are two ways I would have encouraged her to amplify the youth's sense that these discussions represented disciplined forms of the Christian life. First, I would have encouraged her to teach the underlying norms of these moral discussions, noted above, as an explicit *discourse ethic*, offering the youth a set of moral guidelines that could be used to assess dialogue in other settings within and beyond the church. Second, I would have encouraged her to teach the young people the *purpose* of this sort of moral dialogue, why it is an important part of moral discernment in the church and the role it plays in democratic, pluralistic societies.

Moral discussions by the youth group are not the only way that moral education takes place during the secondary phase of the curriculum. Rev. Nichols Hickman makes a special effort to connect with every youth on a personal basis, and many come to trust her enough to share personal issues, allowing her to offer moral guidance in one-to-one relationships. The youth group's yearly mission trips also are a focal point of moral education. Each trip is "framed" in terms of a special theme, which is studied before, during, and after the trip and culminates in a Sunday evening presentation to the congregation. Many youth come away from these trips determined to become more involved in service activities back in Princeton. In recent years, a number have become regular volunteers in congregational outreach programs. Indeed, one recent graduate of the youth group was inspired to raise over $50,000 for "eco-toilets" for a town in Mexico with drinking water polluted by human waste. This is one of the ways the youth group reflects Nassau's commitment to leadership beyond the congregation.

Scanning across the other venues of Nassau's secondary phase of the curriculum, it is not difficult to spot other disciplined approaches to the Christian life. Senior high church school focuses on study of individual books of the Bible in depth and introduces the students to more disciplined approaches to the interpretation of Scripture. Students begin to interpret biblical texts in terms of their historical and literary contexts. Confirmation classes focus on the sort of disciplined study of Christian tradition necessary to make a personal confession of faith—what Nassau refers to as a "step of intention." This includes study of the Apostle's Creed, journaling, conversations with mentors, and participation in discussions that encourage the confirmands to clarify what they believe and are willing to affirm publicly. The Youth Choir achieves an exceptionally high standard of musical performance, which requires a new level of discipline in rehearsal and presentation. Yet performance does not become the single driving force. Teaching the biblical and theological meaning of the musical pieces being learned remains important, as does the choir director's emphasis on musical performance as a form of ministry.

In a variety of venues, thus, Nassau's secondary curriculum introduces youth to more disciplined approaches to the Christian life. I have noted in passing some of the ways the secondary curriculum builds on and reflects certain aspects of the ethos of the congregation as a whole. I now want to explore the relationship between curriculum and ethos more fully.

The Postconventional Phases of the Curriculum

As we turn to Nassau's adult education, I will depart slightly from the format of the previous sections and, rather than beginning with an example, will end with one. I am particularly interested in exploring the relationship between Nassau's identity and ethos, as described in the first part of this chapter, and the endstates that seem to be associated with its curriculum, especially adult education. Nassau has a very strong adult education program. My work as a doctoral student with James Fowler leads me to believe that it is highly likely that the modal level of adult education (the average expected level of faith development) is probably the individuative reflective stage.

The church school is organized around four tracks: (1) Bible, (2) history and theology, (3) faith and family issues, and (4) social and ethical issues. If you look back at the topics covered in these four tracks between 1997 and 2000, you get some idea of the subjects taken up in the adult church school. The classes typically are short-term series and bring in professionals from the congregation and scholars from neighboring institutions of higher education to serve as teachers. The subject matter often is presented at a demanding level, and the quality of discussion is quite high. Indeed, one of Nassau's persistent challenges in recent years has been to develop educational pathways for new members with little background in the Bible or the Reformed tradition that will bring them "up to speed" so they can participate meaningfully in adult education. As my inventory of adult classes and groups makes clear, the church school is not the only venue in which Christian education is offered adults. Yet, in many ways, the short-term series of the church school are the heart and soul of adult education.

I believe that two endstates are closely associated with adult education in the church school: (1) the importance of bringing a thinking faith to bear on the many roles and spheres of life, and (2) the importance of being socially aware and engaged. The first of these points to a well-informed thoughtfulness as a Christian about one's parenting, use of money, appreciation of the arts, and many other areas of life. The second points to Christians' involvement in public life, the importance of understanding contemporary issues in order to make informed decisions and to participate in various volunteer and advocacy programs within and beyond the congregation itself. Both endstates are oriented toward the individual Christian. There is no desire to cultivate a "party line" in terms of the Bible, Reformed theology, or contemporary ideology. The congregation wants its members to be thoughtful and informed but, ultimately, the individual is the arbiter of faith and moral issues. The role of adult education is to inform, challenge, and expose the individual to a wide range of perspectives. Even when the congregation has taken advocacy stances, it has attempted to make it clear that those disagreeing with these stances are welcome and are free to express their dissent in appropriate ways.

It is not difficult to see the close relationship between these endstates of the adult church school and Nassau's ethos. In the first part of this chapter, I portrayed this ethos in terms of four elements: (1) a strong orientation toward leadership beyond the local church, (2) a culture of thinking, (3) an expectation of excellence in all forms of ministry, and (4) ambivalence toward community. Supporting a thinking faith through the curriculum and a culture of thinking in the ethos of the congregation go hand in hand. Similarly, the importance placed on social awareness through the curriculum dovetails with Nassau's commitment to leadership beyond the congregation. The exceptionally high quality of speakers in adult education mirrors Nassau's commitment to excellence in all forms of ministry. To a large extent, thus, Nassau's adult education builds on and deepens its ethos. It is not difficult to see how this filters down to the phases of the curriculum for children and youth as well—in teachers' encouragement of questions, for example, and the sort of moral discussions found in the youth group.

It also is possible to point to the ways Nassau's curriculum reflects the "shadow side" of its ethos. The academic orientation of its curriculum—reflecting its culture of thinking and commitment to excellence—appeals to a highly educated, middle-class constituency and constantly teeters on the brink of elitism. Consistently using world-class scholars as teachers makes it pretty intimidating for the average church member to try his or her hand at teaching in the adult education program. As one of the adults I interviewed put it, "Freeman Dyson (a world-renowned physicist) is a pretty hard act to follow." The fact that this comment was made by a church member who is on the faculty of Princeton University reveals how intimidating it is to teach adult education at Nassau. But perhaps most important of all, its adult curriculum reflects the "shadow side" of the congregation's ambivalence toward community. All adult church school classes are structured as short-term series with many outside speakers, and there is little continuity of participants from one series to the next. Adult education, thus, does not really build a sense of community at Nassau; rather, it offers individuals many rich choices. It mirrors rather than transforms the congregation's ambivalence toward relationships of intimacy, sharing, and fellowship.

I want to end by examining one of the ways adult education *has* altered the ethos of this congregation. This has to do with two educational series between 1986 and 1991 in the social and ethical track of the adult church school. These series began a process of discernment in which Nassau reflected on its stance toward gays and lesbians. While these sessions took place over a decade ago, most had been videotaped and were available for me to view. I also was able to interview a number of participants and leaders of these series. It is helpful to place them in context. In 1978, the General Assembly of the Presbyterian Church (U.S.A.) adopted standards forbidding the ordination of "avowed, practicing homosexuals." Various attempts to overturn what came to be known as the "definitive guidance" ordination standard started to gain momentum in the mid-1980s and have continued to the present. Nassau's wrestling with this issue, thus, took place relatively early in this denomination-wide debate, reflecting the congregation's attention to issues emerging in the national church and its commitment to providing leadership on these issues.

The topic first appeared in Nassau's adult education curriculum in 1986, with a panel discussion led by national church leaders who held different perspectives on this issue. This was followed by a three-week class that continued the discussion. In 1989, the congregation invited Chris Glaser to speak, a gay man who was not able to pursue ordination after completing seminary because of the definitive guidance standard but, nonetheless, worked on the staff of West Hollywood Presbyterian Church. In the spring of 1990, the curriculum included a series, "In Light of Love: The Church and Homosexuality," featuring the following sessions and resource people: (1) "Is There a Word from God? The Bible and Homosexuality,"—Dr. Katherine Sakenfeld, professor at Princeton Theological Seminary, examined biblical passages dealing with homosexuality and principles of biblical interpretation; (2) "Is There a Word from the General Assembly?"—William Thompson, the Stated Clerk of the General Assembly and long-time affiliate of Nassau, covered the recent denominational history and his own change of heart on this issue, leading him to support the removal of the "definitive guidance" standard; (3) "Is There a Word from the Heart?" Parents of gay and lesbian children shared their stories; (4) "Is There a Word from Congregations?"—Members of Prospect Street Presbyterian Church in Trenton, New Jersey, shared the story of their decision to become a "more light" church, joining a network of congregations and individuals seeking the full participation of lesbian, gay, bisexual, and transgender people of faith in the life, ministry, and witness of the Presbyterian Church (U.S.A.).

During the fall of 1990, the adult curriculum included a series, "Do We Need More Light?" which included the following sessions and resource people: (1) "The Story of Third Church, Rochester"—Stephen Ford, a minister of Third Church and former seminary intern at Nassau, described the process Third Church went through in becoming a "more light" congregation; (2) "One Person's Story"—Scott Anderson, a gay Presbyterian minister, shared the story of being blackmailed because of his sexual orientation by two members of his congregation and the ensuing joys and pain of being forced to "come out"; (3) "Theological Perspectives"—Mark Taylor, professor at Princeton Theological Seminary, offered a liberationist perspective on homosexuality, starting with the concrete suffering of gays and lesbians; (4) "The Church's Future"—Chris Glaser explored the possibilities of denominational change.

One thing immediately stands out. Outside of the 1986 panel, every single speaker was in favor of eliminating the "definitive guidance" standard. This one-sidedness is surprising in light of Nassau's ethos, which values open discussion and critical questioning. In my interviews of church members who participated in these series, two quite different perspectives emerged. Some argued that these series prevented any real process of discernment from taking place across the congregation as a whole. It is no accident, they claimed, that only one side of the issue was presented, because these series were part of a carefully orchestrated political process in which key leaders were very intentionally moving the congregation to adopt a more open stance on homosexuality. In sharp contrast, others pointed to the cultural context in which these series were offered. In the late 1980s, they noted, the issue of homosexuality was still unexplored territory in most congregations. Very few members had heard the stories of pain of gays and lesbians, especially from people they knew and respected. The dominant cultural ethos portrayed heterosexuality as normative and homosexuality as a form of perversion. These series, they argued, created an open space to hear the other side of the story in the face of the overwhelmingly negative messages of the dominant culture. How could Nassau really discern this issue unless it first paused to hear this view from the margins?

Let us keep both of these perspectives in mind for the time being. In the following chapter, we will take up the leadership frame, which brings into focus the conflicting values that are likely to emerge when a congregation faces an adaptive challenge that cannot be handled by its present culture. For now, it is enough to point to the impact of these series on Nassau's ethos. Following the second series, the session adopted at its annual retreat "An Affirmation of the Inclusiveness of the Church," which describes the denomination's exclusion of homosexuals from ordination as contradicting the *Book of Order*'s affirmation of "inclusiveness" in congregations. The same year, the congregation sponsored an overture to its presbytery and the General Assembly seeking to invest sessions and presbyteries with the right to make their own, local judgments about the suitability of candidates for ordination and to eliminate any "impediments" in its constitution that imposed standards on these bodies. From this point forward, the ethos of the congregation began to change, adopting an advocacy stance in its leadership on this issue beyond the congregation, welcoming gays and lesbians into all facets of its life, offering counseling to youth who are struggling with their sexual orientation, and developing sexuality programs affirming a variety of sexual orientations. In its own words, Nassau has struggled to become an "inclusive church."

The educational series described above played an important role in these changes. It is an example of the way the education of a congregation's curriculum can contribute to the transformation of its identity and ethos. Yet this process of change involved certain political dynamics and processes that will not be brought into view if we look through the curriculum frame alone. Hence, we turn now to the leadership frame, which brings into focus the educational tasks involved in helping a congregation respond to the adaptive challenges of its own time and place.

Chapter 6

The Uniting Reformed Church of Stellenbosch, South Africa:

Leadership in the Spirit of Belhar

The nails had been distributed to the congregation earlier in this Good Friday worship service. The minister of the congregation, Rev. Jaco Coetsee, now invited the overflow crowd of over eight hundred people to get on their knees and join him in a time of confession, turning around to lean on the pews and holding a nail in their hands. Rev. Coetsee asked them to close their eyes and follow his lead in bringing the concerns of their lives, community, and world before God, to be followed by a time of silence. Prompted by Rev. Coetsee, the congregation concluded each time of silence by saying, "We praise you, O God." During the fourth period of silence, one of the elders hammered a nail into a wooden board. The unexpected bang pierced the silence and echoed throughout the sanctuary. I was kneeling near this elder and my whole body startled. Rev. Coetsee then told the kneeling community that this signified the nailing of the sins they had just confessed to the cross of Christ. Christ bore their sins on the first Good Friday long ago, and they could now return to their lives and world released from the burdens they carried. The congregation rose and sat down in the pews, while the nails were collected. The children were instructed to ask their parents when they returned home why this activity had taken place on this particular day. Throughout this time of confession, the entire congregation was reverent, from the youngest to the oldest.

This brief fragment of a Good Friday worship service in the Cloetesville branch of the Uniting Reformed Church of Stellenbosch is a window on the congregation. Through this window, we begin to see the warmhearted piety of its missionary past and the ways this church is renegotiating its past in the face of the adaptive challenges that it currently faces. We see the enormous burdens carried by the members of this "coloured" community—surrounded on all sides by poverty, violent crime, drug use, the spread of AIDS, and unemployment. When the members of URC Stellenbosch bring their concerns before God, nailing them to the cross of Christ, they are not merely confessing their personal sins but sharing burdened lives of quiet desperation, lives in which they are struggling to do good and cling to hope in the face of very difficult circumstances.

In this chapter we explore the teaching ministry of URC Stellenbosch through the leadership frame, in which the congregation is viewed as participating in God's mission to the world. In order to carry out its mission, the congregation must become a learning organization that faces and responds creatively to the adaptive challenges of its own time and place. The leaders of URC Stellenbosch are quick to point out that theirs is not an extraordinary congregation; many other congregations, they say, were far more prominent in the struggle against apartheid and have higher profiles today. As one member put it, "We're just an ordinary congregation that sometimes does extraordinary things . . . when we follow God's leading hand. Just make sure your readers know that we don't see ourselves as special." While I think they are being a bit modest, they are making a point that is important to this chapter. By using URC Stellenbosch as my case study congregation for the leadership frame, I am not implying that this frame is only relevant for special congregations that stand above other religious communities in their leadership. Rather, the leadership frame brings into focus the ways even "ordinary" congregations can function as learning organizations if they strive to carry out their mission as God's people.

A WINDOW ON THE CONGREGATION'S ETHOS

Good Friday Worship

In South Africa, Easter is similar to the national holiday of Labor Day in the United States. The seasons in these countries are exactly the opposite. What is spring in the United States is fall in South Africa. Easter comes at the end of the hot summer months and marks the transition to cooler weather. Schools typically have an extended break, and university students often travel home. Families use the long Easter weekend as a time to do something special. It felt a bit odd, thus, to a U.S. citizen to have a morning service on Good Friday serve as the highpoint of this liturgical season. Many church members would leave after this service to visit family and would not be present for the much smaller Easter service at the Idas Valley branch of the congregation.

I had already visited the congregation in Cloetesville prior to worshiping there. The building is located across the street from a strip of stores on one of the major streets running through this community. To its rear is a residential neighborhood of neatly kept, small houses. Throughout Cloetesville, however, are pockets of rundown, graffiti-covered apartments and houses. The residents describe these as centers of gang-related activity, often involving the sale of drugs and black market alcohol. Several blocks from the church is a field that serves as a boundary marker of two rival gangs. It is not uncommon for gunfire to be exchanged in this area.

The church building of the Cloetesville branch of this congregation is divided into two separate areas. One part of the building houses offices, classrooms, a kitchen area, and a fellowship hall. This space remains open during the day and many evenings of the week. It is widely used by the community, providing after-school care, a daily meal for poor children, a counseling center for abused women, a weekday preschool, and a meeting place for various sports clubs and exercise groups. Its fellowship hall is frequently used for community-wide events, such as musical performances, local theater, and modeling shows. You must leave this part of the building to enter the sanctuary, which is auditorium-like and holds eight hundred people. The ceiling is quite high, reaching fifty feet at its highest point. Clear windows along both sides allow natural light to enter and create a sense of warmth within and connectedness to the world without. The wooden pews, ceiling, and pulpit furniture are light, natural wood, adding to the feeling of warmth. On the front walls are two chalk pictures: one of Jesus on the cross and a second of Mary tending to Jesus in the manger. Immediately in front of these pictures is a stage-like platform that holds a circular wooden pulpit and baptismal font. Next to this platform is a special block of pews for the elders and deacons.

For this Good Friday service, a table large enough for five adults was placed on the raised area at the front. This contained the Communion elements and was covered by a white linen cloth. Rev. Coetsee sat at this table to lead the service on this particular day, since he had recently torn ligaments in his ankle and needed to sit for the duration of worship. During the serving of the Lord's Supper, two ministers sat to the pastor's left and two elders to his right. All were men, but women elders and deacons provided leadership at various points. Women make up approximately half of the elders and deacons and commonly provide worship leadership. These leaders were distinguishable by what they were wearing: dark clothes with a white shirt/blouse and ties.

As the congregation gathered, a band was playing what is commonly known as "contemporary traditional" gospel music in South Africa. The words were contemporary but the music traditional, interweaving guitar, banjo, and percussion instruments in various rhythmic patterns used for many years in the coloured community. The words were projected on the white wall at the front left of the sanctuary. The congregation joined the band in singing this music as it gathered for worship. As the service unfolded, however, it was apparent that these songs were not sung with nearly the same gusto as the hymns of the rest of service. No printed bulletins were provided, due to financial considerations I later was told. The congregants brought their own hymnals and Bibles and followed the directions of Rev. Coetsee as the service unfolded. Many people were seated long before the service began and joined in singing with the band. The feeling was informal and upbeat, like a family gathering for a holiday meal. All age levels were present, and parents felt free to come and go with their children during the service. At least thirty people arrived after the service began, sitting in the chairs placed on an outdoor patio adjoining the sanctuary.

The service was conducted in Afrikaans, which I do not speak. A translation was offered to me as the service unfolded. I also videotaped the service and viewed it at a later point with a person who provided me a sentence-by-sentence translation. The following is a brief summary of the flow of this service:

- *Call to worship*—Rev. Coetsee asked the members of the congregation to settle down and listen as he offered the call to worship from the Bible.
- *Singing*—Several verses from two hymns were sung. The congregation sang loudly and with much feeling.
- *Prayer*—An elder walked to the front of the church and led the congregation in a time of prayer. He prayed extemporaneously, using simple, straightforward language. He gave thanks to God for not forgetting the congregation and for his gift of love in Jesus Christ.
- *The Apostles' Creed*—This was recited in unison as the congregation stood.
- *Reading Scripture*—Rev. Coetsee read part of Psalm 22. Most in the congregation opened their Bibles and followed while he read. Many left their Bibles open on their laps while he preached (including a number of children and youth), as if they expected him to return to this text over the course of his sermon.
- *Sermon*—Rev. Coetsee preached on Psalm 22, seated at the Communion table. All age levels listened attentively. The sermon focused on the experience of feeling lonely and forsaken by God, even when you are surrounded by friends and loved ones. It spoke to the experience of feeling that God has abandoned your neighborhood and even your country, acknowledging that there may be people in today's service who sometimes feel like crying out, "My God, my God, why have you forsaken me?" Psalm 22 utters these very words to God, and Jesus repeated them on the cross. God has entered into the experience of human pain and loneliness and is not far away from you, even at those moments when you feel most alone and forsaken.
- *Prayer*—Following the sermon, another elder came forward and prayed extemporaneously, thanking God for the gift of redemption in Christ

and asking God to come into their midst today and deepen their faith in him.

- *Singing by the choir*—The choir of thirty-five members sang a song in English in a relatively restrained manner.
- *Invitation to the Lord's Table*—Immediately prior to the invitation to the Lord's Supper, Rev. Coetsee told the congregation that the ushers would pass around collection plates with nails in them. Each person was to take out one nail and hold on to it until later in the service. He explicitly said he wanted the children to participate in this part of the service and gave parents instructions on how they might guide their children so none would hurt themselves with the nails. As the ushers passed out the nails, two women came forward and ceremoniously removed the white linen covering the Communion elements, after which the pastor offered a prayer of consecration.
- *Serving of the children*—Rev. Coetsee invited the children to come forward to several stations where women served them the bread but not the juice. The congregation sang while well over a hundred children came forward.
- *Serving of the adults*—The catechized members of the community were then served both elements while seated. Rev. Coetsee asked the congregation if anyone had been missed, and the ushers took the bread and juice to those who held up their hands. He then served the ushers, participating pastors, and last of all took the elements himself.
- *Responsive prayer and hymn*—A responsive prayer followed, giving thanks to God for the gifts that had just been received. A hymn was sung.
- *Nailing sins to the cross of Christ*—Rev. Coetsee led the community through the special time of confession described at the outset of this chapter. Throughout this entire activity, the congregation was very quiet and reverent.
- *The Lord's Prayer*—The congregation sang the Lord's Prayer together.
- *Benediction*—The pastor, joining hands with the ministers and elders seated with him at the front, offered the benediction.

This worship service provides a window on the ethos of the congregation. My interpretation of the service draws on interviews and observations of other congregational settings, as well as the comparative perspective afforded by attending the worship services of other congregations in the Stellenbosch area. I viewed my videotape of the service with South Africans who are not members of the congregation for their feedback. Drawing on this research, I believe that five elements of the ethos of the congregation are apparent in this Good Friday service.

1. Continuity with the piety of its missionary past. Over the course of the service, the language of a warmhearted piety was used repeatedly—in the music, sermon illustrations, elders' prayers, and the special act of confession. As I have come to know this congregation, I have learned that this is not a highly individualistic "me and Jesus" piety, but one that is rooted in traditional Reformed practices. This congregation still practices catechetical instruction, for example, teaching the Heidelberg Catechism to youth and new members. The traditional distinction between the catechized and uncatechized was evident in the way the Lord's Supper was distributed. The community also still practices certain forms of church discipline. In one of my interviews, for example, a woman shared with me the congregation's response when she had an out-of-wedlock child. She had to appear before the church council, which asked her to refrain from Communion for several months and required her to participate in parenting classes offered in the church. Looking back at this experience, she says, "I didn't feel judged by the church council. I already had a lot of shame about what had happened. I felt supported. The classes I took were really helpful and some older women in the church helped me after my baby arrived." Both catechetical instruction and church discipline are traditional elements of Reformed ecclesiology and are indicative of the continuity the congregation has maintained with its Dutch Reformed missionary heritage.

   2. A combination of old and new: the congregation's break with its past. While the congregation retains elements of continuity with its missionary past, there are numerous signs that it has broken with this heritage in certain ways and continues to struggle with the process of renegotiating its identity as a community. Without any knowledge of the history of the community, these signs would, perhaps, only be available as small "clues" within the worship service itself. A close look, however, reveals a combination of old and new in this worship service, perhaps most apparent in the music. The band, which played "contemporary traditional" gospel music on one of the high holy days of the year, represents the congregation's attempt to interject "new" forms of music into worship, integrating musical traditions long important to the coloured community but not always a part of church life. Yet the "old" hymns of the service were sung with more vigor and seemed to be more meaningful to the worshipers.

   The worship space is a similar amalgamation of old and new. When I first entered the sanctuary, I was struck by how modern it is, especially the baptismal font and pulpit. There are no stained glass windows, steeple, or bell tower. The pews, however, are older than the rest of the building. They were brought to this building from the former sanctuary of the congregation and recall a time of crisis, when the congregation was forced to sell its church building after the apartheid government declared the area in which it was located a "whites only" residential area. During this period, the congregation began to come to terms with the limits of the missionary theology it had been taught, gradually reworking its understanding of God and the church. Its leaders began to criticize the policies of the apartheid government and the denominational patterns that mirrored these policies. The combination of old pews in a new, modern sanctuary stands as a potent sign of the congregation's commitment to its missionary past and its willingness to step into the future in its confrontation with apartheid.

My interviews and observation of the congregation have led me to conclude that the struggle to renegotiate the past remains an important part of the ethos of this community. It is especially apparent in differences across the generations. In my interviews, for example, all adults felt strongly connected to the congregation's worship, but this was true of only one-fourth of the youth, who were particularly critical of the music used in worship and preferred music "with more of a beat." Adults and youth also differed in what they saw as the most important virtues of the Christian life. Older members lifted up integrity, caring, honesty, and forgiveness; youth named being accepting and nonjudgmental, a willingness to speak out about social problems in the community, and following the Golden Rule. While these generational differences are based on a very small sample and may be due to developmental issues, something more may be going on here: the need to find new points of connection to the church now that its important role in opposing apartheid is over.

3. *The participatory and decentralized nature of the congregation.* Also coming to expression in this worship service is the highly participatory and decentralized nature of congregational leadership. As I observed this worship service, I was struck by the large number of people who played different leadership roles. The elders and deacons met in a special room adjoining the sanctuary before the service to go over the business of the coming week and to pray together before the service. Two elders offered prayer during the service and appeared to be quite comfortable praying extemporaneously. Between the band, choir, Communion servers, and ushers, at least fifty people provided some form of leadership. As I got to know this congregation in greater depth, two aspects of its overall administrative organization and style of leadership began to emerge as important components of its ethos.

First, the congregation is organized in a highly decentralized manner. The congregation is divided into neighborhood house-churches, in addition to standing committees, "leagues," and ad hoc prayer groups and Bible study groups. Rev. Coetsee estimates that there are over eighty different administrative units in the congregation, and he encourages these groups to operate according to the following principle: "Every decision that can be made at the 'lowest' level of congregational life should be made at that level."

Second, the congregation has a history of strong leaders and of involving people from many walks of life in leadership roles. Under apartheid, the members of the coloured community were not allowed to hold executive or management positions and were forced to work as domestics, laborers, or workers at the university (a pattern that is now beginning to change). In the church, however, they could play leadership roles denied them in their everyday lives. One of the important educational strategies employed by Rev. Coetsee is to cultivate and equip leaders across this highly decentralized congregation and then to trust the good judgment of those people in these roles.

4. *Social outreach to the community.* In the Good Friday service, Rev. Coetsee's use of Christ's cry of abandonment on the cross to frame his hearers' feeling that

God has abandoned their lives, neighborhood, or country was striking. As I studied this congregation, I came to see how deeply involved it is in outreach to the coloured community of Stellenbosch. Indeed, its pastor is one of the leading forces in a variety of new, ecumenically based outreach initiatives that cross racial and denominational lines. It is no accident that the minister would invite the congregation to bring its own pain and that of the world before God.

In my interviews of adults, many identified the congregation as fairly conservative or traditional in its theology and worship, but liberal or progressive in its social witness. Perhaps something of this division is mirrored in the organization and use of the congregation's space, which is divided into the sanctuary and a multipurpose complex of classes, fellowship hall, offices, and kitchen. For the most part, the sanctuary is locked when worship is not taking place, while the multipurpose complex is open all day long, with a steady stream of people flowing in and out. It is not that the congregation's theology and worship are unrelated to its social outreach, but rather that the church views its "traditional" stance toward Scripture and tradition as pointing it to "progressive" ministries of outreach and justice. As we shall see, holding these two elements together is one of the ways it embodies the spirit of the Confession of Belhar, which played a pivotal role in the denomination's struggle against apartheid.

5. *Creative teaching by the pastor.* The special time of confession designed by the pastor gave all age levels the opportunity to participate in this symbolic act through bodily gestures (kneeling), language (words spoken by the minister and by each person), touch (holding on to the nail), and sound (the loud pounding of a nail into a wooden board). In effect, the worshipers were given the opportunity to link their own lives to Scripture's story of Christ's death—the focal point of this particular service. Especially noteworthy is the sensitivity the minister showed to the presence of young children in the service. He gave special instructions to parents so the children could participate in this activity safely. He also addressed the children directly at one point, inviting them to ask their parents about this activity when they returned home.

Over the course of my time with this congregation, I witnessed this sort of creative teaching and the ability to communicate with all age levels again and again in Rev. Coetsee's leadership. His capacity to draw imaginatively on Scripture and tradition to frame the life circumstances of the members of this community is quite remarkable. His congregation seems to expect him to address them in this way.

Theological Discrimen: Leadership in the Spirit of Belhar

I believe it is possible to capture and sum up the various facets of URC Stellenbosch's identity and ethos in the following theological discrimen: *leadership in the spirit of Belhar*. The reference here is to the Confession of Belhar, which played an important role in the struggle of the coloured Dutch Reformed Mission Church (DRMC) against apartheid and served as a important point of confessional unity when this denomination joined with the black Dutch Reformed Church of South Africa to form the Uniting Reformed Church.[1] As noted in chapter 3, the Confession of Belhar was drafted in 1982 and accepted into the confessional standards of the DRMC four years later, after a period of study and discussion in congregations. It emerged precisely at a time when ecumenical bodies such as the World Alliance of Reformed Churches and the World Council of Churches were attempting to marshal international opposition to the policies of the apartheid government. This culminated in the declaration of a *status confessionis*, condemning as heretical those denominations that condoned the policies of apartheid and calling on all of the churches of the country to take a clear stand against these policies. The coloured DRMC followed with its own declaration of a *status confessionis* in 1982, setting in motion the writing of Belhar. One of URC Stellenbosch's former pastors, Johan Botha, provided leadership in this process at the synod level, and one of the principle drafters of the confession, Dirk Smit, is affiliated with the Idas Valley branch of the congregation. During this period, the draft of the confession was explained to the congregation through preaching and teaching. This was over twenty years ago, however. Is it really plausible to view this confession as continuing to animate the ethos of URC Stellenbosch, shaping its sense of identity and mission today? I believe it is for three basic reasons.

First, the phrase, "the spirit of Belhar," emerged at a number of points in my interviews of adult members of the congregation, especially its leaders, and was used by several theologians in the area to describe this congregation. Belhar remains a part of the living memory of the congregation and is a part of its public profile among those who know something about the Reformed tradition in South Africa.

Second, this confession played a crucial role in the denomination's break with its missionary past, a process that occurred in parallel fashion at the level of this congregation. The congregation had been nurtured in the confessional patterns of Reformed Christianity, including the Heidelberg Catechism. Now, at last, in Belhar it had a confession that spoke directly to its situation, stating unequivocally that the God in whom it believes stands against the policies of apartheid and their legitimization by the DRC "mother" church. As one church member aptly put it, "It spoke to our hearts. It put into words what we had been feeling for a long time." The confession was a *kairotic* event in both the denomination and the congregation and continues to reverberate even two decades later. At present, the white and Indian denominations of the Reformed family have not joined the Uniting Reformed Church that emerged when Belhar was written, but talks of uniting have regained momentum among denominational leaders, keeping Belhar in public view in church circles.

Third, the theological affirmations of Belhar—formulated originally to address the situation of apartheid—continue to provide the congregation with markers of its identity and mission, even in a postapartheid era. The confession affirms three articles, with a prologue and conclusion.

The prologue affirms the triune God's gathering, protecting, and caring of the

church from "the beginning of the world" to "the end" and calls on the church
to resist the practical idolatry of acting as if God were no longer actively involved
in human history. In a very real sense, this affirmation is the basis of URC Stellenbosch's willingness to stay socially and ecumenically engaged in spite of the
massive problems that surround it on all sides.

Article 1 affirms the oneness of the church, which "must become visible." In
the face of a notable decline of interest in ecumenical gatherings and cooperation, the leadership of URC Stellenbosch has rallied the area churches to work
toward new, visible expressions of church unity. In the short time I was with the
congregation, I witnessed no less than four community-wide, ecumenical events.
(I will describe some of these events more fully at a later point.) This commitment to church unity informs the internal life of URC Stellenbosch as well. I
described above the highly decentralized nature of the congregation. Its pastor,
Jaco Coetsee, reports, "Sometimes I wake up in the middle of the night and wonder what holds it all together. More than once, groups have considered breaking
away and going on their own. But someone says, 'No, we are one church. We are
the body of Christ.' I think it's the spirit of Belhar, its call for church unity, that
keeps it all together."

Article 2 affirms the power of God's reconciliation to overcome "irreconcilia-
tion and hatred, bitterness and enmity." We caught a glimpse of the importance
of reconciliation in the congregation's Good Friday confession and church discipline. Moreover, in my interviews I kept hearing stories of "falling away" and
"coming back" to the church through acts of public confession and forgiveness. (I
describe one such story in chapter 7.) This commitment to reconciliation was
embodied in an especially vivid way in Rev. Coetsee's leadership of a special time
of confession by area pastors in which they shared with one another their complicity in the sins of the apartheid regime. This led to a public call via newspapers
for a new spirit of cooperation among the churches in responding to the problems
of the Stellenbosch area. I describe these events at the end of this chapter.

Article 3 articulates God's commitment to justice in all forms of human community, as a God who is "in a special way" the God of the destitute, the poor, the
wronged, and the oppressed. It calls on the church to stand where God stands.
In URC Stellenbosch, this is found in many different ways—its ministries of
compassionate service, its support of public agencies such as the Office of
Employment, its habit of bringing the concerns of the world before God in worship and prayer, its open-door policy on local organizations' use of its building,
and the many small acts of care offered at the grassroots level of its house
churches. It struggles to share God's special concern for those in special need.

Belhar concludes by affirming that Jesus Christ alone is the sole "head" of
all true churches and is to be obeyed "even though the authorities and human
laws might forbid them." In the struggle against apartheid, this reminded the
church that the authority of governments is subordinate to the authority of
God, underwriting their freedom to protest in the face of their own government's injustice. Today the congregation is struggling to rethink its relation-

ship to public life, moving beyond opposition to active participation in shaping the new South Africa.

URC Stellenbosch is a congregation that leads in the spirit of Belhar. Later we will explore the period in which this congregation came to the new theological self-understanding articulated by the Confession of Belhar in response to the crisis of being forced to sell its original church building under apartheid.

THE LEADERSHIP FRAME

The leadership frame brings into focus the congregation as a community that exists in mission. The congregation does not merely *have* a mission; it *is* its mission, a mission of witness in word and deed to God's redemption of the world in Jesus Christ and the glorification of the world in the power of the Holy Spirit. As a community in mission, the congregation stands in a relationship of creative tension to the social context in which it is located. It does not turn its back on the world, but it does not merely adjust to the world as it is. At its best, the church serves as a "critical catalyst" that causes new elements and properties to emerge through its interaction with processes and relationships beyond its internal life.

The leadership frame, thus, invites us to look at leadership along two lines. First, we are to look at the congregation as a whole as a leader in the community, standing in a relationship of creative tension with its social context because of its mission. To pursue its mission, the congregation must learn to understand the particular adaptive challenges of its community and the particular resources it might bring to bear on these challenges. Second, we are to examine the ways leadership is carried out within the congregation itself, through both formal and informal channels. We are to picture the congregation as a learning organization, which fosters (or not) a culture of thinking, mutual learning, and innovation across its various activities.

Theological Perspective: The Congregation as Mission

An important theological theme to emerge in the second half of the twentieth century was the *missio Dei*, the missions of God.[2] In large part, this theme was prompted by new thinking about the doctrine of the Trinity and the importance of viewing the "work" of the divine persons in the economy of salvation as missionary in character. The church finds its identity and purpose within the missions of the triune God, looking backward to its christological center, outward to the world Christ came to seek and save, and forward to God's promised future for creation. This perspective has engendered fresh thinking about congregations along four lines.

First, it invites congregations to view their reason for being as participation in God's seeking and saving love for the world. As Dietrich Bonhoeffer put it, the church is a community for others.[3] Congregations do not serve their own needs and interests but are caught up in the movement of God's outpouring of love in Christ and the Spirit. It is not enough, thus, to think of mission exclusively in terms of evangelism or compassionate outreach. Rather, all facets of congregational life are to reflect this missionary character. The gathering, upbuilding, and sending of congregations are one integral whole.

Second, to carry out their missions, congregations must seek to understand in some depth their social contexts. Across the centuries and in various cultural contexts, they have carried out their missions in markedly different ways. Their enduring witness to God's seeking and saving love has been responsive to the specific problems and possibilities of their own social and historical contexts. As Hans Küng aptly puts it, "Loyalty to its original nature is something the Church must preserve through all changing history. . . . But it can only do that through change, not through immobility."[4] The particular shape of a congregation's mission will take form as it understands and responds to the particular challenges of its own time and place.

Third, both the missionary witness of congregations and their need to understand their own social context necessarily lead them to enter into a dialogue with the world. This does not preclude evangelism and conversion at appropriate times and places. But dialogue is fundamentally different. In a dialogue, the congregation listens and learns from its partner. It respects the partner as an other who has dignity and is worthy of respect. The capacity to enter into dialogue in this sense is especially important in our highly pluralistic, globalizing social context. When a congregation demonstrates its willingness to listen with respect and openness, it gains the right to be heard and contributes to the overall atmosphere of trust in the community as a whole.

Fourth, congregations are to serve as leaders in their communities. This presupposes everything that has been said to this point. If congregations view all facets of their life as serving their mission, strive to understand the challenges of their social context, and demonstrate a willingness to engage others in dialogue, then they cannot avoid providing some form of leadership in their local, national, or international communities. As we shall see below, leadership involves more than merely wielding influence and power. It has to do with calling attention to the adaptive challenges that a community faces at any given time. It risks the conflict that often emerges when issues are raised that many in the community would just as soon avoid. Leadership in this sense is a necessary part of the congregation as a missionary community.

Conversation Partners: Organizational Learning and Leadership Theories

In recent decades, organizational learning has become a topic of increasing interest across a number of fields, from corporations to charitable organizations to educational institutions to religious communities. In part, this has been prompted by an awareness that the world is in the midst of a period of rapid and comprehensive change. Important institutions such as the family, national government, and the economy currently are in the midst of major transitions. Inherited models and practices no longer seem to work in the ways they once did.

Organizational Learning

In the face of such changes, some social scientists have begun to conceptualize the core challenge facing contemporary institutions and communities as one of *organizational learning*. This is not merely a matter of adjusting to the various changes that are taking place in our world. Some of these trends are harmful and cause great suffering for many people. Rather, it is the challenge of *learning*—forming an accurate understanding of changes in the environment, reflecting critically on the norms and practices that have guided an organization or community in the past, and forming a response that is based on the values it deems most important to its purpose. Learning, viewed along these lines, is more than adjustment. It involves what some call "adaptive work"—the ability to face the tough issues before the organization or community and to forge an informed, values-driven response. Within contemporary organizational learning theory, three broad schools of thought have emerged.[5] I will briefly describe each of these and then illustrate their helpfulness with an example.

The first school of thought focuses on the *mental models* that people use to understand the complexity of an organization and its relationship to the environment. This perspective draws heavily on cognitive science and systems theory.[6] It argues that organizations fail to learn in large measure because their members use simplistic models to understand complicated systems. It has some affinity with Howard Gardner's portrait of the continuing power of the "intuitive theories" of the unschooled mind examined in chapter 5. By the time people reach the age of five, they have formed a mental model of causality that views cause and effect as closely related to one another. If you drop a glass on a hard surface (cause), then it will shatter into many pieces (effect). In this model, we learn through direct and immediate experience. In complex systems, however, cause and effect are not this closely related. They are related through feedback loops that are spread out across time and space, making it impossible to experience directly the consequences of many of our decisions and actions. Moreover, we often cannot see directly the ways other systems are influencing our behavior or that of the group to which we belong. Organizational learning, thus, requires pressing beyond simplistic mental models and learning to think in terms of patterns of systems.

The second school of organizational learning focuses on *individual and group defenses* that inhibit problem solving in organizations.[7] Both individuals and groups within organizations have a tendency to use protective strategies that make it very difficult for them to gain an accurate picture of the problems they face. They cover up their mistakes and bad decisions, for example, setting in motion an escalating cycle of deception. Or they refuse to question the assumptions shaping the organization's rules, roles, or goals. Such assumptions are taboo in the organization—they are off-limits for discussion. Or they espouse one ratio-nale for their action (their espoused theory), while employing a quite different rationale in actuality (their theory-in-use). Some of these defensive strategies are intentional and represent an attempt to protect an individual's or group's posi-tion in the organization. Others appear to be unconscious. In either case, orga-nizational learning can only take place when these protective strategies are subject to discussion and critical reflection and, eventually, are overcome, freeing the organization to better understand and respond to the problems it faces.

A third school of thought focuses on *the ways the culture of an organization* supports or inhibits learning.[8] Organizations are viewed as forming cultures that are based on rituals, stories, values, heroes, and myths, with both rational and irrational components. Such cultures may support a considerable amount of learning as long as the problems facing an organization are familiar. But if the organization faces new adaptive challenges, then the culture itself must change. Only then will it be in a position to learn how to respond effectively to these challenges.

These three schools of thought are not mutually exclusive, and it is not uncommon for them to be combined in a given theory.[9] Those who lead con-gregations will not find it difficult to see the usefulness of all three perspectives. Imagine the following scenario. Shady Grove Church has become increasingly concerned in recent years with its failure to "hold on" to the youth of the con-gregation. While there are many young people in the church and the surround-ing community, very few remain actively involved in the congregation once they have completed confirmation in the ninth grade. This is widely perceived as "caused" by certain failures on the part of the youth group leader and the high school Sunday school teachers, although few can pinpoint exactly what they are doing wrong. No attention is given to the broader, systemic factors shaping ado-lescent participation in church life across contemporary U.S. culture. The men-tal models used to understand this problem, thus, are inadequate. Focusing exclusively on the "failures" of the youth program, moreover, serves as a kind of defense against raising questions about the contributions of the senior minister and choir director to this problem. In effect, it functions as a protective strategy. Attention is deflected away from the fact that many of the youth find the church music on Sunday morning completely unappealing and never feel that their issues are addressed in the senior minister's preaching. The culture of Shady Grove, moreover, rests on stories, rituals, and an ethos formed several generations ago, when the surrounding community was predominantly a rural, farming area. Many of the youth no longer identify with this past. This puzzles the older mem-bers of the congregation, who think of the church and Christianity generally in terms of the culture and ethos with which they are familiar.

For this congregation to learn what it would take to involve its youth in the church it would need to question its mental models, protective strategies, and congregational culture as a whole. This would not be an easy task. It would call for a new understanding of congregational leadership that places a premium on the educational tasks of leaders. *Leaders must focus on helping congregations become learning organizations that can face the adaptive challenges confronting their community at any given time.* Viewing leadership along these lines entails giving up some of the ways we commonly think about who leaders are and what they do.

Leadership and Organizational Learning

If one were to ask people in a congregation or faculty who its leaders are, chances are good that many would name those people with the most power and influence or those in established positions of authority. In contrast, the perspective followed here builds on the thinking of social scientists who define leadership normatively.[10] Proponents of normative theories of leadership argue that identifying leadership with the ability to influence others or with occupancy of a position of authority begs the question of what constitutes genuine leadership. Many individuals have influenced large numbers of people to follow their vision and pursue goals that have proved harmful. If influence alone is the criterion of leadership, then Adolf Hitler, Idi Amin, and Jim Jones qualify. Moreover, identifying leadership with those who hold established positions of authority eliminates people such as Mahatma Gandhi and Martin Luther King, Jr. Yet these individuals have led whole societies through important periods of social change without holding elected office or working in an established position of authority.

The alternative is to define leadership normatively. In what follows, I draw on the thinking of Ronald Heifetz. According to Heifetz, leaders are those who challenge an organization or community to engage in "adaptive work."[11] They help a community confront the difficult issues before it at any given time, manage the conflicting values evoked by such issues, and design a process of learning that allows the community to forge a response consistent with the values it holds most dear. People in positions of authority who sidestep such issues do not qualify as leaders in this sense. Nor do people who deflect attention from tough issues through "work avoidance" mechanisms such as scapegoating, distracting the group with an irrelevant issue, or mobilizing their energies by focusing on an external enemy. Though people who use these strategies might have great influence in an organization or community, they would not be helping it engage in adaptive work. Heifetz draws on evolutionary and systems thinking to form his understanding of adaptive work. It is worth examining the larger framework in which he develops this concept, for it allows us to see the ways his theory incorporates some of the dimensions of organizational learning theory described above.

All living systems, Heifetz notes, are embedded in broader natural and social systems. They are open systems that exchange information with other systems in their environments. To understand these complex patterns of interaction, people must use *mental models* based on systems thinking. Living systems, he goes on to point out, seek equilibrium. They respond to stress by seeking to restore balance to the system. In a relatively stable environment, the established patterns of a system retain the ability to bring it back to a state of equilibrium. Sometimes, however, changes in the environment pose adaptive challenges that make the older patterns of a system inadequate. Among nonhuman species, the ability to respond successfully to such challenges largely is a function of a species' genetic inheritance. Random variations in the genes of a particular species population allow some to adapt more successfully than others. This places them in a better position to pass on their genes to the next generation. In human societies, however, cultural patterns play a much larger role in the success or failure of adaptation. Cultures adapt in large part through a process of learning. They can resist change by stubbornly clinging to patterns, roles, and values with which they are familiar, resorting to various *defensive strategies* to restore social equilibrium as quickly as possible. Or they can respond to adaptive challenges by attempting to learn new patterns and roles. In other words, learning both draws on the existent culture of a community and involves *changes in this culture*. Learning that involves extensive cultural change inevitably thrusts a community into a period of disequilibrium.

One of the most important dimensions of Heifetz's theory is his emphasis on values. Since human beings generate purposes that go beyond mere survival, adaptive work typically includes a period of conflict over values. Different ways of interpreting and responding to an adaptive challenge reflect different values held by different individuals or groups in the community. These often are based on different narratives that define the identity of the community and its mission. As Heifetz succinctly puts it:

> In human societies, adaptive work consists of efforts to close the gap between reality and a host of values not restricted to survival. We perceive problems whenever circumstances do not conform to the way we think things ought to be. Thus adaptive work involves not only the assessment of reality but also the clarification of values.[12]

An important part of the organization's adaptive work, thus, is the educational process by which people gain insight into the values and narratives that frame their understanding of the challenge before the community. This often includes a period of conflict based on different values and perspectives. In chapter 5, for example, we saw conflicting values and perspectives emerge in Nassau Presbyterian Church as it struggled to rework its stance toward gays and lesbians. If handled properly, such conflict ultimately contributes to the community's learning.

In short, leadership is the ability to engage an organization or community in adaptive work. This involves a process of learning in which the organization or community (1) forms an understanding of the adaptive challenges it faces, drawing on mental models that allow it to grasp the systemic dimensions of these challenges; (2) avoids protective strategies that seek to restore equilibrium prematurely; and (3) explores various ways of responding to these challenges that both draw on and change the values and core narratives of its culture.

Rethinking Catechesis, Exhortation, and Discernment in the Leadership Frame

What do the three tasks of the teaching ministry look like in the leadership frame? My perspective is summarized below, and it may be helpful to examine this chart before proceeding. Since we will explore several extended examples of catechesis, exhortation, and discernment in URC Stellenbosch in the remainder of this chapter, my comments are brief.

Catechesis, Exhortation, and Discernment in the Leadership Frame

	Learning Tasks	*Teaching Tasks*
Catechesis	• Interpreting the issues before the community in terms of theology and the Bible • Reflecting critically on the theological assumptions of the community	• Framing issues in terms of constructive analogies based on Scripture and tradition • Facilitating a process of reflecting on assumptions and considering alternative perspectives in the community, Scripture, and tradition
Exhortation	• Discovering moral exemplars from the past and/or present, who have responded to similar situations • Reflecting critically on personal and communal moral norms • Participating appropriately in a process of moral deliberation and discussion	• Scanning for relevant exemplars from a community's past, the tradition, etc. • Articulating ethical assumptions • Facilitating and modeling open discussion, productive use of conflict, and clarifying what is at stake in values differences • Facilitating links between ethical ideals and a strategic plan of action
Discernment	• Trusting in the guidance of God's Spirit as the congregation steps into the future • Becoming adept in practices of discernment in the context of decision making	• Modeling confidence in the Spirit's guidance of the community • Introduction of practices of discernment into the organizational processes of the community

In the leadership frame, *catechesis* focuses on the task of drawing on Scripture and tradition to help a congregation clarify its identity and mission in relation to the adaptive challenges it faces. Teaching, thus, centers on helping the community frame the issues before it in terms of its core narratives and values, facilitating the construction of analogies between the Bible and tradition and the present situation. It also includes facilitating critical reflection on the assumptive frameworks the members of the congregation are using, opening up the possibility of new ways of thinking.

Exhortation focuses on the task of discovering the ethical issues at stake in the adaptive challenge. The congregation is viewed as a community of moral discourse, deliberation, and decision making. Teaching, thus, centers on facilitating a process of moral conversation in the community, clarifying the moral assumptions being articulated, interjecting new perspectives when needed, and fostering critical reflection on the moral norms being used. An extremely important teaching role is modeling the attitudes and communicative skills necessary for moral deliberation and decision making, especially in situations where strong feelings and conflicting perspectives are present. Moreover, it often is helpful to invite the community to consider moral exemplars who have responded to similar situations in the past or are doing so in the present.

Discernment focuses on the task of using various practices of discernment in the congregation's decision-making process. Adaptive challenges press the community to trust God's Spirit as it steps into the future. An important facet of teaching, thus, is serving as a "living reminder" of the many times God has called congregations to a new place and provided for them on their journeys. This entails modeling confidence in the guiding and sustaining presence of God's Spirit in the community's midst. It also points to the importance of facilitating the use of practices of discernment in the community's deliberation. If such practices are not a part of the life of the congregation already, an important teaching task is the introduction of such practices into the process. A helpful and growing literature on discernment in congregational life has emerged in recent years, providing important models that might be emulated.[13]

Focus Questions of the Leadership Frame

In the remainder of this chapter, we will examine three examples of the teaching ministry of URC Stellenbosch brought into focus by the leadership frame, developing further our rethinking of catechesis, exhortation, and discernment. My selection of these examples is informed by three focal questions:

1. Do the leaders of the congregation facilitate learning across its organizational life, especially in response to the significant adaptive challenges before it at any given time? This question invites us to think of catechesis, exhortation, and discernment in terms of the educational tasks of leadership when congregations face a significant adaptive challenge. It includes such teaching activities as drawing on Scripture, theology, and ethics to frame the issues before the community and reflecting critically on the narratives and norms that already inform its life.

2. Does the congregation support an explicit program of leadership development, helping its members acquire the attitudes, knowledge, and skills necessary for genuine leadership? This question has in mind leadership in Heifetz's sense: doing more than solving problems within the assumptive framework and procedures of the community, but facing up to the tough issues and adaptive challenges before it. In congregations this includes a biblical, theological, and ethical knowledge base and the ability to connect this knowledge to contemporary life. It also includes a bundle of skills in communication and group process. Perhaps most important of all, it involves the formation of the character of leaders, allowing them to serve as models of the attitudes and dispositions desired in the community as a whole as it faces significant adaptive work.

3. *Do the leaders of the congregation both model and draw on practices that embody a spirit of openness to the creative presence of the Holy Spirit in the community's midst?* This question construes the work of the Spirit as new creation, opening out to the important place of creativity in the congregation's organizational life. While this is perhaps most directly involved in the congregation's willingness to discern the "new thing" God is calling it to do and be, it also is present in creative links between past traditions and present context that are ultimately the gift of the Spirit.

URC STELLENBOSCH THROUGH THE LEADERSHIP FRAME: THREE EXAMPLES

Facilitating Organizational Learning

In this section, we explore an example from the history of URC Stellenbosch in which the leadership of this congregation facilitated catechesis, exhortation, and discernment along the lines described above. The example focuses on the leadership of Johan Botha in helping the congregation question certain beliefs and practices of its missionary past and develop new ways of thinking and acting in the spirit of Belhar. It highlights Rev. Botha's role in facilitating a *process* that unfolded over the eighteen months he was pastor of the congregation and continued after he stepped down.

It is important to recall events of the decade immediately preceding Rev. Botha's arrival as pastor in 1980. In 1970, the congregation had been forced to turn over its original church building to the government when the government passed laws declaring the area in which it was located a "whites only" region. The task of planning for a new church building in Cloetesville involved much conflict. Firsthand reports of those participating in this process lead me to believe that the insights of organization learning may be helpful in understanding what was going on in this conflict. Obviously, the congregation faced an adaptive challenge of monumental proportions. Not only had it lost its beloved church building, but it faced the task of erecting a new one with extremely limited financial resources.

Some in the congregation responded by holding fast to mental models of the past, arguing vociferously that the congregation should erect a new building that reduplicated certain features of the old church. Others argued that the proposed modern sanctuary represented a fitting break with this past and looked toward the future. While the latter position eventually prevailed, the church council accommodated those advocating continuity by moving the pews from the old building into the new sanctuary. During this period, there seem to be relatively few indications that either group was able to draw on theological and ethical models that allowed it to reflect on the systemic evil of apartheid or the church's mission in the face of this system. Moreover, there are signs that a variety of individual and group defenses were operative during this period. Members directed their anger and frustration toward one another, deflecting them from the apartheid government that had forced them to hand over their original church building. Their white pastor was the object of a certain amount of scapegoating, as some in the congregation asserted that if he had only "fought harder," then these tragic events might have been averted. While the culture of the congregation began to change during this period—becoming less dependent on the white, DRC "mother church" of Stellenbosch and becoming more democratic in its decision making—the congregation remained cautious in its relationship to the white community. The church council was guarded in responding to the riots and school closings following the 1976 Soweto uprising.

When Johan Botha became the pastor of the congregation in 1980, thus, the church had experienced over a decade of turmoil following its exile from its original church building. As mentioned in chapter 3, one of the older adults I interviewed portrayed Rev. Botha as "the one who took us from a phase of religious childhood to religious adulthood in our thinking." He helped the congregation to respond to the adaptive challenge before it by breaking with its missionary past and learning a new set of theological assumptions with which to understand its identity and mission. Three forms of organizational learning emerged under Rev. Botha's leadership.

Learning One: A New Theological Identity

The congregation began to question the missionary theology of its past and to forge a new theological identity through Rev. Botha's catechesis of the community during this period. He worked on two fronts simultaneously, surfacing an inadequate model of God's providential care of the world and replacing it with the theological perspective of Belhar. The former is captured nicely by one of my interviewees as he looked back at this period: "We had been taught to think, 'God's will be done.' We were not supposed to think about what was going on in our community. We weren't supposed to get involved. We were just supposed to get down on our knees and pray about it. We were almost brainwashed." In this older theological perspective, the events of history—including the congregation's exile from its original building—were portrayed as somehow mysteriously the will of God, placing the church "on its knees" rather than "on its feet" to confront the evils of its social context. As we have seen, the Confession of Belhar portrays both God and the church along markedly different lines. The triune God is described as desiring visible unity, reconciliation, and justice and as unequivocally opposed to racial segregation of church and society and the enmity and injustice this inevitably breeds. It calls the church to "stand where God stands" on these matters.

How did Rev. Botha catechize the community on these matters? It was not through the formal teaching of a catechism class but through his preaching, informal conversations with congregational leaders, and the feedback loops he created between events going on in the synod and the congregation. The first two of these are fairly straightforward. They depend on a leader who is aware of the assumptive theology of his congregation and has made it a priority to alter this framework by consistently teaching new ways of thinking in various venues. Over time, through sermons and informal conversations, change is effected.

The notion of "feedback loops" deserves comment. Throughout the period of time when Rev. Botha was pastor, the denomination was still the Dutch Reformed Missionary Church. It had entered a new phase of struggle against apartheid, declaring a *status confessionis*, calling for the unification of all denominations in the Reformed family, and beginning the process of discussing the draft of Belhar. One of Rev. Botha's most important educational strategies was to create feedback loops between processes going on at the synod level and in the congregation. For example, Rev. Botha always discussed policy statements and declarations of the synod in the church council and in sermons. Members of the congregation were recruited to participate in all facets of the synod's work and asked to report back to the congregation. Rev. Botha framed his own role in the synod as that of representing the *congregation's* point of view. In effect, the congregation was asked to rethink its theology as part of a larger rethinking taking place across the denomination as a whole.

Learning Two: From Recipients to Agents of Mission

This shift in theological assumptions had important ramifications for the congregation's understanding of mission. Throughout the congregation's history, the "mother" church of the DRC in Stellenbosch was viewed not only as a key player in founding the congregation but also as the dominant "partner" in continuing support and guidance. The roles were now reversed, as the congregation began to frame its mission in terms of Belhar. It was the "mother" church who was in need of mission from its coloured and black partners, confronting her with the need to break with the policies of apartheid and the false understandings of God, the church, and society supporting her complicity.

Rev. Botha fostered this shift from being the object of mission to being an agent of mission in a variety of ways. One educational strategy focused on the internal life of the church. Rev. Botha began a process of leadership development for pastoral care, writing a training manual and offering classes to equip caregivers to pursue this ministry across the congregation. This was the first of several initiatives along these lines in the congregation, which have continued under Rev. Jaco Coetsee's leadership. A second educational strategy focused on Rev. Botha's modeling of active involvement in social service beyond the congregation. He was deeply involved in the local branch of the Council of Church Cooperation, an ecumenical body that drew attention to the needs of the community and sponsored various initiatives to meet these needs. Slowly the congregation began to view its mission as including engagement of social issues at the local level. If God "in a special way" cares for the poor, destitute, and oppressed—as Belhar puts it—then the congregation was learning to embody this theological perspective. Following the lead of Rev. Botha, its members were learning to view the problems of their community in terms of larger systems. They began to think in terms of ministries of advocacy as well as of service.

Learning Three: Testifying to the White Christian Community

A third important area of learning during this period focused on the acquisition of communicative competencies and attitudes necessary for the leaders of the congregation to testify to their white fellow Christians. Much of this centered on the participation of congregational leaders in special meetings during Pentecost, designed to bring together church councils of all congregations in the Dutch Reformed family of churches—white, coloured, and black—in order to foster better understanding across all racial groups. They included times of testimony, discussion, and worship. One of the adults I interviewed, who was a firsthand participant in these meetings, describes their significance as follows: "The Pentecost meetings became a burning point. We opened our hearts and the anger came out as never before. We grew up respecting white people and not answering back. But now, for the first time, we said what we really felt."

Rev. Botha's role in facilitating learning through the church council's participation in these meetings was twofold. First, he encouraged council members to participate and challenged them "to testify boldly and openly" about their own personal experiences under apartheid in light of the gospel. Often such testimony was quite powerful. One member still recalls vividly moments when "old mothers, with absolutely no education at all, stood up before the group and said, 'Let me tell you the story of my son and what the government has done to him. How can you stand by and let this happen?'" This was the first time that many members of this coloured congregation were empowered to share openly with their fellow white Christians the pain and frustration they felt under apartheid. Rev. Botha's encouragement of their participation in this process was an important first step. Second, he often engaged the church council and individuals in times of reflection after these meetings. As he put it, "It wasn't enough just to vent emotions. I wanted them to discern the issues at stake." He was helping the church's leaders to think their way into a new theology that allowed them to discern the political dimensions of the adaptive challenges they faced.

Rev. Botha's role in URC Stellenbosch during the time he was pastor is a particularly good example of the sort of education brought into focus by the leadership frame. Through a variety of educational strategies and processes, he placed the adaptive challenge before the congregation: It needed to rethink its identity and mission as the church in ways that addressed more directly the evils of the apartheid government. The congregation had survived exile from its original church building, but this was not enough. It had to learn new ways of thinking about God and the church's role as a missionary community. This sort of learning did not emerge overnight, but as a result of Rev. Botha's leadership a marked shift began to take place in the identity and mission of URC Stellenbosch. The assumptive theology of the congregation began to change.

Leadership Education in the Congregation

The second example brings into focus the ways the congregation equips its members to provide leadership in some form of ministry, developing both their gifts and their ability to guide others who also are involved in this ministry. I have pointed briefly to one example of leadership education in the ministry of Rev. Botha: his training program for caregivers. The congregation's current pastor, Rev. Coetsee, has built on and expanded this program of leadership education, establishing the Stellenbosch Bible Academy six years ago. The academy's target audience has evolved somewhat over the years. Initially it focused on leadership development within the congregation, but gradually it has been opened up to the coloured community as a whole. This reflects the congregation's commitment to building ecumenical cooperation across the Christian churches of Stellenbosch and is one of many ways it embodies Belhar's call for visible unity in the Christian community.

A sampling of courses offered in the academy since its inception include the following, drawing on Rev. Coetsee's own descriptions:

- *An Introduction to Biblical Interpretation.* Target audience: the leaders of house churches. Content: creating a message through the study of the Bible.
- *An Introduction to Theology.* Target audience: elders, deacons, and other interested members of the community. Content: an introduction to themes in dogmatics.
- *Understanding Yourself.* Target audience: all members of the church and community. Content: deepening self-understanding through the Myers-Briggs personality inventory.
- *The Life of Prayer.* Target audience: all members of the church and community. Content: prayer and inner healing in the context of personal and social brokenness.
- *Communication and Conflict.* Target audience: all members of the church and community. Content: a simple framework to understand human communication and to improve skills in communication, especially in situations of conflict.

Projected courses for the coming year include:

- *Learning to Care.* Target audience: elders, deacons, and leaders of other organizations in the congregation but open to the community. Content: counseling and care toward the chronically and terminally ill (e.g., those with AIDS), unemployed, elderly, alcoholics, unwed mothers, widows, those in stressed marriages.

- *Leadership Skills.* Target audience: all interested parties in the congregation and community. Content: definitions of leadership, servant leadership, planning, communication, effectiveness, excellence.
- *Prayer.* Target audience: all interested parties in the congregation and community. Content: prayer as lifestyle, principles, example of Jesus.
- *Teaching Skills.* Target audience: Sunday school teachers, parents, and those working with children. Content: personal and spiritual qualities of "good" teachers, skills.
- *Youth Alive.* Target audience: teens and young adults. Content: friendship formation, "voices and choices,"AIDS and sexuality, music, etc.

It is not uncommon for Rev. Coetsee to draw on resource people from the congregation and professors from the University of Stellenbosch to teach these classes. He sets the pedagogical agenda, however, which is characterized by the creative, participatory style I observed in the special confession of the Good Friday service. In the class I observed, for example, he used handouts, role play, and a combination of discussion and personal reflection. It seemed to me that the group trusted him and one another to the point of feeling safe to share personal experiences.

It is not difficult to identify elements of catechesis, exhortation, and discernment at the level of content in the various course offerings listed above. The important point to underscore, however, is the academy's goal of equipping the participants with knowledge and skills that are useful *in their own ministries.* This is reflected in the pedagogical aims and methods typically used. They are highly interactive and seek to help the participants make connections between the subject matter and their leadership roles or their everyday lives, focusing on *knowledge and skills the participants will use.* The classes are designed to equip leaders and members of the congregation (as well as the broader community) with (1) biblical, theological, and ethical knowledge; (2) skills in communication, caring, and teaching; and (3) facility in the leadership of practices such as prayer and democratic decision making that participants can use in their ministries in the congregation.

Openness to the Guidance of the Holy Spirit

Our final example takes us on holy ground. It invites us into the very heart of Jaco Coetsee's spiritual life and makes me deeply aware of the difficulties inherent in rendering an account of such matters. It began as a gentle prompting in Rev. Coetsee's prayer life. Throughout the struggle years, a spirit of ecumenical cooperation had been present in many of the congregations of the Stellenbosch area. The Council of Church Cooperation was founded in 1980 and had attempted to promote interracial understanding and to respond to social needs such as chronic unemployment, alcoholism, malnutrition, and health care that were present in the local community. Now, almost two decades later, the spirit of ecumenical cooperation had departed. As Rev. Coetsee puts it, "We had a new South Africa but, socially, no bridges were being built across the racial divisions that continued to determine our everyday lives." He began to make this concern a part of his prayer life: "Lord, please do something. Things are getting worse, not better. Your people are losing their jobs. Gangs and drugs are everywhere. We're scared of violence even in our own homes. Black and coloured people don't trust each other. Whites are indifferent. Lord, do something!" Rev. Coetsee struggled with this in prayer for almost a year. Slowly an inner conviction began to grow in his heart, but the answer was not what he expected: "You do something. You are the one!"

This was not easy to hear. Rev. Coetsee describes himself as a "sideline" person in the public life of Stellenbosch and the denomination. He is shy and rarely puts himself forward in public gatherings beyond the congregation. As a white pastor of a coloured congregation, he is marginalized socially. He is viewed with suspicion by many whites and, in spite of the great affection his congregation has for him, he realizes that he will never truly be a member of the coloured community. Yet this inner prompting that *he* was to do something would not let him go. It gradually began to take more definite shape. As he describes it, "the Spirit" led him to realize that nothing would change until the Christians of Stellenbosch came to terms with their own history, openly confessing to one another the guilt of the past.

Rev. Coetsee invited a group of five ministers to gather and shared with them his sense of what needed to be done. Together they drafted a document called *Testimony*. The document states four things: The signers (1) have humbled themselves before God and confessed to one another the injustice of the past, as well as the estrangement and suspicion that it engendered, and have offered one another forgiveness and the chance to start anew; (2) confess their failure to give visible expression to the unity of the church and preoccupation with their own congregations; (3) pledge they will work together to combat unemployment, crime, and violence in the home and across the community; and (4) promise that they will pray for each other as friends and work for greater understanding and cooperation across the Christian community of Stellenbosch. These affirmations were followed by a call from the pastors for the members of their congregations to follow their lead toward reconciliation, unity, and justice.

Subsequently, this group invited the pastors of the area to gather on October 10, 2000, at the Cloetesville branch of URC Stellenbosch, not merely to read and sign this document but, more importantly, to do what it called for. Twenty-five pastors came. The purpose of the gathering was explained and the *Testimony* document read, inviting those gathered to revise the document and turn it into something they could affirm publicly. One by one the pastors rose, confessed their own complicity in the sins of the past, including sins of silence and omission, and then went forward to sign the document. A key moment in this time of confession centered around the comments of a prominent coloured pastor. He had played a strong oppositional role in the struggle against apartheid and had suffered accordingly. He rose and said to the group, "I forgive you. It is time for us to move forward. But I too have sin to confess," continuing with his own testimony. The *Testimony* document was published in local and regional newspapers, and after it was published, more ministers endorsed it. To date, more than forty have done so, virtually all of the ministers of Stellenbosch. Similar processes of reconciliation began to take place in Cape Town and other towns in the Western Cape. This movement came to be known as the transformation movement of Cape Town.

In Stellenbosch, it spawned new ecumenical initiatives that are still unfolding. The pastors held a community-wide service of reconciliation on December 16, 2000, for all area congregations in which over a thousand people participated. The *Testimony* document served as the basis of a litany in which those gathered confessed, forgave, and pledged to work together in a new spirit of cooperation. This was the first time large numbers of Roman Catholics, charismatics, Messianic Jews, and Protestants had worshiped together in Stellenbosch. The service was followed by a procession through the streets of the town to an open-air meeting for carol singing. The Roman Catholic priest spoke; a charismatic pastor served as the master of ceremonies.

In the months following this gathering, the congregations of Stellenbosch have continued to come together in various ecumenical events. When I was with the congregation, I attended several such gatherings. They included a large worship service in the town hall, led by the Messianic Jewish community. I participated in a Palm Sunday parade in the Idas Valley suburb in which members of different congregations processed through the streets, led by a brass band, stopping before each church and offering a prayer together before its members pealed off to attend their own services. I took part in an Ash Wednesday Agape meal in which the members of many coloured congregations participated. Since the time of my stay with URC Stellenbosch, the congregation has joined other area churches to establish the Stellenbosch Christian Network, which coordinates activities like those described above, as well as channeling money and volunteers to the various local social service agencies already in existence in the Stellenbosch area.

The leadership frame helps us to recognize the educational dimension of these events. At a local level, Rev. Coetsee has provided leadership for an educational process that has confronted both his own congregation and those of the Stellenbosch area with an important adaptive challenge: Now that the struggle years are over, will congregations turn inward or will they stay socially engaged, working together to address the many problems that threaten to engulf the new South Africa? This process began by bringing to the surface conflicting values that kept the churches divided, namely, the quite different stances they had taken in the past in the struggle against apartheid. It also helped the leaders of these congregations to develop a common vision of church unity and social engagement in the *Testimony* document. It set in motion organizational processes and roles that put flesh and bones on this vision in a series of ecumenical events. Not only have the leaders of different congregations learned to trust each other and to work together, but also the members of their congregations have learned to understand and trust each other beyond their racial, theological, and denominational differences. Public gatherings of various sorts have dramatized this vision of cooperation, giving momentum to the more practical initiatives that have begun to emerge. No doubt, these will continue to unfold in the months and years ahead.

Viewing these events exclusively through the lens of social science, however, is not enough. A theological perspective invites us to take seriously the "insiders' perspective" of the participants, the religious meanings they bring to these events. These include their understanding of the mission of the church and how they, as members of the church, ought to respond to the residue of guilt and suspicion that used to keep the area churches apart. Reflecting theologically on the meaning of these events draws our attention to Rev. Coetsee's personal struggle in prayer and his willingness to follow the promptings of the Holy Spirit in search of ways the churches might better carry out their mission in the Stellenbosch area. It reminds us of the Christian tradition's affirmation of the power of confession and forgiveness to break cycles of enmity and suspicion. It helps us to see how one congregation's reworking of its identity several decades earlier would enable it to offer leadership for a movement that calls for visible church unity, reconciliation, and social justice—precisely the core affirmations of Belhar.

Chapter 7

The Pilgrimage Frame:

Evoking and Nurturing the Vocations of Individuals

The pilgrimage frame brings into focus *individuals* in congregations. It invites us to take seriously the changes that are likely to take place in their sense of vocation over the course of their lives.[1] In recent years, Sharon Daloz Parks has explored the theme of pilgrimage in helpful ways.[2] She notes that the journey metaphor—when developed along the lines of a heroic quest—seems closer to the experience of men than women, with its portrayal of the self as leaving home, facing a series of tests, suffering losses, and even doing battle. The journey metaphor understood along these lines captures the pattern of separation and differentiation but not connection and relationality. In contrast, Parks portrays the metaphor of pilgrimage as including both venturing forth and abiding. It better holds together the need of women and men both to leave the familiar, take risks, explore new inner and outer geographies *and* find a lasting center, build a home in which to dwell, sustain lasting relationships, and find continuity in their lives over time. There is a kind of rhythm to our lives: Sometimes the need to venture forth is strongest; sometimes the need to abide.[3] In this chapter, I explore this rhythm as it unfolds in the lives of two individuals from each of the case study congregations studied in previous chapters. I give special attention to patterns of continuity and discontinuity in their sense of vocation as these unfold across their pilgrimages of faith.

THE PILGRIMAGE FRAME

Reconstructing the Reformers' Concept of Vocation

One of the most important concepts developed by Martin Luther to guide his reformation of the church was the concept of vocation. *Vocatio*, from the Latin *vocare*, means "calling." It had long been used in Christian theology to translate the Greek term *klesis*, which was frequently used by Paul to refer to God's calling of individuals to a life of faith through the preaching of the gospel, resulting in their entry into the Christian community and their service of God in their everyday lives. During the Middle Ages, the concept of vocation came to be closely associated with the special calling of those who enter monastic communities, who are set apart from the world and devoted entirely to lives of prayer and service. Luther was especially interested in recovering Paul's use of this term to refer to God's calling of *all* Christians, not just ministers, priests, or monastics. This was part of his affirmation of the priesthood of all believers, in which all baptized members of the congregation are viewed as sharing equally in the one priestly ministry of Jesus Christ and as appointed to the particular ministry God has given them to do.

Luther also emphasized that Christian vocation is not to be seen as dealing only with Christian ministry within the congregation. Rather, it points to the Christian calling to serve God in everyday life—in contradistinction to the supposedly "higher" calling of monastic vocations.[4] He developed the idea of the *double vocation* of every Christian. The *spiritual vocation* is the inward response of faith to the proclamation of the gospel, leading to entry into God's spiritual kingdom. The *external vocation* is the call to serve God in the worldly kingdom, through the particular station or profession in which a person works and through his or her various responsibilities as a parent, citizen, and neighbor. While the former is common to all Christians, the latter varies in relation to the particular circumstances of an individual's life.

While Luther's twofold understanding of vocation had the beneficial effects of eradicating the very sharp medieval distinction between priests and monastics on the one hand, and the laity on the other, and of portraying the service of God as taking place through work, parenting, and so forth, it was not without problems. Perhaps most fundamentally, Luther tended to link it to a protological view of creation in which various "orders" of life are viewed along the lines of static "prototypes" laid down when God created the world. The roles of government, of men and women, and of the church are portrayed in relatively fixed terms. Vocation is limited to serving God *within* the orders of creation. This has the effect of drawing attention away from the highly malleable institutions that shape the social and gender roles of a given society. Sometimes the most important task of Christian congregations is to try and change these institutional patterns, not merely to encourage their members to serve God within the roles these institutions prescribe.

If we are to retrieve the idea of vocation, thus, we must reconstruct it in certain ways.[5] I find the theological perspectives of Jürgen Moltmann and Miroslav Volf to be particularly helpful in this regard. Moltmann invites us to think beyond protological accounts of creation, reminding us that the Christian tradition speaks not only of God's original creation of the world but also of God's continuing creation and of the promise of new creation.[6] He also develops a picture of the "work" of the Holy Spirit that is broader than most Western theology. The Spirit not only communicates the knowledge and love of Christ, but also is God's "immanent transcendence" in creation and the mediator of God's promised future of new creation. We will examine both of these dimensions of Moltmann's theology more fully in chapter 8. At this point, it is enough to indicate two ways Moltmann begins to rethink the meaning of vocation within this theological framework.[7]

First, he associates vocation with a dynamic understanding of creation that views new patterns of social life as part of God's continuing creation. Vocation, thus, is not to be identified as serving God within preestablished "orders" or "estates." In principle, God can be served and glorified in a wide variety of cultural roles and patterns that change and evolve throughout history. Second, he describes vocation as life in the Spirit, whom Moltmann portrays as active in original, continuing, and new creation. This perspective has a twofold effect on his understanding of vocation: (1) It allows him to portray our vocation in *any* sphere of life (and not just in congregations) as life in the Spirit, and (2) it places vocation within an eschatological horizon, portraying life in the Spirit as an anticipation of God's future completion and perfection of the world in the consummation. Moltmann, thus, preserves the Reformers' understanding of vocation as encompassing all spheres of life, while placing it in a more dynamic understanding of creation and a richer understanding of the Holy Spirit.

Building on Moltmann's seminal insights, Miroslav Volf has developed a theology of the *charismata*—the gifts of the Spirit—that adds three important insights to our discussion of vocation.[8] First, he develops an *interactional* model of *charismata*. He argues that it is not helpful to think of spiritual gifts on the model of supernatural "additions" to natural endowments. Rather, *charismata* are best viewed as natural gifts and energies that are evoked, revitalized, expanded, and given new direction as they interact with the Spirit's work in continuing and new creation.

Second, Volf distinguishes between the fruit of the Spirit and the gifts of the Spirit. As he puts it, "The fruit of the Spirit designates the general character of Christian existence, 'the lifestyle of those who are indwelled and energized by the Spirit.' The gifts of the Spirit are related to the specific tasks or functions to which God calls and fits each Christian."[9] All Christians are called to bear the fruit of the Spirit. In their interaction with the Spirit, however, individuals find themselves in different circumstances and with different natural endowments and tasks. Accordingly, different spiritual gifts are evoked in concert with their discernment of what God is calling them to do and be within their specific life circumstances. While the fruit of the Spirit is common to all Christians, the gifts of the Spirit are particular to individuals.

Third, Volf extends the scope of the *charismata* to Christians' involvement in all spheres of life. In their roles and relationships as parents, citizens, workers, friends, and church members, Christians interact with the Spirit's work of continuing and new creation. The *charismata*, thus, are not confined to congregational life. Volf's primary focus in *Work in the Spirit* is the economic sphere. He argues that human labor can and should be construed as a form of participation in the Spirit, as an avenue of creativity and self-expression and a way of contributing to the common good. In this sphere, natural endowments may interact with the Spirit in ways that are life giving and that participate in the dynamism of continuing creation. Yet Volf also makes the very important point that serving God in the sphere of work is not to be equated with the patterns of economic life as they presently exist in a society, for too often such patterns have represented institutionalized forms of injustice, which rob workers of their dignity and enrich some people at the expense of others. In such circumstances, the vocation of Christians in relation to the sphere of work may mean attempting to alter the economy so that it might anticipate more nearly the justice and righteousness of God's future kingdom.

Building on the frameworks offered by Moltmann and Volf, I define vocation as follows: *Vocation refers to individuals' calling to partnership with God in which particular gifts are evoked and developed in concert with their discernment of the particular role God has given them to play during a certain period of their lives.* Like Moltmann and Volf, I view vocation as encompassing many spheres of life, potentially including work, volunteer activities, parenting, and so forth. If the Spirit is present throughout creation, then participation in its continuing and transforming activity can potentially take place in relation to any sphere of life. Moreover, I accept Volf's interactional model of *charismata*, in which individuals' natural endowments and particular life circumstances are viewed as vitalized and redirected as they are responsive to the Spirit. *Charismata*, thus, emerge in concert with particular situations and talents; they include gifts that appear as God is served and glorified in any sphere of life. However, I believe we gain a clearer understanding of the meaning of vocation if we view it from a dramatological perspective, which I explain more fully in the introduction to part 3 in terms of Hans Urs von Balthasar's concept of Theo-drama. At this point, it is enough to indicate three important ways that this framework shapes my understanding of vocation.

First, a dramatological perspective clarifies what I mean by the term "role" in the definition offered above. What I have in mind is something analogous to a part an actor plays within a drama. We can best make sense of the idea of vocation if we think of each individual's life as analogous to an unfolding drama in which freedom and fate, choice and circumstance interact. Balthasar invites Christians to view these dramatic patterns as unfolding within a more encompassing Theo-drama in which the triune God, the church, and the community of creation are part of the ensemble. An individual's vocation, thus, is the role she believes God is calling her to play at a given point in her life. It may include her roles as mother, lawyer, church member, volunteer, and tennis player, but it is more than any of these. It is the animating center that "orchestrates" her participation in these many different activities.[10] It is the "master role" or "role of roles" that guides and directs her investment of energy in accordance with what she believes God is calling her to do and be—the part or role she is given to play—at a particular point in her life.

Second, a dramatological perspective allows us to view an individual's sense of vocation as temporally bounded. Drama portrays actions unfolding through time. Roles and characters may change markedly in response to other actors and events. This is true of the dramatic patterns of an individual's life as well. The center of our energies at a given point in time may change markedly over the course of our lives, bringing with it a corresponding change in our understanding of the role God is calling us to play. Children grow up and leave home; parents age and become dependent; jobs are lost or become more demanding; a car accident leaves us disabled; cancer strikes. Such changes are the ordinary fare of individuals' lives, and their sense of vocation is apt to shift accordingly. An individual's vocation may assume a variety of patterns over time.

Third, a dramatological view of vocation acknowledges the many different patterns an individual's vocation may take. This is analogous to the many different roles actors may play in a drama. Four prominent patterns are the following:

1. *Vocation as clearly distinguished from job.* Individuals earn a living through jobs that put food on the table, while they pursue their vocations in other parts of their lives. Artists often have followed this pattern, as have immigrants and ethnic minorities who have been forced into menial labor but in their congregations have been drawn into forms of leadership and creative expression that have served as the center of their vocations.

2. *Vocation as closely related to one's job or career.* The workplace is the center of vocation. Individuals may be deeply involved in a demanding helping profession and have little energy to give to volunteer activities, including the ministries of the congregation. Such people often look to their congregations for various forms of "creative dependency"—supportive friendships, spiritual guidance, and moral inspiration—that sustain them in their intense, demanding professions.

3. *Vocation as closely related to participation in volunteer activities or social movements beyond the congregation.* Individuals are deeply involved in a social movement that is attempting to change some aspect of contemporary society, or they give an enormous amount of their time to voluntary organizations not related to a church but that provide important social services. Neither their jobs nor the ministries of their congregations are the center of their sense of calling. Here too

the congregation provides them with encouragement, inspiration, and moral reasons that sustain them in their efforts to make this world a better place.

4. Vocation as the attempt to balance multiple responsibilities across many spheres of life. In this pattern, individuals view the "role" they are called to play at this point in their lives as finding ways of balancing in a fair and responsible fashion the commitments of their parenting, volunteer activities, household maintenance, and jobs. Such people often look to congregations for help in evolving new, more egalitarian family patterns that often are quite different from those of their families of origin.

These vocational patterns are varied, and others could be added. But this is precisely the point. The pilgrimage frame brings into focus individuals and their changing sense of vocation over the course of their pilgrimages of faith. It acknowledges process and movement over the course of individuals' lives, that life patterns and circumstances shift markedly. What is often missing in the lives of contemporary people, however, is the opportunity to appropriate these kinds of changes in terms of the emergence of a new understanding of their vocations— what they believe God is calling them to do and be at this point in their lives.

The congregation's role in helping individuals claim and rework their sense of vocation over the course of their lives stands at the very heart of the pilgrimage frame. To recall Sharon Parks' depiction of the inner rhythm of pilgrimage, sometimes this involves helping people "venture forth," supporting and encouraging them to explore new territory, to take risks, to let go of the old and make room for the new beginning God's Spirit is opening up for them. Sometimes it involves helping them "abide," supporting them in returning home, staying with commitments, and building a lasting center or gestalt that gives form to their lives. There is no way of knowing in advance what sort of support and encouragement an individual will find most helpful. This is why the pilgrimage frame challenges congregations to take individuals seriously and not to be satisfied with a one-size-fits-all approach to the teaching ministry.

In addition to developing a theological understanding of vocation, it also is important to understand the larger social forces that have created the "open space" in which individuals find room to discern what God is calling them to do and be at different points in their lives. These forces are best understood in terms of the various social processes associated with modernization and, more recently, globalization.

Interdisciplinary Dialogue Partner: Sociological Theories of Individualization

An important concept in sociological theories of modernization is *institutional differentiation*.[11] This concept describes the way the systems of the economy, family, education, government, religion, and other institutions operate relatively independently of one another in modern societies. Each institution develops its own goals, media of communication, and moral "logics." Institutional differentiation creates social conditions in which the phenomenon of *individualization* is widespread, especially when combined with urbanization and ex-urbanization. More freedom and burden is placed on individuals and nuclear families in the task of constructing what Peter Berger calls a meaningful "life project," the task of knitting together a coherent pattern of life.[12]

This is best understood by way of contrast. In the small rural villages or towns of the past, social roles were relatively stable and individuals interacted with overlapping groups of people at work, church, the grocery store, and town meetings. In a modern city, the roles individuals must play as they move from one institution to another are segmented into different compartments. They know one group of people at work, another at church, and still others in their apartment. Each of these segmented roles calls for different knowledge, attitudes, and skills. A person may be extremely analytical and competitive at work, emotional and generous at church, and fun-loving and erotic at home. In a differentiated society of segmented roles, more freedom and responsibility falls on individuals and nuclear families to knit together a meaningful pattern across the different spheres of life and across the life cycle. This is what is meant by individualization.

As societies modernize and their institutions become more differentiated, individualization begins to interact with and reshape long-standing cultural norms. Consider South Korea. This society passed through an intense period of modernization between 1960 to 1990, which saw the rise of new, more autonomous systems of the economy, education, government, and religion. It also became more urban. Individualization has accompanied these trends, interacting with and reshaping the strong sense of corporate identity and the kind of kinship obligations associated with neo-Confucianism. A weakening of ties across the generations has begun to occur, both within families and more generally. Generational discontinuity has become more pronounced, that is, the values, beliefs, and life experiences of youth are often quite different from those of their parents and grandparents. Youth culture is now characterized by more expressive values; higher education emphasizes critical thinking; kinship obligations such as the oldest son's care of aging parents and the continuing prominence of the son's mother after he has married have begun to weaken; more egalitarian patterns of marriage have emerged among some; the divorce rate has risen. In short, more freedom and responsibility now fall on individuals and nuclear families to form a meaningful life project.

Today we must view individualization not only in terms of modernization theory but also in terms of globalization theory in order to broaden our perspective beyond national societies to the transnational systems with which individuals must cope. The globalization of the economy, polity, and culture in recent decades has had the effect of intensifying individualization in many parts of the world. The power of local cultures to shape young people has diminished as children and youth have participated in the cultural flows of the global media, studied other cultures and languages in school, interacted with others through the Internet, made friends with exchange students, and traveled abroad. Local cultures remain important forces of socialization, to be sure, but they now are relativized and experienced as one option among many. Here again, more freedom and a greater burden is placed on individuals to knit together a meaningful life project in the face of their experience of a multicultural world.

Individualization represents both a challenge and opportunity for contemporary congregations. The greater freedom of individuals in differentiated societies makes affiliation with a congregation a matter of *choice*. It is no longer simply a matter of being raised in the church or particular denomination. Congregations must demonstrate that they have something meaningful and life giving to offer individuals, especially as they reach late adolescence and young adulthood and are free to choose for themselves. But this freedom also is an opportunity for congregations. In the "open space" of differentiated societies, individuals have greater freedom to choose the values and commitments that will shape the pattern of their lives. The pilgrimage frame invites congregations to take this opportunity seriously and to provide contexts that give individuals the chance to develop a sense of vocation . Individuals now have greater freedom to choose how they will live, but will they choose a lifestyle of careerism and consumerism, or a life project animated by the calling to serve God and God's world?

Interdisciplinary Dialogue Partner:
New Perspectives on Life Cycle Theory

In addition to the macroperspective of social theory, the pilgrimage frame also draws on the microperspective of various psychological theories, for they deepen our understanding of individual differences in cognitive development, learning style, gender, race/ethnicity, and personal biography. In the twentieth century, psychological theories sensitized educators to the fact that children, youth, and adults bring different cognitive capacities and issues to education. This insight resulted in the formation of age-level classes and developmentally appropriate curriculum materials.

These insights have been extended in important ways in recent theories of human development. One of the most important of these is Howard Gardner's theory of multiple intelligences. Gardner's pluralized view of the mind/brain and his recognition that its bio-psychological potentials are amplified in markedly different ways in various cultural contexts can help us recognize the very different profiles of intelligence that individuals possess. Often children have hidden strengths that go unnoticed by teachers and parents.[13] The same is true of adolescents and adults who frequently have gifts that go unrecognized at school or on the job. Such potentials need supportive, personalized contexts if they are to have a chance to blossom. Gardner's theory thus remains an important dialogue partner for the pilgrimage frame. It brings into focus the need for in-depth understanding of the individuals in a congregation and the importance of contexts that will support them in recognizing and claiming potential strengths they might not even realize they have.

The pilgrimage frame also is enriched by new thinking about the human life cycle. Some psychologists and practical theologians have begun to raise important questions about life cycle theories that have long been central to religious education.[14] Especially important is their critique of influential theories such as Erik Erikson's "eight ages of man" and Daniel Levinson's "seasons" of men's and women's lives.[15] Critics argue that in highly differentiated, pluralistic social contexts, these sorts of life cycle theories have not taken into account the wide variety of paths individuals travel over the course of their lives. They point to the need for postmodern perspectives on the life cycle that are richer and more open to variety than the standard literature. They explore the complexity of social and cultural factors that shape the life cycle in different groups. Two perspectives will help us to see what is at stake in their critique: (1) an analysis of gender and (2) an analysis of the impact of "life chances" on the life cycle.

Gender Studies

Some of the most important criticisms of standard accounts of the life cycle have been offered by feminists who have studied closely the patterns of women's lives long neglected by researchers. Two of the earliest critiques were offered by Jean Baker Miller in *Toward a New Psychology of Women* and Carol Gilligan in *In a Different Voice*.[16] In her early work, Miller raised important questions about accounts of the life cycle like Erikson's that portray growth toward maturity in terms of increased separation and autonomy, a criticism that has been sharpened by research she and her colleagues at the Stone Center have conducted on adolescent girls and young women. They discovered that the construction of personal identity is not merely a matter of standing over against significant others. Rather, it is a matter both of renegotiating relationships toward more complex forms of relatedness and constructing a clearer sense of agency and voice.[17] The process of growth toward maturity by girls and women is better pictured in terms of growth-in-connection than separation-for-autonomy.

Carol Gilligan raised similarly important questions about the lack of attention to the experience of girls and women in dominant theories of psychology. Focusing her criticism initially on Lawrence Kohlberg's theory of moral development, Gilligan's research on the moral deliberation of adolescent girls and young women led her to conclude that Kohlberg's theory was unable to account for the ways they matured in their moral thinking, consistently scoring them at the conventional level. This led Gilligan to develop an alternative account of moral development, which acknowledges the contextual and relational modes of thinking that women and girls commonly employ. In subsequent research, she and her colleagues have continued to argue that paying closer attention to the dynamics of women's experience can yield important insights into the very different paths that development can take, with important implications for education.[18]

The groundbreaking work of Miller and Gilligan opened a floodgate of new research on the psychology of gender. Some scholars have built on their early work, calling attention to the markedly different paths traveled by girls and women in contradistinction to boys and men.[19] Others have raised questions about overemphasizing the differences between females and males, asking if this simply legitimates socially constructed differences in ways that are ultimately pernicious.[20] Still others have called attention to the distinctive communicative patterns of men and women or explored the roots of gender identity from the perspectives of depth psychology or evolutionary psychology.[21] This burgeoning literature also has given rise to new research on boys and men, calling attention to the potential contribution of fathers to parenting and to the special issues males face over the course of their lives.[22]

This growing body of research on gender raises important questions about life cycle theories of the past century. Do they take into account gender differences in their portraits of human growth and development? Is it really possible to posit a single account of the life cycle for women and men? Must not congregations do a better job of taking gender differences into account in order to develop educational contexts and relationships that support the discernment of vocation across women's and men's lives?

The Effect of "Life Chances" on the Life Cycle

A second critical perspective on recent life cycle theories deepens the force of these questions.[23] Its varied proponents argue that social structures such as race, ethnicity, and class have a pervasive impact on the "life chances" of specific populations and shape the patterns of the life cycle among these groups. Erikson's theory, for example, seems to assume certain social conditions that do not obtain among many sectors of the world population. His description of adolescence as a time of moratorium—in which young people are free to explore a range of possible identities—is a case in point. It appears to assume a level of material wellbeing and cultural freedom that does not accurately capture the "life chances" of many people. What of those adolescents in many parts of the world who grow up in crushing poverty and are forced into menial labor early in childhood? What of the many girls who have children out of wedlock during early adolescence? What of those African American and Latino adolescent males who despair of their life chances as they become aware of the pervasiveness of racism in their society? The concept of psychosocial moratorium does not seem adequate to these groups' experience of adolescence.

Proponents of this sort of critique of standard accounts of life cycle theory point to a wide variety of social and economic factors that shape the course of life.[24] They argue, for example, that material well-being and physical well-being interact, shaping life expectancy, infant mortality rates, and the prevalence of serious diseases, disabilities, developmental deficiencies, and mental illness. As David Held notes, such negative factors "tend to be correlated directly with geography, class, gender, and race, and, accordingly, with particular clusters of deprivation found—most dramatically—among countries of the South, among non-whites, among the poor and working classes and among women."[25]

Attention to the ways "life chances" are impacted by factors of this sort should give the leaders of congregations pause about relying too heavily on life cycle theories that bracket out such considerations. Instead of relying on generalized accounts of the psychological issues that supposedly face all people in a certain age group, they must work harder to understand the patterns of their own particular communities. And within these patterns, they must allow for individual differences. One of the most promising lines of thinking to emerge in this regard uses the category of narrative to conceptualize individual identity, calling attention to the ways it is uniquely suited to holding together the past, present, and future dimensions of the self-in-time.[26] Individuals are portrayed as reworking their personal identity narratives over the course of their lives, a perspective that has much to offer the pilgrimage frame and its emphasis on the reworking of the individual's sense of vocation as his or her life circumstances change.

Focus Questions of the Pilgrimage Frame

1. Does the congregation make room for individuals at very different points on their unfolding pilgrimages of faith? This question asks about the ways a congregation takes account of the diversity of paths its individual members follow on their pilgrimages of faith. It underscores the importance of a teaching ministry that is not driven exclusively by a one-size-fits-all program and allows room for diversity.

2. Does the congregation acknowledge the increased freedom and burden placed on individuals in the contemporary world by offering educational contexts for vocational discernment in an ongoing fashion? A sense of vocation does not spring forth automatically; it needs the support of contexts that give individuals the opportunity to renarrate their lives as pilgrimages of faith and to discern the particular "role" God is calling them to play in the present. Such contexts are highly personalized and give individuals the opportunity to explore their biographies, gifts, and life circumstances.

3. Does the congregation support the discernment of vocation in relation to many spheres of life and not merely in terms of meeting its own institutional needs? An individual's vocation can take a variety of patterns in relation to many spheres of life and is likely to change over the course of his or her life. It is quite possible that an individual will not view the ministries of the congregation as the center of his or her vocational energies. For this reason, it is important that congregations be clear about the difference between meeting their own needs as institutions and vocational discernment, especially in an era when volunteers are in such short supply.

4. Does the congregation communicate the importance of developing a sense of vocation to all of its members? In a highly differentiated and pluralistic social context, individuals have great freedom to decide whether or not they will affiliate with a religious community. It is tempting for congregations to simply accommodate the felt needs and interests of their long-term, new, or prospective members. While congregations must develop programs that are responsive to felt needs, they must be viewed as a first step toward more demanding forms of vocational discernment. This question invites church leaders to determine if their congregation communicates the expectation that all members will wrestle seriously with the issues surrounding their calling to partnership with God and the ways this may reorder the patterns and priorities of their lives.

VOCATION AS PILGRIMAGE: SIX EXAMPLES

In the remainder of this chapter, I portray six individuals from the case study congregations who exemplify a variety of patterns of vocation. Their understanding of their calling to partnership with God has shifted over the course of their pilgrimages of faith. Sometimes they have ventured forth and sometimes they have abided. I have changed the names and some of the life circumstances of these individuals in order to preserve their anonymity. Over the course of my description, passages that appear in quotation marks are taken directly from my interviews.

Sung-young Lee is a shy and quiet woman in her mid-fifties. She was born in Taegu in the southeast of South Korea into a family of seven children. She was not raised in the church, but became a Christian while attending Ehwa Women's University. After graduation, Mrs. Lee married, moved back to Taegu for two years, and finally settled with her family in Seoul. Mrs. Lee describes the early years of her marriage as very hard, leading her to "forget" Christianity. Her husband's family was "very Confucian," and since she was married to the eldest son in the family, she was under pressure to conform to the expectations of a "dutiful daughter-in-law." The pressure mounted when she gave birth to two daughters, failing to provide her husband's family with a highly desired grandson. When her third child, also a daughter, was stillborn, Mrs. Lee experienced a tremendous amount of inner turmoil. Her self-esteem and self-confidence began slipping away.

Around this time, her sister-in-law invited her to go to a Christian fellowship group. The group was pentecostal, and Mrs. Lee received the gift of ecstatic utterance. It was a transforming moment in her life, motivating her to venture forth in a new and deeper appreciation of Christianity. As she put it:

> I now had a sense of joy that was deeper than any pain or sorrow. I think, looking back, that my third child being stillborn was a sign calling me back to God. And my personality began to change. I was always quiet and shy. Now I felt God's energy flowing through me, and I felt brave. . . . Several years later, one of my childhood friends who now lives in the U.S. came home for a visit and we ran into each other. "You've changed," she told me. "You're more confident and outgoing now." I think faith has the power to change you. I know it has changed me! When my fourth child was a daughter, I viewed her as a gift of God. It didn't matter, now that I was a Christian, that my in-laws so desperately wanted a son. I saw this as the leading hand of God.

Even many years later, Mrs. Lee looks back at this period as a turning point in her life. When she moved to Seoul in 1980, she joined Somang Presbyterian Church at the invitation of her older sister, who was among its earliest members. Since then her understanding of Christianity has changed, especially under the influence of Rev. Kwak. From Rev. Kwak's preaching, she says, she has acquired a "much better understanding of the eschatological ethics of the New Testament." Unlike the pentecostals who brought her back to the faith, she has come to realize that being a Christian is not about "receiving blessings." "I now look at that as almost being Shamanistic," she says. "Our final destiny is not in this worldly life. We must open our eyes to the blessings that we already have, and we must seek the ministry that God gives us."

In the twenty-two years that Mrs. Lee has been a member of Somang, she has carried out a number of ministries in the congregation. In recent years, she has been the key lay leader of one of the congregation's ministry zones, coordinating funeral arrangements, leading a weekly Bible study for its members, and other activities. She currently is the moderator of one of its mission groups, composed of around two hundred members. This group supports a variety of outreach projects, including the remodeling of houses for homeless families and raising money for the college tuition of poor youth.

Mrs. Lee is a leader in Somang, acknowledged by her election as a Kwonsa. What I find particularly remarkable about her leadership is not her administrative gifts, as strong as they are, but her gifts as a public speaker and prayer leader. How was it possible for such a shy and modest woman to develop gifts in these areas? Mrs. Lee harks back to the changes that began to take place when she received the gift of ecstatic utterance many years ago. While her original "boldness" has "calmed down" and she has gradually relinquished the "spiritual pride" that accompanied her initial return to Christianity, changes of lasting importance began to unfold during this part of her life. Looking back at the way her natural endowments have been reshaped across the years, she points out that her love of reading and her ability to memorize large amounts of material have come to play an important role in her public speaking. She has read the Bible from cover to cover three times and is constantly reading other books besides the Bible. According to others, there is a richness and depth to her public speaking, and her prayers are "full of wisdom" and bring to expression the "spiritual longings and needs" of those for whom she is praying.

How ironic that one who is so quiet and shy in relating to others would develop the reputation as a gifted speaker and prayer leader in her congregation. Clearly we see here something of the way the Spirit evokes and vitalizes natural endowments as these gifts are placed in the service of God. We also gain insight into the ways the Spirit can break the deadening grip of cultural scripts that might rob someone like Mrs. Lee of her self-esteem and prevent her from discovering her hidden leadership abilities. At present, Mrs. Lee's sense of vocation is centered on her ministry at Somang. In light of the self-respect and leadership experience she has gained in this setting, it is easy for me to imagine her using these considerable gifts in other venues in the future.

Sangkeun Kim is an energetic, thoughtful man in his sixties. Over three decades ago, he made a life-changing shift in careers that reflected a profound vocational commitment to the reunification of North and South Korea. This has remained the animating center of his vocation across his adult life. In his early thirties at the time, Dr. Kim was employed by the government. He also was in school part-time, pursuing a doctorate in political science. He began to write books on North Korea and reunification. During this period, he was asked to give a lecture at a national conference on reunification, attended by administrators and professors from universities across Korea. His lecture was so well received that he immediately was offered invitations from several universities to join their faculty.

Dr. Kim was faced with two decisions that were likely to shape the rest of his life. First, should he change careers? Becoming a professor would lower significantly his income, and as a father with young children this was not a decision to be taken lightly. Second, if he changed careers, which university invitation should he accept? Several were located in the Seoul area, the center of political, cultural, and economic life in South Korea. The only Christian university extending an offer was located five hours outside of Seoul. While he had already written several books, he was not sure that the academic life really suited him, and there was no promise of tenure. The one thing he *was* clear about was his passion for the reunification of North and South Korea.

Dr. Kim had grown up in Incheon, about an hour west of Seoul. His family was not Christian. As a high school student, he taught elementary children in a Sunday school but did not attend church himself. He taught because he loved children and wanted to learn how to teach. During this period, his father unexpectedly and suddenly died, and Dr. Kim was overcome with grief. Even the children in his Sunday school class noticed. They began to ask him, "Why don't you go to church? Come with us, if you want someone to sit with." So he did. And he became a Christian. While serving in the military, he was stationed in Seoul, where he belonged to several churches before joining Somang, which had been in existence for only three years at that time.

When Dr. Kim stood at the crossroads of two career paths in his early thirties, he did so in the context of a community of faith. He received the counsel and prayers of trusted Christian friends during this period. He and his wife prayed together about the decisions that lay before him. Gradually it became clear that his passion for the reunification of North and South Korea stood at the very center of what he believed God was calling him to do with his life and that the best place to follow this sense of calling was in the Christian university located far from Seoul. Though the financial risks and career uncertainty were daunting, Dr. Kim chose to venture into the unknown.

It is important for us not to interpret what has happened to Dr. Kim since he chose this path in his early thirties along the lines of an American or Asian success story. The financial costs to his family have been real. Since he has continued to live in Seoul, he must drive five hours to the university where he teaches every week and live apart from his family. He did not become a "superstar" in mediating relations between the North and South. Yet there are many signs that confirm Dr. Kim's decision to abide in this vocation throughout his adult life.

First, his natural gifts have proven to be exceptionally helpful in the pursuit of this vocation. He has become a very creative teacher and public speaker, with an uncanny ability to shape his presentation to the educational level and questions of his audience. These gifts have allowed him to become a very able interpreter of the complex issues of reunification to the Christian community, which comprises 25 percent of the South Korean population. Second, his decision to teach in a Christian university has allowed him to integrate his work as a political scientist with his Christian convictions, which would have been more difficult in a secular university. Because of his expertise, he has served in a variety of leadership roles for the denomination on the issue of reunification. Third, a kind of synchronicity can be discerned between Dr. Kim's lifelong passion for reunification and his participation in Somang Church. Somang was still in its infancy when Dr. Kim joined it, and it was only later that the "happy coincidence" of his vocational passion and Rev. Kwak's emphasis on outreach to the North became apparent.

Dr. Kim ventured forth at a key moment during young adulthood in order to pursue his passion for the reunification of North and South Korea. He took this step because he believed that this was the role God was asking him to play at that point in his life. Since then, he has abided in this understanding of his vocation, making it central to his work at Somang, the university, and his volunteer activities. By staying with and deepening his commitment to reunification over many years, Dr. Kim has developed a depth of knowledge and a network of colleagues that otherwise would not have been possible. As relations between the North and South continue to be problematic and as North Korea seeks to develop nuclear weapons, the church is fortunate to have a person with Dr. Kim's experience to provide it with guidance in how it might best respond to the crisis events that once again threaten the Korean peninsula.

Sharon Ofendahl is a large, thirty-five-year-old, coloured woman. She was born and raised in Stellenbosch and has participated in URC Stellenbosch her entire life. Along with her adult sisters—none of whom are married—she continues to live with her parents. Home is a prominent theme in her sense of vocation. Yet this does not mean that she has not grown or taken risks. Indeed, staying where God has "put her" entails certain sacrifices on her part, as we shall see.

Sharon was blessed with a very strong, intact family that shaped her core values and beliefs. Her parents were teachers in the public school system, and Sharon became a primary school teacher when she reached adulthood. Her parents were actively involved in URC Stellenbosch, and Sharon has carved out a very important role in the church as one of the congregation's most important catechists. As public school teachers, her parents are better educated and have a higher income then most of the members of URC Stellenbosch. Yet it was made clear to Sharon throughout her childhood that the family chose to stay involved in this congregation rather than attend the middle-class, coloured congregation in downtown Stellenbosch. They were needed here, her parents said, for both financial and leadership reasons. This made a lasting impression on Sharon and continues to shape her sense of vocation.

Sharon teaches in a primary school in a very poor farming area outside of Stellenbosch. Her students' parents work as day laborers on farms and vineyards and are paid only when their work is needed. Alcoholism is widespread. Most families live and sleep in one-room shacks, and children commonly come to school without having eaten breakfast. Sharon has had many opportunities to take teaching positions in schools located in more prosperous areas and even to relocate overseas. But she chooses to stay in this school. It is an important part of her sense of calling. She puts it like this:

> God gave this job to me. In the Bible, it tells us we are to go on with the talent he gives you. The talent he gave me is teaching. Teaching at this school is hard. I have classes of forty to fifty students. Most of their families are broken. You need a higher hand to guide you if you are going to make it there. . . . Most of them don't know what love is. I want them to know that when I put my arm around them or reprimand them, it's because I love them. I want them to get the idea, "I love you as a fellow human being, I love you as your teacher, and I love you because you are one of God's children."

Sharon tries to communicate this love to her students through both the subjects she teaches and the way she relates to them. For example, when teaching English as a second language, she makes love one of the organizing themes, giving her the opportunity to talk about what love is. As she puts it, "I sometimes can talk about God if he's a part of a poem or book. But most of the time, I try to help them see that love means caring about another person, respecting them. I also try to help them learn the Golden Rule and to love their neighbor as themselves. I know it might sound odd, but the hardest thing for them is to love *themselves*." She goes on:

> I know that just *talking* about love doesn't mean as much as *showing* it. So I try to do that too, by encouraging them to believe in themselves. For some of them, I'm the only adult in their lives who really expects anything from them and really believes that they could do something with their lives. And I listen to their problems. They know I'm always willing to stay late to talk with them. I've even had to get the authorities to step in and stop some violence and other things that the children have shared. And that has been scary sometimes too. I had a father try and jump me after school. He was drunk. . . . But I stay at this school because I think God has put me there.

Sharon chooses to abide where she believes God has put her. She learned this from her parents, and it is an important part of her sense of vocation.

A second part of Sharon's sense of vocation is her teaching as a catechist in URC Stellenbosch. She is one of seven catechists in the church, and her special responsibility is the first year of confirmation. She is generally viewed as one of the congregation's best teachers, and parents go out of their way to get their children in her class. She is seen as a kind of "mother figure" to the youth. She has their trust and teaches in a way that engages them in conversation about real-life issues. But she also is an authority figure who expects her students to study their confirmation lessons. As Sharon puts it, "I want them to come out of confirmation knowing the gist of Christianity. If I can plant seeds that will grow, that's good enough for me. This is a really important time in their lives. They're still open. When the mind is set, the mind is set."

Several years ago, Sharon was in a terrible car accident that threatened to leave her blind. She had a major operation that restored her vision. In this first major crisis of her life, she received support from her family and congregation, but still, she acknowledges, it was a "really, really hard time" because it threatened to end her career as a teacher. As Sharon pointed out, "I don't know too many blind teachers with fifty students. It's hard enough to keep on top of things when you can *see* what's going on!" As she reflects back on this experience, she says that it gave her a new "passion" in her teaching: "I realize how precious time is and how you have to use each moment of your life. I became more passionate in my teaching at school and at the church. And my students felt this. They could tell I really believed what I was saying—my heart speaking to their hearts."

Home is a prominent theme in Sharon's sense of vocation: building on the foundation laid in the home; abiding in her school and church when she might have gone elsewhere; building a life that is filled with children, though none of them are her own; and finding a renewed passion for the place and tasks that have long stood at the center of her vocation.

We find a very different sort of pilgrimage of faith in the story of *Claudia van der Hoost*, also from URC Stellenbosch. For Claudia, "huge leaps" of faith have been followed by times of "falling down." According to Rev. Coetsee, her story is more typical of the members of the congregation than is Sharon's. As he put it, "Few people in this church have typical middle class ethics. They have a hard life, where a lot of give and take takes place. But they know that the church will always be the one place where they can find grace."

Claudia was married in URC Stellenbosch in 1984, the church of her childhood. "We were *so* in love," she recalls. "My mother was against the marriage, but he was my true soul mate. We had a daughter. I was so happy. And he was really good to me. He belonged to another church but was willing to join mine. And he was hard working. He drove a huge lorry for a factory. Every morning he left at 4:00 a.m." A year after they were married, her husband was killed in a truck accident at work. "I remember that morning as if it were yesterday," Claudia says. "I was sick with grief. I kept asking the Lord, 'Why? Why? Why?'"

As a child, Claudia's home life offered none of the stability and security of Sharon's. She did not know her biological father. Her stepfather was an alcoholic who often was physically violent. "When he drank, he was mean," Claudia remembers. "If he turned on one of us children and my mother tried to help us, she would get it ten times worse. It was hard, very hard, for all of us . . . living in fear. This is why I took my husband's death so hard. I finally had what I'd always dreamed of. And it was gone in a second."

Claudia's life since her husband's death has been "one struggle after another." As she puts it, "I was a widow, you see, and a single mother. So people were always trying to take advantage of me." When her husband was killed on the job, the head of the company union tried to cheat Claudia out of her insurance money, and she had to fight to get it. After this, she dropped out of the church for a while. When she returned, she became very involved in a parachurch organization called the Bible Mission Group, which has branches in many congregations throughout the country. Her gifts of leadership and public speaking soon became evident. She became a deacon in URC Stellenbosch and was frequently asked to speak at public events. According to Rev. Coetsee, people would go out of their way to hear her preach.

During this period, she grew close to a leader in the Bible Mission Group. Though he was married, they had an affair, and Claudia became pregnant. They decided that she would have an abortion, and when this became known in the community, they were both publicly shamed. She dropped out of church and the Bible Mission Group. Several years later, she attended URC Stellenbosch's annual summer camp meeting, and this proved to be a new turning point for her. "I came to the point of repentance," she says. "I confessed everything and received true forgiveness and healing." The congregation welcomed her back into the community, and she "rose quickly," soon being asked to preach at various church gatherings. For the past nine years, she has worked for a large construction company, beginning as a cashier but gradually working her way up to become an accountant. But even that has been challenging. She was fired from her job when a jealous coworker made false accusations against her, forcing her to take the company to court in order to prove her innocence and get her job back.

Claudia's story is filled with crises and hardship. Her venturing forth is not a heroic quest in which she chose to leave home to face the challenges of the wider world. Suffering and pain have come to her, sometimes through her own bad choices but more often for no good reason at all. Yet Claudia, like many other members of URC Stellenboch whose stories are similar, has found comfort, strength, and hope in her faith and the church. Her life is not a simple tragedy; it is a pilgrimage of faith in which she has discovered God traveling with her through the extreme ups and downs of life. Claudia describes this in terms of her prayer life. It is in prayer, she says, that she has learned to be completely open with God and has developed a vivid sense of God's presence. She puts it like this:

> My mother taught me to pray and we often prayed together when I was a child. But it was when my husband died that prayer became real. I argued with the Lord. I was so angry and hurt. And slowly I learned to hear him talk back to me. It took a long time. I heard him tell me: "You are my child and I love you so much; trust me and I will show you how much I love you." In my prayer group we talk about being emotionally involved with the Lord. I know things are bad for me spiritually when that's not there—not when

I'm angry or disappointed or frustrated. That's when I really start talking to God. . . . At work, people know I'm a church sister. They know I pray. Sometimes, they say, "Sister Claudia, I've got this problem. Will you pray for me?" Sometimes they lay out a dream for me and ask me to interpret it for them.

Sharon Ofendahl and Claudia van der Hoost both grew up in the same congregation in the same community. They are both women and both coloured. Yet their stories are remarkably different. Paying attention to these kinds of differences lies at the heart of the pilgrimage frame.

Carla Thompson is a member of Nassau Presbyterian Church. At the very heart of her present sense of vocation is her participation in a wide range of service activities. Though a well-respected social worker and therapist in the Princeton area, she finds the time and energy to take part in numerous volunteer activities, both in the congregation and beyond. She has served on the board, as a client assistant, and home delivery server for the Crisis Ministry of Princeton and Trenton, which provides assistance to low-income families. She has served as an elder at Nassau and as a member of its Reconciliation Committee. As an elder, she spearheaded the congregation's effort to bring affordable housing to Princeton. She has run a support group for breast cancer survivors at the local YWCA. She has served as an adult leader on several of the youth group's mission trips. Single-handedly, she started a photography class for African American inner-city children in Trenton and Latino children in Princeton. Indeed, virtually every time I attended a special function at Nassau, there was Carla, serving coffee, cleaning up, donating money, or providing support in some other way.

In my conversation with her, Carla shared the enormous sense of personal satisfaction and creativity that she derives from these activities. "I receive a lot more than I give," she says. "I've even started telling people who come to me for counseling, 'Do something outside yourself. Try to stop being so self-focused. It keeps you stuck in a victim condition.' I've found that to be true for myself, and I think it has proven true for them as well." Over the course of my interview with Carla, a number of stories emerged that illustrate quite vividly what Carla "receives" from her own volunteer activities. Let me share just two.

One of Carla's favorite volunteer activities is delivering food to shut-ins for the Crisis Ministry. Once a month, Carla gets bags of groceries from the Crisis Ministry office and off she goes to visit her "friends." She describes these times as follows:

I'd say about half of the eight women I visit have become my friends. I look forward to seeing them, and we always spend time talking. There is a beauty and kindness and wisdom about these women. You'd never know it was there if you didn't spend time with them. I almost always feel better after these visits than when I arrived. It's close to a religious thing for me.

Carla describes the photography program she started in similar ways. She and her husband, Thomas, made a pact several years ago that they would develop new hobbies. Thomas took up painting; Carla, photography. Both have become quite good. Serendipitously, Carla heard about a program called Shooting Back, which teaches inner-city children photography skills as a way of helping them discover their creative abilities. Carla contacted the founder and arranged to meet with him to learn more about the program. She then started her own version, linking it initially to Nassau's after-school program in Trenton and subsequently to the low-income, after-school program in Princeton. She recruits church youth to work with her on this project whom she has gotten to know as a volunteer on the youth group's mission trips. She mentors these students as they work with her on the project. Here is how she describes the project itself:

> The kids love learning how to take pictures and to develop them. I take them through the whole process. I ask them to write about their pictures and we display them every so often at the church. We talk about their pictures—what they see; what's important to them; and they really share. It helps them to see their environment in a different way. It gives them something concrete that they can have and be in control of. They're not just victims; they're empowered. . . . They learn certain skills, and I can see them improve. Some have been really gifted too. They have the eyes of an artist. They learn to see and frame their pictures in ways that I find pretty amazing.

Throughout our conversation, Carla lit up when she shared these kinds of stories. Clearly, she finds her volunteer activities to be a major source of personal fulfillment and creativity. One of the things that struck me later as I listened to the tape of our interview was the remarkable absence of "oughts" in our conversation. She kept coming back to what she gets out of these activities. She pointed out that over the years she has learned to drop those activities that she does not find energizing. Volunteering has become more central to Carla's sense of vocation since she has entered the latter part of mid-life. Her children have long left home; she is well-established as a professional and continues to gain satisfaction from her work with clients. But it is her volunteer work that seems to be the greatest source of creativity and vitality at this point in her life. It is one of the ways she continues to venture forth, even as she abides in the same congregation, profession, and community. It takes her across racial and age boundaries. It allows her to feel that she is using her gifts to make the world a better place. As Carla might put it, she "receives" even as she "gives."

Charles Atwater was born in Raleigh, North Carolina, where he was raised in a United Methodist church. He attended North Carolina State University and did graduate work in a technical college, deepening his knowledge of computers and preparing him to work as a systems analyst. Shortly after graduation, he began to work for a large multinational corporation whose headquarters are located in New York City. Charles worked out of one of the larger offices located just outside of Princeton. He was employed by this company for twenty-two years, eventually becoming the director of an applications development team with thirty people under his supervision. His team had the job of designing systems that allow the company to better handle emerging opportunities.

Not long after moving to the Princeton area, Charles began attending Nassau Presbyterian Church. He describes his first experience of worship at Nassau as deeply meaningful. "Wallace Alston was preaching, and he gave me a sense of the realness of God," Charles says. "I already had a vague notion of God. But the whole experience 'penetrated' me. It gave me a feeling that God really does exist. It set me on a course of investigation." In the twenty years Charles has participated in Nassau, he has come to appreciate especially the adult education program and the overall intellectual atmosphere of the congregation. As he puts it, "I have deep respect for the many thinkers we have in this congregation. If you're looking for intellectual stimulation and are willing to ponder what you've heard in church, then this is the right congregation for you."

Of the various people I interviewed for this part of the book, Charles is the only one *presently* in the midst of a major crisis of vocation. Approximately eighteen months before our interview, he lost his job. The story is long and complex, and my account here will not go into all of the details. Suffice it to say that a superior at work pressured Charles to misrepresent his professional judgment about the viability of a $30 million project that his company was considering investing in. When he refused and continued to vocalize his opposition, he was silenced by his immediate boss, subjected to rumors in an attempt to discredit him, and finally let go. His dismissal was carried out under the guise of corporate layoffs necessitated by the downturn of the economy following the attack on the World Trade Center. Charles had worked for this company for over twenty years. He had never received a negative work report, and his development team had created some of the most innovative systems for the company as it moved into the global economy. When his dismissal became public knowledge, some of the members of his team started circulating a petition to protest his "unfair treatment," something virtually unheard of in the corporate world. Yet here Charles was, eighteen months later, unable to find a comparable position. His unemployment and health benefits had just run out.

This whole experience has precipitated a crisis of vocation for Charles that goes well beyond losing one job and going through the process of finding another. It has to do with whether or not he can continue to function in the current corporate culture and still maintain his professional and ethical integrity. This issue emerged several times over the course of our conversation, and each time Charles framed it in similar ways. On the one hand, he loves the challenge of his former position. "Where else can you do the kind of work I was doing?" he said. "Large, multinational corporations are the only places that allow you to tackle intellectual problems of the complexity I was dealing with and to develop systems applications at the very cutting edge of information technology." He also spoke with pride about the collaborative managerial style he developed while director of his applications team. On the other hand, the whole experience of being asked to compromise his professional integrity and to provide, in effect, a dishonest assessment of a proposal being pushed by his boss has brought to the fore issues simmering just beneath the surface for many years. "To be honest," he says, "I always felt like a fish out of water in corporate America. There's always been a conflict, but it's been a managed conflict." He worries especially that in the highly competitive environment of the global marketplace, it has become "easier to steal than to create." When asked to explain what this means, Charles put it like this:

> Remember Alvin Toffler's book, *Future Shock?* I know it was written a long time ago, but a lot of what he says has come true. The world is changing so rapidly and the level of adaptation is so great that people can't adjust to the speed of the world. But people still have to survive. So how do they compete? More and more, they're using strategies that are immoral and unethical. It's a whole lot easier to steal somebody's ideas and work than to pay the price of creating them. More and more, I think that's what's going on in corporate culture. People are stealing or taking over other people's work. . . . I guess that is my biggest fear about getting back into this culture. He who is good may be free, but can he pay the mortgage?

Charles is struggling to make sense of the recent events of his life. When asked about the support of his congregation in this process, his initial response was to say, "I'm not looking for help from the church. It's not Nassau's responsibility." But then he qualified this, saying, "It's not the church's job to help me personally. But it *is* the church's job—and I mean the church in general—to do a better job of connecting to what its flock is dealing with. There are a lot of people out there who believe in God and yet they're out there duking it out on their own in their everyday lives. There's pretty much a total disconnect with corporate America." I cannot help but wonder if Charles has picked up on Nassau's ambivalence toward community (described in chapter 5), leading him to expect little in the way of personal support in working through the vocational issues he now faces.

Yet Charles does point to one significant way the church has helped him during this period—his volunteer work three days a week in one of the congregation's outreach ministries. He describes this as being both "an education and an awakening." As an economics major, he had a long-term interest in the inequitable distribution of wealth, but now, for the first time, he is coming "face-to-face with the realities of poverty." He describes what he has learned from this experience as follows: "It pretty much crushes your preconceived notions that poor people are just societal freeloaders who could pull themselves up by their bootstraps. There are so many dimensions to their problems. It's not just a matter of personal initiative." Charles has found his volunteer work in this ministry to be so stimulating that he has even considered making a career shift into the volunteer sector. But he wonders if this would really be possible: "It's difficult to justify a complete career change, especially in our current economic environment; you need a track record in an area to get a job."

It is fitting that we should end this chapter with Charles Atkins. He brings into focus many of the reasons that congregations must pay more attention to the pilgrimage frame in their teaching ministries. The life structure that Charles built over the course of young adulthood has begun to unravel. Vocational questions of great importance have come to the fore in his life. Should he return to corporate America or follow a different career path? Are there alternative vocational patterns open to Charles? These kinds of questions cannot be answered through generic, one-size-fits-all Christian education programs. They require educational contexts and personal relationships that give individuals the freedom and encouragement to explore their own stories and life circumstances in the context of faith. Should they abide, or should they venture forth at this point in their pilgrimages of faith? What is God calling them to do and be?

PART THREE
INSIDE THE ARTIST'S STUDIO:
Refashioning Your Congregation's Teaching Ministry

Introduction to Part Three

In part 3, I focus on the normative and pragmatic tasks of practical theology. While practical theologians do not always draw a close connection between these two tasks, I think it is appropriate to do so in a book on the teaching ministry of congregations. As pastors and Christian educators know firsthand, congregational patterns tend to be self-perpetuating once they are established. It is important, thus, to periodically stand back and assess these patterns critically, testing them against a theological account of the church. This sort of critical reflection and assessment is what a normative framework in practical theology is designed to support.

But developing a sense of the way things ought to be in a congregation and knowing how to bring them about are not the same thing. *Why* and *how to* are distinguishable, even when closely related. *How to* is the focus of the pragmatic task of practical theology, the formulation of models of praxis and "rules of art" that provide concrete and practical guidance in how to carry out some action or practice. As the phrase "rules of art" implies, such models and guidelines cannot be applied in a mechanical or rote fashion; they assume the artistry of reflective practice, which takes account of context, timing, resources, and a host of other factors that can never be determined in advance. In chapters 9, 10, and 11, I offer rules of art for the teaching ministry. In this introduction, I begin to present the normative framework developed in chapter 8.

In recent decades, a number of contemporary practical theologians have begun to describe the "generative problematic" of the normative task of practical theology in terms of the construction of models of divine and human action. This has been given special attention in the United States by James Fowler, James Loder, and Don Browning. In the case of Fowler, H. Richard Niebuhr's influence has been especially important and has led him to emphasize the role of narrative and metaphor in the construal of God's creating, governing, liberating, and redeeming praxis in the world and human responsiveness to divine action.[1] For Loder, Søren Kierkegaard and Karl Barth have carried greater weight, leading him to develop a model of divine and human action based on the bipolar, relational unity of Chalcedon's Christology and to emphasize the role of transformation.[2] Don Browning has drawn on Reinhold Niebuhr's theology to describe the "narrative envelope" of Christian ethics.[3] The key point is that all of these practical theologians have developed theological models of divine and human action that can critique and guide Christian praxis. I find this to be a helpful way of thinking about the normative task of practical theology. It takes the form not of church doctrines as in dogmatics, or of exegesis and commentary on texts as in biblical studies, but of the construction of models of divine and human action that can guide Christian praxis in the present.

In my own thinking about the normative task of practical theology, I am increasingly drawn to the possibilities of a dramatological perspective in which aesthetics and drama are important. It supplements practical theology's tendency to rely on models of action taken over from the social sciences with models developed in the humanities and arts. The fruitfulness of this sort of dialogue between theology and the humanities has become evident in recent decades in the emergence of narrative as an important category in theology and ethics. The metaphorical complex of drama retains the gains of narratology. Dramas are "storied," with plots that unfold the unity of action through time. But they go further by placing in the foreground the role of action in dramatic realization. Dramas are not merely read; they are performed.

Moreover, the metaphor of the world as a theater has a long history in Western philosophy and theology. During the Reformation period both Luther and Calvin used this metaphor at points, Calvin quite extensively to describe creation as the theater of God's glory.[4] In recent American Protestant theology, Reinhold Niebuhr developed the categories of drama to portray the interplay of human freedom and destiny in history.[5] Yet it is a contemporary Roman Catholic theologian, Hans Urs von Balthasar, who has reflected most extensively on the theological possibilities of conceptualizing the world as a theater in which divine and human dramas are played out. Balthasar develops this perspective in *Theo-Drama: Theological Dramatic Theory* (five volumes), which articulates Christian ethics as a dramatological theory of the Good.

People go to serious theater, Balthasar argues, out of a twofold need and pleasure: (1) The drama is analogous to the dramatic tensions of their own lives and serves as a kind of mirror that clarifies and interprets their life's patterns, and (2) the drama as a whole presents a "solution" or "insight" into the dramatic tensions the members of the audience face.[6] This is a helpful way of thinking about the Christian life, he contends, for in the Theo-drama of God's entry onto the stage of the world in Jesus Christ, Christians find the dramatic patterns of their own lives clarified and interpreted. Indeed, they find themselves not merely in the spectator role of the audience but as actors in the drama with a particular role to play.

Balthasar invites us to think of this "Theo-drama" in trinitarian terms: God the Father is analogous to the author of the Theo-drama, the Son to the lead actor, and the Spirit to the director of the ensemble. Christians, thus, find themselves caught up in a Theo-drama that is not of their own making and being directed by someone other than themselves. Nor do they have the lead role. Nonetheless, the parts they are given to play are real and take all of their skill and creativity.

Balthasar encourages us to think of our parts or roles in this Theo-drama as analogous to the "active receiving" of the actors in a play.[7] On the one hand, the actors *receive* from the author a particular part within an ensemble of roles, themes, and unfolding action composing the drama as a whole. They must give themselves to and "serve" the particular part for which they are cast, be it central or minor. On the other hand, they are *active*, for the success of their performance depends on their own creativity and skill, making use of the resources of their physical, emotional, and spiritual selves to bring their particular role to life. Indeed, the playwright's script remains unactualized without the dramatic realization of the actors who bring it to life in a dramatic performance. Analogously, Balthasar argues, the Christian life is one of active receptivity, a matter of discovering the particular role we are given to play—a role likely to shift over the course of our lives—and of making full use of our gifts in the dramatic realization of this role.

In the remainder of this book, I develop a dramatological model to portray the patterns of divine and human action as taking the form of a Theo-drama. The substantive account I develop of this Theo-drama will take its bearings from the theology of Jürgen Moltmann. In dialogue with his writings, I chart three decisive acts in the Theo-drama of God's dealings with the world: creation, redemption, and glorification. Since I draw so extensively on Moltmann's writings in the final part of this book, it may be helpful to conclude this introduction with a brief overview of his life and theology.

JÜRGEN MOLTMANN: AN INTRODUCTION

Jürgen Moltmann was born in 1926.[8] By his own account, the initial source of his theology was his experience as a prisoner of war from 1945 to 1948. Two central themes of his early theology emerged from this experience: the power of God in hope and God's presence in suffering. After the war, he was a student of theology at Göttingen University, where he studied with Otto Weber, Ernst Wolf, Hans Iwand, Gerhard von Rad, and Ernst Käseman. Upon the completion of his studies, he was ordained and served for five years as the pastor of a small Protestant community in Wasserhorst, a suburb of Bremen. In 1958, he became an academic teacher while still a pastor. From 1967 to 1994, he served as professor of systematic theology at Tübingen University. It would take a chapter or even a book to trace the wide range of conversation partners Moltmann has engaged over the course of his theological career. Such partners have included figures such as Karl Barth, Ernst Bloch, and Abraham Heschel, as well as theological traditions as diverse as neo-orthodoxy, liberation and feminist theology, Orthodox theology, and process thought.

Moltmann characterizes his various theological writings as falling into two major series of works. The first series is a trilogy that focuses on three complementary perspectives on Christian theology. In *The Theology of Hope*, he attempts to develop an eschatological interpretation of the Christian life as a whole. In *The Crucified God*, he focuses on the cross of Christ as the key to understanding God as Trinity and as the criterion of all Christian theology. In *The Church in the Power of the Spirit*, he focuses on the church as a messianic and pneumatological fellowship. His second major series of works is more systematic and addresses the traditional doctrinal loci in a planned order. This series includes books on God (*The Trinity and the Kingdom of God*, 1980), creation (*God in Creation*, 1985), Jesus Christ (*The Way of Jesus Christ*, 1989), the Holy Spirit (*The Spirit of Life*, 1991), eschatology (*The Coming of God*, 1995), and the tasks and methods of theology (*Experiences in Theology*, 2000). While my dialogue with Moltmann's theology will primarily draw on his second series, I will place it against the backdrop of his earlier theology when appropriate.

Chapter 8

Theo-Drama

Divine and Human Action

In this chapter, I explore what it means for congregations to find their own particular stories within the Theo-drama of God's creation, redemption, and glorification of the world. Jürgen Moltmann, my primary dialogue partner, has often described theology as *imagination for the kingdom of God* in this world, and, accordingly, I begin each section with images that attempt to engage the imagination, helping you see and feel theological issues before they are developed in conceptual terms.[1] At points, I refer to music, and it might enhance your reading to listen to this music as you read. Most of it is readily available through the Internet or in libraries.

BEFORE THE CURTAIN RISES: TRINITY

In classical theater, it was not uncommon for a play to include a prologue before the chorus entered and the dramatic action began; a narrator would offer a short poem, speech, or song introducing the audience to the themes of the play. In our Theo-drama, think of the prologue as taking place behind the curtain. No words are spoken. All that you can hear is the most beautiful music imaginable. If you watch closely, you can faintly discern the thin curtain billowing from the movement of three Persons dancing to the music, which, mysteriously, is not being played by the musicians in the orchestra pit, whose instruments are resting idly on their laps. The strange and beautiful music you hear flows instead out of the movement of the dancers, reflecting perfectly the varied patterns of their dance.

You will only be able to gain insight into what is going on behind the curtain when two of these dancers come on stage to play their roles. As you observe the relationship of these figures to one another and to the other actors in this "theater of the world," you will begin to form an understanding of what was going on behind the curtain before the play of life began. But even then, you must be cautious, for you can never behold directly the divine dance unfolding behind the curtain.

Christian theology begins with an affirmation of God. Before creation, God alone exists. The theater of the world and its dramatic action come into being out of God. But God is of a different order than the created world. God is the author of the play that is about to unfold—the creative source of its materials, characters, and defining horizon. But the meaning of this unfolding Theo-drama becomes clear only with the entry of Jesus Christ onto the stage of the world. Jesus Christ is Immanuel—God with us—the "only begotten of the Father," as John's prologue puts it (KJV). Here the secret of creation stands revealed. It now becomes clear that the divine Author of the drama of life has desired communion with creation from the very beginning.

Alongside Christ within the theater of the world, Christian theology also discerns another center of divine agency at work: the Holy Spirit.[2] Though her presence is elusive, she is already present in all places and at all times on the world stage, preparing the way for the Son's arrival. She is the power and divine energy at work over the course of Christ's public ministry, and when he departs, she is poured out on "all flesh," animating the church and creation as a whole with the vitalities and possibilities of new creation.

Just as the theology of the Hebrew Scriptures takes its bearings from the salvific experiences of exodus and covenant, Christian theology takes its bearings from the patterns of divine action discerned in the Son and Spirit that leads it to form a trinitarian understanding of God. Long before church councils and theologians forged an explicit doctrine of the Trinity, the early church was developing trinitarian practices that gave expression to the mystery at the heart of the Christian understanding of God. As early as the Gospel of Matthew, Christ is portrayed as telling his disciples that they are to baptize new converts "in the name of the Father and of the Son and of the Holy Spirit" (Matt. 28:19). Prayers are offered to the Son and the Spirit, and they are worshiped along with the Father. The Spirit is portrayed as uniting disciples to Christ and through him to the Father.

A trinitarian understanding of God is basic to Christian belief and practice. This brings us face to face with important questions about how the Trinity should be portrayed in Christian theology. The classical formulation of the Trinity to emerge out of the great ecumenical councils of the fourth and fifth centuries was "one God in three Persons." In this formulation, the church attempted to hold together two affirmations found in the New Testament: (1) The church stands in continuity with Israel's monotheistic faith in one God, and (2) the church recognizes distinct centers of divine activity within the economy of salvation. The oneness and threeness of the Godhead are held in tension.

Throughout the centuries, Christian theologians have struggled to find ways of honoring both the unity and differentiation of the Trinity. I follow the lead of Jürgen Moltmann, emphasizing the distinct personhood of each member of the Trinity. This is commonly known as a *social doctrine of the Trinity*. Unity is pictured as being like a fellowship of persons who are so closely related to one another that the actions and "subjectivity" of one always impact and influence the others. The divine Persons are bound together in a community of mutual love.

The unity of the three divine Persons is also described in terms of the ancient concept of *perichoresis*: their mutual interpenetration and indwelling. One of the etymological roots of this term is "to dance," and perichoresis expresses the dynamic motion and reciprocal relations of the members of the Trinity. The image of a dance going on behind the curtain at the beginning of this section is an attempt to help us imagine this relationality.[3] Even on a strictly human level, we know something of what it is like to "lose" ourselves in a dance. Music and motion, action and reciprocal action sweep us into something that is larger than our individual selves. We become a part of the dance. This is a helpful way of describing the unity of the three Persons of the Trinity. They exist in and for each other. They interpenetrate and coinhere in a dance of mutual love.

This dynamic and relational understanding of the Trinity allows us to portray each of the divine Persons as leading the divine dance at different points, without losing the sense that at every moment the one leading continues to stand in reciprocal relations with the other divine Persons. Or to shift metaphors, different members of the Trinity play the "lead role" at different points in the Theo-drama that is about to unfold.[4] In *creation* and *continuing creation*, the pattern is: *Creation is by the Father through the Son in the Holy Spirit*.[5] In this pattern, the Father "leads" the divine dance as it makes room for creation. The Son, God's eternal counterpart, is the mediator of creation: the divine Logos or Wisdom of the pattern by which creation as "other" is related to the Creator. Creation takes place through the operation of the Holy Spirit, God's immanent transcendence in the world, the energies by which it is originally brought into being and continues to unfold. In *redemption*, the order shifts. Here it is the Son who "leads" the divine dance. The pattern of redemption may be described as *by the Son in the Spirit to the Father*. In *glorification*, the order shifts once more. Here the Holy Spirit takes the "lead." In this act of the Theo-drama, the eschatological Spirit carries out the work of new creation within the conditions of an unredeemed world, creating anticipations of the world's transfiguration at the consummation. The pattern of glorification may be described as *by the Spirit through the Son to the Father*.[6]

CREATION BY THE FATHER THROUGH THE SON IN THE HOLY SPIRIT

As the curtain rises, a single figure appears at the very back of the stage. She is out of the spotlight and somewhat difficult to see in the darkness of the stage. The only light that illumines this figure seems to emanate from her shimmering, translucent gown. It irradiates her form with many colors that shift at her slightest movement—blues, greens, reds and pinks, light brown, golden white. Closing her eyes, this figure tilts her head almost imperceptibly to one side as if she is listening intently to a voice that only she can hear. She bends her body forward and inward slightly, gathering herself to draw in a deep breath. Gracefully, her whole body moves backward and upward as she opens her mouth and blows out the breath of creation. Beautiful golden particles begin to flow out of her mouth and slowly scatter around the stage. As the particles travel beyond the force of her exhalation they move randomly in all directions, bumping into one another and careening wildly in a strange, chaotic dance as they slowly fill the stage.

The figure opens her eyes and pauses for a long, pregnant moment to behold what she has created. Suddenly she lifts the hands dangling loosely at her side, drawing them inward and upward across the center of her upper torso and then thrusting them outward and upward in a brief gesture of praise. Her entire body gently follows the upward arc of her hands, elevating from the stage and moving forward into the very center of the random dance of golden particles. Her form explodes in a sudden burst of light into thousands of luminous, golden-red particles that flow outward among the other particles careening wildly about the stage. Immediately a change takes place. The particles abandon their chaotic dance and begin to form themselves into a series of heliocentric circles of various sizes, which flow in many directions and angles around an empty center. Suddenly all motion ceases and the beautiful, heliocentric pattern lies suspended above the stage. The largest and densest circle encompassing all others begins to vibrate, and for the briefest of moments sitar-like music fills the theater. All at once, the many circles implode to their common center and the particles melt together in a fiery ball suspended above the stage. This ball throbs brighter and brighter, and then in a sudden, powerful flash explodes outward, filling the stage with the space and time of first creation.

These images invite us to consider two dimensions of creation that are important to our understanding of God's action in the world: (1) the role of the Holy Spirit in original and continuing creation and (2) the dialogue between science and theology in our understanding of the world. Scholars have long noted that the Bible contains diverse accounts of creation forged in different eras, which in part reflect new understandings of the natural world.[7] Our task in this section is to carry out a dialogue with contemporary scientific knowledge of the evolution of the universe. Theology learns from science, but it also speaks back critically to science on the basis of its own convictions. As Moltmann puts it, "The sciences have shown us how to understand creation as nature. Now theology must show how nature is to be understood as God's creation."[8]

The Evolution of the Universe

Keith Ward describes the origin of the universe as follows:

> The galaxy of stars to which our sun belongs is one of millions of galaxies, scattered throughout a space-time system which has itself expanded from a primeval burst of energy thousands of millions of years ago. This vast cosmos, awesome in beauty and in extent, began in a sudden blaze of energy from one singularity, a point of infinitely compressed gravitational force and density, which exploded in the primeval "Big Bang."[9]

For intelligent life to emerge on our planet, crucial thresholds were crossed in the evolution of the universe, beginning with the emergence of simple nuclear particles from an earlier mass of superheated energy, then crossing the threshold of the formation of simple molecules out of atoms with protons, neutrons, and electrons, followed by the emergence of chains of molecules with the capacity to build copies of themselves, then the emergence of organic life with DNA giving rise to bodies with differentiated parts and a central nervous system, and finally the emergence of *homo sapiens*, with nervous systems complex enough to allow human consciousness and culture to emerge.[10] Each threshold represents the emergence of a new order of complexity in the evolution toward intelligent life.

Scientists now believe that the universe is around 13.7 billion years old. When we place human life and culture on our planet against the backdrop of the evolution of the universe, we cannot help but be struck by their relative brevity. The beginnings of human evolution extend back six million years, but the "big bang" of human culture occurred as recently as 60,000 years ago.[11] Imagine that you are watching a three-hour play of the evolution of the universe from the big bang to the present. If you happened to blink at the wrong moment, you would miss the entire part of the drama covering human life on our planet. This should give us pause. Is it really adequate for us to think of creation in highly anthropocentric terms? Is not nature far more than the impersonal backdrop of divine and human action? How might we conceptualize God's relationship to the evolutionary processes of nature? These are questions that practical theology cannot avoid if it is to take seriously contemporary science's understanding of the universe.

Creation: An Unfolding Drama

Christian theologians who have engaged modern science's account of the evolution of the universe are virtually unanimous in their judgment that contemporary thinking about creation must now distinguish more clearly between *original* and *continuing* creation. While both have been a part of Christian theology across the centuries, the accent has primarily fallen on original creation, with continuing creation largely treated in terms of God's preservation and providential care of creation. In the tradition's description of original creation, nature and human culture have often been described as conforming to *prototypes* established by God in first creation, with a static, hierarchical order: Animals are subordinate to humans, children to parents, women to men, servants to masters, subjects to rulers, and so forth in a great chain of being leading all the way up to God. This sort of protological account of creation must be revised in light of what we have learned from modern evolutionary science. A world populated with intelligent life did not come into being instantaneously but evolved over billions of years. We must learn to think not only in terms of original creation but also in terms of continuing creation. How might we think of God's activity in and through the unfolding drama of an evolving universe? Here I will explore the model of *trinitarian panentheism* developed by Jürgen Moltmann in *God in Creation*.

It is important not to confuse pan*en*theism with pantheism. Pantheism identifies God with the forces of nature and abandons any notion of God's transcendence. In contrast, *panentheism* literally means "the whole (pan) within (en) God (theism)." Moltmann's model of panentheism is explicitly trinitarian, which allows him to affirm God's active participation in the processes of continuing creation through the Holy Spirit while also affirming God's transcendence of the world as its Creator, who is not to be confused with the order of created, contingent being. He sometimes uses a brief epigram to describe God's transcendence and immanence: *The world is in God and God is in the world*.[12]

The first part of this epigram—*the world is in God*—indicates Moltmann's portrait of the preexistent, triune God as making time and space for a created other. Recall the image of *perichoresis* as a divine dance of mutual love. As love, the divine Persons of the Trinity are open to relations of mutuality and reciprocity with one another. As love, the triune God is open also to relations of mutuality and reciprocity with the *created* other. This picture of God's relationship to creation is quite different from those parts of the Christian tradition that have portrayed God as "unchanging" and "apathetic" (as unresponsive and unaffected by creation). In an act of creative and ecstatic love, God brings creation into being out of nothing, restricting the divine presence to make room for this created other in the divine dance of *perichoresis*.[13] While God's being transcends this new partner, God takes account of creation's movements and responds to them. Moltmann is even willing to say that God "experiences" creation and is affected by it, grounding his important concept of the Trinitarian history of God's dealings with world.[14] Creation's becoming is *within* God's triune being and becoming.

The second part of this epigram—*God is in the world*—points to Moltmann's portrait of God's immanence in creation. While maintaining the theological "grammar" of creation as by the Father through the Son in the Holy Spirit, he gives most of his attention in *God in Creation* to the activity of the Holy Spirit in continuing creation. Having created the world, God indwells it in the Spirit. The image with which we began this section portrays the Spirit as listening to the Word of the Father in original creation, serving as his efficacious agent. But she then indwells what she has helped create, actively participating in its evolving forms and emergent order.

But how are we to picture the Spirit's participation in continuing creation? Moltmann, along with other contemporary theologians, offers two important models: the Spirit's kenosis in creation and the Spirit's opening of creation to God's future. In a sense, these are the passive and active sides of the Spirit's activity in creation. *Kenosis* in Christian theology refers to the self-emptying of God. Traditionally, theologians have used this concept to describe God's condescension in entering fully into created existence in the incarnation, drawing on Philippians 2:7. Moltmann extends this concept to the activity of the Spirit in continuing creation. The Spirit's indwelling of creation respects its contingent order and freedom. She works within both the regularities and indeterminacies of the created other, even to the point of making herself vulnerable to creation's suffering. The Spirit's suffering with creation is an important theme in *God in Creation*.

The more active side of the Spirit's role in continuing creation is described in terms of her opening of creation to God's future. Modern science no longer pictures the world in terms of the fixed, mechanical "laws" of a closed, Newtonian universe. This is a result of the discovery in physics that matter at the quantum level is characterized by a certain degree of indeterminacy.[15] Instead of fixed laws, science now thinks in terms of open systems, relatively stable "gestalts" of dynamic, interacting parts that are open to new information from the environment. In light of the best available accounts we have of contemporary science, Moltmann argues that we are warranted in interpreting the universe as a whole as an open system. He places this new picture of the world within his trinitarian panentheistic framework:

> The world in its different parts and as a whole is a system open to God. God is its extra-worldly encompassing *milieu*, from which and in which, it lives. God is its extra-worldly *forecourt*, into which it is evolving. God is the origin of the new possibilities out of which its realities are won. We then have to understand God, for his part, as a Being open to the world. He encompasses the world with the possibilities of his Being, and interpenetrates it with the powers of his Spirit. Through the energies of his Spirit, he is present in the world and immanent in each individual system.[16]

By portraying creation as an open system in which the Spirit is actively involved, Moltmann has moved toward a more dynamic understanding of creation and the Spirit's active presence within it. God is not portrayed merely as *preserving* an already completed and static world. Rather, continuing creation is a part of an unfolding, dynamic Theo-drama.

Humans Beings: Created in God's Image

When Charles Darwin's theory of evolution burst on the scene in the 1870s, it drew a response of fear and outrage in many church circles, in part because it contained the "dangerous idea" that human beings share a common ancestry with the animal world. This appeared to represent a direct assault on a central tenet of the Christian tradition: Human beings are created in the image of God. Throughout much of Christian history, the *imago Dei* has been interpreted in terms of the ways human beings are *different* from the animal world. They were portrayed as endowed by their Creator with immortal souls or with reason, free will, conscience, or some other "faculty" that animals do not possess.[17] How are we to think of the *imago Dei* if we take with full seriousness the "naturalization" of human beings, placing them within the unfolding drama of the evolution of the universe? Are we to abandon any notion of human uniqueness? Moltmann's twofold response to these questions is highly creative.

First, he emphasizes the *continuity-within-discontinuity* of human beings' participation in the evolving systems of nature. He portrays human beings as a part of the *community of creation*.[18] They are not the only actors who participate in the Theo-drama of creation. They are part of an ensemble that includes the various systems and species of nature. By portraying human beings as standing in continuity with this community of creation, Moltmann hopes to help the church break free of the anthropocentrism that has sometimes characterized Christian theology and stands at the very heart of the worldview of modernity. The metadrama of the modern way of life has largely cast human beings as the chief actors on the stage of life and portrayed the rest of nature as something to be dominated and exploited for human purposes. To develop an alternative to this anthropocentric drama, Moltmann takes a fresh look at the accounts of creation in Genesis. Contrary to what the church may have taught in the past, the creation stories do not portray human beings as the apex of God's creation. Rather, they portray the Sabbath as the culminating point—God's rest and enjoyment of the created other. Moltmann then places this in an eschatological and messianic framework in light of the messianic "work" of Jesus Christ. *The "end" of creation is the eschatological Sabbath*, when God will indwell fully a transfigured creation and when creation will find perfect repose and enjoyment in God. Humans are not the center of the unfolding Theo-drama of creation. They are part of the community of creation, which is on its way toward God's eschatological Sabbath.

Second, Moltmann describes human uniqueness in terms of the *discontinuity-within-continuity* of an evolutionary perspective. Nature crossed a threshold with the emergence of human beings. While *homo sapiens* are not alone in possessing central nervous systems, they are unique in the complexity of these systems. They are equipped with brains that give rise to human consciousness and culture, which have continued to evolve since the "modern mind" first appeared approximately 60,000 years ago. They represent a new order of freedom and self-transcendence within the open systems of the natural world.

Building on these two moves, Moltmann refashions traditional accounts of the *imago Dei* along two lines. First, he portrays human beings as God's *counterpart* on earth, "the counterpart to whom he [God] wants to talk and who is intended to respond to him."[19] Only human beings have the freedom and self-transcendence necessary to enter into an I-Thou relationship with their Creator. Alone among God's creatures, they are free to "give the seeking love of God the sought-for-response."[20] While they are not the only actors on the stage of life, they have the capacity to receive in freedom and responsibility the role they have been given to play. What is this role?

This leads us to the next move Moltmann makes. He portrays human beings as God's *representatives* on earth. They are stewards of God's creation and are to care for the community of creation in ways that reflect the mutual care and reciprocity of the triune God. Just as the Trinity is not to be understood as a hierarchy in which one of the divine Persons dominates the others but in terms of *perichoretic* relations of equality, mutuality, and interpenetration, so too human beings reflect God's likeness when their stewardship of the earth is characterized by mutual indwelling and care. As Moltmann puts it, "The true human community is designed to be the *imago Trinitatis*."[21] As God's representatives on earth, human beings have a degree of freedom and self-transcendence not found in other systems of life. But along with this freedom comes responsibility. They are to love and care for the community of creation in ways that reflect God's love.

Implications for the Teaching Ministry: Inside the Artist's Studio

Let us pause to reflect on some of the implications of this understanding of creation for the teaching ministry of congregations. Imagine that you have entered the artist's studio of your own teaching ministry. What might you bring into this studio from our conversation with Jürgen Moltmann? One learning is a broader sense of perspective. In painting or drawing, perspective is the presentation on a plane of the spatial relations of objects as they might appear to the eye. Perspective in this sense did not really appear in Western art until the Renaissance.

Moltmann's account of continuing creation as a dynamic, evolving system in which the Holy Spirit is a participant invites us to widen the perspective we bring to our teaching ministries in congregations. We are learning to view this ministry not only in relation to the congregation as a whole but also in terms of the congregation's relationship to God's world. The subject matter and relationships we are learning to see is the congregation in context. Sometimes the perspective we adopt views the congregation in terms of its immediate context—the relationships and events in the local community that impact the church and its members. At other times, we look beyond the local context to broader events, trends, and systems. In either case, we are learning to look at the congregation as part of God's continuing creation, which encompasses all of life and not just the congregation in isolation.

We might make this same point in dramatological terms. Sometimes we think of the Christian drama solely as encompassing the roles and dramatic action that take place *within* the congregation. Moltmann invites us to imagine a Theo-drama in which the ensemble and dramatic action encompasses the world as a whole. If we take seriously his understanding of the Holy Spirit as an active participant in continuing creation, then we begin to realize that God is already out there in the world ahead of us. In our teaching, therefore, we must do more than merely help people learn how to be good church members. We are directors preparing people for roles in a drama that encompasses every part of their lives. At least one of our goals is to help them learn to understand themselves as actors in the drama of continuing creation.

This brings us to a second learning: the challenging nature of teaching contemporary people to view this world as God's creation. Earlier I quoted Moltmann's reminder that modern science has taught us to interpret the world as *nature* but that the church's task is to teach its members how to interpret the world as God's *creation*. We should not underestimate the challenge this represents. From the time they enter school, children are socialized into a scientific worldview that teaches them to view nature as an object to be dominated and exploited. They are taught to live in a disenchanted world in which the dramas of life are construed almost exclusively in terms of human utility. Learning to view this world differently—as God's creation in which the Spirit is present and active—will take nothing less than a conversion of the imagination.

In the face of the all-encompassing impact of modern science and technology on our world, it is especially important for us to teach our students to respect the inherent worth and dignity of the nonhuman species of our planet as members of the community of creation. The world of nature is not merely to be exploited for our own human purposes. It is sacred in God's sight and part of the divine creativity in which we live and move and have our being. We have reached a crisis point in the unfolding drama of our modern scientific, technological civilization. Already whole species are being wiped out, and over the next hundred years the biodiversity of our planet will be radically reduced unless steps are taken now to shape an alternative future.[22] Surely we cannot teach the members of our congregations to affirm God as the "maker of heaven and earth" in worship and then ignore this crisis when they return to everyday life.

These are just a few of the issues Moltmann raises in his portrait of the drama of creation, issues that we would do well to take with us when we enter the artist's studio of our teaching ministries in congregations. Let us continue our conversation with Moltmann and see what else we might learn.

REDEMPTION BY THE SON IN THE SPIRIT TO THE FATHER

We turn now to the second act of this Theo-drama, beginning once more with a series of images. Imagine yourself standing in the lobby of a brightly painted, old theater. The lights blink several times, signaling the end of the first intermission, so you return to your seat for the second act. When the audience has settled down and the lights have dimmed, an old, wizened man comes onto the stage and tells the audience, "In this scene, you are more than spectators. You are perpetrators too. You must leave your seats and step onto the aisle of life. It will take you into the darkness of the stage to see what you will see." A moving sidewalk of the sort commonly found in modern airports suddenly springs into life, running down the center of the stage and disappearing into the darkness at the back.

After an anxious moment, you summon up your courage, walk to the front, step onto the aisle, and travel into darkness. As you move into the void at the back of the stage, it is as if you are suddenly transported into another dimension of time and space. Peering into the darkness ahead, you can make out pools of light emanating from three, dome-like structures facing the moving walkway. As you draw close to the first of these domes, you hear music, a tune you have known since childhood, "All Things Bright and Beautiful." It sounds like carousel music, and the words are sung at a high-pitched, rapid pace by munchkin-like voices.

When the walkway has taken you directly in front of the first lighted area, it stops. You can now peer directly into what appears to be a minitheater. A small platform springs out of the front of the stage, beckoning you to step from the walkway onto the stage itself. When you do so, your senses are suddenly disoriented and your head begins to spin. You lose your balance and fall, only to find yourself sprawled on a carpet of thick green grass. As your senses clear, you look around and discover that you are in a grassy meadow on the side of a hill overlooking a sandy beach. The view is breathtaking, and the warmth of the sun begins to relax your body. As you look toward the ocean, you notice birds circling over one part of the beach. The circular motion reminds you of the heliocentric circles of gold and red particles in the first act of this Theo-drama. "How beautiful," you whisper to yourself.

As the birds begin to swoop toward the beach, your eyes follow their downward path. Suddenly you shudder with horror as you begin to take in the tragedy unfolding before you. Scattered along the beach are the remnants of shells. As the newborn turtles struggle toward the ocean, the diving birds grab them in their claws, swing over jagged rocks, and drop them to their deaths. As each bird releases one of the newborns to smash against the rocks below, it follows the falling turtle downward in a kind of death spiral to prevent another bird from grabbing its mangled prize. Only seven of the thirty who are born make it to the safety of the water.

As this drama comes to an end, you lean back in the grass, drained by the scene you have just witnessed. As you lie there, you feel something crawling gently across your hand. It is a caterpillar, with stripes of yellow and dark brown. As the caterpillar leaves your hand and slowly makes its way through the grass, you are struck by its beauty. Suddenly you become aware of a buzzing sound and glance up to locate its source—a large, swollen wasp. In a slow, circular motion, the wasp descends to the caterpillar and stings it. Almost immediately, the caterpillar is paralyzed, but you can tell that it is not dead because its antennae continue to twitch slightly. Slowly the wasp lays her eggs on top of the caterpillar's back. As you watch, it is as if you have entered a wrinkle in time with events unfolding more quickly than in real time. As the wasp eggs hatch, the larvae begin to devour the paralyzed caterpillar, burrowing their way inward to eat it from the inside out. They are careful to leave the heart and other vital organs for the last, lest the caterpillar decay too soon and spoil their first source of food.

You have been staring at all this in a kind of trance, unable to pull yourself away. Slightly nauseous, you get up from the ground, turn away from the ocean, and suddenly find yourself back on the stage of the minitheater. You step back onto the walkway. As it slowly takes you away, munchkin-like voices echo in your ears:

> All things bright and beautiful,
> All creatures great and small,
> All things wise and wonderful:
> The Lord God made them all.
>
> He gave us eyes to see them,
> And lips that we might tell
> How great is God Almighty,
> Who has made all things well.

Gradually the music fades away, and you travel in silence. Only as you reach the very edge of light emanating from the next dome do you begin to make out a very different sort of music. The music is quite faint at first, but you recognize it immediately. It is Henryk Gorecki's Symphony no. 3—the *Symphony of Sorrowful Songs*. As the moving walkway stops in front of the second minitheater, you recall the texts of lamentation that Gorecki weaves into his own lyrics. The second movement builds on a simple inscription originally scrawled on a Gestapo prison cell wall in 1944 by an eighteen-year-old girl: "Oh, mama, do not cry— Immaculate Queen of Heaven support me always. Hail Mary."[23] In Gorecki's symphony, these words are put in Christ's mouth to answer Mary's plea to her son who is dying on the cross, a plea based on the fourth verse of a fifteenth-century Polish prayer known as the Lamentation of the Holy Cross:[24]

> My son, my chosen and beloved,
> Share your wounds with your mother;
> And because, dear son,
> I have always carried you in my heart,
> And always served you faithfully,
> Speak to your mother, to make her happy,
> Although you are already leaving me,
> my cherished hope.

This music has always moved you. But now, as the end of the second movement nears, you are filled with a deep sense of dread. A small platform springs out of the front of the minitheater, and as you step onto it, the platform suddenly drops slightly, leading you to look downward momentarily as you catch your balance. When you look up, the stage has been transformed into a kind of courtroom. As you watch the proceedings from your vantage point at the rear, you realize that this is not a court of law. The commissioners seated at a long table at the front and presiding over the proceedings are not judges; the people testifying are not cross-examined but are gently urged to tell their stories. Sometimes the people who are presiding weep as the witnesses speak. But strangest of all, television monitors are located all around the large room where a large crowd is seated. As the witnesses tell their stories, the events they are describing mysteriously appear on the TV screens.

Commissioner: You were a leader of a student group that was organizing protests against the government's educational policies in the late 1970s?

Witness: Yes. We were being forced to learn all our subjects in Afrikaans. We might have known English and Xhosa or some other language. Nobody spoke Afrikaans where I lived.

Commissioner: Tell us what happened. Tell us your story.

Witness: I was first picked up by the security branch while protesting at school and ended up in Queenstown. They kept asking me about Mr. Sondlo, claiming that he was trying to promote the aims of the ANC. I told him I was part of a student organization and knew nothing about this. This happened to me every day for almost three months. Sometimes they would beat me and pull plastic bags over my face. One day they took me from my cell in the afternoon after dressing me in police camouflage and putting a balaclava over my face. They drove me to some place—I don't know where—and took me out of the police van. They began asking me the same old questions and said they'd shoot me if I didn't tell them what I knew. They said they'd tell the public that I had run away from the police station a long time ago and had come back as a well-trained ANC terrorist. One of the security men moved about twenty meters from me and pointed a gun at me. But I told him that I didn't have any information for them. He shot at my feet, but I still was silent. Finally, they took me back to the station and I was kept in solitary confinement for about two more months. Later I was part of a group of eleven people charged with terrorism, but three of us were set free after the trial because they didn't have any evidence against us.

Commissioner: Then what happened?

Witness: I started working in my student organization again. After several months, I was picked up again. They asked me to become their informer and told me I would be paid for this work. I told them I was not looking for employment, that I was a student. So they released me. Several weeks later, I heard from some of the other leaders of my organization that they had been paid a visit by the security police. One of the police dropped a receipt during the visit for six hundred rand with my signature on it. Some of the leaders thought I had become an informer; others thought it was a trick. Word got out in the community, and I was humiliated. I had to lie low for a long time because I didn't want to be necklaced.

This witness continues his story and then the commission breaks for lunch. When it reconvenes, two women come to the front, a grandmother (GM) and a granddaughter (GD), who begins to tell the story of her mother's death.

Commissioner: How did you find out that your mother was dead?

GD: I received a telegram from my grandmother that my mother had passed away. She had been burned to death. (*Begins to weep.*) For a long time, we didn't know what had happened. We heard that they were looking for my uncle, who was a policeman, and when they couldn't find him, they took my mother instead. Others said it was because she bought meat at a butcher shop during a boycott; others said she was an informer. She was pregnant when this happened.

Commissioner: How did you find out what happened?

GM: We found a man who was there.

Commissioner: Is he here?

GM: Yes. (*Man comes forward.*)

Commissioner: Can you tell us what happened?

As the man begins to talk, you watch the events unfold on the TV monitor near the back of the room. You see a woman walking by herself down a dusty street. Five young men emerge from a side street and begin to follow her. She suddenly runs into a nearby house, but they drag her back into the street, calling out in loud voices: "Informer! Informer!" They force her to the ground, kicking and beating her, and then pull off her clothes. While three of them hold her down, the others begin to pour gasoline over her naked body. (You hear the sobs of the grandmother and granddaughter in the background.) They jerk the woman roughly to her feet and necklace her, jamming a tire over her head and onto her body, which holds her arms tight. After pouring more gasoline over the tire, they set her on fire. The woman stumbles back and forth in the street, crying out: "Help me! Somebody, please help me!" Some in the crowd reach out to her, but the young men push them back, saying she is an informer. At last the police arrive and load her into the back of a van. She is alive and still conscious.

GM: They took her to a hospital, and she lived for three days. After she died, we were told that we couldn't bury her in Colesberg, where she was from. They threatened to burn down the church if she were buried there, because they thought she was an informer.

GD: We can tell you this story, but this is a wound that will never heal.

As the story continues, you close your eyes, resting your forehead on your left hand. Slowly the voices fade away and you find yourself standing alone on the stage. You step back onto the walkway, which gently begins to move, taking you out of the pool of light. As you pass into darkness, the music of the third movement of Gorecki's *Symphony of Sorrows* begins to play. The lyrics accompanying this music are based on a Polish folk song, which reads in part:[25]

> Where has he gone,
> My dearest son?
> Perhaps during the uprising
> The guards killed him.
> Ah, you bad people,
> In the name of God, the most Holy,
> Tell me, why you killed
> My son . . .
> He lies in his grave
> And I know not where
> Though I keep asking people
> Everywhere.
> Perhaps, the poor child
> Lies in a rough ditch
> And instead he could have been
> Lying in his warm bed.

As the moving walkway draws near to the last pool of light, your apprehension grows. Nonetheless, as the walkway comes to a stop, you peer into the third and final minitheater. Standing in the center of the stage surrounded by a semicircle of children sitting on the floor is a beautiful woman. She appears to be telling them a story. Her translucent gown and face remind you immediately of the lone actor to appear in the first act of this Theo-drama. As the moving walkway comes to a halt, the woman stops her storytelling and looks directly into your eyes. "Two questions," she says, "will help you decide whether to return for the final act. Do you still love the fantasy stories written for children? Do you long for justice in this world of evil, or is your heart too numbed by what you have seen and done?" Without waiting for your reply, she turns back to her storytelling, and the walkway begins to move. Suddenly it drops away, and you find yourself falling down a chute, which gently drops you to one side of the theater lobby.

Beyond Evolution

While the above images are my own, they are based on true accounts of events that have taken place in our world.[26] They bring us face to face with the suffering of creation—the suffering of nature and the suffering that humans inflict upon one another. In light of our dialogue with evolutionary thinking in the first act of this Theo-drama, it is especially important to begin this second act with the realities of suffering and evil before us. In the past century, the religious education theorists most attuned to evolutionary thinking often drew on this framework to eliminate what they portrayed as the "pessimistic" side of Christianity. In George Albert Coe's *A Social Theory of Religious Education*, for example, human sin is reduced to the remediable flaws of social systems; the eschatological kingdom of God is transformed into the personalizing and democratizing processes of history; the cross of Christ becomes an example of prophetic human love. Moltmann's assessment of the evolutionary theology of Teilhard de Chardin is equally applicable to Coe and religious educators who followed his lead:

> Teilhard does seem to have overlooked the ambiguity of evolution itself, and therefore to have paid no attention to evolution's victims. Evolution always means *selection*. Many living things are sacrificed in order that "the fittest"—which means the most effective and the most adaptable—may survive. In this way higher and increasingly complex life systems . . . develop. But in the same process milliards of living things fall by the wayside and disappear into evolution's rubbish bin. Evolution is not merely a constructive affair on nature's part. It is a cruel one too. It is a kind of biological execution of the Last Judgment on the weak, the sick and the "unfit."[27]

When Teilhard, Coe, and others gloss over the suffering of nature and humanity in evolution, they eliminate the need for its redemption. As Moltmann puts it, "A *Christus evolutor* without *Christus redemptor* is nothing more than a cruel, unfeeling *Christus selector*, a historical world-judge without compassion for the weak, and a breeder of life uninterested in the victims."[28]

If you grew up in the church, perhaps, you too learned to sing "All Things Bright and Beautiful" as a child. Its highly idealized picture of the natural world ignores the fact that nature is littered with the mangled bodies of baby turtles and with the desiccated skins of caterpillars devoured alive by the larvae of wasps. Human history also is filled with stories of suffering and evil like those offered above based on transcripts of the proceedings of South Africa's Truth and Reconciliation Commission. Where is God in the face of the suffering of nature and human history? Ultimately, I believe, we will find him where Gorecki points us: on the cross, killed by the guards as part of the uprising, and lying unknown in a rough ditch, instead of lying, as he might, in a warm bed. Only a God who has entered fully into the suffering of the world—enduring the transience of nature and the cruelty of human history—is capable of offering us a compelling and loving redemption.

The Entry of the Son of God into the Theater of the World

Every serious drama has its climactic scene: Themes converge; the true nature of the characters is revealed; the end comes into view. So it is with the entry of God's Son into the theater of the world. This is the climactic moment in the history of the triune God's dealings with the world, for it deals with God's redemption.

The etymological roots of the term *redemption* are to buy back or purchase the freedom of someone in captivity. In the Greco-Roman world, it often was used to describe the payment made to gain a slave's freedom. Moltmann uses this term quite broadly to refer to Christ's work as freeing creation from suffering, sin, and death. His understanding of Christ's redemption is holistic in two ways. First, it includes nature as well as human history, the human body as well as the mind and spirit. Second, it encompasses not only the reconciliation of those who are estranged but also the healing of those who are afflicted, the freeing of those who are in bondage, and the "softening" of those who are hard-hearted. Redemption in its fullness, thus, is eschatological. It will only be completed with Christ's parousia and the transformation of this world into a new creation.

A German who became a Christian in a prisoner of war camp during World War II, Moltmann has wrestled from the beginning with issues of collective guilt, the human capacity for evil, and God's apparent indifference to massive human suffering. In his first two major books, *A Theology of Hope* and *The Crucified God*, he began to develop an account of redemption that focused primarily on the relationship of the cross and resurrection.[29] I do not believe that Moltmann has moved away from the fundamental insights formed during this period, even though he has deepened and broadened this early understanding of redemption over the course of his later writings.

In both of these early books, Moltmann describes Christ's redemption of creation in terms of a *dialectical* relationship between the cross and resurrection.[30] Think of this in dramatological terms. If Christ's entry into the theater of the world represents the central act of this Theo-drama, then the decisive and climactic scenes of this act are his death and resurrection. To describe these two scenes as dialectically related is to see them as *opposites that contradict one another.* In his death on the cross, Jesus identifies with the present reality of the world in all of its negativity—its subjection to sin, suffering, and death. In God's resurrection of Jesus from the dead, the promise of the eschatological kingdom shines forth—when sin, suffering, and death will be annihilated and God will be "all in all."[31] Redemption encompasses both of these scenes: God's full and complete entry into the conditions of a world suffering in sin and death and God's resurrection of Jesus to new life, as the firstborn of the new creation.

Moltmann makes use of this dialectical pattern in a particularly interesting way in *The Crucified God*, portraying the significance of Christ's death in much broader terms than do atonement theologies that focus primarily on the forgiveness of individual sin. He addresses the systemic dimensions of evil and sin and portrays Jesus as dying the death of all people who are the victims of these systems.[32] Jesus is executed as a *rebel* by the political authorities; he is condemned as a *blasphemer* who abrogates the law by the dominant religious authorities; he dies as one who is *forsaken* by God, crying out to his Father, "My God, my God, why have you forsaken me?" (Mark 15:34). In his suffering and death on the cross, Moltmann argues, the Son of God participates fully in the suffering of human history in an act of loving solidarity with its victims. Moreover, the Father suffers the loss of his only begotten Son. In the mutual surrender of the Son and Father, the suffering of this world is taken into the very life of God.

In the first act of this Theo-drama, we observed the kenosis of the Spirit in creation, how she respects the contingent freedom and regularities of the created other. Unless we are willing to adopt a model of providence in which God "over-rules" this contingent freedom (ultimately making God directly responsible for evil and suffering), then we must accept natural and human suffering as part of finite existence and view the human capacity to inflict evil as the distorted outcome of this contingent freedom.

Whatever else the suffering and death of Christ might mean, however, it is clear that God is not indifferent to the victims of history, a passive spectator sitting on the heavenly sidelines. God in Jesus Christ has entered fully into this suffering and made it his own. Redemption initially takes its bearings from this suffering love. We can trust the love of God because we know the extent to which God is willing to go to share in our plight. When we turn to the next scene of redemption—God's resurrection of Jesus from the dead—we now understand why Moltmann describes the resurrection as standing in a dialectical relationship to the cross. What God has suffered—the evil and transience of creation—God has now overcome. As the firstborn of the new creation, the resurrected Christ is the embodied promise of God's ultimate triumph over sin and death.

Moltmann does not abandon this dialectical pattern in his later treatment of Christ's redemption of creation in *The Way of Jesus Christ*, but he modifies it in three important ways. First, he portrays the redemptive mission of Christ not only in terms of the dialectical *contradiction* of the cross and resurrection but also in terms of the way Christ's messianic life *anticipates* and *corresponds* to God's promised future.[33] Without softening his recognition of the realities of suffering and evil, he begins to explore more fully the ways redemptive possibilities of new creation can break into the present under the conditions of an unredeemed world. This leads him to place greater emphasis on Jesus' earthly ministry as an embodiment of these possibilities and to explore the ways the church (and other institutions) can participate in these redemptive possibilities in anticipatory and provisional ways.

Second, Moltmann pays greater attention to the suffering of nature, which leads him to accentuate the cosmic dimensions of redemption. Human beings are not the only ones in need of God's redemption; the whole of creation suffers and groans under the transience of life. Today, moreover, nature suffers greatly at the hands of human beings, who treat it as an object to be exploited or even eradicated merely to serve human purposes.

Third, Moltmann extends his account of the storyline of redemption beyond the cross and resurrection. He develops the image of the "way" of Jesus Christ to describe the drama of his redemption. The scenes of this part of the Theo-drama are now extended backward to include Christ's public ministry and forward to his parousia:

Scene One: Jesus' Messianic Ministry—As the Messiah, Jesus brings near God's coming kingdom in his proclamation of glad tidings to the poor, his forgiveness of the guilty, his healing of the sick, and his acceptance of social outcasts.[34] This is one of the most important ways that Moltmann develops the theme of anticipation in his Christology. Jesus' public ministry anticipates the liberation, reconciliation, and healing of creation that the final redemption of the consummation will bring.

Scene Two: Jesus' Apocalyptic Suffering and Death—Focusing on the apocalyptic nature of Christ's death, Moltmann now emphasizes its cosmic scope, which includes his suffering in solidarity with nature as well as the victims of human history.[35] His death represents the "trials and tribulations" of the end time, marking the end of transient and suffering creation and the birth pangs of the new creation.

Scene Three: Jesus' Eschatological Resurrection—In his treatment of the resurrection, Moltmann retains the dialectical pattern of cross and resurrection found in his earlier writings. The cross is a historical event; the resurrection is an eschatological event. As such, Jesus' resurrection is the splendor and beauty cast ahead of the coming glory of God. It is the "preliminary radiance" of the imminent dawn of God's new creation, pointing us toward the future of life and the "freeing of human beings and the whole sighing creation from the forces of annihilation and death."[36]

Scene Four: The Lordship of Christ—Following his resurrection and ascension to the right hand of the Father, Christ reigns as the Lord of creation. What is new and important in Moltmann's description of this part of the drama of redemption is the continuity he now draws between the messianic shape of Jesus' earthly ministry and his postresurrection lordship, with important implications for his picture of the community of disciples living under Christ's lordship. God's reign, as it is effected through Jesus' messianic ministry, comes up against conflict, contradiction, and contention because it calls into question the world's status quo. The fact that this ministry will ultimately defeat evil and transform the present world is hidden. So too, Christ's postresurrection lordship remains hidden from the world. The community of disciples who live under the rule of the risen Lord is called to embody the same anticipation-in-contradiction of Jesus' earthly ministry. They are to serve as a "contrast society" that "calls into question the world's systems of violence and injustice."[37]

Scene Five: Christ's Parousia—In his treatment of Christ's parousia in *The Way of Jesus Christ*, Moltmann begins to deal with themes he takes up more fully in *The Coming of God*. Jesus Christ is on his way to the promised redemption of the world. Though sin and death have been defeated, redemption in its fullness remains an eschatological hope. Only when the king returns will this part of the Theo-drama be played out.

The Congregation: A Community of Christopraxis

Throughout *The Way of Jesus Christ*, Moltmann describes the congregation as a community of disciples engaging in *Christopraxis,* that is, the praxis of a community that participates in Jesus' mission of redemption. He describes the church as a "contrast society" that struggles to hold before the world a way of life that is an alternative to its systems of sin and death. Moltmann does not, however, develop these ecclesiological themes systematically in this book, especially in comparison to his earlier treatment of the church in *The Church in the Power of the Spirit*. In this section, thus, I will draw on both of these books to develop a theology of congregations.[38] We will do well to keep in mind the nomenclature from the discussion of Reinhard Hütter's *Suffering Divine Things* in chapter 4. Following Hütter, I defined *praxis* as the comprehensive way of life of a community, and *practices* as the discrete, tradition-bearing patterns of action that give concrete shape and form to its praxis. I also distinguished between *core* and *mediating* practices. The former describe practices that are constitutive of a congregation's very being as the church; the latter are local or regional practices only found in some contexts.

In *The Church in the Power of the Spirit*, Moltmann develops his ecclesiology in conjunction with a highly creative reworking of the traditional Reformed doctrine of the *munus triplex*, a way of looking at the "work" or "mission" of Christ in terms of his threefold office as prophet, priest, and king. Looking at Moltmann's reworking of the *munus triplex* will provide a helpful link between his Christology in *The Way of Jesus Christ* and his fuller description of the church in *The Church in the Power of the Spirit*. An important part of Moltmann's reappropriation of the *munus triplex* is his addition of two new dimensions to his description of Christ's mission: Christ as transfigured humanity and Christ as friend. Thus, we find correspondence between Christ's work of redemption and congregations' participation in this work:

Christ's Fivefold Office	Congregational Christopraxis
Prophetic	*Marturia*
Priestly	*Diakonia*
Transfigured	*Doxology*
Royal	*Didache*
Open fellowship	*Koinonia*

While this fivefold office of Christ in *The Church in the Power of the Spirit* does not precisely parallel Moltmann's treatment of the five dimensions of Christ's "way" in *The Way of Jesus Christ*, I find enough similarities to warrant a reworking of this concept to bring it in line with his later Christology. My purpose here is twofold: (1) to provide a christologically grounded, normative perspective on the Christopraxis of congregations; and (2) to offer an account of the core practices of congregations that embodies this Christopraxis. As I take up each aspect of Christ's mission of redemption, thus, I relate it to a corresponding dimension of congregational Christopraxis and the core practices associated with this dimension.

The prophetic dimension of Christ's mission lies at the heart of Jesus' *messianic, earthly ministry* and points to Jesus' *announcement of the glad tidings* of the dawn of God's reign. Jesus is the long-awaited Messiah who brings the good news of God's seeking, forgiving love to a world in captivity to sin, suffering, and death. To the victims of the world's systems of violence, this good news brings divine acceptance, dignity, and the promise of freedom. To the perpetrators and beneficiaries of systems of injustice and evil, it brings a call to repentance and conversion to a new way of life.

Those who respond in faith to Jesus' prophetic announcement of joyful tidings are commissioned to serve as witnesses. I use the term *marturia* to refer to this dimension of the congregation's Christopraxis. Core practices that embody *marturia* in congregations are (1) kerygmatic preaching—the proclamation of the gospel in the context of worship; (2) testimony—the communication of the gospel in personal forms of sharing; and (3) evangelism—witnessing to the gospel to those outside the community of faith.

The priestly dimension of Christ's mission focuses on Christ's self-giving love, which frees the world from sin and death and sets it in a right relationship with God. While this encompasses the entirety of Christ's incarnation and earthly ministry, it culminates in his *apocalyptic death on the cross.* Not only does Jesus suffer in solidarity with the victims of history, but he also dies the death of all transient, mortal life. In his self-giving love on the cross, he takes into the life of God the suffering of history and nature, as well as the guilt of human sin, and overcomes them.

The Christopraxis of the community of disciples that follows Christ on his way to the cross opens itself to the suffering of the world and voluntarily shares in this suffering. It is active suffering that seeks to break the grip of systems of violence and oppression and to allow the light of the new creation to break in. I refer to this dimension of the Christopraxis of congregations as *diakonia*: self-giving service in the name of Christ that opens itself in solidarity to the pain and suffering of the world. Core practices that embody *diakonia* in the congregation are: (1) Eucharist—the ritual in which the congregation recalls and gives thanks for Christ's self-giving love on the cross; (2) burden bearing—the congregation's care of its members in times of pain and need; and (3) social outreach—ministries of service and advocacy that provide concrete help to those in need and advocate their cause in the face of social injustice.

The dimension of transfiguration in Christ's mission points to the glory and beauty of *Christ's eschatological resurrection*, which Moltmann typically treats in aesthetic categories.[39] Christ's transfiguration in the resurrection points to the radiance of his glorified body and his transformation from the form of a slave, crushed in death, into the divine beauty of one who lives in eternal life. As the transfigured one, he is the embodied promise of the new creation.

I refer to this dimension of Christopraxis as *doxology*, participation in the transfiguration of the risen Christ through the praise and enjoyment of God. Core practices of doxology are (1) Sabbath keeping—setting aside a day of "rest" for the worship and enjoyment of God; (2) the praise of God through music, prayer, psalmody, song, dance, poetry, and other forms of creative self-expression in the context of the gathered community; and (3) recreation—activities affording the enjoyment of God's creation and the development of the individual's creative gifts through play, the arts, and so forth.

The royal dimension of Christ's mission focuses on the eschatological *Lordship of the risen and exalted Christ,* which stands in continuity with the reign of God as it was redefined in Jesus' earthly ministry. It entails a radical reversal of our conventional notions of royal rule, for it does not primarily take the form of command/obedience. The Lord is the servant of all. His "rule" takes the form of persuasion, teaching, and example, giving his disciples the time and space to grow in their understanding of his messiahship and their own roles in his mission.

I view the Christopraxis of congregations that corresponds with Christ's lordship in terms of *didache,* the teaching and learning through which the congregation deepens its understanding of and participation in Christ's messianic way of life. Congregations are communities that grow in faith, hope, and love. Core practices of *didache* are those described in the first part of this book: (1) catechesis—handing on Christian Scripture and tradition; (2) exhortation—moral formation and education that enables the congregation to serve as a "contrast society"; and (3) discernment—learning to "test" the spirits to determine the guiding light of the Holy Spirit.

The open friendship and fellowship of Christ's mission as it is treated in Moltmann's creative reworking of the *munus triplex* does not, at first glance, appear to correspond to any facet of the Christology he sets forth in *The Way of Jesus Christ.* This is largely because he describes this theme in terms of Jesus' public friendship and fellowship meals with tax collectors and sinners. Upon further reflection, however, it is not difficult to see how central this is to Moltmann's treatment of *Christ's parousia.* As we have seen, his social doctrine of the Trinity portrays the three divine Persons as an open fellowship—open to the creation of the world, open to "experiencing" the world in its unfolding, and open to the perfecting and completing of the world in the consummation. The open fellowship of Jesus' public friendship with tax collectors and sinners, thus, points us to the periochoretic community at the heart of the triune God. In the time of creation, the world's participation in this fellowship is indirect, because God "restricts" the divine presence to give creation its own time and space; at the consummation, participation will be direct, for God will be "all in all."

I describe this dimension of Christopraxis in terms of *koinonia,* the fellowship of the congregation as a community and its fellowship and dialogue with its partners in history. Across his various writings, Moltmann has described the periochoretic fellowship of the triune God as a model for human communities, taking the form of equality and mutuality in love. Core practices that embody *koinonia* are (1) baptism—initiation into the fellowship of the community; (2) the affirmation of spiritual gifts—the identification and nurture of the *charismata* of all members of the community; and (3) hospitality—extending to strangers kindness usually reserved for friends and family and demonstrating goodwill in the public sphere through open dialogue with the church's non-Christian partners in history.

The following table summarizes the preceding discussion:

Congregational Christopraxis	Core Practices
Marturia	Preaching, testimony, evangelism
Diakonia	Eucharist, burden bearing, social outreach
Doxology	Sabbath keeping, praise, recreation
Didache	Catechesis, exhortation, discernment
Koinonia	Baptism, affirmation of spiritual gifts, hospitality

Implications for the Teaching Ministry: Inside the Artist's Studio

Why is it important in one's leadership of congregations to draw on a normative perspective of the sort I have offered above? There is one basic reason: A normative theology of the congregation affords a perspective with which to assess the relative strengths and weaknesses of the Christopraxis of one's own congregation. If some of the core practices are missing or distorted beyond recognition, then it is quite likely that the congregation's identity and mission will be at risk in certain ways. We need a normative framework to test critically the adequacy of our congregation's Christopraxis. While I make no claim to have developed the one definitive account of the core practices of the congregation—recall the alternative perspectives offered by Reinhard Hütter, John Howard Yoder, and Richard Foster that are described in chapter 4—I do believe that critical theological reflection on the practices of a congregation is a key task of congregational leadership.

GLORIFICATION BY THE SPIRIT THROUGH THE SON TO THE FATHER

Let us begin by picking up the story line of the images with which we began the second act of this Theo-drama. Imagine yourself standing in the lobby of the theater waiting for the final act to begin. Your attention is gently drawn to the music playing in the background. You know this song; it's Roberta Flack singing "Killing Me Softly." The song is about a person who goes to hear a nightclub singer and experiences a shock of recognition while listening to the lyrics of the music, which seem to be telling the story of her own painful relationships. You hum the words of the chorus along with her.

The lights blink off and on, and the music follows you as you move toward the entrance of the theater. As you enter, you are handed a pair of cardboard glasses like the 3–D glasses used in the 1950s. When all audience members have returned to their seats, the old man from the second act reappears. "In a moment," he says, "a screen will descend to the stage. Put on your glasses, for each one of you will see what only you need to see. Prepare to enter the zone of soft killing in order to receive the greater gift of real healing. Prepare to be blessed!" As he exits the stage, a huge flat-screen monitor is slowly lowered to the stage. You put on your glasses and begin to peer into it.

As images gradually begin to take shape, you let out a small gasp, and then a smile comes across your face. There you are once more in the backyard of the house where you lived while a graduate student. You are pushing your four-year-old son on his swing set. "Higher, Daddy," he calls out in glee. With all the nimbleness and daring of a preschooler, he jumps out of the swing at its highest point, lands on his feet, races across the yard, and grabs a light saber that is lying on the ground. "Prepare to defend yourself, Darth Vader," he calls out. You quickly grab a stick lying at your feet and ready yourself to be cast down by the goodness of the rebel force rushing toward you through the warm Georgia air.

The scene dissolves, and a rush of images of you and your son come in and out of focus. He scores the winning goal in the overtime of a soccer game, and you jump for joy. You are running together along the wide sandy beaches of South Carolina. One image lingers a bit. He is now a high school student and asking you what you think about Plato's *Sophist*. He is not reading this for school but for a book club that he and his friends have formed. Again, you smile. The images continue to flash by, taking you in and out of memories—until at last tragedy strikes. These scenes are too painful for you ever to forget. There you are in that old car, having just picked your son up at the airport for spring break during his freshman year of college. He babbles on incoherently about the fast he has been on for the past month and all sorts of ideas that make no sense. This scene gives way to a dark office where you and your wife sit while the doctor tells you that your son suffers from schizophrenia. He is very sorry, but he does not think your son can handle college right now or maybe ever. In rapid succession, images of your son pacing back and forth come in and out of focus—in the ward of a psychiatric hospital, in your home, in the lobby of a movie theater. As tears run down your cheeks, you hear others crying softly as they relive their own personal tragedies.

But then something strange and wonderful happens. The monitor blinks and every single person in the theater draws in a deep breath. Through your glasses, a new and different scene slowly begins to take form. This is nothing from your past. The colors are more vivid and the scene more real. You are standing with your son in a small circle of men and women. They are dressed in the clothing of people from many historical periods and cultures and are talking together in an intense but good-natured way. As you overhear their conversation, your son turns to an older man, dressed in the garb of the ancient Greeks, his countenance not altogether handsome, and asks him, "Tell me, Socrates. Did Plato really get it right? Did you really have all those questions about the sophists? And what do you think now that you know the truth?" As Socrates smiles and begins to answer, you smile with him, and the scene slowly dissolves.

The old man reappears at the side of the stage and tells the audience to remove their glasses. "Join me now for two endings," he says. "Perhaps you know them. But even if you are unfamiliar with the stories they bring to a close, you will know enough to understand. After all, they point ahead to the ending of us all and the new beginning too." The stage begins to rotate. When it stops, a man is sitting alone with a bare wooden cross for company. He sings:

> Alone I wait in shadows
> I count the hours till I can sleep
> . . . God on high
> Hear my prayer
> Take me now
> To thy care
> Where You are
> Let me be
> Take me now
> Take me there
> Bring me home
> Bring me home.

You know this ending. It comes at the close of *Les Misérables*, the musical based on Victor Hugo's novel. It tells the story of Jean Valjean, who learns the meaning of grace through an unmerited act of kindness by a bishop from whom he has stolen precious silver candlesticks. Over the course of this drama, Valjean gradually comes to embody the power of forgiveness and self-giving love beyond the harsh and unrelenting rule of law. The play also gives expression to the yearnings of the poor and of idealistic youth for freedom and justice in prerevolutionary France. The scene described above comes near the end of the play, as Valjean nears his death. He is joined on stage by the spirits of two characters who died at earlier points in the play, Fantine and Eponine. They also embody self-giving love even as their lives are broken on the rack of poverty and political repression. The spirit of Fantine sings to Valjean:

> Come with me
> Where chains will never bind you
> All your grief
> At last, at last, behind you
> Lord in Heaven
> Look down on him in mercy.

Valjean responds:

> Forgive me all my trespasses
> And take me to your glory.

The three characters then sing together:

> Take my hand
> And lead me to salvation
> Take my love
> For love is everlasting
> And remember

The truth that once was spoken,
To love another person
Is to see the face of God.

The drama ends with a chorus, which is sung by the entire ensemble to a musical motif that has been associated with revolutionary aspirations throughout the play. It goes in part:

Do you hear the people sing
Lost in the valley of the night?
It is the music of a people
Who are climbing to the light.
For the wretched of the earth
There is a flame that never dies.
Even the darkest night will end
And the sun will rise.

They will live again in freedom
In the garden of the Lord.
They will walk behind the plough-share.
They will put away the sword.
The chain will be broken
And all men will have their reward.

Will you join in our crusade?
Who will be strong and stand with me?
Somewhere beyond the barricade
Is there a world you long to see?
Do you hear the people sing
Say, do you hear the distant drums?
It is the future that they bring
When tomorrow comes!

As this final chorus ends, the stage slowly begins to rotate, taking the actors out of view. When it has completed its half-revolution, the lovely woman who has appeared in each scene of this Theo-drama stands in the center of the stage. When you last saw her, she was reading to a group of children, and this is what she is doing now. She is reading from *The Last Battle*, the final book in C. S. Lewis's *Chronicles of Narnia* series. She is not at the very end of the story but quite near it. The characters have seen the end of their old world of Narnia and passed through a door into a new one. They suddenly realize that this new world is like the old Narnia they have always known, but it is unlike it in many ways as well. The audience overhears the woman reading to the children:

It was the Unicorn who summed up what everyone was feeling. He stamped his right fore-hood on the ground and neighed and then cried: "I have come home at last! This is my real country! I belong here. This is the land I have been looking for all my life, though I never knew it till now. The reason why we loved the old Narnia is that it sometimes looked a little like this. Bree-hee-hee! Come further up, come further in!"[40]

At the end of this passage, the woman looks up and says to the children and to the audience as well: "Good children's stories, like good art, can help us imagine things that are not easy to see or believe. This story helps us imagine the new beginning of our world that God will one day bring. It will be like entering the land we've always longed for. All suffering and injustice will come to an end. God will heal and forgive and redeem all things. This is a great mystery. Until that day, I will be with you even though you will not be able to see me. If you let me, I will help you remember God's promise of a new beginning." She pauses and smiles, "Well, that's enough for now. Let's finish the rest of this story. I wonder what else Aslan has in store for them?" As the woman begins to read, the stage slowly turns, taking the group out of sight. The curtain falls, and the images of this Theo-drama come to an end.

The Holy Spirit and the Glorification of God

In the previous section, I described the congregation as a community of Christo-praxis. My task now is to describe it as a community that lives in the fellowship of the Holy Spirit. Here again, we will enter into a dialogue with Jürgen Molt-mann, particularly his thinking about the Holy Spirit in *The Spirit of Life*. One of the most important ways Moltmann describes the work of the Holy Spirit in the world is with the theme of the glorification of God. Throughout Scripture, the glory of the Lord is used in a wide variety of ways to depict the splendor, beauty, and majesty of God's revealed presence in nature and history.[41] Molt-mann's use of glorification reflects this diversity in Scripture. Sometimes he uses glorification as a *comprehensive* way of describing the work of the Holy Spirit.[42] At other points, he uses it to describe *one facet* of the Christian life: the praise and enjoyment of God for God's own sake. In this second line of thinking, glorifica-tion (or transfiguration) is portrayed in aesthetic categories and is contrasted to the ethical dimensions of the Christian life.[43]

In the remainder of this chapter, I follow the first line of Moltmann's think-ing, using glorification comprehensively to describe the Spirit's work of gather-ing, uniting, and freeing God's creation in ways that anticipate the radiance, beauty, and splendor of the new creation. I reserve his second line of thinking—the praise and enjoyment of God for God's own sake—to descriptions of *dox-ology* as outlined in my discussion of Christopraxis in the previous section. I am particularly interested in Moltmann's depiction of our experience of the Spirit within the experiences of life. This opens up a new perspective on one of the more troubling impasses of American Protestant Christian education in the past century.

Over the course of the twentieth century, Christian education in mainline Protestant congregations was caught on the horns of a dilemma.[44] On the one hand, it was deeply influenced by progressive education as this was mediated to the church by the religious education movement. This approach to education placed great emphasis on learning through experience, leading educators to emphasize the active participation of the learner in the construction of knowledge and the importance of using pedagogies that drew on students' experience and helped them to reflect on it. "Transmission" models of Christian education were viewed with deep suspicion. On the other hand, during the middle of the twentieth century some Christian education theorists reacted strongly against this approach. Under the influence of European crisis theology and American Christian realism, they argued that the study of Scripture and Christian tradition are central to Christian education. For example, James Smart, under the influence of Karl Barth, contended that the Word of God cannot be derived from human experience. God's Word entered the world in a unique and unsurpassable way in the incarnation of Jesus Christ, and this Word continues to break into our experience through the preaching and teaching of the church. The religious education movement's preoccupation with present experience was seen as cutting the church off from the collective wisdom of its own traditions and from hearing the living Word of God through the proclamation of the church based on Scripture's portrait of Jesus, the early church, and Israel.

In their extreme forms, these two perspectives presented Christian educators with a choice. They could either focus on present human experience—making the issues currently facing individuals and societies the central subject matter and drawing on pedagogies that actively engage students in the construction of knowledge—or they could focus on the Word of God—by making Scripture and Christian tradition the determinant content of Christian education and using pedagogies that cultivate knowledge of these subject matters. In what follows, I will explore the ways Moltmann's theology can help us find a place in Christian education for *both* our experience of the Spirit within the experiences of life *and* our encounter of God's Word as it is mediated through the special events of God's history with Israel and in Jesus Christ. As Moltmann puts it:

> There are no words of God without human experiences of God's Spirit. So the words of proclamation spoken by the Bible and the church must also be related to the experiences of people today. . . . But this is only possible if Word and Spirit are seen as existing in a *mutual relationship,* not as a one-way street.[45]

I will describe Moltmann's account of the Spirit's role in the Christian life in two steps: first, a summary of his understanding of experience within a trinitarian panentheistic framework; second, an account of "signs" of the Spirit's presence in human experience, giving special attention to congregations.

Experiences of the Spirit within the Experiences of Life

Moltmann develops his account of human experience on the basis of certain assumptions that are grounded in his theological anthropology. The most important of these is his depiction of human beings as "beings-in-relation." Human beings move and live and have their being within the community of creation.

They do not merely *have* relations; they *are* their relations. Their very selves are constituted by their transactions with the world. In large measure, Moltmann develops this picture of human beings to counter the philosophy of consciousness that dominates the intellectual traditions of the modern West and the anthropocentrism of our contemporary scientific and technological culture.[46] Both place the human subject—especially the knowing subject—at the center of experience. Moltmann is particularly critical of the modern tendency to generalize the model of experience found in the empirical sciences. As he puts it, "Experiment puts nature on the rack, in order to extort her secrets from her and make her compliant. The concept of experience is reduced to the domination of nature, and nature is dominated so that she may be of utility for human life."[47]

This should give us pause at pragmatism's understanding of experience, particularly as it was developed in the educational philosophy of John Dewey, which had an enormous impact on the religious education movement and continues to be important in mainline Protestant Christian education.[48] While Dewey's educational theory shares certain features of Moltmann's relational and transactional view of human beings, he develops this in the direction of problem-solving reason, which is portrayed as lying at the heart of the modern experimental sciences. "Having" an experience is triggered by the advent of a problematic situation, which subsequently is "developed" through a series of steps that mirror the processes of experimental reason. Experience, thus, is narrowed sharply in the direction of "reflective" experience, oriented toward providing human beings with greater control over the "problems" of life.

To counter this sort of truncated model of experience, Moltmann emphasizes both the active and passive sides of experience. We "suffer" and "receive" experiences, as well as actively create and manage them. Reciprocity, thus, lies at the heart of the human experience of being-in-relation. Potentially this reciprocity can take the form of an I-Thou relationship in which nature and other human beings are experienced as having an integrity of their own, which we "receive" in our experience of them and are, thereby, changed. Moreover, Moltmann argues that our capacity to experience life in this way is ultimately dependent on the religious horizon that shapes our experience, the centers of value and meaning that orient us to life and give definition to our ultimate concerns.[49]

Building on this rich understanding of experience, Moltmann goes on to describe experiences of the Holy Spirit within the experiences of life, returning to his panentheistic framework: God in all things and all things in God. *To experience God in all things* is to acknowledge the "transcendence which is immanent" in all of life.[50] All of life moves and lives and has its being in God's Spirit, who is the creating, sustaining, and renewing source of all things. This should foster an attitude of reverence toward life, leading us to acknowledge the value and worth of every member of the community of God's creation. *To experience all things in God* is to view life in terms of its transcendent horizon. In Moltmann's theology, this always takes the form of an eschatological horizon. Experience of the Spirit is never simply a matter of affirming life as it is. This would be inconceivable in light of Moltmann's consistent attention to the suffering of creation. Rather, it is a matter of perceiving and experiencing creation within the horizon of what it will one day be, the horizon of new creation.

Experiencing life in terms of this eschatological horizon has both positive and negative dimensions.[51] Positively, the Spirit offers a foretaste of the freedom and new life of the consummation. It is our experience of the *novum* of God's inbreaking kingdom: the entry of something qualitatively new and different into our present experience. Negatively, such experiences make us more aware of the ways creation is captive to sin and death. "When freedom is close, the chains begin to hurt," as Moltmann puts it. The Spirit heightens our awareness of the "negations of life" that we take for granted and fosters a determined "negation of the negative," an affirmation of life even in the face of suffering and evil.

The way Moltmann holds together the Spirit's "immanent transcendence" in creation and her mediation of the *novum* of new creation brings before us a fundamental tenet of his theology of the Holy Spirit. The Spirit of life is also the Spirit of new creation. New creation is not the annihilation of present creation but its transformation.[52] Our experience of God's Spirit, thus, is not the experience of a disembodied, immaterial, ghostly being who draws us away from life in this world. Rather, it is the experience of a renewed vitality in our experiences of life in this world, which will be taken up, perfected, and completed in the new creation. When this occurs, God is glorified.

We will explore the implications of Moltmann's theology of the Spirit for Christian education in the final chapters of this book. In the following section, the focus is broader. What are the "signs" of the Spirit's presence within our experiences of life? What does spiritual vitality look like in a congregation?

Signs of the Spirit's Presence

To this point, my discussion necessarily has been one-sided, focusing exclusively on the activity of the Holy Spirit. This might leave the impression that Moltmann's theology of the Spirit has nothing to do with his Christology. Moltmann is interested in describing Spirit and Word as standing in a genuinely reciprocal relationship, however, not in opposition to one another or running along parallel tracks. He consistently thinks in terms of patterns of mutual interaction and interpenetration of the divine Persons. In his Christology, thus, he invites us to view Christ's work of redemption as empowered by the Holy Spirit. In his pneumatology, he invites us to think of the Spirit's work of glorification as participation in Christ's messianic way and as anticipating the glory of Christ's future parousia at the new creation. Our experiences of the Spirit within the experiences of life are a foretaste of Christ's redemption. What are the signs of the Spirit's mediation of new creation?

Moltmann helps to answer this question in his creative reworking of the *ordo salutis*, the order of salvation.[53] Traditionally, Protestant theology has used this theological category to describe the individual's subjective appropriation of the work of Christ. Often this has taken the form of an ordered pattern: justification, calling, regeneration, sanctification, good works, and so forth. Moltmann redescribes these themes in terms of experiences that accompany our glorification of God in the fellowship of the Holy Spirit.[54] They are signs of the vitality that accompanies life in the Spirit, indicators of her presence in the lives of individuals, congregations, and other social institutions. As I describe these signs of spiritual vitality, I will recall examples from the congregations examined in part 2.

Experiences of Freedom in the Spirit

Throughout Scripture, one of the first and primary experiences people have of God's Spirit is an immense sense of freedom.[55] They are liberated from social and personal forms of bondage. At the individual level, we might recall Sung-young Lee, described in chapter 7. Mrs. Lee had a dramatic, pentecostal experience of the Spirit following the birth of a third daughter, who was stillborn. This experience granted her a new sense of freedom from the cultural oppression of familial Confucianism, which had driven her to strive endlessly to become the perfect wife and daughter-in-law. At the congregational level, we might recall the new sense of freedom that emerged in URC Stellenbosch when the members of its church council took part in interracial and ecumenical pentecostal gatherings during the early 1980s. For the first time, these coloured Christians were liberated from social norms that had kept them from speaking openly and forcefully to white Christians about their pain under the system of apartheid.

While these two examples reflect diverse cultures and circumstances, they have one thing in common: the experience of freedom that opens people up to a new set of possibilities beyond the bondage of their former lives. As you consider your own congregation, you might ask: Do the practices of this congregation breathe the Spirit of freedom into its members? Do they liberate them from various forms of social bondage and open up new possibilities?

Differentiated Experiences of Justification

A second sign of the Spirit's presence is her mediation of Christ's justification of life in the face of the realities of evil and suffering.[56] One of the hallmarks of Moltmann's treatment of this topic is the way he acknowledges the universal reality of human sin without eradicating the very real differences between the circumstances of people who benefit from structural sin and those who are stripped of their dignity by systemic evil. People who are the beneficiaries of unjust systems experience justification as freeing them from the need to repress their guilt, as the offer of forgiveness, and as conversion to a new way of life. Those who live under the crushing weight of injustice and oppression experience justification as granting them a new sense of dignity within the rectifying work of God in which their cause is set right and justice is established.

The Spirit's mediation of the experience of justification, thus, takes a wide variety of forms depending on the circumstances of individuals and congregations. In my research, the importance of working with this sort of differentiated understanding of the experience of justification became particularly evident as I came to know URC Stellenbosch. Time and time again, this congregation brought before me a different facet of the experience of justification. We can recall Jaco Coetsee's gathering of the pastors of the Stellenbosch area, leading to a moment of mutual confession and forgiveness. We also can recall the special role played by the Confession of Belhar, which helped the members of this congregation receive a new sense of their own dignity within God's special love for those who are oppressed. Within this congregation, moreover, individuals still bear their own burdens of guilt. Fathers abuse their daughters; adolescents struggle with sexual promiscuity; persons with AIDS are shunned by their families. This congregation knows the importance of confession and forgiveness that free people to start anew.

As you consider your own congregation, you might ask: Do you find in this particular community signs of the diversity of ways the Spirit mediates justification, or does one, routinized pattern prevail? Are people given the opportunity to struggle with their personal and/or collective guilt? Does the congregation offer the downtrodden the opportunity to receive a new sense of dignity within the righteousness of God?

Regeneration: Experiences of New Beginnings

Regeneration is the experience of a new beginning in the Spirit. Moltmann describes this in eschatological terms, as analogous to the first signs of spring or the first light of dawn. It is our experience of new creation breaking in and opening up our lives in ways that point ahead to the new beginning that awaits all of life in the consummation. The eschatological nature of regeneration should lead us to expect new beginnings to occur many times over the course of our lives and to take many different forms. We are being made new in ways that anticipate God's promised future for creation.

While there are many examples in the case study congregations of new beginnings in the Spirit, nowhere was this more evident than in Somang. Over half of the members of this congregation are new Christians—people who have a clear sense of the new beginning of their life in Christ. In my interviews of Somang's children, youth, and adults, moreover, the delight and enjoyment of God within the experiences of life was a theme that emerged again and again. Something new had entered the lives of people who live in a society with an exceptionally strong work ethic and who labor under the burden of bringing honor to their families.

Somang's way of lifting up the possibilities of new beginnings in the Spirit is not identical to the way this takes place at Nassau or URC Stellenbosch. As you consider your own congregation, thus, you will do well to remain open to the variety of ways new beginnings occur. Consider questions like these: How does this congregation hold before its members the possibilities of new beginnings in the Holy Spirit? Is it open to the regenerating presence of the Spirit in both its corporate life and in the lives of individuals? Does it frame such new beginnings eschatologically, teaching its members to view signs of new life in their midst as anticipations of the new creation that is yet to come?

Sanctification: Experiences of Growth in the Spirit

"Every life that is born wants to grow. . . . The life we say has been 'born again' or 'born anew' from God's eternal Spirit also wants to grow, and to arrive at its proper form, configuration, or Gestalt."[57] So writes Jürgen Moltmann as he takes up the theme of sanctification. If regeneration calls attention to the many new beginnings of life in the Spirit, then sanctification points to the patterns of growth and development marking progression toward maturity in the Christian life. Life in the Spirit encompasses both.

It is not easy for Christians today to use the language of sanctification to describe their experiences of growth in the Spirit. For many, it has come to be associated with a narrow and rigid piety that crushes the vitality and spontaneity out of life. But is this really what sanctification means? Moltmann, I believe, gets to the heart of the matter: "'Sanctification today' means first of all rediscovering *the sanctity of life* and *the divine mystery of creation*, and defending them from life's manipulation, the secularization of nature, and the destruction of the world through human violence."[58] There is, thus, a moral dimension to sanctification, slow and steady growth in practicing a discipleship ethic that takes seriously the sanctity of life, love of neighbor, Christian nonviolence, and other aspects of the Christian moral life that make congregations "contrast societies" in our contemporary world. Sanctification also encompasses growth toward maturity in spiritual discernment. It takes maturity of judgment to determine the right course of action in circumstances that are confusing and complex. It takes a disciplined imagination to discern new possibilities for the present in light of God's promised future.

Viewing sanctification along these lines has the effect of humanizing our understanding of the sanctified life. I am reminded of some of the people we have already encountered in this book. I think of Sharon Ofendahl, a school teacher in South Africa who views her teaching as an opportunity to help her impoverished students discover their own worth and dignity. I think of Sangkeun Kim, who has shaped his entire career around a passion for the reunification of North and South Korea. I think of Carla Thompson, a therapist by profession, who invests an enormous amount of her free time in volunteer activities that serve others, including a photography program designed to help low-income children discover their creative gifts. These are the "ordinary saints" found in many congregations. Their simple respect for the sanctity of life leads them to discern possibilities for service and caring in their everyday lives. It is no accident that each of these individuals is a member of a congregation that communicates to its members that they should expect to find the Holy Spirit leading them toward the service of others and that they will grow if they are willing to embrace the challenges this poses.

One last time, think in terms of the artistry of your own work as a teacher or leader of congregations. Ask yourself questions like these: Is the ethos of your congregation one of service and mission? Are its members encouraged to expect that the Holy Spirit will lead them toward the service of others? What specific practices cultivate maturity in the Christian moral life and in spiritual discernment? What images of mature and responsible discipleship are operative in this congregation? Do the leaders embody these qualities?

In the chapters that follow, I will spell out more fully the implications for the teaching ministry of the trinitarian framework developed over the course of this chapter. As we shall discover, catechesis, exhortation, and discernment acquire a new richness and depth when they are viewed as forms of participation in the triune God's creating, redeeming, and glorifying of the world.

Chapter 9

Catechesis:

A Dramatological Model

Building on our examination of Paul in part 1 and the theological perspective of chapter 8, this chapter develops a dramatological model of catechesis. It begins with a definition of catechesis and then identifies four different patterns of interpretation used by this model, giving rise to four patterns of teaching. Finally, it explores the ways catechesis might be carried out in contemporary congregations through the leadership, practices, pilgrimage, and curriculum frames.

CATECHESIS DEFINED

The core elements of the dramatological model of catechesis developed in this chapter are contained in the following definition: *Catechesis is an interpretive activity undertaken by congregations and their individual members who see themselves as participants in the Theo-drama of the triune God and are seeking to better understand their roles in this drama by deepening their understanding of Scripture and Christian tradition.* In part 1, we found Paul "handing on" Israel's Scripture and early Christian tradition in ways that addressed the particular circumstances of the congregations to which he was writing. This is what I mean by describing catechesis *as an interpretive activity*. It is a matter of finding meaning and new understanding in the texts of Scripture and tradition as we allow them to address our lives and world. The biblical scholar Stephen Fowl describes this interpretive activity as a form of *phronesis*, or practical reasoning, because it involves the interpretation not only of the texts of Scripture and tradition but also of our contemporary world.[1] Learning how to engage in practical reasoning that interprets text and context in a responsible fashion lies at the heart of catechesis.

Catechesis is an interpretive activity *undertaken by congregations and their individual members*. Empirical research reveals that many contemporary Christians view Bible study in individualistic and devotional terms, as drawing them closer to God and providing them with inner peace and personal meaning.[2] In my earlier discussion of the pilgrimage frame, I explained why I believe congregations need to take seriously the individuals in their midst and would do well to teach their members how to read Scripture devotionally. Yet this focus on the individual has its proper place within catechesis that is oriented toward building up the congregation as a whole, edifying the community so that its way of life better embodies its calling as God's people.

We come to the heart of a dramatological model of catechesis when it is described as an interpretive activity carried out by people *who see themselves as participants in the Theo-drama of the triune God*. The purpose of catechesis is to help congregations and their members better understand their identity, mission, and vocations as God's people within an unfolding Theo-drama. While catechesis gives special attention to the interpretation of the texts of Scripture and tradition, the Theo-drama that these sources unfold extends beyond the "world of the text" to God's involvement in our world today through continuing creation, the present activity of the Holy Spirit, and the congregation's Christopraxis. Catechesis, thus, nurtures practical reasoning that attends to the interpretation of the contemporary context, the Holy Spirit, and congregational praxis.

If the Theo-drama unfolded by Scripture and tradition extends beyond the "world of the text" to our life and world, then a primary goal of catechesis is helping congregations and their individual members *better understand their roles in this drama*. It is helpful to think of this as analogous to the ways the actors in a drama *actively receive* their roles, as described by Balthasar. We receive the roles we are given to play because we are participants in a drama that is not of our own making. The Theo-drama of creation, redemption, and glorification was unfolding long before we entered the stage to play our particular parts. It is important, thus, for us to gain a sense of the story line of this longer drama through catechesis. Moreover, our different parts are received within a broader ensemble of players with varied gifts, backgrounds, and life circumstances. Yet the active side of this process also is important. If we take seriously the emergent qualities of continuing creation and the inbreaking character of new creation, then the roles we play are not laid out in advance along the lines of a protological account of creation or a mechanical model of providence; they are fashioned in part through our creativity, freedom, and choices.

This active receiving occurs as we *deepen our understanding of Scripture and Christian tradition.* In a dramatological model of catechesis, these sources of the Christian faith are taught and engaged in ways that are analogous to the "mirror function" of serious drama. Just as the members of the audience go to the theater with the need and hope that they will find the dramatic tensions of their own lives reflected in the play and find "insights" and "solutions," so too Scripture and tradition are taught in ways that "mirror" our lives and world. They are not studied exclusively as historical artifacts, great literature, or collections of timeless spiritual truths, but as part of the drama of God's dealings with the world, which involves us and claims us as God's people.

PATTERNS OF INTERPRETATION AND TEACHING IN CATECHESIS

In the definition offered above, catechesis is portrayed as "handing on" Scripture and tradition in ways that allow the members of a congregation to interpret their lives and world as part of an unfolding Theo-drama. This has important implications for our understanding of the interpretive activity, or practical reasoning, that is nurtured in catechesis. The Theo-drama to which the texts of Scripture and tradition point extends beyond the world of these texts to the contemporary world in which God continues to be involved through continuing creation, the Christopraxis of congregations, and the new creation of the Holy Spirit.

A dramatological model of catechesis, thus, invites the members of congregations to interpret not only the texts of Scripture and tradition but also the contemporary world as the scene of God's present activity. As we shall see, this is consistent with Paul's practice of reinterpreting Israel's Scripture and early Christian tradition in relation to the "new thing" God's Spirit was doing in his congregations; it also is consistent with the attention he gave to the interpretation of the praxis of his congregations, which he commonly reframed in terms of his interpretation of the gospel. In this section, I identify four *patterns of interpretation* that are nurtured in a dramatological model of catechesis:

1. Interpreting the texts of Scripture and tradition: exegesis and mimesis
2. Interpreting the present activity of the Holy Spirit: reading with the Spirit and reading the Spirit
3. Interpreting the praxis of the congregation: the practices of the congregation as the embodied interpretation of Scripture and tradition
4. Interpreting the contemporary context: congregations as participants in continuing creation

Following my description of each pattern of interpretation, I develop a model of teaching that is consistent with this pattern. While I present these teaching models as a sequence of "steps," it is best to think of these steps along the lines of rules of art. They are open-ended guidelines about how to teach in ways that attend to the key elements of an interpretive pattern. These steps, thus, can be organized differently in a particular teaching event or series. They call for reflection and good judgment on the part of teachers and leaders. These teaching models are summarized as follows:

Four Patterns of Teaching in Catechesis

Primary Focus	Step One	Step Two	Step Three
Interpreting texts of Scripture and tradition	Preunderstanding	Exegesis of texts	Appropriation
Interpreting present activity of the Spirit	Experience of the Spirit	Searching Scripture and tradition	Integration
Interpreting congregational Christopraxis	Attending to congregational praxis	Interpreting and testing in relation to Scripture and tradition	Deeper understanding or reform of praxis
Interpreting continuing creation	Engaging the present context with openness	Dialogue with Scripture and tradition	Informed judgment

INTERPRETING TEXTS OF SCRIPTURE AND TRADITION: EXEGESIS AND MIMESIS

In this interpretive pattern, catechesis gives primary attention to interpreting texts of the Bible and tradition (e.g., creeds, catechisms, doctrines). This pattern involves three activities: (1) exegeting texts, (2) placing them in their canonical or confessional contexts, and (3) appropriating these texts mimetically. Exegesis is the task of examining a text closely, often under the guidance of scholarly commentaries and aids. Mimesis involves appropriating a text by creating analogies between its world and our own.

Teaching people how to exegete the texts of Scripture and tradition in a manner that is appropriate to their developmental level is an important goal of catechesis. Over time, we hope that youth and adults will learn how to approach these texts with the tools of modern critical scholarship: placing them in their original historical and cultural context, understanding the genre or literary form in which they were written, and so forth. It is also important to place particular texts in their canonical or confessional contexts, viewing them in relation to the multiplicity of perspectives found in Scripture and tradition. All of these interpretive skills and perspectives are worthy goals of catechesis.

Yet they are only part of what we hope to accomplish in catechesis. We also seek to cultivate the interpretive skills necessary to appropriate the texts of Scripture and tradition in ways that open new possibilities for our life and world. With regard to the Bible, this is the difference between interpreting it as merely a historical artifact or a piece of great literature and interpreting it as the sacred Scripture of our own community of faith. As Richard Hays puts it, "When we say that a text is 'Scripture' for our community, we are committing ourselves to a diligent effort to discern analogical relations between the text and our community's life—but that is not all. We are also committing ourselves to form—and reform—our communal life in such a way that the analogies will be made more clearly visible."[3]

Construing the Bible as Scripture, thus, commits us to the identity-shaping and identity-breaking dimensions of interpretation. It takes seriously the claims that Scripture makes on our lives as God's people. In contemporary interpretation theory, the task of appropriating Scripture in ways that allow it to reshape our lives is described by Paul Ricoeur as the *mimetic* dimension of text interpretation.[4] Following our careful exegesis of texts, we seek to discover analogies between its world and our own. While the term *mimesis* means to imitate, Ricoeur describes it as a process of metaphor making.[5]

Metaphors draw on a familiar field of experience to understand another field of experience. In creating an analogy between two fields, both similarity and difference are maintained. A basketball player, for example, might be described as "choking" when he misses a foul shot at a crucial time in the game. The experience of having one's breath cut off when an object is lodged in the windpipe is applied analogically to the effects of pressure on a player's ability to perform. Metaphor making lies at the heart of the mimetic process of appropriation. Having entered the world of the text, interpreters construct metaphorical relations between that world and their own. Appropriation, thus, is not a matter of literal application but of the discovery of similarity-in-difference. It involves a creative, imaginative leap.

A model of teaching that is based on this pattern of interpretation can be conceptualized as following three steps. The first step focuses on the *preunderstanding* of students, the horizon of expectation they bring to the interpretation of a text. Once teachers have spent time studying the text that is the subject of their teaching, they must determine the interpretive focus of their session. The richness of many texts means that teachers must be selective in choosing what they will cover in any given session. Once they have done so, they then should reflect on the experience and background of their students in order to determine if the students are familiar with situations, issues, or problems that are similar to those brought to the fore by the text. Suppose a biblical text focuses on forgiveness, as in Mark 2:3–12. Learning activities that tap into the students' own experience of forgiveness, guilt, and release from the burden of sin serve as entry points that help them move into the text.

The second step involves learning activities that allow students to examine the text closely, to *exegete* it. Teachers must take account of the developmental readiness of their students in designing these learning activities. They also will do well to consider activities that involve more than verbal-linguistic and mathematical intelligences, as described by Gardner. Children, for example, examine a text closely when they act it out in role play or a puppet show. The important point is to give them the opportunity to look closely at the text in a responsible, age-appropriate fashion.

The third step involves the process of mimetic *appropriation* as described above. A text is not really understood until students are given the chance to construct analogies and metaphorical relations between its world and their own. This step requires activities that foster the creativity of students, for the texts of Scripture and tradition are similar to the contemporary world in some ways and quite different in others. For example, in dealing with a text on forgiveness like the one mentioned above, this involves giving them the opportunity to discover new insights about their own need for forgiveness or their possible role as agents of forgiveness in their families, friendships, and other relationships.

Interpreting the Present Activity of the Holy Spirit: Reading the Spirit and Reading with the Spirit

A second pattern of interpretation also important in catechesis focuses on interpreting the present activity of the Holy Spirit. This pattern has received extensive attention in the writings of contemporary biblical scholars such as Richard Hays, Stephen Fowl, and Luke Johnson. In *Scripture and Discernment*, Johnson explores this pattern as it comes to expression in Acts. He calls attention especially to the important role that testimony to the Spirit's presence among Gentile Christians played in the Jerusalem Council.[6] The "circumcision party" drew on Israel's traditions to argue that Gentiles ought to be circumcised and accept certain dietary regulations when they joined the church. In contrast, Peter testified to the Spirit's presence among Cornelius and his household and the way this had changed his own thinking about this issue. Likewise, Barnabas and Paul offered testimony to the "signs and wonders" the Spirit was effecting among Gentile Christians. In rendering the council's decision, James is portrayed by Acts as citing Amos 9:11–12 and then *reinterpreting* this passage in light of this testimony to the Spirit's work among Gentile Christians. Johnson comments: "As Peter had come to a new understanding of Jesus' words because of the gift of the Spirit, so here the Old Testament is illuminated and interpreted by the narrative of God's activity in the present."[7]

Similarly, in *The Echoes of Scripture in the Letters of Paul*, Hays examines the ways Paul reinterprets Israel's Scripture in light of the Spirit's presence among his congregations. Hays poses the interpretive question this raises: "But does the experience of the Spirit have a *hermeneutical* function? To state the issue broadly, is the scriptural text to be illuminated in the light of Spirit-experience, or is Spirit-experience to be measured by normative constraints laid down by the text?"[8] "Paul's unflinching answer," Hays contends, "is to opt for the hermeneutical priority of Spirit-experience."[9]

In reflecting on the insights of Johnson and Hays, Fowl argues that if contemporary Christian communities are to interpret Scripture and tradition in ways that are analogous to the interpretive practices of the early church, then they must pay more attention to the hermeneutical significance of their present experience of the Holy Spirit. They must learn to "read with" the Spirit, that is, to reason *from* testimony and personal experience of the present activity of the Spirit *to* the texts of Scripture and tradition. But Fowl also offers a cautionary note: "The Spirit's activity is no more self-interpreting than a passage of scripture is. Understanding and interpreting the Spirit's movement is a matter of communal debate and discernment over time."[10] This pattern of interpretation, thus, is circular. We learn to "read" the Spirit, to discern the signs of her presence in our contemporary experience, as we study Scripture's accounts of her prior activity. We learn to "read with" the Spirit, to discover new meaning in biblical texts and traditions, as we attend to her present activity in our lives and world.

A model of teaching that is based on this pattern of interpretation can be conceptualized as following three steps. The first step gives people the chance *to share their experience, to give testimony to the Spirit's active presence in their lives and world.* In dialogue with Moltmann in the previous chapter, I described some of the signs of the Spirit's presence within the experiences of life: freedom from forces holding us in bondage, no longer hiding from our guilt, a newfound sense of dignity within the righteousness of God, a deeper appreciation of the sanctity of life, and new beginnings. These sorts of experiences of the Spirit within experiences of life are an important starting point of this model of teaching.

When Nassau's youth and adults take part in mission trips, for example, it is not uncommon for them to begin to wrestle with a sense of guilt about their privileged lives and the materialism of the American way of life. New Christians at Somang often feel a profound sense of release and freedom from the cultural patterns dominating their family relations and their work habits. Crushed by poverty and violence, the members of URC Stellenbosch sometimes experience a new sense of their own dignity and worth within the compassion and righteousness of God. This model of teaching takes these experiences of the Spirit seriously and begins by giving people the opportunity to testify to their experiences. Putting such experiences into words and having trusted others receive them is an important first step.

The second step grants people the opportunity to *deepen and to test critically such experiences by bringing them into dialogue with Scripture and tradition.* Experiences of the Spirit often have the effect of bringing the Bible to life in new ways, as people now understand firsthand what it means when describing experiences of forgiveness, being comforted, or receiving unexpected courage. Helping people build connections between their experiences of the Spirit and Scripture or tradition allows them to see their lives as part of the Theo-drama of which these sources speak. But it also is important for people to test critically their experiences. Many have claimed to speak and act on behalf of the Spirit of God in ways that, in retrospect, appear self-deceptive. We must test our experiences of the Spirit in the context of community and against the patterns of her work found in Scripture, tradition, and the testimony of those who are mature in such matters.

The third step is *integration,* helping people refashion the patterns of their lives in ways that build on what they have learned. This is different from appropriating a biblical text, for it gives greater attention to firsthand experience of the Spirit and to the testimony of others. If a member of Nassau's youth group were to experience on a mission trip a profound sense of being "convicted" by the Spirit about the materialism of her life and were given the opportunity to reflect on biblical texts dealing with the dangers of wealth, then the task of integration is to allow this conviction to reshape the pattern of her life when she returns home. Concrete commitments, accountability, and continuing encouragement are often crucial to this sort of integration.

Interpreting the Praxis of the Congregation

A third pattern of interpretation focuses on the praxis of the congregation. Here again, we find a pattern that was also used by Paul in his letters. Paul would remind his readers of creeds or practices that already were an integral part of his readers' praxis as a Christian community. He then would attempt to deepen their understanding of this praxis by explicating it in light of the gospel, Israel's Scripture, or early Christian tradition. He often would conclude by challenging his readers to do a better job of embodying the gospel in some facet of their shared life. Often the chiasmic (ABA) structure of a block of material in a letter is a signal that this pattern of interpretation is being used by Paul. We saw this, for example, in Paul's treatment of spiritual gifts in the Corinthians' practice of worship (1 Cor. 12), followed by his "ode to love" (1 Cor. 13), and his return to the proper use of spiritual gifts in worship (1 Cor. 14).

Within a dramatological model of catechesis, this pattern of interpretation is important, for it takes seriously the Christopraxis of congregations. It is here that Christians learn what it means to live as Jesus' disciples, as part of a community that is struggling to embody the drama of redemption in the practices of a shared life and mission. In a very real sense, the praxis of a congregation provides its members with their first interpretation of Scripture and tradition. It is here that they build up habits, perceptions, and expectations about a life of discipleship, for better and for worse. This is why catechesis must include the ongoing interpretation of the praxis of the congregation in the light of Scripture and tradition—in order to *deepen* the congregation's understanding of practices in which they already are participating and to *test them critically* against the norms of Scripture and tradition.

A model of teaching that is based on this pattern of interpretation can be conceptualized as following three steps. The first step is *to pay careful attention to some aspect of the congregation's current praxis.* If the goal is simply to deepen people's understanding of the meaning of an established congregational practice, it is usually enough to draw attention to how it is already being practiced and to explain what this involves. In worship education of children, for example, this might involve identifying the different parts of the worship service. Sometimes, however, this first step takes its bearings from the perception of a problem in congregational praxis, prompted by a variety of possible sources: prophetic voices outside the community, threats to the congregation's long-term survival, fresh insights of new members, conflict in the congregation, and so forth. It is not crucial that this problem receive clear definition at this point. Nor is it necessary for the perception of a problem to be widely shared in the congregation or recognized by those in authority, at least initially. But at least some in the community must share this perception, setting in motion a process of learning.

The second step is *to interpret the meaning of the particular practice in light of Scripture or tradition.* If the goal is simply to deepen understanding of this practice, it is enough to offer teaching that explains its meaning: This is why we baptize children or confirm adolescents; this is why we begin with the call to worship. If the goal is to respond to the perception of a problem in present praxis, then this second step involves *searching for guidance on this matter in Scripture and tradition.* In a sense, the process involves a kind of "reverse mimesis." Instead of moving analogically from Scripture and tradition to the contemporary world, we move from the perception of present problems to explore analogous situations in Scripture and tradition.

It is important to add one caveat about this movement from problem to Scripture. Proponents of problem-solving reasoning often encourage people to make "problem-definition" the first step in this process. In contrast, I believe it is important to hold open our definition of the problem until this second step in order to allow Scripture and tradition to reframe our initial perceptions. Time and time again, Paul reframed his congregations' definitions of the issues they faced by portraying them very differently in light of the gospel or Israel's Scripture. We too should be open to this sort of reframing process by listening with openness to the voices of Scripture and tradition and not approaching them merely to confirm our own prior perceptions.

The third step in this model of teaching is *to deepen understanding of present practice or to initiate a process of reforming present practice.* Achieving deepened understanding involves giving the participants a chance to respond to the teaching offered in step two. In worship education, for example, this might involve asking teams of children to create a worship bulletin appropriate for Sunday morning worship. Initiating reform of some aspect of congregational praxis is more complex and often involves additional steps that can only be determined in the face of a concrete situation. If the worship committee, for example, decided that certain changes should be made in the practice of worship, then this would affect the entire congregation. Its members would also need to participate in a learning process that would take them through the first two steps. Reform of praxis often falters precisely because a group has come to certain insights through a process of learning and then has mistakenly assumed that it can simply present the outcome of its learning to others. It is more appropriate for the group to view its own learning as the first step in an educational process involving the congregation as a whole.

Interpreting the Contemporary Context: Congregations and Continuing Creation

A fourth pattern of catechesis focuses on congregations' interpretation of the contemporary context as the scene of continuing creation. This is best conceptualized as a *mutually critical dialogue*. Knowledge and insights that emerge out of the contemporary context have the capacity to challenge certain features of Scripture and tradition. Earlier we explored some of the ways the science of evolution challenges certain features of traditional Christian anthropology, which portrays human beings as the apex of creation and as totally discontinuous with nature. The Bible and tradition often reflect the cultural and historical assumptions of their age: the subordinate role of women, the acceptance of slavery, the hierarchical relationship between rulers and ruled, and so forth. New knowledge and social patterns emerging over the course of history or out of the contemporary context have the potential of challenging these assumptions.[11]

At the same time, however, the Christian community speaks back critically to the contemporary context, drawing on its own beliefs and commitments. For example, I have pointed to some of the ways the Christian interpretation of our world as God's *creation* raises questions about the anthropocentrism of modernity, its willingness to crush nature to produce an endless stream of trivial consumer products. Likewise, I would hope that the Christian community's understanding of justice and *oikumene* might lead it to bring a critical perspective to many of the trends currently characterizing globalization. Learning to interpret our contemporary world as the scene of God's continuing creation, thus, requires both openness and criticism on the part of congregations—the capacity for a mutually critical conversation that is learned through catechesis.

A model of teaching that is based on this pattern of interpretation can be conceptualized as following three steps. The first step is to *engage with openness new knowledge, social movements, and cultural patterns of the contemporary context*. Often this is simply a matter of listening carefully to the questions and issues that people bring with them to the congregation. Can I believe in science and still believe in the stories of creation? Why has our congregation never had a woman minister? Should we still refer to God as Father? Is the spread of global capitalism a good thing? To what extent should we support the manipulation of the genetic code of plants, animals, and human beings?

This first step also includes providing members with the chance to deepen their understanding of these questions by engaging the relevant literature and "experts." This often means that catechesis uses resources that have little to do with either the Bible or Christian tradition but a great deal to do with learning to better understand and interpret the knowledge, movements, and issues of a particular sociohistorical context. We begin by listening and learning—not immediately rushing to judgment.

The second step involves *bringing the perspectives of Scripture and tradition into dialogue with the contextual issue under study.* This puts at risk inherited beliefs and practices, but also raises critical questions about contemporary trends on the basis of an interpretation of the normative beliefs and values of Scripture and tradition.

The third step involves *helping the participants crystallize what they have learned by identifying new insights and forms of action.* On many issues, all participants need not come to the same conclusion. Is it really necessary, for example, for all people to think the same way about praying to God as Father or referring to the Holy Spirit with feminine pronouns? The process of renegotiating tradition in dialogue with the contemporary context often occurs over an extended period of time and, even then, only a rough consensus may be reached. In the meantime, catechesis that supports an open and critical dialogue with the contemporary context should strive to enable people to make informed judgments about what they believe and value. It provides them with opportunities to develop good reasons for their beliefs and actions and to dialogue with people whose beliefs and values may be quite different from their own.

INSIDE THE ARTIST'S STUDIO: CATECHESIS THROUGH FOUR FRAMES

In a dramatological model of catechesis, different patterns of Scripture interpretation inform different models of teaching. This final section invites you to enter the artist's studio where you will explore ways of using this framework to guide catechesis in your own congregation. Those readers who are not currently in a position of leadership in a congregation are asked to keep in mind a congregation with which they are familiar. Students might consider their home church or their field education placements.

Reflecting on concrete situations is the focus of the pragmatic task of practical theological reflection. Conceptual models and categories of the sort developed in this book can only take you so far. It takes creativity and good judgment to draw on these tools in an actual situation. You might think of yourself as an artist in a studio who is attempting to fashion a unique creation on the basis of his skills, tools, and imagination. The art of leading and teaching a particular congregation takes the same sort of imagination, skill, and good judgment. To facilitate the creative process, I offer examples of catechesis brought into focus by the four frames developed in part 2. My goal is to encourage you to expand your imagination, to recognize the many opportunities for catechesis beyond formal educational settings. These examples are followed by questions designed to help you identify analogous forms of teaching that might be carried out in your own congregation.

Catechesis through the Leadership Frame

The leadership frame brings into focus the ways a congregation is a "learning organization" that faces adaptive challenges. These challenges are of various sorts. They might call into question the congregation's very identity and mission or might involve issues that are less encompassing—but still potentially rife with conflict—such as choosing a new hymnal, changing the atmosphere of the worship service, or starting a weekday preschool program. These are important opportunities for congregations and their working committees to deepen their understanding of Scripture and tradition as they draw on these sources to understand and respond to the challenges they face.

In chapter 6, I identified an adaptive challenge facing the churches of South Africa: Now that the struggle against apartheid is over, will congregations turn inward to the exclusion of ecumenical cooperation in dealing with poverty, violence, drugs, and AIDS? This concern became a centerpoint of Rev. Coetsee's prayer life for almost a year, as he wrestled with the Spirit's gentle prompting that *he* must be the one to take the lead. He gathered the area pastors together in a dramatic moment of confession and forgiveness, giving rise to a new spirit of ecumenical cooperation across their congregations. During my time with URC Stellenbosch, I had the opportunity to witness firsthand a number of ecumenical events that emerged out of this new spirit of cooperation. One such gathering was an Ash Wednesday agape meal in the Idas Valley branch of URC Stellenbosch, open to the members of all area congregations.

As families entered the fellowship hall of the congregation, they spread out a blanket and sat on the hard linoleum floor. In his typically creative fashion, Rev. Coetsee structured their time together in ways that emphasized the unity of those gathered. Each family introduced itself and then moved around the fellowship hall to greet one another, singing a familiar welcome song. After announcements and further singing, Rev. Coetsee distributed candles to each family. The lights were turned off and, kneeling next to a lighted candle in the middle of the hall, he read 1 Corinthians 12:4–7, which emphasizes the one Lord and Spirit who lies behind the diversity of spiritual gifts and ministries. He then spoke briefly to the group about their oneness in Christ:

> In spite of the differences of our churches, we have one Savior, who gave himself for us all, and one Lord, whom we all serve. We are called to give visible expression to our common faith, working together to overcome the many problems that Stellenbosch and our nation face. Together we can light a candle of hope in the darkness of crime and unemployment and violence. Sharing what we have with one another, we are strengthened to show the love of God in a world of hate and suspicion.

He then invited children from every family to come to the center of the hall, light their candle from the single candle next to him, and carry the light back to their families. Slowly the darkness of the hall gave way to the light of many candles.

Rev. Coetsee then instructed the group to share with one another the food they had brought for the agape meal.

This is a wonderful example of catechesis through the leadership frame. In the face of an adaptive challenge before the congregations of Stellenbosch, Rev. Coetsee interpreted this challenge with a passage of Scripture. The real issue at stake, he implied, is Christian unity and cooperation, born of a common faith in one Lord and Savior. He involved the group in parabolic actions—spreading small pockets of light around the dark hall from a single candle and sharing food with one another. I view the pattern of interpretation and teaching he used here in terms of the second one described in the previous section, which begins with our present experience of the Holy Spirit and then moves to Scripture or tradition in order to deepen our understanding of what we are experiencing. Experiences of the Spirit in the present were important starting points of catechesis: in Rev. Coetsee's personal struggle in prayer, in the time of confession among the area pastors, and in the new beginning of cooperation among area congregations. In the agape meal, Rev. Coetsee was attempting to help those gathered to interpret these experiences in light of a text of Scripture and to enact parabolically the need for visible unity and mutual care across the Christian community.

It is not difficult to imagine other patterns of interpretation and teaching being used in concert with the leadership frame. I have known more than a few pastors and educators, for example, who have turned the perception of a problem in congregational praxis (the starting point of the third pattern) into opportunities for catechesis, dealing with such questions as: Why do so many of our youth drop out of the congregation as soon as confirmation is over? Should our minister marry nonmembers who are divorced and cannot be married in their former churches? When viewed through the leadership frame, these are not just administrative issues (i.e., setting church policies) but opportunities for teaching and learning. In attempting to identify opportunities for catechesis through the leadership frame, consider questions like these:

- What are the adaptive challenges before your congregation at this point in time? Are these primarily experienced by the congregation as internal or external issues, that is, as driven by problems within congregational praxis or by changes in the social context? As you pray, meditate, study Scripture, and talk with others about these challenges, what images, stories, or concepts of Scripture and tradition begin to help you interpret them?
- Where are the winds of new creation blowing in the lives of individual members, in the congregation, in the local community, and in the world? How might you help your congregation and its members connect with these sources of spiritual vitality? How might you connect such experiences with new understandings of Scripture and tradition?
- In leadership education, how might you prepare congregational leaders

to draw on Scripture and tradition when they face major adaptive challenges? Are there "easier," less controversial issues that might first be engaged in order to help them learn how to draw on these sources before they face more difficult challenges in the future?

Catechesis through the Practices Frame

I know of a small, Midwestern congregation—I will call it Fourth Church—that is located almost directly across the street from a mental health center. Though relatively small in number (150 members) and with limited financial resources, this congregation has a large sense of mission. It has developed an informal partnership with the mental health center to provide support for the mentally ill who receive treatment there. Several decades ago, the psychiatric hospital serving the community in which this congregation is located was shut down, discharging all patients with chronic mental illness. Advances in psychotropic drugs and new community mental health centers supposedly meant that it was no longer necessary to "warehouse" the mentally ill. Several decades later, however, it is apparent that the promised support from the federal and state governments has not materialized in many communities. The mentally ill now make up a disproportionately large percentage of the homeless in the United States and, increasingly, the prison population.

Fourth Church has stepped into the breach in its own little corner of the world. It has set up a system to help patients locate low-income housing and to involve them in the vocational rehabilitation program of the mental health center. It has devised a program that connects its members and local college students with the mentally ill, serving as the front line of care and monitoring their needs. It regularly sponsors workshops led by mental health professionals to train those who participate in this program. It also hosts social events at the church for the program's "clients."

Fourth Church does not have much of a church school; there are relatively few children and teenagers in this congregation. Yet it is a community of catechesis in a particularly striking way. Through its practices of mission, it embodies the story of God's people in ways that form the identities of its members. Its members learn Scripture and tradition as they reflect on the praxis of their congregation, deepening their understanding of what it means to serve in the name of Christ and wrestling with the problems that emerge as they carry out their mission to the mentally ill. I believe this sort of catechesis is best described in terms of the third pattern of interpretation and teaching developed in the previous section, which takes its bearings initially from the praxis of the congregation and learns Scripture and tradition to understand and guide this praxis. Let me offer an example of how this takes place at Fourth Church.

Every year the congregation has a special commissioning service for those members and college students who will serve as caregivers of the mentally ill during the coming year. It uses a special liturgy of commissioning in the middle of the service with a covenantal structure. The caregivers make certain promises, and the congregation promises to offer them support and training that will help them carry out their ministries. The liturgy places this promise making within God's promise to meet the caregivers as they serve those in special need, building on Matthew 25:35–36: "I was hungry and you gave me food, I was thirsty and you gave me something to drink, I was a stranger and you welcomed me, I was naked and you gave me clothing, I was sick and you took care of me, I was in prison and you visited me." The minister typically preaches on a biblical passage in which the theme of covenant is prominent.

In effect, the entire worship service interprets the meaning of the congregation's missional praxis with Scripture and tradition. This is one of the ways that catechesis takes place through the practices frame: teaching that interprets to the members of a congregation the meaning of practices in which they are already participating. It has the potential of helping a congregation understand its way of life as a continuation of the story of God's people. It also may help a congregation move beyond simply taking for granted practices that are habitual and long-established.

I will mention in passing another form of catechesis brought into focus by the practices frame, for it is one we have examined extensively already: catechesis that is woven into a practice which does not have education as its primary focus. Dawn Prayer at Somang is a good example, affording its participants the opportunity to work their way through the entire Bible in a systematic fashion as they gather to worship God. Weaving catechesis into established practices may be easier than you think. You might offer a series of sermons on one of the traditional catechetical subjects: the Apostles' Creed, Lord's Prayer, or Ten Commandments—an important practice in Reformation churches of the past. Or you might weave intergenerational Bible studies into family camping retreats, or study a biblical theme before, during, and after a mission trip. In attempting to identify opportunities for catechesis through the practices frame, consider questions like these:

- When you view your congregation as a community in which catechesis takes place through the formation, or identity-shaping impact, of its practices, how adequate is this formation? As members participate in the practices of your congregation, what do they learn about the life of discipleship? Do certain practices need to be reformed or added for your congregation to become a community of disciples?
- Are there occasions when you might interpret the meaning of practices in which the members of the congregation are already participating? How might you make better use of the teaching potential of such interpretive moments?
- Are there ways to weave teaching and learning into practices whose primary purpose is not education? Think of Dawn Prayer and catechetical preaching as examples.

Catechesis through the Pilgrimage Frame

The pilgrimage frame brings into focus the individuals of a congregation and the diverse journeys of faith they are traveling. Increasingly around the world, it has become less likely that people will remain a member of only one congregation over the course of their lives. This is particularly true in countries like the United States with a high degree of mobility and where denominational and interreligious switching are prevalent. Pastors and Christian educators often are aware of the diverse backgrounds, interests, and needs of their church members, but they sometimes are perplexed about how to respond. Here I explore two of the challenges this diversity poses to catechesis: (1) new members' classes and (2) groups or relationships that allow individuals to build their own connections to Scripture and tradition.

New Members' Classes

Research indicates that the first six to twelve months after people affiliate with a congregation are crucial to their assimilation into this community.[12] By and large, patterns established during this period set the stage for future participation. The stakes are high, thus, for thinking through the sort of catechesis that is offered to new members. But the sheer diversity of backgrounds and interests of newcomers leave many pastors struggling with questions such as: What sort of catechesis is appropriate for new members? Is it even possible to devise a single program of catechesis for such a diverse group of people? Is there any place left for the cultivation of denominational identity in this elementary catechesis? Two different but equally viable approaches have emerged among congregations.

One approach reaches back to the adult catechumenate of the third and fourth centuries and, accordingly, is sometimes called a *catechumenal* approach. It prolongs and intensifies the catechesis of new members in a program that often lasts for a year or two. In large measure, this approach has been sparked by the RCIA (the Rites of the Christian Initiation of Adults) in the Roman Catholic Church, but it also is practiced by churches in the Anglican and Lutheran traditions and has been adapted by other branches of Protestantism.[13] Like the catechumenate of old, this form of catechesis goes well beyond a quick introduction to denomination beliefs and polity. It engages new members in a process of formation as they participate in certain practices of the Christian life. Often these include personal prayer under the guidance of a spiritual director; serious study of the Bible, church catechisms, and liturgy; regular participation in worship; and involvement in the congregation's outreach programs. Every individual receives special attention and mentoring as he or she moves through the process.

A second, equally effective approach places much less emphasis on new members' classes per se and more on helping people become a part of ongoing classes, groups, and ministries that will assimilate them into the congregation during the first few months of their membership. This is sometimes called an *incorporation* approach. Catechesis takes the form of helping people reflect on their pilgrimages of faith to this point in their lives, to identify the issues of the current stage of their faith journeys, and to receive guidance about those parts of the congregation's life they are apt to find most meaningful. Some congregations do this by running new members' classes like small groups, placing emphasis on structured sharing under the guidance of an experienced leader; others use "gifts" inventories in these classes, helping individuals identify their particular talents, needs, and interests. It is common for a minister to visit each individual or couple participating in the class to explore these issues in a more personal way. Often this minister follows up several months later in order to make sure these new members have connected with some part of the congregation's life.

These two approaches to the catechesis of new members are quite different, but both have proven to be effective. One raises the bar at the threshold of the congregation; the other makes it relatively easy to cross this threshold but works very hard to incorporate new members into some facet of the congregation's life. The important point to underscore is that *both* approaches take seriously the diversity of backgrounds and needs individuals bring to congregations, and they shape their catechesis accordingly.

Personalized Contexts and Relationships

A second challenge facing many congregations today is developing educational contexts and relationships that are sensitive to the particular needs of individual members. Even relatively small congregations today are apt to have youth and adults at very different points on their pilgrimages of faith. Some youth are in full rebellion against the church as a way of separating from the parents; others come from broken homes and look to the church for friends and trusted adults. Some adults are recently divorced; others are newlyweds. Some are bored to death with their jobs; others are facing retirement and wonder what life will be like when they are no longer working. Some are refugees from conservative Christianity and blanch at the slightest hint of any "ought"; others are searching for solid answers after many years of wallowing in a shallow and narcissistic relativism. How can a congregation possibly create an educational program that is responsive to the needs of people so different?

At one level, a congregation cannot possibly respond to all of the needs and interests of its members. It can, however, develop personalized educational contexts in which individuals are given the opportunity to create their own connections between the particular circumstances of their lives and Scripture and tradition. One of the most effective contexts in which this takes place is small groups, especially small group Bible studies. If an inductive method of teaching is employed, such groups allow individuals to share their stories and, with the support of the group, to discern connections between their stories and biblical texts.

But at another level, attention to the diverse and changing needs of church members ought to be part of the planning process of the Christian education program. Instead of repeating the same classes and programs year after year, a concerted effort can be made to identify people whose needs and interests are not currently reflected in the curriculum. Congregations that plan in this way are constantly adding new classes and groups and dropping those that are faltering or have fallen into ruts.

But what about those individuals who are just not going to participate in the educational program at this point in their lives? Empirical research repeatedly has discovered that people who are not affiliated with a religious institution or participate in such institutions marginally continue to think about spiritual and faith issues.[14] Should not the teaching ministry find ways of reaching out to them? Not long ago, a student of mine wrote up a case study of the youth group she had helped lead before coming to seminary. The group is outstanding in many different ways, but what really caught my attention is how the youth minister (Sherry) develops relationships with youth who do not participate in any part of the program. As my student put it, "Sherry never stops reaching out, but she does not try to convince them that they need to get involved. In a thousand little ways, she tells them that she is there for them if they need her. She even has e-mail relationships with some of them." I happen to know Sherry, so I asked her about these e-mail relationships. She told me, "You know, I actually have deeper conversations with some of these youth than with those who come faithfully every Sunday evening. They ask me the hardest questions. Sometimes I have to tell them, 'I don't know the answer, but I'll think about it.'"

This is the catechesis of personal relationships. The word "gospel" may be spoken infrequently, but it is being communicated through the loving acceptance and interest that this youth minister is offering these young people. Moreover, she is taking their intellectual questions seriously, reminding us that those on the margins of the congregation often continue to think about the big questions of life. We would do well not to confine the catechesis of personal relationships to our work with youth, but to include children and adults. Treating everyone with respect and taking their questions, issues, and needs seriously is an important dimension of the catechesis of congregations. As you think about the catechesis of your own congregation through the pilgrimage frame, consider questions like these:

- How does this congregation handle new members' classes? If it were up to you and time and resources were not a consideration, how would you change these classes to better take account of the diverse needs and interests of individual participants? Would they become closer to the catechumenal or incorporation approaches discussed above?
- Does your congregation have small groups that give individuals the chance to build connections between their life circumstances and Scripture or tradition? If not, how might you start a small group ministry?
- Bring to mind some of the people in your congregation who do not participate in its educational program but are likely to be thinking about important spiritual and ethical issues. How does the "catechesis of per-

sonal relationships" alter the way you think about your relationship with such people?

Catechesis through the Curriculum Frame

I have intentionally left the congregational curriculum for last, in part because it is what usually comes to mind when we think about catechesis—the church school, Bible studies, and so forth. But I also left it for last for several other reasons. Many small congregations will never be able to develop high-powered educational programs, and it is important for their leaders to take note of the many opportunities for catechesis that are available when it is viewed through the leadership, practices, and pilgrimage frames. Moreover, it is often difficult for pastors—regardless of the size of their congregation—to participate regularly in the Sunday morning church school. It is important that they too recognize the many ways they can offer catechesis beyond this venue.

In chapter 5, I developed a set of categories in dialogue with Howard Gardner and James Fowler to help you think about the congregational curriculum. It will be helpful to review this earlier discussion, not only for this chapter but also for the two that follow:

- *Endstates* are the valued roles, activities, and products for which education is preparing people.
- *Development* is primarily nonuniversal and context dependent, for it involves growth in competencies necessary to function well in a particular culture, domain, or discipline.
- *Educational pathways* are lines of development and cumulative learning that are supported by the curriculum over time.
- *Developmental readiness* focuses on the individual's psychological readiness to acquire certain kinds of knowledge, attitudes, and skills.
- *Phases of the curriculum* are distinct periods of learning in the curriculum, based on the sequencing of the subject matter and people's developmental readiness. Five phases were projected, presented here with catechesis in mind:

  1. *Natural learner:* Supporting the emergence of "intuitive" models of God and the church built up through relationships, simple stories, and an elementary vocabulary; learning simple action scripts for practices such as prayer, worship, and sharing that are important in the Christian way of life.
  2. *Primary phase:* Fostering biblical and theological literacies in the context of a "community of faith in miniature," a community that turns to the Bible for guidance, uses theological language to understand the drama of God's relationship to the world, and worships God as a gathered and scattered community.

3. *Secondary phase*: Apprenticing young people in more "disciplined" approaches to the Christian way of life, especially those having to do with the interpretation of Scripture and tradition as ways of understanding their lives and world.

4. *Critical phase*: Providing adults opportunities to reflect on the values and beliefs into which they were socialized and to explore systems of belief and action in order to form a critical, self-chosen faith stance.

5. *Postcritical phase*: Providing adults opportunities to recognize the limits of any system of beliefs and practices and the need to engage perspectives different from their own.

As noted in my discussion of the curriculum frame in chapter 5, I believe that every congregation's curriculum must be *local,* that is, tailored to the particular resources, membership, and needs of a specific congregation. "Thinking local," however, does not rule out thinking normatively. The curriculum frame invites you to view the educational program of your congregation as promoting cumulative growth and learning in a systematic, intentional, and sustained fashion. This means that you must reflect on the endstates toward which the curriculum is "leading people out"—the core meaning of *education* (from the Latin, *e* = out and *ducare* = to lead). You must first identify the desired endstates of the congregational curriculum and then design a systematic plan that will allow people to acquire the knowledge, attitudes, and skills that are needed for them to participate with maturity in certain roles and practices or to fashion certain products.

At different points in this book, I have identified several possible endstates that might spark your own thinking about these issues. In chapter 5, for example, I discussed some of the theological reasons the Protestant Reformers offered to justify their emphasis on education. Conceptualized as the endstates of a curriculum, they would include helping people move from an implicit to an explicit faith, equipping all members of the congregation for ministry, helping individuals develop a sense of their personal vocations, and nurturing maturity in the freedom and good judgment of individual conscience. In dialogue with James Fowler's theory of faith development, a somewhat different endstate came into view: educating people toward postconventional forms of Christian identity in a globalizing context that is increasingly multicultural and multireligious. Drawing on the discussion of catechesis in the first two sections of the present chapter, I might add the endstate of wise *phronesis* in the interpretation of Scripture and tradition. This takes account not only of the interpretation of the texts of Scripture and tradition but also interpretation of the present activity of the Holy Spirit, the praxis of the congregation, and the contemporary context as the scene of continuing creation. Gaining the knowledge, attitudes, and skills involved in this sort of complex interpretive activity would certainly be a worthy goal of catechesis. In reflecting on the curriculum of catechesis in your own congregation, consider questions like these:

- What are the implicit endstates of your congregation's curriculum, and what roles do Scripture and tradition play in them? Are these adequate when viewed normatively?
- Identify venues (e.g., classes, groups) in which catechesis is strong. Are they confined to a certain age level? Are there ways of strengthening connections between these venues, especially those in different phases, in order to create educational pathways across the curriculum?
- On the assumption that small changes can sometimes bring about large results, what is one initiative that would improve the catechesis of your congregation? Consider such things as starting a programmatic Bible study such as *Bethel* or *Kerygma*, upgrading the confirmation program, using the *Logos* program in a midweek, after-school class for children, or beginning a small group Bible study. What might this initiative contribute to the endstates of the curriculum? How is it related to the ethos of the congregation?

In this chapter, I have developed a dramatological model of catechesis in which congregations and their individual members interpret Scripture and tradition in order to deepen their understanding of the roles they actively receive within the Theo-drama of God's creating, redeeming, and glorifying of the world. As I extend this model to exhortation and discernment in the chapters that follow, it will become evident that a symbiotic relationship exists between the three core tasks of the teaching ministry. Strengths in one task often interact in supportive and positive ways with strengths in other tasks. But the converse also is true. Deficiencies in biblical and theological knowledge make it difficult to interweave biblical and contemporary story lines in discernment or to develop moral capacities in exhortation. While core tasks of the teaching ministry can be separated for analytical and practical purposes, it is important to keep their symbiotic relationship in mind in the chapters that follow.

Chapter 10

Exhortation

Moral Formation and Education in the Congregation

In our examination of Paul's letters in part 1, we found him giving attention to the distinctive moral ethos, identity, and mission of his congregations. The social composition and roles of these communities were relatively unique in the Greco-Roman world. This often created tensions and confusion as they struggled to form a way of life that embodied the moral claims of the gospel. Paul responded to their difficulties in a variety of ways. One of his most important strategies was to point to moral exemplars who embodied certain facets of the Christian moral life and to link such exemplars to Jesus Christ, who was portrayed as the paradigm of a life pleasing to God. Paul also offered his congregations explicit moral teachings and would often remind his readers of these teachings as he applied them to new issues.

Throughout Paul's writings, these sorts of strategies of moral formation and education were animated by his theological understanding of the church as God's people who are called, justified, and sanctified in Christ Jesus. He portrayed his congregations as caught up in an apocalyptic drama in which Christ is the centerpoint of the turn of the ages and the Holy Spirit is poured out on Jews and Gentiles alike, bringing them together in a community of the new covenant. Paul reminds his congregations who they are as God's people and then exhorts them to more fully embody this identity.

The dramatological model of exhortation developed in this chapter maintains this close relationship between identity and morality. It views the task of moral formation and education as helping the members of congregations to find their identities within the Theo-drama of God's creating, redeeming, and glorifying love, and to view their moral lives in terms of what God is calling them to do and be within this unfolding drama. I begin by developing an account of moral formation and education that draws on the thinking of Paul Ricoeur.[1] I then place Ricoeur's account of the moral life in a Christian ethical framework and use it to describe the moral formation and education of congregations through the practices, curriculum, leadership, and pilgrimage frames.

CONGREGATIONS AS COMMUNITIES OF MORAL FORMATION AND EDUCATION

In *Oneself as Another*, Paul Ricoeur proposes a three-part account of the moral life that is helpful in thinking about the teaching ministry of exhortation: (1) the identity-shaping ethos of a moral community that is embodied in its practices, narratives, relationships, and models; (2) the universal ethical principles a moral community uses to test its moral practices and vision and to take account of the moral claims of others beyond this community; and (3) the *phronesis*, or practical moral reasoning, that is needed to apply moral convictions to particular situations. While Ricoeur's account is in principle applicable to *all* moral communities, I will use it to describe the key elements of moral formation and education in Christian congregations.

Identity-Shaping Practices, Narratives, Relationships, and Models

Since the Enlightenment, it has been common in Western moral philosophy to portray the moral life in terms of the capacity for abstract moral reasoning that is universal in two senses: It is available to all human beings, and it strives for impartiality, adopting principles and perspectives that treat the claims of all parties in a just and fair manner.[2] This account of the moral life has exerted great influence on modern theories of moral education, which have tended to focus on moral reasoning and abstract ethical principles supposedly shared by all "rational" people.

One of the most important flaws of this approach to moral formation and education might be summarized as follows: *Ethics without ethos is empty.* Learning abstract ethical principles does not motivate people to act in moral ways, nor does it take into account the moral competencies needed to engage in effective moral action in actual situations. Throughout this book, I have drawn attention to the identity-shaping nature of the ethos of congregations: the habits of thought, feeling, and action that are gradually built up as people participate in the practices of a community and learn its way of life. This is the starting point of Ricoeur's account of the moral life—the shaping force of the ethos of particular moral communities. He describes this in terms of the "thick" practices, narratives, relationships, and models of particular moral communities. It is here that our natural prosocial impulses are interpreted and shaped toward the moral vision and values of the communities to which we belong and with which we identify.

We gain a better understanding of the formative role of a community's ethos if we bring Ricoeur's perspective into dialogue with certain lines of research on the moral self found in contemporary psychology. This research identifies three building blocks of the moral self: the moral emotions, moral knowledge, and moral actions.

The moral emotions take root initially in infants' feeling states, which attune them to their inner and outer worlds. Over the course of childhood, these relatively fleeting feelings evolve into more stable emotional patterns, or dispositions, that take shape in children's interaction with others. Some of these emotional patterns play an important role in the moral life, attuning us to others and providing us with an assessment of events, relationships, and situations. There are numerous moral emotions, and the following list simply points to some of the primary ones:

- *Empathy* is the capacity to respond to another person's feelings with similar emotions.[3] There is a link between empathy and prosocial behavior such as helping and sharing.
- *Shame* is an other-directed emotion rooted in feelings of embarrassment or being "exposed" before significant others who view one's behavior as unacceptable.
- *Guilt* is commonly viewed as an inner-directed emotion that is oriented to internal moral standards or rules of propriety and the feelings of remorse accompanying their violation.[4]
- *Outrage* is rooted in feelings of anger evoked when children perceive that they have been wronged or harm has been done to others. As they develop a sense of fairness through participating in games with rules, outrage may be evoked when they believe the structure of fairness has been violated.
- *Caring* is rooted in feelings of warmth, trust, and positive regard that emerge in healthy attachment relationships. Feeling valued and cared for is the building block of the capacity to offer care to others later in life.
- *Pleasure*, as a moral emotion, is rooted in the feelings of delight that accompany children's exploration of the world, animated by their natural curiosity and playfulness. It funds creativity and the unwillingness to settle for rote answers in the moral life.

Moral knowledge focuses on both the development of *cognitive capacities* that are important to moral reasoning and perspective taking and the *acquisition of moral contents.* The role of cognitive development in the moral life has been the focus of influential theorists who build on the work of Jean Piaget, such as Lawrence Kohlberg, Robert Selman, James Rest, and Jürgen Habermas.[5] While cognitive development is an important building block of the moral self, I tend to view it as a necessary but not sufficient way of describing growth in the moral life. Cognitive development does not in and of itself guarantee that people will use their emerging cognitive abilities in moral ways. People often use advances in their perspective-taking abilities, for example, to manipulate others toward their own selfish ends. Growth of general cognitive capacities, thus, must be viewed as closely related to the *moral contents* that give them substance and direction—something not found in Piaget's perspective.

This leads me to a second perspective on moral knowledge, known as *cognitive semantics,* which grants greater importance to the interaction of moral contents and cognitive processes. This is developed in the work of George Lakoff, Mark Johnson, and other scholars.[6] Johnson argues that a key building block of the moral self is the *moral imagination* and describes six, content-rich cognitive structures that are basic to its operation, some of which were mentioned in earlier chapters.[7]

Prototypes. We categorize moral situations and persons on the basis of prototypes, the typical instances or members of a category.[8] Children, for example, begin to form the category of fairness on the basis of prototypical situations in which fairness is enacted: sharing cookies at story time, taking turns on the swing, following the rules of a game.

Frames. These are generalized frameworks used to understand the kinds of situations we encounter.[9] They activate specific vocabularies, prototypes, and action schemes that are associated with that frame. The arrest and detention without trial of people of Middle Eastern descent following September 11, 2001, for example, might be framed in terms of war (as an extraordinary wartime measure), the law (as a matter of due process), or human rights (as the humane treatment of all regardless of their citizenship). Each way of framing this situation brings different moral issues into focus.

Metaphors/metaphorical mapping. Metaphors draw on domains with which we are familiar so that we may understand experiences with which we are less familiar. Metaphorical mapping draws on a primary or root metaphor to structure in a sustained manner our understanding of events, relationships, or social systems. For example, we might use the "contract" metaphor taken from the business world to understand our marriage, leading us to "map" this relationship along the lines of a fair bargain in which each partner gives and receives certain services. This same relationship could be mapped in terms of other metaphors: covenant, hierarchical obligation, companionship, or self-fulfillment.

Narrative. While Johnson notes that narratives are only one of many cognitive structures that shape the moral imagination, he underscores their importance, building on Paul Ricoeur's thought and arguing that "*narrative* provides the most comprehensive structure for grasping the temporal dimension of our moral selfhood and action."[10] Narrative allows us to synthesize the temporal flow of our experience into a meaningful pattern, to construct a long-term identity, and to construe particular situations as episodes of moral choice, conflict, or action within an unfolding story. Our cultures and religious traditions provide us with a stock of stories to construct both our personal and corporate identities.

Rules and principles. Johnson treats rules and principles together, and I will do so here.[11] Moral rules are practical guides closely related to lived experience that offer guidance in recurrent, conventional situations. Ethical principles are inclusive, moral ideals that keep before us the most cherished values of the communities and traditions to which we belong. They bring before us the values that are likely to be at stake in many different kinds of circumstances and the sorts of procedures we might follow to actualize these values in a particular situation.

Moral action includes three elements: habituation, self-control, and actional competence. Habituation and self-control as moral capacities are similar to cognitive development in moral knowledge: They are necessary but not sufficient. Criminals acquire habits and practice self-control as defined here. As such, habits and self-control are necessary behavioral capacities that must be shaped toward certain moral ends if they are to acquire a positive role in the moral life.

Habituation is defined by Johannes van der Ven as "the formation of behavioral habits, actions that are marked by their repetitive, routine character."[12] Habit formation is motivated both positively and negatively. To acquire habits, children must be induced to perform certain activities they find undesirable (e.g., going to bed, eating a nutritional meal, doing homework). Many habits, however, are built up through the performance of activities they find intrinsically satisfying (shooting a basketball, playing the guitar). In both cases, the repetition of the activities over time results in the internalization of a behavioral script that is followed in a quasi-automatic fashion. At a very young age, children begin to ascribe moral "oughtness" to some of the habits of action they have acquired, leading them to make certain moral judgments about their own behaviors and those of others.

Self-control is the capacity to delay immediate gratification for goals realized in the future.[13] This is an important behavioral capacity in the moral life, for most important moral ends require that we forego immediate satisfaction in order to procure more enduring goods. Deficits in the capacity for self-control are an important factor in many of the problems facing contemporary American society, contributing to the rise of youth violence, peer cruelty, and sexual promiscuity. Moreover, studies indicate a correlation between low impulse control during childhood and delinquency during adolescence.[14]

Van der Ven argues that the long-term goal of both habituation and self-control in the moral life is *self-regulation,* the capacity to steer and monitor one's actions in ways that are self-directed and informed by personal judgment.[15] Young people must develop capacities for moral agency beyond following blindly the moral habits and customs of the groups to which they belong. Research indicates that the adult-child relationships that foster a morality of self-regulation are those in which clear control and guidance are offered, on the one hand, and support is given to children's emerging independence and personal judgments, on the other.[16]

Actional competence is the acquisition of particular skills that enable one to act effectively in situations of moral import to achieve a valued end. It is one thing, for example, to want to help a friend who is severely depressed, and quite another to have the sorts of skills that would enable one to be of genuine assistance. Actional competence is the acquisition of particular skills that enable one to act effectively in situations of moral import. Obviously, no one can be omnicompetent, especially in our highly specialized and complex world. Moral skills, thus, often must be learned in relation to specific roles, tasks, and contexts.

This brief examination of the moral emotions, knowledge, and actions helps us to better understand the formative power of the ethos of moral communities, the starting point of Ricoeur's model. These three building blocks of the moral self are a natural substratum of human sociality that is shaped and interpreted by the communities to which we belong. Rationalistic moral theories that focus solely on abstract ethical principles are flawed because they detach the moral life from its grounding in primary relationships and communities of identification. In short, ethics without ethos is empty.

While the moral emotions, knowledge, and actions can be distinguished for analytical purposes, they are almost never found in isolation from one another in real life. Indeed, one of the reasons our participation in moral practices is such an important source of formation is the way they "package" our emotions, knowledge, and actions into integrated patterns. When we participate in the practice of confession in public worship, for example, we undertake certain actions, reflect on our lives and world in order to acknowledge our complicity in evil, and experience a range of possible emotions such as guilt, shame, sadness, and release. Over time, our participation in practices of this sort cultivates what I call *moral capacities*.

Testing Our Community's Moral Ethos against Universal Ethical Principles

In the second part of Ricoeur's model, he argues that moral communities must be willing to test their practices and norms against universal ethical principles. Do they regard the moral worth of others as equal to their own? When the interests of their community conflict with the interests of others, are they committed to procedures that are fair and open to all parties? Can they enter sympathetically into the perspectives of persons and groups different from themselves culturally, racially, and religiously?

Why is it important for communities to subject their moral practices and norms to these kinds of moral tests? In a nutshell, *practices without principles become provincial.* It is not difficult to see why this is the case. The fact that our moral capacities are shaped by those closest to us, by the communities and individuals with whom we identify, is precisely what makes it so easy to confine our circle of moral concern to those most like ourselves. In situations of moral conflict, human beings are apt to put the interests of their families and local communities above those outside these groups. Unless moral communities are vigilant in testing their moral ethos against universal ethical principles that widen the circle of moral concern to the entire human community and to the community of creation, they are apt to settle for moral answers and actions that are too provincial and self-serving.

But where do we get these universal ethical principles? This is a very complex question, and I will not give it the extended answer it deserves. Suffice it to say that I do not follow Riceour's attempt to derive universal principles from the moral claims implicit in the construction of human identity in relation to an "other." This is sometimes referred to as the "Kantian moment" of Ricoeur's theory, for it follows Immanuel Kant's strategy of deriving universal principles from generic features of human existence.[17] In contrast, I adopt what might be called a hermeneutical strategy that views universal ethical principles as derived from the historical experience of particular moral communities and the ethical traditions they have developed over an extended period of time.

This hermeneutical strategy is compatible with the understanding of ethical principles described above in Mark Johnson's account of the moral imagination. It views such principles as *inclusive moral ideals* that remind a community of the most important values that have emerged out of its experience and been articulated in its moral traditions.[18] It works with a different understanding of universality than is found in the Kantian tradition. Principles are universal in terms of their inclusivity and scope; they direct us outward to other human beings and species who are seen as having moral worth and dignity. But they are not universal in derivation, that is, they are not grounded in generic features of our common human existence.

Cultivating Practical Moral Reasoning in Particular Situations

The third part of Ricoeur's model is practical moral reasoning, or moral phronesis. In chapter 9, we examined phronesis in relation to the various interpretive activities involved in catechesis. Ricoeur's model draws our attention to the sort of practical moral reasoning that is needed to act wisely in particular circumstances. It is one thing to acquire moral knowledge, habits, and general principles, and quite another to use them well in the midst of an unfolding situation in which we have something at stake. We must have the ability to see the relevant factors involved in a particular situation, to make judgments about the actual choices available to us, and to determine courses of action that might be efficacious under these circumstances. Without the capacity to make such judgments, moral knowledge and principles play a small role in our lives. In other words, *principles without phronesis lie fallow.*

While holding on to the importance of practical moral reasoning, I want to expand somewhat Ricoeur's portrait of moral phronesis, using James Wilson's notion of *moral sense*.[19] The ability to function well in a specific situation of moral import does indeed involve our practical moral reasoning. But it also involves our emotional assessments, moral imagination, and competence as moral actors. This complex constellation of feeling, thinking, and acting work together to make up our moral sense, that is, our ability to interpret and respond to concrete circumstances in a morally responsible fashion.

In the remainder of this chapter, I draw on Ricoeur's model to examine the ministry of exhortation in Christian congregations. First, I portray Christian congregations as communities of moral formation that interpret and shape the natural substratum of moral emotions, knowledge, and actions into moral capacities through their practices, narratives, relationships, and models. Second, I examine the role of moral education in teaching the members of congregations universal ethical principles that can guide their everyday lives and serve as critical tests of the communities to which they belong. Third, I describe ways congregations can cultivate the moral phronesis of their members, helping them to draw on their moral capacities in spheres of life beyond the church. I view moral formation primarily through the practices frame, moral education through the curriculum frame, and moral phronesis through the pilgrimage and leadership frames.

CONGREGATIONAL MORAL FORMATION: ETHICS WITHOUT ETHOS IS EMPTY

In this section I portray Christian congregations as covenant communities which cultivate the moral capacities of their members through practices that embody certain aspects of their covenant with God as Creator, Redeemer, and Glorifier of the world.[20] In the Bible a covenant is a pact between two or more parties that defines the nature of their relationship and stipulates their mutual obligations and responsibilities within this relationship. Scholars have identified two somewhat different understandings of *covenant* in the Bible.[21]

One understanding features the *promissory and unconditional nature of God's covenant*. God is portrayed as the initiator and guarantor of the covenant, which is not dependent on the special goodness or capacities of the participants. Rather, it depends solely on the faithfulness and generosity of God. The other understanding features *historically particular and conditional special covenants* in which the parties involved enter into an agreement that defines the nature of their relationship and their mutual responsibilities as these are shaped by their common relationship with God. The covenant is conditional in the sense that both parties are expected to live up to the terms of their agreement.

Contemporary covenant ethicists draw on both of these biblical traditions.[22] They draw on the biblical traditions of historically particular, conditional covenants to portray our responsibilities to God and one another in terms of the various special covenants in which we participate. This allows these ethicists to distinguish the rights and responsibilities of our covenants in different relationships and spheres of life—the differences between marriage and friendship, for example.[23] This also allows these ethicists to acknowledge that the shape of these covenants will change in different social and historical circumstances, reflecting the emergent qualities of continuing creation and the dynamic character of God's relationship to the world.

Contemporary covenant ethicists also draw on those biblical traditions that portray God's unconditional, promissory covenants for two closely related purposes. First, they view these traditions as making a fundamental point about what it means to be human. As relational and social beings, humans are inherently covenantal; we are involved in relationships of mutual trust and commitment that shape our patterns of personal identity, interpersonal relationships, and communities. Second, they interpret these traditions as portraying the universal and inclusive scope of God's covenant love. In the ethical perspective I develop here, this universality is seen as taking three forms, which build on the theological framework developed in chapter 8: the covenants of creation, redemption, and glorification.

In the *covenant of creation,* God affirms the universal moral worth and dignity of all human beings, who are created in God's image, as well as the sanctity of the other members of the community of creation. This is the basis of an ethic of equal regard in which we consider other human beings as having moral worth that is equal to our own and regard the nonhuman species who are our partners in the community of creation as having moral worth beyond their instrumental value to human needs and purposes. In the *covenant of redemption,* God offers a world caught in the clutches of suffering and evil the redemptive possibilities of forgiveness, freedom, and restoration of right-relatedness. This is the basis of an ethic of reconciliation which seeks to bring peace to relationships and systems that are torn apart by mutual violence and enmity. In the *covenant of glorification,* God promises that the transfigured beauty of Christ's resurrection is the ultimate future of creation, pointing ahead to an encompassing transformation that preserves, completes, and harmonizes the many fragments of goodness and beauty already found in nature and human culture through the present activity of the Holy Spirit. This is the basis of an ethic of glorification in which we seek to behold and love our neighbor within the eschatological beauty of God.

In what follows, I give primary attention to key *moral capacities* involved in our assent to and participation in the covenants of creation, redemption, and glorification, and to the *moral practices* that cultivate these capacities. The various practices described in this section are examples, not a comprehensive list, and range across families, congregations, and Christians' participation in public life. I view this account of moral capacities cultivated through practices as describing only half of a dramatological model of exhortation. The other half has to do with our willingness to receive anew the roles and vocations God gives us to carry out within the unfolding dramas of our personal and corporate lives. Here we have to do with God's call and command, which is received anew and in freedom. Moral capacities put us in a position to hear and receive; they attune us to God's call and command. But in and of themselves, they offer no guarantee that this call will be heard and heeded. The moral formation and education of congregations can shape our moral capacities, but that is as far as they can go.

God's Inclusive Covenant Love in Creation: An Ethic of Equal Regard

An ethic of creation draws on those biblical traditions that portray God's creation of the world as an act of sheer love in which God makes time and space for a created "other," affirms the essential goodness of creation, promises to love and care for the created "other" without violating its creaturely freedom, and awaits the creature's answering response. As Joseph Allen puts it, in the covenant of creation, God loves creation *inclusively,* affirming the moral worth and dignity of the members of the community of creation.[24] Human beings in their stewardship of creation are to reflect the inclusive, universal nature of God's covenant love for all creatures.

Throughout the Christian tradition, a wide variety of ethical perspectives have attempted to spell out the moral implications of this affirmation of God's inclusive covenant love for creation. Within contemporary Christian ethics, the framework that I find most helpful is articulated by Don Browning and others in terms of an *ethic of equal regard*.[25] Acknowledging God's inclusive covenant love for creation entails regarding our neighbors as having moral worth and dignity that is equal to our own. This is summarized in the Christian tradition in terms of the Golden Rule—"Do to others as you would have them do to you"— and Jesus' "summary" of the law and commandments: "Love God with all your heart, soul, and strength, and your neighbor as yourself." In both of these moral teachings, love is defined as treating our neighbor with the same respect and care that we would hope to receive ourselves. Moreover, the second teaching implies that we are to regard ourselves as having moral worth because God does. This is an important counterpoint to social definitions that ascribe lesser moral worth to persons or groups on the basis of their race, ethnicity, gender, or religious membership. In an ethic of equal regard, there are three core capacities of the Christian moral life that are responsive to God's inclusive covenant love: fairness, compassion, and fidelity.

Fairness is best understood in terms of the moral capacity to participate in practices of *communicative justice*. If we regard the moral worth of other human beings as equal to our own, then we commit ourselves to allowing our special covenants with them to be shaped by a moral conversation in which the needs and interests of all parties are treated fairly and given their due. In this sort of conversation, all are treated as equals. Each party's needs and interests are taken seriously, as is their right to influence the course of the conversation. No one person or group has undue power to control the issues raised or the outcomes achieved. Participation in practices of communicative justice in our families and congregation has the effect of cultivating a basic sense of fairness that can guide us in relationships and institutions beyond the church. The following are several examples.

- *Family meetings.* The goal of family meetings is to help children and youth learn how to make decisions and set family rules through a fair and open process.[26] Such meetings help children learn how to express their thoughts and feelings, to listen to others, and to understand the reasons for family rules.
- *Congregational governance.* Decision-making practices at many levels of congregational life can teach communicative justice through debate and discussion, fair representation, civility among those who disagree, and the articulation of good reasons.
- *Practices of advocacy.* These are practices in which the members of a congregation seek to influence public policies that impact disadvantaged groups. Congregations give voice and political clout to people with little voice, thereby, bringing about a closer approximation of communicative justice in the public sphere.

Compassion includes empathetic understanding essential for the sort of moral conversation that has just been described.[27] But it goes further, for it involves the moral capacity for sympathy: the readiness to identify with the special needs of vulnerable people and, potentially, to suffer in solidarity with them. This tilts our understanding of communicative justice away from an exclusive reliance on notions of justice as impartial fairness (to each according to their due) or "rough justice" (fair trade-offs that balance conflicting interests). Compassion leads us to give those in greatest need their special due. Practices of compassion cultivate sympathy when they invite us to enter into the plight of others, both literally and imaginatively.

- *Family helping projects.* When families offer assistance to people beyond the home, this may cultivate compassion, especially if parents talk with their children about their experiences and evoke their capacities for empathy, sympathy, and perspective taking.
- *Practices of service.* Members of congregations participate directly in some form of service within the congregation, in the local community, or beyond. Compassion is enhanced by linking these experiences to opportunities to think, feel, and understand in greater depth the plight of those being served.

Fidelity is the moral capacity to honor the commitments and promises of the various special covenants in which we participate. Much of the time, the promissory nature of our covenanting is most directly evident in our interpersonal relationships and voluntary associations. We make certain promises, for example, when we baptize our children, are confirmed, enter into a marriage, join a new church, or are ordained as an officer of a congregation. Yet promise making and promise keeping are implicitly a part of our membership in other communities as well. We also implicitly promise to fulfill our responsibilities as citizens of a nation, as members of a profession, as workers for a company. One of the tasks of moral formation is to help the members of a congregation better understand the fiduciary nature of their membership in communities of this sort.

- *Family chores and discipline.* When all members of the family carry out their fair share of the household chores and live within the rules set up through family meetings then the capacity for fidelity is nurtured in the home.
- *Practices of financial giving.* These practices cultivate fidelity if they are linked to stewardship of the earth's resources and the virtue of simplicity.[28] Christians in affluent nations must be especially encouraged to simplify their way of life in order to break with the infidelity of materialism, which results in their disproportionate consumption of the world's resources and binds them to unjust economic and political systems.

God's Inclusive Covenant Love in Redemption: An Ethic of Reconciliation

God's inclusive covenant of redemption comes to expression in the seeking love of Christ, which reaches out to a world caught in systems of suffering and evil and reconciles it to God inclusively and universally in an act of unmerited grace. It is appropriate, thus, to describe the moral dimensions of our assent to and participation in this covenant in terms of an ethic of reconciliation. We are to love our neighbors as those for whom Christ has given himself in love. An ethic of reconciliation assumes the moral framework of equal regard described above, but it recognizes the depths of creation's estrangement from God and the cost of reconciliation in a world of sin and death. It orients us in ways that are fundamentally different from an ethic of creation and requires of us a different set of moral capacities. If an ethic of equal regard seeks to balance fairly the rights of all parties, an ethic of reconciliation calls us to the "higher righteousness" of sacrificial, nonretaliatory love that is basic to reconciliation.

It is important to recognize that an ethic of reconciliation addresses many different levels of life beyond the interpersonal sphere.[29] *Theological reconciliation* has to do with the reconciliation between God and humanity and what this means in terms of human relations. *Interpersonal reconciliation* addresses broken relations between individuals such as family members, neighbors, church members, or coworkers. *Social reconciliation* addresses problems of enmity between communities at a local level, such as racial tensions in a high school or religious conflicts in a neighborhood. *Political reconciliation* addresses conflicts at a national or international level, such as those of Northern Ireland, postapartheid South Africa, or the Middle East. The three core moral capacities I associate with an ethic of reconciliation—peacemaking, forbearance, and forgiveness—contribute to reconciliation at all of these levels.

Peacemaking is the capacity to instigate transforming initiatives in the face of conditions of "negative peace," that is, a state of hostility, violence, and enmity.[30] I have taken the concept of transforming initiatives from the writings of Glen Stassen and others who challenge the church to respond to relationships of enmity and violence with practices that seek to alter the context of relationships between conflicting parties and to initiate the first steps toward reconciliation.[31] Some of the essential ingredients of such initiatives are: (1) The participants are proactive, not merely reactive or passive; (2) they acknowledge their own contribution to the conditions of negative peace or the contribution of the communities to which they belong; (3) they affirm the dignity and interests of their enemies, even while rejecting their sinful or wrong behavior; (4) they offer the estranged "other" the invitation to work together toward peace and justice; and (5) they seek to take the first steps toward new forms of community that include, rather than exclude, former enemies and outcasts.[32]

- *Covenants of peacemaking.* Some denominations encourage their congregations to form an explicit peacemaking covenant to signify their commitment to this ideal.[33]
- *Practicing nonviolent resolution of conflict.* One practice that has been adapted to a variety of settings is cooperative conflict resolution, commonly used in peer mediation at schools, community mediation in neighborhoods, out-of-court divorce mediation, and the peacemaking initiatives of diplomats, envoys, and political leaders in situations where violence and war have broken out.[34]
- *Practicing generosity toward those who have done you harm.* In a situation of negative peace, taking the initiative in acts of generosity toward those who have done you harm is sometimes the first step toward reconciliation. It can play an important role in interpersonal reconciliation, but it also can have a powerful effect on social and political reconciliation—readily apparent in the behavior of people such as Nelson Mandela.
- *Practices of nonviolent protest.* Boycotts, strikes, marches, civil disobedience, and many other forms of nonviolent protest are used by social movements as a way of responding to the negative peace of institutional violence and oppression.

Forbearance is the moral capacity to resist retaliation and despair in the face of hostility or violence and to remain patient in working toward reconciliation and peace. It is not to be confused with the passive acceptance of injustice, which would be contrary to the notion of transforming initiatives. Rather, it interjects a note of realism into our understanding of what is involved in working for peace and reconciliation in a world of sin and death. Such initiatives are often met with resistance and violence, and the temptation will be great to return violence in kind. Forbearance resists this temptation and seeks to embody the possibilities of healing, peace, and reconciliation even in the face of such opposition.

- *The practice of praying for our enemies.* In the New Testament, Christians are told to pray for those who persecute them, especially when they are exhorted to love their enemies and not to return harm in kind.[35]
- *Practices of threat reduction.* These practices embody the positive side of forbearance in the form of actions that seek to break long-standing cycles of mutual distrust and conflict.[36] Rather than waiting for some sort of negotiated resolution of the conflict, one of the parties undertakes a series of visible and verifiable actions designed to reduce the enemy's perception of the threat it poses and to demonstrate goodwill.

Confession and Forgiveness can be distinguished, but I will treat them together, for they often are closely related in the process of reconciliation. Confession is the capacity to face up to our guilt and to undertake acts of repentance; forgiveness is the capacity to accept such confession, to release the guilty party from his or her debt, and to take the risk of starting anew.[37] John de Gruchy helps us to recognize different types of guilt that may be the focus of confession.[38] *Criminal guilt* involves breaking the law; *political guilt* has to do with the responsibility of citizens for their government's unjust policies and actions; *personal guilt* involves the individual's breach of ethical standards through acts of commission or omission; *collective guilt* has to do with the systemic moral failures of the communities to which we belong; *ontological guilt* has to do with humanity's alienation and estrangement from God. Recognizing these different forms of guilt helps us to better understand the various forms confession can take. While confession may sometimes focus on our guilt as individuals, it also focuses on our collective guilt as members of churches, corporations, and nations, even though we may be "good" personally by conventional moral standards. We need practices that help us face up to our guilt. But we also need practices that help us to receive anew the promise of forgiveness we are offered in Christ, which grants us the courage to make amends and start anew.

- *Learning to apologize.* One of the building blocks of confession and forgiveness is learning to offer and receive apologies in the home. Admitting that we have made a mistake, saying we are sorry, promising to make amends, and receiving the forgiveness of trusted others are the starting points of our capacities for confession and forgiveness.
- *Practices of confession.* Many congregations make corporate confession and forgiveness a regular part of worship. If this addresses the various

forms of guilt outlined above, it is an important way of cultivating our capacity to acknowledge our guilt.

- *Practices of vicarious confession.* These are practices in which those who are struggling against injustice or oppression bring the sins of their community before God. Just as Christ acted vicariously for a humanity caught in sin and evil, so too, vicarious confession is offered to God in the face of the unwillingness of the majority community to face up to its guilt. The German Confessing Church offered vicarious confession in the Stuttgart Confession of Guilt in 1945, as did churches in South Africa under apartheid.[39]
- *Practices of social and national reconciliation.* The single best example of this sort of practice in recent decades is the Truth and Reconciliation Commission of South Africa. The TRC did not seek to establish guilt and apportion punishment through legal means; it attempted to elicit national healing and reconciliation by giving voice to the stories of those who suffered under apartheid and by giving perpetrators the opportunity to confess their guilt publicly.[40]

God's Inclusive Covenant Love in Glorification: Loving Our Neighbors within the Eschatological Beauty of God

An *ethic of glorification* takes its bearings from the embodied promise of Christ's resurrection from the dead, which points ahead to God's future transformation of creation, and from Christ's promise that the Holy Spirit will be present to mediate this new creation until his parousia.[41] These promises and the covenant to which they point are universal, for new creation is cosmic in scope and encompasses the transitory fragments of beauty emerging and disappearing over the course of creation's unfolding. Our recognition and assent to this covenant commits us to the task and joy of loving our neighbors within the eschatological beauty of God.

My thinking about what this ethic entails has been stimulated by the work of Frank Brown, who has written, "To enjoy another's enjoyment is already an act of love."[42] He is calling our attention to the moral challenge of learning to appreciate the aesthetic tastes of our neighbors whose cultural and religious backgrounds may be quite different than our own. For example, all three of the congregations studied in the second part of this book embody a Reformed aesthetic of worship, emphasizing the arts of oral communication and music. Those who worship in these congregations will gradually build up a particular set of tastes and may find it difficult or even repulsive to worship in ways that are markedly different. They may find the use of incense in a Catholic cathedral disgusting, the lusty singing of "The Old Rugged Cross" in a rural congregation sentimental, or the presence of icons in an Orthodox church bewildering. Yet these may be mediators of God's beauty to those who worship in these different communities.

Denigration of our neighbor's enjoyments on the basis of our own set of tastes is a kind of violence to our neighbor, manifesting a lack of understanding, empathy, and, ultimately, love. It reveals a failure to behold our neighbor within the eschatological beauty of God, which preserves, completes, and transforms the diverse fragments of human beauty into an encompassing and harmonious whole. Three moral capacities lie at the heart of an ethic of glorification: delight, hospitality, and hopeful imagination.

Delight is the capacity to find pleasure in praising and enjoying God for God's own sake. It is cultivated especially by a congregation's practices of doxology. Potentially, our experiences of delight can break the spell of everyday life and remind us that the ultimate end of creation lies in God's eschatological beauty, not the patterns of work, family, or political power that shape our present world. Moreover, delight evoked by doxology often expands outward to enhance our appreciation of the contingent goods of creation: the beauty of nature, good company, sexuality, artistic creation, and our own creativity—now experienced as enjoyments that are a foretaste of a fuller enjoyment yet to come. Our present experiences of delight have the potential of attracting, rather than compelling, us toward the goodness of God and, as such, play an important role in the moral life.[43]

- *Recreation on the Sabbath.* This practice was explored in chapter 4 on Somang. The Sabbath as a day of rest is used by families for recreational activities that renew the bonds of family life. It might easily be used in comparable ways by friends.
- *Practices of worship eliciting delight.* Cultivating delight through public worship is important but difficult to accomplish, especially across the generations, which often have different tastes in music and styles of participation. Unless worship brings delight to its participants, however, it will be unlikely to attract and motivate them toward the goodness of God.

Hospitality in Christian Scripture and tradition involves "extending to strangers a quality of kindness usually reserved for friends and family."[44] It often is explicitly distinguished from forms of hospitality in which the host seeks to gain the favor of those to whom hospitality is extended. Rather, it is offered to strangers, outcasts, and the poor, who are not in a position to return the favor. In this way, it reflects the gracious hospitality of Christ, who crossed boundaries to extend God's love to those who were marginal and vulnerable in society and to affirm their worth and dignity in God's sight. As Christine Pohl points out, hospitality in this sense is not quaint or tame; it is risky and subversive.[45] It is a way of recognizing the strangers in our midst and of affirming the worth of those whom the dominant culture may view as unworthy because of their race, ethnicity, religion, or sexual orientation. In extending hospitality to such persons, Christians are offering it to Christ, who is present in their vulnerable neighbor.

- *Hospitality in the home.* This is not a matter of entertaining our friends; it involves welcoming those who may be far from home, new to our neighborhood, or just passing through by inviting them into our homes for meals, offering them lodging, or performing other acts of generosity and welcome.
- *Practicing hospitality in social service.* Many congregations provide social services for the homeless, the disabled, unwed mothers, drug addicts, and other vulnerable and needy people. Hospitality takes us beyond charity; it seeks to offer help in ways that recognize and affirm the dignity of those being served.
- *Hospitality to marginalized groups.* When congregations intentionally cross social boundaries to offer hospitality to groups that are marginalized in their social context, they reflect the pattern of Jesus' earthly ministry. This may include welcoming them into the the congregation or hosting gatherings that foster fellowship between communities.

Hopeful Imagination stands at the very heart of an ethic of glorification. To hope is a capacity of the imagination in which we transcend the limits of the present out of a longing for something new and different.[46] Christian hope takes its bearings from eschatological images of God's promised future that help us to imagine a world in which suffering is healed, captives are set free, justice is done, and peace is established among humans and with nature. As Richard Bauckham and Trevor Hart point out, the capacity to "imagine otherwise" is "the source of our ability as humans to protest in the face of the given, to refuse to accept its limitations and lacks and unacceptable features, to reject the inevitability of the intolerable."[47] Far from encouraging us to escape from our world, we are encouraged to imagine our world differently and to open ourselves to the sort of personal and social transformation that corresponds to God's promised future.

- *Care for people in circumstances beyond repair.* In the face of extreme suffering, even the most empathetic of people are apt to turn away. Yet some congregations cultivate the capacity to walk with those who are terminally ill or chronically disabled and to see them within the eschatological beauty of God.
- *Practices of hopeful witness.* These witnessing practices work for social change even in the face of seemingly impossible circumstances such as the spread of AIDS in Africa, the crushing poverty of many underdeveloped countries, and the proliferation of weapons of mass destruction. They keep hope alive by offering direct assistance, advocating changes in public policy, and modeling alternatives to the present structures.
- *Practices engaging the arts.* The arts can play a special role in practices nurturing the capacities of a hopeful imagination, for they shock us out of our refusal to see the harsher realities of life and help us imagine alternatives to the present.

In this section, I have portrayed the moral formation of congregations primarily through the practices frame. Practices that embody the covenants of creation, redemption, and glorification create a congregational ethos that cultivates moral capacities among its members. Since my examples were brief and designed to help you imagine some of the ways congregational formation might shape the core capacities of the Christian moral life, it is important to end this section by calling attention to what is assumed in this account. Practices include narratives, relationships, and models, key elements of a community's moral ethos as described by Ricoeur. The practice of confession in the context of worship, for example, does more than engage people in a series of rote actions. It typically interprets such actions with references to the story of God's seeking love and the promise of forgiveness. It invites people to consider their relationships or offers them models with which to consider their collective guilt as members of larger communities. It is this sort of "bundling" of practice, narrative, relationships, and models that serve as the focal point of moral formation in congregations.

MORAL EDUCATION: PRACTICES WITHOUT PRINCIPLES BECOME PROVINCIAL

We now turn to moral education, dealing with issues brought into focus by the curriculum frame. It is primarily here that I will take up the important role given to universal ethical principles by Ricoeur. At the end of chapter 9, I reviewed categories of the curriculum frame derived from our earlier dialogue with Howard Gardner. In these categories, the threefold covenant ethic described above is conceptualized as the *endstates* of moral education, which guide a congregation in forming educational pathways. As people grow toward these endstates, they gain the capacity to assess critically their congregations and other communities against the universal scope of God's covenant love, raising questions like: Do these communities acknowledge the equal moral worth of all human beings in practices and policies that are just and fair? Are they committed to peacemaking as a form of settling conflicts? Do they encourage us to enjoy our neighbors' enjoyments as a form of love? As I have noted, designing a curriculum can only be done locally, taking account of the particular resources, people, and circumstances of a specific congregation. What follows, thus, are guidelines for thinking through the sorts of issues this involves.

 1. *View moral education in terms of the image of a widening circle of moral concern that extends outward to the universal, inclusive scope of God's covenant love.* This guideline portrays the educational pathways of moral education with the image of a widening circle that is rooted in the primary relationships of our family and friends and gradually expands outward to the community of creation. Attitudes, knowledge, and actional competencies are gradually widened to new social spheres and relationships as people move from one phase of the curriculum to another. To provide a example of what this involves, I will describe an

educational pathway that takes its bearings from an ethic of equal regard. This is based on God's covenant with creation, which affirms the equal moral worth of all human beings who are created in God's image and the sanctity of all of life. I will focus on communicative justice, a form of power sharing and decision making in which people are treated with fairness along three lines: (1) All relevant parties affected by a decision or policy have the opportunity to articulate their points of view, which are not caricatured or marginalized; (2) all parties have the opportunity to influence the outcome through procedures that are open and fair; and (3) the resulting decisions or policies are recognized by all parties as the fair outcome of their deliberations, even if they disagree with actual decisions or policies that are made. As a moral ideal, communicative justice is unlikely to be found in pure form in any actual social relationship or organization. Yet it alerts those who hold this ideal to problems in the power-sharing and decision-making practices of their relationships, organizations, and political communities, serving as a critical test.

What sort of educational pathway might teach the participants of a congregation the attitudes, knowledge, and skills of communicative justice? An important first step takes place in the home in the form of family meetings in which children and parents participate together in setting family rules, making decisions, and dividing up the chores of household maintenance in a fair and nonsexist manner. In the church school during the *primary phase,* this sort of participatory rule setting and decision making is extended beyond the family along two lines.[48] First, children are included in the task of setting rules for their classes, even though the teacher retains responsibility for enforcing these rules. Second, teachers use times of discussion and sharing to help their students develop their listening and perspective-taking skills, as well as their capacities for empathy, taking turns, and expressing disagreements in ways that are respectful.

During the *secondary phase* of the curriculum, youth play a more active role in the planning and governance of the youth group and classes (e.g., the topics discussed, the focus of retreats, standards of behavior for mission trips). The goal is to allow youth to participate in decision-making processes that are open and fair. The moral discussion method of teaching also is important during this phase, and we explored an example of this in our examination of Nassau's youth group in chapter 5. It is an approach in which the teacher does not give answers but encourages students to articulate their own perspectives, to listen closely to one another, and to reconsider their initial insights in light of the insights of others. The emergence of abstract reasoning makes it possible to teach young people the principles and procedures of this sort of moral conversation as an explicit discourse ethic, which subsequently can be used to reflect critically on spheres and relationships beyond the church.

During the *critical phase* of moral education, a central task is supporting the development of a self-chosen system of ethical thinking. Studying the biblical and theological foundations of an ethic of equal regard along these lines, thus, is important. It is also important that people be given the opportunity to use this ethic to evaluate other spheres of life, exploring its relevance to families, public policies, cultural patterns, and economic systems. Debate and discussion of controversial social issues is a teaching approach that may be especially useful during this phase, for it gives people the opportunity to practice moral argumentation in which they give moral reasons for their position and hear the challenges of others. Such discussions work best if they are guided by an explicit set of rules and procedures that embody the fundamental tenets of communicative justice.

In the *postcritical phase* of moral education, the ethical principle of equal regard is taught as an inclusive moral ideal that articulates central values of the Christian tradition, but recognition also is given to the complexity of this tradition and the ways it supports ethical perspectives beyond this ideal alone. The limits of equal regard in both theory and practice are explored. This phase gives people the opportunity to dialogue with individuals and communities that challenge this perspective, nurturing their capacity to participate in the pluralistic social contexts of civil society and in the political arena.

Projecting educational pathways of this sort takes systematic and intentional planning on the part of the leaders of a congregation's educational ministry. They must start with a picture of the endstates desired and then design a curriculum of moral education that builds up moral capacities and expands them to new social spheres as people move from one phase to another.

2. Present particular moral teachings in a holistic framework that relates them to a narrative of God's covenants in creation, redemption, and glorification. Too often, moral education in the church takes place in small increments that focus on particular Bible stories or moral rules. This breaks the connection between our identity as God's new covenant people and the moral responsibilities that flow from this identity. An overriding curricular goal of moral education, thus, is to relate particular moral teachings to a narrative of the congregation as a covenant community, within the longer story of Israel and the church. If teachers are given the opportunity to learn this narrative framework through programmatic Bible studies such as *Kerygma* or *Bethel* or through teacher education, they will be able to help their students relate particular Bible stories and moral rules to other parts of this story. They also will be able to offer their students brief summaries of this larger narrative, integrating learning from year to year.

3. Cultivate the moral emotions. This curricular goal has two basic dimensions: (1) the intentional use of a language of the moral emotions in teaching, introducing terms such as *empathy, guilt, shame, pleasure,* or *outrage*; and (2) fostering moral emotional intelligence. The second of these dimensions focuses on helping students learn to recognize their own emotions and those of others in situations where something is at stake morally. When exploring a Bible story, case study, or role play, thus, it is not enough to state some general moral rule or principle. It also is necessary to explore what other people might be feeling in such situations and the students' own emotional responses. This gives students the opportunity to become more attuned to their emotions as ways of assessing the moral significance of situations. It also gives them the chance to develop their capacities for empathy, sympathy, outrage, and other moral emotions. Learning to name and use the moral emotions prepares students to assess critically the communities to which they belong in two key ways: (1) by cultivating insight into the emotional patterns taking shape in their families and primary relationships, and (2) by fostering moral dispositions that stand in tension with the dominant culture.

4. *Teach moral knowledge in its variety but cultivate it systematically.* In my earlier discussion of moral knowledge, I drew attention to the variety of cognitive structures employed by the moral imagination. Moral rules and principles have a role, but they are not as fundamental as prototypes, frames, metaphorical mapping, and narratives in our moral knowledge. From childhood through adulthood, for example, we will categorize moral situations in terms of prototypes—paradigmatic instances of justice, peacemaking, and hospitality—and will reason analogically from these prototypes to situations that are both similar and dissimilar (metaphorical mapping).

With this varied mix of moral contents in mind, it is quite important for congregations to develop a systematic plan of the central moral ideals that will be taught throughout the curriculum, from grade to grade and from phase to phase. Teachers might learn this plan through teacher education. In light of the three-fold covenant ethic developed in this chapter, I would include moral ideals such as these: Love your neighbor as yourself. Do to others as you would have them do to you. Just as God in Christ has accepted and forgiven you, so you are to accept and forgive others. Do not repay evil for evil, but overcome evil with goodness. Show hospitality to strangers, for God's people were once strangers in a strange land.

Children in the primary phase will not understand these moral ideals abstractly, but they will develop knowledge of the values they represent if they are taught in conjunction with concrete, prototypical situations and stories. By introducing these sorts of moral ideals at an early age and returning to them repeatedly throughout the curriculum, students develop a much clearer understanding of the central moral commitments of their congregation. As they grow older, these moral ideals can be taught as abstract ethical principles and as part of an ethical system of beliefs and values.

5. *Teach the skills and roles of moral action.* As I noted in my original discussion of moral action, it is one thing to know what you ought to do and quite another to have the skills to bring this about. Many Christian values, moreover, stand in tension with the surrounding culture. Peacemaking, fidelity in relationships, and other Christian values will seem unrealistic and therefore irrelevant unless students are given the chance to practice strategies that might be used to actualize these values in their everyday lives. Children and youth, for example, can learn ways of dealing with bullies that do not resort to violence. Youth and adults, likewise, can learn strategies of nonviolent communication and protest. When they learn and practice these skills in the church, they are far more likely to use them in other parts of their lives.

6. Use both didactic and eductive teaching methods. The distinction between didactic and eductive teaching methods is crude but makes an important point. *Didactic* methods focus on the transmission of the core features of a particular subject matter, based on the teacher's advanced study or prior knowledge. Teachers do, in fact, have something to "hand on," to use Paul's language, or at least they should. But this is only part of the story. "To educe" means to draw out or elicit, and accordingly, *eductive* teaching methods attempt to draw out the emotions, reasoning, and actional competencies that students already possess and to deepen them in certain ways. This might include teaching strategies such as asking questions that evoke thinking or encouraging students to "feel into" the point of view of others. Moral education involves both didactic and eductive teaching methods, transmitting the subject matter to students and also drawing out their capacities to feel, think, and act.

7. Make ample use of stories of moral exemplars that appeal to the imagination. One of the most important ways moral emotions, knowledge, and actions are cultivated *together* in Christian moral education is through the use of stories of moral exemplars, especially through the use of stories, films, and dramas that *show* us exemplars in ways that surpass our ability to *say* the moral qualities such persons possess. The remarkable popularity of the Harry Potter series and J. R. R. Tolkien's *Lord of the Rings* should alert us to the possibilities of using literature in moral education. These books represent the genre of secondary world fantasy literature, which invites readers to enter imaginatively into a coherent, alternative world quite different from their own.[49] In using this sort of literature in moral education, the first and most important task is to travel with people into these alternative worlds, resisting the temptation to reduce their meaning to "the moral" of the story. This involves helping them explore different characters, key moments of decision, dramatic patterns, and other aspects of the world and plot created by the story. Only then, as a second step, do we encourage our students to return from this alternative world to discover analogous choices, situations, and persons in their own lives and world.

This sort of use of literature in moral education makes a broader point. Within the many different roles the arts might play, one of the most important is the provision of moral exemplars with whom our students can identify. Such figures are not necessarily perfect or without faults. But that is the point. They help us imagine the possibilities of the Christian moral life in a world of complexity and ambiguity, in which the realities of guilt and tragic choice are real.

In this section, I have provided guidelines for moral education as it is seen through the curriculum frame. In a systematic, intentional, and sustained program of Christian moral education, people gradually acquire the universal ethical principles, or what I prefer to call universal moral ideals, that allow them to test critically the practices and commitments of their congregation, voluntary associations, country, and other communities. Moral education, thus, plays a special and important role in congregational life. Ideally, it gradually broadens members' circle of moral concern in ways that reflect the universal scope of God's covenant love in creation, redemption, and glorification. It provides congregations with moral principles or ideals that keep them from becoming too provincial, from ascribing moral worth only to those people or groups most like themselves.

PRINCIPLES WITHOUT PHRONESIS LIE FALLOW: THE PILGRIMAGE AND LEADERSHIP FRAMES

In this final section, we take up the third dimension of Ricoeur's model: moral phronesis. Without the ability to draw on our ethical principles or ideals in real-life situations, they will lie fallow, playing little role in guiding our everyday lives. Earlier I argued that we should broaden our understanding of moral phronesis beyond moral reasoning to include our moral emotions, the moral imagination, and our competence as moral actors. These too contribute to the task of making moral sense of particular situations.

Moral Phronesis through the Pilgrimage Frame

In this book, I have argued that congregations must give greater attention to the diverse individuals in their midst. How can congregations do a better job of supporting the moral phronesis of individuals? Here are three guidelines.

1. *Use teaching strategies to give individuals the opportunity to relate Christian morality to the particular circumstances of their lives.* This guideline may seem fairly obvious. Yet its importance is not always acknowledged in the actual moral education of congregations. Adult education classes in particular tend to overuse the lecture method. Even when the discussion method is used, it often treats moral themes or issues at a level far removed from individuals' lives. Little attention is given to learning activities that make it safe for individuals to bring their life circumstances into the discussion. This requires thinking through how the class might be broken up into small groups or giving time for personal reflection, journaling, and so forth. In a class for parents of teenagers, for example, it is not enough to provide general information about teen drug use, sexual activity, and peer pressure, for these will mean very different things to the parents involved, depending on their particular teenager. Participants need the chance to make moral sense of their very different circumstances.

2. *Develop personal relationships that support individuals' moral phronesis.* In the past, pastors, elders, and other leaders of the congregation served as moral guides.[50] This sort of relationship is neglected in many contemporary churches for a variety of reasons. American culture, for example, is highly individualistic, and many people resist having religious leaders tell them how they ought to think and act. Moreover, therapeutic perspectives have become more prominent, leading pastors to bracket out moral guidance in order to forge the sort of nonjudgmental relationship that is important in counseling. I have no desire to turn back

the clock and throw out the many gains of pastoral care's dialogue with the therapeutic disciplines. Rather, I am calling our attention to relationships of a different sort, relationships in which moral guidance is asked for and needed.

This requires leaders who are adept at moral reflection on contemporary issues and have the capacity to listen, hold confidences in trust, and to provide moral guidance eductively. In many congregations, youth pastors, church school teachers, and confirmation leaders are playing this role already; they communicate a willingness to stay after class and talk if this is something a student desires. These kinds of one-on-one moral conversations should not be confined to children and youth; adults also need this sort of support for their moral phronesis.

3. *Offer personalized education in conjunction with rituals of covenanting.* A Christian congregation is one of the few moral communities in contemporary society that offers rituals with an explicit covenantal structure in which promises are made before God and the Christian community. These include baptism, confirmation, marriage, marriage renewal, commissioning for mission, and small group covenants.[51] They often are important markers of an individual's transition to a new stage on her pilgrimage of faith, and signal new rights and responsibilities. If linked to personalized forms of education, these rituals of covenant making are potentially an important way of cultivating moral phronesis. In prebaptismal or premarriage counseling, for example, this might include a close examination of the promises that will be made in the ritual and exploration of the moral implications of these promises for the particular people involved. It may well be that the best people to engage in this sort of moral conversation are not pastors but members similar in age and circumstance to those entering into these covenants.

Moral Phronesis through the Leadership Frame

My interviews for this book have convinced me that leaders play an important role as moral exemplars in a congregation's response to the adaptive challenges of its own time and place. Interviewees consistently lifted up such persons as exemplifying the values of the Christian moral life. At URC Stellenbosch, this included people such as Nelson Mandela and Desmond Tutu, who were described as embodying the hopes of national reconciliation. While comparable national leaders were absent in my interviews at Somang and Nassau, local leaders were identified as moral exemplars—in the congregation, parachurch organizations, or local communities. On the basis of this research, I want to underscore two important points: (1) Formal and informal leaders set the tone of the ethos of a congregation, for better and for worse, and (2) they play a particularly important role as models of moral phronesis in the face of adaptive challenges.

First, the influence of leaders as moral exemplars is a double-edged sword. In service-oriented congregations such as Somang, Nassau, and URC Stellenbosch, they serve as models close at hand of a life of service and giving, which can be imitated and can set the tone for the moral ethos of the congregation. Yet leaders can also serve as negative models of the Christian moral life, fostering a moral ethos of low-commitment Christianity, uncritical patriotism, or a lifestyle driven by personal success and conspicuous consumption. Ministers and nominating committees will do well to seek out leaders who exemplify the sort of moral values they hope the congregation as a whole will embody. They must use criteria other than success in secular careers.

Second, leaders play an especially important role in the ways a congregation handles adaptive challenges. They can model the sort of wise phronesis needed in such circumstances, or they can cut off the creativity and conflict that often comes to the fore at such times. It is rare that a lay leader will acquire by osmosis the dispositions, moral reasoning, and communication skills needed to handle adaptive challenges. These capacities are nurtured through an intentional program of leadership education that gives people opportunities to practice making moral sense of such challenges before they face them in an actual situation.

In the following chapter, we explore some of the ways discernment can be integrated into the mundane work of church committees in order to lay a foundation for handling more difficult issues before the congregation. When we explore these practices, recall this chapter's discussion of the important role of leaders in modeling moral phronesis.

Chapter 11

Discernment:

New Practices for Contemporary Congregations

Winking at gross sexual misconduct by a leader of the church; Christians taking other Christians to court to settle their differences; intense debate over contemporary social issues that seem to violate long-standing religious norms; a faction that views itself as especially wise, knowledgeable, and mature creating problems for the "less advanced" members of church—does this sound like a synopsis of the headlines of the religious section of our newspapers? It very well could be. Yet this list simply reminds us of some of the issues with which Paul struggled in his Corinthian correspondence. We examined them in part 1 when we looked at how Paul attempted to teach the Corinthian community to engage in discernment. As we struggle with similar issues, we need to look over Paul's shoulder and discover how we might do a better job of teaching our own congregations to engage in the task of discernment today. Let us begin by recalling some of the things we learned in our exploration of Paul.

KEY ELEMENTS OF DIVERSE PRACTICES OF DISCERNMENT

The etymological roots of *discernment* lie in terms meaning "to judge," "sift," or "render a decision." Paul uses *discernment* to refer to the kinds of judgments his congregations face as they try to determine God's will in their everyday lives. He gave special attention to the importance of discernment in the face of confusing, complex, or contentious issues. He encouraged his congregations to integrate practices of discernment into their lives so that when they faced especially difficult issues they would have a repertoire of socially shared activities they might draw on. Having learned to discern small matters, they would be better prepared to discern big ones.

The metaphor we used to understand Paul's picture of discernment was *bifocal vision,* which captured his attempt to teach his predominantly Gentile congregations how to think and live eschatologically. On the one hand, this involved learning to see "things near" as a battleground in which the Spirit is engaged in a struggle, attempting to give birth proleptically to the new creation in the face of the continuing power of sin and death. On the other hand, this involved learning to see "things far," remembering in hope the promise of God's future for creation revealed in the death and resurrection of Jesus Christ.

We also examined discernment as the weaving together of several story lines in a multilayered plot. Paul invited his congregations to weave their own story lines into the longer story of Israel and, even more importantly, into the story line of the corporate person, Jesus Christ. In their baptisms, the Spirit brought them into fellowship (*koinonia*) with Christ, and as they participated "in" him the pattern of their everyday lives was reshaped toward his likeness. Discernment, thus, is a weaving together of stories, learning to see the unfolding dramas of our lives within the larger Theo-drama of God's dealings with the world.

Finally, we explored the variety of practices of discernment Paul commended to the Corinthians. At one end of the continuum was the kind of open debate and discussion characterizing his treatment of meat sacrificed to idols. Here he articulated a variety of perspectives found in the Corinthian community and afforded a measure of freedom to individual conscience. At the other end of the continuum was the weighty discernment involved in expelling a man from the community who was engaged in egregious sexual immorality. In between these two extremes, he chided the community because it had not established "judges" to settle conflicts in-house but had taken its disputes to the secular courts. Paul also invited the Corinthians to join him in moral reflection on the significance of life in the body.

Key Elements of Discernment

If we pause and reflect on this summary, we can identify several key elements of discernment:

- *Judgment*—Discernment is not needed when prescribed rules or roles provide us with adequate guidance in determining what we should do. It is needed in circumstances that are complex or confusing, when we are uncertain how we should proceed and must sift through various factors in coming to a judgment.

- *The Spirit's guidance*—Discernment is not simply a matter of human agency or reasoning. It is actively seeking the Spirit's guidance in making judgments about how we should proceed. This involves a range of truth-seeking mechanisms, including (a) the emotions, (b) rational debate, discussion, and consensus formation, (c) consultation of relevant authorities, especially Scripture and tradition, and (d) the creative imagination.
- *Testing the spirits*—In recognition of the seductive power of evil and the capacity for human self-deception, discernment involves testing the spirits vying for our attention. Insights and ideas are not to be immediately trusted. Even the insights of the prophets must be discerned. This critical testing also is necessary because choices must sometimes be made between several worthy values that cannot be pursued simultaneously.
- *Orientation toward the future in hope*—Discernment as bifocal vision involves learning to view the present in light of God's promised future. In hope, it discerns hidden possibilities of change that may be latent within the present but as yet unrealized. Imaginative discernment is a goad of creative transformation.
- *Judging according to standards of reversal*—Discernment is not merely a species of problem-solving reasoning or utilitarian calculation common in our contemporary world. It judges according to the reversal at the heart of the cross and resurrection.
- *The interweaving of stories*—Discernment involves weaving together the stories of everyday life, including the life of the congregation, and the stories of Israel, the church, and the corporate person, Jesus Christ.

I believe that it would be misleading to draw together these elements of discernment into a single, integrated model, largely because they have been organized into such different patterns in the practices of discernment found in the Christian tradition. In the early centuries of Christianity, for example, a tradition of discernment emerged among the desert fathers that influenced various forms of monasticism. It involved testing the spirits within the context of an ascetic way of life, focusing on the individual's inner spiritual struggle to live a life undistracted from worldly pleasures and temptations. Later, Ignatius developed a structured process of discernment as part of an extended retreat, which in recent years has been used by Christians who are not part of a monastic community. American Reformed theologian Jonathan Edwards developed a framework to discern the operation of the Holy Spirit in individuals' lives in the face of the emotional upheavals of the Great Awakening. He and other Christian pastors faced the task of helping their church members sort out emotions and inner promptings that were genuinely inspired by the Spirit from those that were counterfeit and the result of group hysteria. The Quakers have developed practices of discernment for the decision making of the community, which includes "talking up" the issue within the community, attending to the inner light of the Spirit within individual participants, spending time in prayer and silence, and working toward consensus. This diversity cannot legitimately be boiled down to a single model, and we would do well to acknowledge at the outset the richness and variety of the Christian tradition of discernment.

Why Problem-Solving Reasoning Is Not Enough

For much of the past century in the United States, religious education in both mainline Protestantism and liberal Roman Catholicism were deeply influenced by philosophical pragmatism, especially as formulated by John Dewey. At the heart of Dewey's program of progressive education is an understanding of problem-solving reasoning that includes six elements: (1) the experience of being brought up short when our normal habits and perceptions encounter a situation that is puzzling or confusing; (2) problem-definition that brings some measure of initial clarity to what is problematic in the situation; (3) investigation of the problem, gathering information that is relevant to our understanding of the situation and how we might proceed; (4) consideration of a variety of possible responses; (5) choice and implementation of a particular course of action; and (6) openness to assess the consequences of our course of action and a willingness to make future revisions in light of this feedback.[1]

Dewey argued that these steps reflected the core of experimental, scientific reasoning but were also found in the problem solving of everyday life. He believed that democratic societies facilitate problem-solving reasoning through shared communication, which allows people to debate and discuss possible courses of action from a wide range of perspectives. Educators, thus, should approach their classes as "democracies in miniature," fostering this sort of reasoning, shared communication, and decision making.

In light of the pervasive influence of problem-solving reasoning on American culture in general and religious education in particular, it is important to distinguish between discernment and this form of rationality. It is not that Christian discernment eschews altogether problem-solving reasoning, but as we saw in chapter 8, it draws on a richer understanding of experience than the relatively narrow range of "reflective experience" championed in Dewey's approach. Another way of putting this is to say that discernment uses truth-seeking mechanisms that are typically marginalized in problem solving, which often slides into technical rationality—the sort of means-ends calculation appropriate to the marketplace. These truth-seeking mechanisms include the following four aspects:

1. *The truth we feel.* Recent research on the human brain has revealed the crucial role of the emotions in both everyday life and the higher mental functions.[2] Our capacity to "feel a feeling" is a complex, second-order activity, providing access not only to our internal states but also to our evaluation of external events. In ordinary human communication, for example, our capacity to "read" the emotional context of verbal contents is crucial to understanding. Discern-

ment typically has included attention to our emotional states as a truth-seeking mechanism. It has provided a language to describe the religious affections and an interpretive framework with which to make sense of what they are telling us. These include emotions as diverse as a sense of utter desolation, a diffuse sense of guilt, a sense of inner peace, and feelings of ecstatic bliss. The Spirit of God is interpreted as speaking to us through such emotions. Taking them into account, as well as scrutinizing and testing them, is a part of the informed judgment of discernment.

2. *The truth we receive.* Tradition is anathema to problem-solving reasoning, for it is viewed as the dead weight of the past that prevents us from making autonomous judgments in the present. In contrast, discernment is dependent on both the collective wisdom of tradition and the revelatory capacity of the stories of Scripture to provide us with a truthful account of our lives and world. Weaving together the stories we have received and those of our everyday lives allows us to discern insights and actions likely to be overlooked if we rely solely on our own reflective capacities or contemporary culture. Wise judgment is not viewed as antithetical to tradition but as its creative reappropriation in new and different contexts.

3. *The truth we reason together.* Reason plays an important role in discernment, and it is here that problem solving has its place, though it is contextualized within a richer understanding of human rationality. Today the natural and social sciences acknowledge that reason always works within a matrix of assumptions that includes particular values, procedures, and patterns of communication. The focus has shifted from reason as one universal pattern of truth seeking to a communicative model of rationality whose patterns vary in different cultures and disciplines. This broader and richer understanding of human reason helps us to see that discernment and rationality are not antithetical. Like other forms of reasoning, discernment works within a set of values and procedures that are shared by a specific Christian community and have been developed to allow its members to arrive at reasoned judgments. These rational procedures have taken different forms in various practices of discernment.

4. *The truth we imagine.* One of the severest limits of problem-solving reasoning is its relative inattention to the role of the imagination. By teaching us to think primarily in terms of problems that have solutions, such reasoning draws attention away from the imaginative frames that shape what we see as "problems" in the first place. In recent years, greater attention has been paid to the aesthetic dimension of scientific discovery, acknowledging the role of the imagination in human creativity and new insights. Christian discernment has long given attention to this aesthetic dimension, orienting the members of the Christian community to alternative frames with which to see and act in everyday life. Jonathan Edwards, for example, gave great attention to the beauty of God, which led him to describe the religious affections as providing a "taste" of the divine beauty that reorders our experience of everyday life. More recently, various Christian scholars have called attention to the role of the eschatological symbols of the faith in

reorienting the imagination of the community of faith. Walter Brueggemann, for example, has described the prophetic imagination of ancient Israel along these lines.[3] Discernment, thus, is oriented to the truth we can imagine, shaping our particular judgments in the present toward the possibilities disclosed by an alternative imagination.

In short, Christian discernment uses a wide range of truth-seeking mechanisms. It draws on forms of experience that are much broader and richer than the "reflective experience" of problem-solving reasoning and accesses the truth we feel, receive, reason together, and imagine. In the Christian tradition, these truth-seeking mechanisms have been organized in quite different patterns in various practices of discernment.

CULTIVATING A CONGREGATIONAL ETHOS OF DISCERNMENT

Building up a congregation that is a community of discernment involves two basic tasks. One task is to help the members of a congregation understand why discernment is an important part of the Christian life and to offer them concrete models of discernment that they might use. (Later we examine three discernment practices that might be used by contemporary congregations.) The second task is more indirect. It involves cultivating a congregational ethos that sets the stage for participation in more intentional and focused practices of discernment. I will begin by examining three ways the congregational curriculum might build up this sort of ethos: (1) by cultivating the intimacy of Christian friendship, (2) by valuing the creativity with which people appropriate Scripture and Christian tradition, and (3) by teaching the gospel as a word of love that lays a foundation for prayer. Once you see what each of these entails, it will not be difficult to think of ways ethos building might take place in other parts of your congregation's life.

Cultivating the Intimacy of Friendship

Many church school teachers and youth group leaders realize that how they relate to children and youth is every bit as important as what they teach, perhaps even more important. If you were raised in the church, recall your experience of Sunday school or the youth group. You may have difficulty remembering specific ideas that you learned in a particular class, but you will have little trouble remembering the special teacher or youth group leader who let you know they cared. You probably also will be able to remember the names of some of your closest church friends.

Usually we think of friendship in terms of such qualities as mutual attraction, shared interests, and enjoyment of time spent together. While this is true, Paul Wadell argues that the core of friendship is intimacy: "An undying need of every human being is the need to communicate our self, to share our soul and spirit with others in the hope that we might live in communion with them. This reciprocal communication of selves is the most humanizing and life-giving activity, and it is the lifeblood of friendship—whether it be friendship with God, the special friendship of marriage, or friendship with others."[4] Discernment depends in fundamental ways on the intimacy of friendship.

Why is this the case? In the presence of others whom I trust, I access my feelings and may find the freedom to explore my secret fears and flights of fancy. Among friends, I may even speak aloud the deepest truths of my life and how I wish things might be. Conversation with friends sometimes allows me to bring to expression insights and connections that I never would have discovered by myself. It affords the kind of mutuality that allows insight to build on insight until an entirely new way of thinking is given birth. Real friendship allows me to share in ways I dare not do with others. I know that my confidences will be kept in trust. I am afforded the sort of acceptance that allows me to be who I am and yet calls me to my best self.

A curriculum can build up an ethos of friendship in at least five ways:

1. *Group-building activities*—These activities are not extraneous fluff but are important ways of cultivating a sense that the congregation is a place where people get to know one another and may even become friends.
2. *Opportunities for appropriate self-disclosure among peers*—These range from the nonthreatening sharing of highs and lows to more risky sharing of personal dreams and problems, which involves greater intimacy.
3. *Relationships between teachers and students*—These relationships often are different from peer-peer relationships. They may be closer to mentoring relationships, which include the mutual affection and enjoyment that characterizes friendship.
4. *Cooperative learning*—This teaching approach encourages people to work together and to learn from each other, rather than by themselves and in competition.
5. *Teachers who model caring relationships*—As teachers care for their students, students learn to care for one another.

At first, friendship nurtured through the curriculum might involve little more than shared interests and just plain fun. But gradually, a deeper and harder form of Christian friendship may emerge that includes honest disagreements, genuine sharing, and calls to accountability. But this is likely to occur only if a foundation of mutual trust and sharing is first laid.

Valuing Creativity in the Appropriation of Scripture and Christian Tradition

A second important way the congregational curriculum prepares people to participate in practices of discernment is by affirming their creative application of

Scripture and Christian tradition to contemporary life. In the chapter on cate-chesis, I discussed this idea extensively. Here I simply note the possibility of a pos-itive *symbiotic* relationship between discernment and teaching the Bible and tradition. The interpretive activities of catechesis include attention to contem-porary life—in the mimetic appropriation of texts, in attentiveness to the present activity of the Holy Spirit, and in the interpretation of congregational praxis and the contemporary context. These sorts of interpretive activities lie at the heart of weaving together the stories of the Bible and our own stories that is so important to discernment.

With this in mind, teachers might consider the following four guidelines:

1. In balancing the responsible interpretation of texts and individuals' creative appropriation, priority should not automatically be given to responsible interpreta-tion. Teachers who have studied a text carefully in preparation for their teaching realize that people of all ages often depart markedly from a responsible interpre-tation of textual meaning as they make a creative leap into the present. Teachers are faced with a dilemma. Should they correct the students' interpretation of the text or affirm their creativity? As a rule of thumb, it seems best to me to allow great latitude for the creative process, for it prepares students for the kind of cre-ativity that is so important to discernment. Obviously, good judgment is called for here. Children deserve the greatest degree of latitude. Adolescents and adults have greater readiness to make critical judgments about the meaning of texts and might be encouraged to think again.

2. A helpful way to correct and expand the interpretive insights of students is for other members of the class or group to share their creative appropriation of a text. One of the most effective ways a teacher can guide students who are "overly creative" in their appropriation of biblical texts is to allow them to listen to the applica-tions of others. This takes the teacher out of the role of class expert and prepares students for the kind of cooperative sharing and rational discussion important to discernment.

3. Engaging multiple intelligences in the appropriation of Scripture and tradition is an important way of schooling people in the use of truth-seeking mechanisms beyond problem-solving reasoning. Earlier I noted that discernment makes use of a wide range of truth-seeking mechanisms beyond problem-solving reasoning. This guideline links this to our discussion of multiple intelligence theory in chap-ter 5, which called attention to the importance of teaching activities that engage people's varied forms of intelligence. This sort of multimodal teaching prepares students for the art of discernment by cultivating forms of intelligence beyond logical-mathematical reasoning alone.

4. Building connections between the Bible, tradition, and other spheres of life pre-pares students for the kind of connection making involved in discernment. Through-out modernity, religion often has been confined to the private sphere—to the congregation, the family, and the individual's personal search for meaning. In contrast, discernment may be directed to any area of life—from prophetic discernment of politics to ethical dilemmas at work. Learning to make these sorts of connections should start early in the congregational curriculum and should gradually be broadened as young people's boundaries of social awareness expand.

The Gospel of Love and the Foundation of Prayer

A third way the curriculum helps create an ethos that prepares the members of a congregation to participate in discernment is by presenting the gospel in ways that lay a foundation for prayer. If children and youth gain nothing more from the Sunday school and youth group, they should come away with an understanding of the gracious nature of God's love in Christ, a love that is offered to them as a free gift and invites them into a relationship in which they can trust the guiding, supportive presence of God's Spirit. God desires their friendship, and the personal conversation of prayer is the simplest way of building this friendship. Prayer is our response to God's seeking love; it is friendship returned.

Discernment finds one of its most important grounding points here. Our willingness to share ourselves with God in the intimacy of personal conversation and our desire to please God and discern God's will are born of our sense that we are loved by Another who knows us far better than we know ourselves. Prayer can lead us to a hard and lonely place where God seems more like an enemy or an aching absence than a loving parent or friend. But at its most elemental starting point, prayer takes root in hearing the gospel of God's gracious love; we prepare church members for more demanding practices of discernment when we communicate this good news through the congregational curriculum.

In short, the congregational curriculum can help build up an ethos that supports practices of discernment by cultivating friendship, affirming the creative appropriation of Scripture and tradition, and communicating the gospel of love as a foundation of the personal conversation of prayer. Imagine all three of these as integrated into the primary and secondary phases of your congregation's curriculum. A kind of readiness to engage in practices of discernment would be cultivated among the children and youth of the church. Now imagine them present in the adult curriculum. I believe it would have the same effect.

In the remainder of this chapter, I explore three practices of discernment that might be established in contemporary congregations. Each practice is closely related to one of the frames that emerged in part 2. *Practices of vocational discernment* give special attention to the unfolding pilgrimages of individuals, helping people to discern what God is calling them to do and be at a particular point in their lives. *Practices of discernment in the decision making of congregational leaders* give special attention to the issues brought into focus by the leadership frame. By learning how to integrate discernment into the ordinary work of church committees, it prepares leaders for the major adaptive challenges the congregation may face. *Practices of prayer as a form of discernment* are examined through the

curriculum frame, identifying some of the ways a life of prayer might be cultivated in a systematic, intentional, and sustained manner.

PRACTICES OF VOCATIONAL DISCERNMENT

Vocational discernment gives special attention to the kinds of issues identified by
the pilgrimage frame. It recognizes that the incorporation of individual members
into the life of a congregation is especially challenging in our highly differentiated, pluralistic social context and that the life circumstances of individuals
change markedly over the course of their lives. This practice seeks to respond to
these realities by providing a context in which individuals can discover or rework
their sense of vocation, their calling to partnership with God at a particular point
in their lives.

When first establishing vocational discernment in your congregation, it may
be helpful to think in terms of target groups. These are people who face similar
changes of major proportions in their lives. They often are especially receptive to
participating in practices of vocational discernment that are oriented toward their
particular needs. The following are five potential target groups.

1. High school students beginning the application process for college—This is a
time of high stress for youth and their families. They now face the realities of
financial resources, grade point average, peer pressure, and the prospects of leaving home. They must cope with deciding where to apply and the possibility of
having their hopes dashed. Congregations might turn this difficult period into a
meaningful process of discernment with a program that combines practical decision-making tools, meetings with a guidance counselor and/or college admis-
sions officer, instruction in how to write an application, and a small group of
peers who work together to discern the spiritual and ethical issues at stake in
choosing a college.

2. Church members facing retirement—Men and women who are nearing
retirement face complex issues: Where will they live? What sort of financial
resources will they have? How will they spend their time? Some congregations
help their members engage the challenges and possibilities of this transition by
inviting them to enter a process of structured discernment that gives special
attention to the new role God might be giving them to play during this period
of their life.

3. Couples with newborns—Families with newborns not only face high stress,
but they also are frequently sorting out new family patterns. Who will work?
Who will stay at home? What about day care? How can I teach my child good
values right from the start? Small groups of couples in similar circumstances are
a potentially potent context for discernment, giving them the chance to explore
the values at stake in giving answer to these kinds of questions and to consider a
range of possible family patterns beyond their families of origin.

4. Divorce support groups—There are many therapy groups designed to help the recently divorced survive the breakup of a marriage. There are far fewer church-based groups that allow them to engage this time of loss and transition as a process of discernment. Yet the church can offer spiritual resources that are not provided by therapy alone: confession and forgiveness, companionship with God, and the promise of new beginnings beyond the loss of old relationships. Depending on the participants, such groups might give attention to practical considerations if its members are now learning for the first time how to handle taxes, plan for retirement, and save for college education.

5. *Youth involved in service learning*—Increasingly, high schools across the United States are requiring young people to participate in some form of community service as a condition of graduation. Many congregations, moreover, involve their youth in various mission projects. Research indicates that these kinds of experience are most meaningful when the service component involves challenging tasks that go beyond busy work and the learning component includes time to process what they are experiencing and to reflect on related reading.[5] Some congregations involve youth in discernment groups that are closely related to service projects, giving them the opportunity to consider career paths and vocational patterns that include significant forms of service.

Many congregations have people who fall into these kinds of groups. In the face of a major transition or decision, they often are open to the sort of issues taken up in the practice of vocational discernment. In designing a practice for one of these target groups, it is important to include both individual and corporate components, with structured activities for individuals on their own and regular meetings of a small group. (I will return to this below.) It also is helpful to think of this practice as including three key elements: self-exploration, vocational clarification, and vocational actualization.

Self-exploration focuses on helping individuals discern patterns in their past and present lives. It may be useful to think of this in dramatological terms. What are the different acts of the drama of the participants' lives to the present? What scenes particularly stand out? What are the dramatic patterns, the moments of choice, conflict, and decision? What roles have they played in their partnership with God? This sort of life review and discernment of patterns enables participants to construct a longer and richer perspective on their lives in which to make such decisions as the college they should attend, the focus of their energies in retirement, or how they will handle the care of a newborn. Self-exploration provides people with the opportunity to pause, go deeper into themselves, and discern God's involvement in their particular life story.

Vocational clarification involves two tasks: helping individuals to identify their spiritual gifts and giving them the opportunity to explore a new sense of vocation. My understanding of both of these things draws on the theology of spiritual gifts and vocation developed in chapter 7. Spiritual gifts are not supernatural "additions" but are an individual's natural endowments as they are given vitality and direction in interaction with the Holy Spirit. But identifying our spiritual gifts is not as straightforward as it might seem. Often we have natural gifts that lie fallow because of other commitments, or go unrecognized at school, work, or home. Sometimes it is only when we are given a new task to do that they come to the fore, often in surprising ways. An important part of vocational clarification is giving individuals the opportunity to explore their gifts, recalling parts of themselves that may have been put on the shelf for many years, or discovering gifts through involvement in new activities or projects.

The second task involves giving people the chance to explore what they believe God is calling them to do and be at this point in their lives. For young people, this may be their first opportunity to develop a sense of vocation and to explore the many different patterns this might take. For adults, it may involve remembering lost passions and dreams or forming new ones that are now possible in light of changes in their life circumstances. Or it may mean staying with long-term commitments or shifting the center of their energies within established patterns, from work to volunteer activities, for example. As we saw in chapter 7, vocation can take a wide variety of forms, and a key task of vocational clarification is to give people the chance to explore what this might mean for their lives in the present.

Vocational actualization turns from the present to the future, helping people take concrete steps toward actualizing their emerging sense of vocation. One of the most important roles a group can play is to help people visualize how to move from here to there and to serve as a source of accountability. For example, a high school junior might have begun to gain a clearer sense of the sort of college she would like to attend. But she needs to sit down with her parents to consider realistically the financial resources that are available. She also needs to line up several visits during the fall or coming months. One of the things a small group can do is help her to specify tasks to be done and hold her accountable for their accomplishment.

I indicated earlier that the practice of vocational discernment works best when it unfolds along two tracks simultaneously: structured times for individuals' discernment of certain issues on their own and participation in an ongoing small group. Even though individuals are largely looking at their own lives and exploring their own sense of calling, they need the help of others who offer encouragement and accountability and can save them from self-deception. The small group, moreover, provides a pattern to the discernment process, laying out a series of structured activities in which all participate. The fact that individuals are to share the fruits of these activities with others often motivates them to carry them out. A variety of good books on small groups have emerged in recent decades.[6] In working to establish the practice of vocational discernment in your congregation, it will be helpful to consult this literature. Training and supporting small group leaders will play an important role in the success of this practice.

DISCERNMENT AND LEADERSHIP

Here we examine discernment through the leadership frame, which focuses on the congregation in mission, caught up in the movement of God's self-giving love for the world. As such, the community of faith is directed beyond its own inner life to the surrounding social context, seeking to better understand this context, entering into a respectful dialogue with its partners in the human community, and working with them to respond to the common challenges they face. This theological under-standing of the missionary nature of the congregation led us in chapter 6 to enter into a dialogue with theories of organizational learning and leadership, which por-tray leaders as those people in a community who enable it to respond to the adap-tive challenges of its own time and place. Adaptive work, by definition, involves a significant challenge to a community's established identity and way of life. It rep-resents precisely the sort of situation in which congregations must discern the guid-ing light of the Spirit as they make judgments about how best to respond to a major challenge before them at a particular moment in time.

Yet it is somewhat misleading to portray the connection between discernment and leadership in these terms alone. One of the limits of Ronald Heifetz's theory is its description of leadership almost exclusively in terms of moments of signifi-cant adaptive challenge. But pastors and Christian educators do not spend most of their time helping their congregations come to terms with issues that challenge their identities and way of life. They face the more mundane administrative tasks of planning, recruiting, motivating, and implementing—the sorts of tasks involved in building and maintaining an open, well-functioning congregational system. Does not their leadership in these ordinary tasks have something to do with discernment?

I think it does. Integrating practices of discernment into the ongoing, ordi-nary work of congregational life may well be the most important way congrega-tions are schooled in the sort of discernment that will be needed when they face significant adaptive challenges. It is helpful, thus, to view leadership in terms of a continuum. At one end are the leadership tasks involved in significant adaptive work, the sorts of tasks described by Heifetz. At the other end of the continuum are the leadership tasks involved in system formation and maintenance. Since we have examined Heifetz's theory already, our focus here will be on system forma-tion and maintenance.

In recent decades, a helpful literature has emerged that explores the congre-gation in terms of systems thinking, providing insight into the tasks of system formation and maintenance.[7] One of the key points made in this literature is the importance of patterns of interaction and roles that structure a group's relation-ships and tasks. These patterns constitute a whole that is greater than the sum of its parts. When individuals become a part of an organization or group, they must learn the explicit and implicit norms that are embedded in its organizational structures and roles, patterns of communication, and procedures.

Discernment through the Leadership Frame

Adaptive Work	System Formation and Maintenance

Leadership as
-Identifying an adaptive challenge
-Creating a holding environment
-Creating procedures to examine the issues
-Framing the issues
-Orchestrating conflicting perspectives
-Choosing a decision-making process

Leadership as
-Identifying potential leaders
-Leadership education
-Creating values-based systems
-Cultivating a spiritual culture
-Sharing administrative burdens
-Ongoing nurture of leaders

Since most work in congregations is carried out by relatively small groups, it is helpful to think in terms of categories that are used to analyze small group systems. These categories identify two different types of system norms. *Task norms* have to do with the procedures and roles developed by the group to carry out its work. *Relationship norms* have to do with the patterns of interaction within the group, such as the style and flow of communication, power dynamics, level of group cohesion, and the level of individual satisfaction. In many organizations, task norms dominate. Small groups are nestled within a larger organization, and their specific tasks are largely determined by their particular function within this larger system. Relationship norms are viewed as important only to the extent that they impact positively or negatively the group's ability to accomplish its tasks. In many organizations, thus, people do not form a "whole person" orientation to other members of their group, but relate to one another in terms of their specific roles. Relational dynamics and personal needs only come to the fore as they impinge upon role performance.

Church members bring their experiences of small groups in other areas of life with them to their work on the councils and committees of their congregation. Unless they are given the chance to learn a different set of norms, they are apt to carry out their work in the congregation with the same task orientation they have learned elsewhere. Yet many church members know intuitively that this is not what they are looking for in their congregations. They do not merely want to accomplish a particular task that is needed by the larger congregational system. They hope to find friendship, to grow spiritually, to use gifts lying fallow in other parts of their lives, and to be part of a worthwhile cause that is larger than themselves. Reframing church councils and committees in terms of the practice of discernment allows room for all of these things.

It does so by a figure-ground shift that reverses the priority typically given to task over relationship. Most working groups place the task in the foreground and relationships in the background, but communities of discernment reverse this pattern. The primary "work" of church groups is not to accomplish certain tasks that are predetermined by the larger organization, but to become a particular kind of community, a community with enough trust and intimacy to discern together the guidance of the Spirit in their work on the congregation's behalf. In a sense, the particular goals they accomplish are less important than the good that flows from their participation in a church committee or council—the friendships they make, the feeling of vitality and creativity that is fostered, the chance to explore different perspectives with honesty, and the opportunity to pray with others and to be with them in silence.

Some denominations have well-established traditions of discernment that inform the ongoing decision making and work of the leaders of congregations.[8] Most mainline Protestant congregations, however, are apt to rely on some combination of parliamentary procedure and problem-solving reasoning. It is important, thus, to explore alternative models. One of the most interesting models put forward in recent years is offered by Charles Olsen.[9] Olsen's proposal is particularly interesting to practical theologians because he carries out the sort of empirical, normative, and pragmatic work that is important to this perspective. While Olsen's model is not the only way the work of church councils and committees might be reoriented around discernment, it represents an approach that has been researched empirically and tested pragmatically in American congregations.

Olsen identifies four core elements in his model: (1) history giving and storytelling, (2) biblical-theological reflection, (3) prayerful discernment, and (4) visioning the future.[10] It is not difficult to see analogues to each of these elements in my earlier account of Paul's understanding of discernment. Taken seriously, sustained attention to these elements will give rise to a qualitatively different experience of church work based on a qualitatively different form of community.

History giving and storytelling are the sorts of activities that are apt to be viewed as a waste of time in our hurry-up, task-oriented culture. Yet taking the time to get to know the other members of a committee, building a corporate memory about the history of the congregation and a committee's prior work, and giving people the chance to bring to expression the spiritual dimensions of their everyday lives is a key part of building the sort of community that can engage in discernment. Incorporating time for the sharing of stories is an important way of making sure that the relationship task of the group is primary.

For example, when a committee first meets, one of its most important relationship tasks is helping the group members get to know each other through structured sharing of some part of their life stories. New members may need to hear some of the history of this particular committee. When the committee begins to focus on a particular task, it is important to take the time to rehearse the "story behind the problem"—building a deeper sense of why this task is something the committee needs to give its time and energy to. Some committees find it helpful to have brief "check in" times at the beginning or end of the meeting, giving people the chance to share snippets of how their lives are going. History giving and storytelling, thus, are not a matter of one particular method but of sensitivity to the importance of building a community of memory and sharing. This is not extraneous to the work of the committee. It *is* the work of the committee.

Biblical and theological reflection involve what Olsen calls the "distilling of wisdom." This is not a matter of a brief devotional at the beginning of a committee meeting. Rather, it involves two things. First, it focuses on cultivating the use of the primary languages of the church—the languages of the Bible, theology, and ethics—to frame and reflect on the committee's work. Some committees ask their members to read a book over the summer in preparation for the coming year. Others search for particular passages of Scripture that may throw light on issues before them. The goal is to move away from the language and concepts of the marketplace, therapy, or some other sphere of life in order to use the primary languages of the church in conducting its work.

The second task focuses on beginning to use these languages to discern particular goals or lines of action that are a part of committee work. This is where "distilling wisdom" comes to the fore. It is similar to the tasks of constructing analogies and metaphor making in catechesis. The members of the group work together to discern analogies between the Bible, tradition, or moral exemplars and the particular issues they are dealing with as a committee. When done well, this is a highly creative process and goes far toward helping the group to see its work as guided by the Spirit and to rely on the "piece of wisdom" that each member has to offer.

Prayerful discernment includes the integration of prayer into the work of the committee as it attempts to make decisions as a group. This means overcoming the embarrassment that many feel about praying with others. It also involves learning a variety of creative formats that can be woven into the committee's time together. But perhaps most important of all, it has to do with the cultivation of certain dispositions that should permeate every aspect of a committee's work—a general attitude of receptivity to the guidance of the Spirit through the insights of others, through times of honest sharing and silence, through insights emerging outside of the committee, and so forth. These sorts of "prayerful dispositions" are the basis of the group's ability to hear the Spirit and to test the spirits.

Visioning the future involves the imaginative work of considering the possibilities and challenges of the present in light of God's promised future for creation. Putting it this way may sound too grandiose for the mundane work of church committees. What can this possibly have to do with deciding on a curriculum for the vacation Bible school or deciding if the first-grade Sunday school class can use a room that has long been the meeting place of a dwindling group of older adults? Yet is this not what is involved in learning to use bifocal vision—seeing our everyday lives in light of God's promised future? The key is seeing the link between the imagination, creativity, and new creation. It is a matter of schooling the imagination in the creative discernment of hidden possibilities of change that are apt to be overlooked if we stay within the safe confines of our ordinary frames of reference. Decisions do not have to be big in order to be creative.

Again, Olsen's model is not the only one that might be used to integrate discernment into the ordinary work of church leaders. His research, however, makes a larger point: Congregations are often revitalized when they alter their way of carrying out their work from models grounded in the business world or in parliamentary procedures to approaches that draw on the language and practices of the church.

TEACHING THE PRACTICES OF PRAYER IN THE CURRICULUM

I conclude this chapter by returning to the curriculum frame and describing how congregations might teach prayer in a systematic, intentional, and sustained way in their formal educational offerings. I was surprised to discover in my research on the three case study congregations how neglected this is in the educational program, even in congregations with strong teaching ministries. This is puzzling to me, for recent decades have seen a resurgence of interest in spirituality and prayer.[11] It was not so much that children and youth were not encouraged to pray; prayer played an important role in the lives of many of the people I interviewed in the three case study congregations. For the most part, however, it was not something that they had ever been taught. They saw their parents pray and prayed at church. In times of crisis, they were encouraged by others to pray or had friends tell them that they would keep them in their prayers. But it was rare for them to be able to recall a time when someone had taught them how to pray or shared with them how they themselves pray. There were almost no designated guides in their congregations to whom they could turn if they wanted to learn more about prayer. It is almost as if they were expected to learn how to pray by osmosis through their informal participation in moments of prayer and by seeing and imitating others.

Firsthand participation in prayer and imitation of others may well be an important way we learn how to pray. But if this is the *only* way prayer is learned, then children, youth, and adults are cut off from the rich traditions of prayer that have been developed in the Christian community. They do not have the chance to study this practice—to reflect theologically on its meaning and to experiment with different ways of praying found in the Christian tradition. They are not provided with an educational pathway through which they might grow in the knowledge and skills of this practice. Far too many adults have cognitive models of prayer trapped in the "unschooled mind" of the religious child. They still think of prayer as asking God to meet their needs, especially in times of trouble.

It is important to state at the outset that prayer involves more than discernment. It includes such things as the adoration and praise of God's beauty that lift our sights beyond ordinary life and give us a taste of communion with the divine being. Yet prayer is one of the most important ways of weaving discernment into our everyday lives. It helps us to see our ordinary decisions and daily interactions as participation in the life of the Spirit. Few have captured this important link between discernment and prayer with the simple profundity of Marjorie Thompson, Rose Mary Dougherty, and Kenneth Leech.

Thompson defines the spiritual life as "simply the increasing vitality and sway of God's Spirit in us" that is seeking to form and transform us toward the image of Christ.[12] Spiritual growth, thus, is "essentially a work of divine grace with which we are called to cooperate."[13] She describes our role as like navigating a sailboat. We cannot control the coming and going of the wind, but we can shift the position of the boat by adjusting the tiller and letting the sails in or out. We can put our craft in a position to catch the wind when it blows and be prepared to travel where it takes us. A disciplined and conscious attentiveness to the movement of the Spirit, thus, is one of the central purposes of prayer.

Dougherty explicitly describes this disciplined attentiveness to the Spirit in prayer in terms of discernment, giving special attention to the ways group spiritual direction can support this process. The key element of group spiritual direction, she believes, is the intention shared by all participants "to rely on God, to seek God actively and wait for God's leading."[14] At the heart of spiritual direction, thus, is the task of discernment: "seeing what God gives us to see."[15] She goes on:

> Prayer, then, is the starting place of discernment as well as the atmosphere in which it happens. Prayer for our part is our way of honoring our relationship with God. It fine-tunes the heart to the prayer of God in us, God's desire for us. Gradually we come to live out of that desire in all of life. . . . Discernment, then, must always include prayer, and intentional prayer must become the subject of our discernment from time to time.[16]

Kenneth Leech describes spiritual direction in the practice of prayer along similar lines as "the guidance of individuals in the life of the Spirit." But he draws an important connection between prayer and prophetic discernment. Prayer teaches us to discern the ways our daily lives are caught up in a spiritual struggle against the powers and principalities that seek to bend us toward evil. He writes:

> Spiritual direction is an activity within the sphere of the Kingdom of God, the liberated zone of God's movement. . . . The Kingdom is the standard by which the Christian disciple lives, and by that standard he discerns the signs of the times. . . . It is this which determines true prayer, and this fact needs to disturb us. . . . It is the new age which is one of righteousness and *shalom* and joy in the Spirit, which only the spiritually-born can see, and which is to transform the face of the earth. Spirituality which is centred in this hope cannot then be escapist or individualistic, for it is a hope for human society and for the common life. . . . No spiritual direction can be seen as adequate in Christian terms unless it is preparing men and women for the struggle of love against spiritual wickedness in the structures of the fallen world and in the depths of the heart.[17]

Authentic prayer does not lead us away from social transformation. Rather, it helps us to discern the ways our everyday lives are caught up in larger systems of suffering and evil that seek to win our allegiance and draw us away from God's kingdom. And it helps us to discern the "signs of the times," the possibilities of social change that come to light when seen through the lens of God's promised future.

How then might we do a better job of teaching the members of our congregations how to pray? I will cast my suggestions in the form of six guidelines that might inform the curriculum of a congregation.

1. Project a curriculum plan. Just as we might be intentional about covering certain stories of the Bible in different phases of the curriculum, we should become intentional about projecting a plan that teaches our children, youth, adults, and new members how to pray. We also must provide opportunities for long-term members to deepen their understanding of various forms of prayer and to expand their repertoire of prayer practices.

2. The first school of prayer is the home, but many parents today need education in how to integrate prayer into family life. It is no secret that the foundations of prayer are laid in the home, as children pray with their families before meals and at bedtime and participate in family devotions. For a variety of reasons, many parents today are failing to establish these simple practices in the home. It is important for congregations to forge a kind of partnership with the parents of young children, working together to plan parenting and intergenerational classes in which families learn to pray together.

3. Families with preschool and early elementary age children should work together to reinforce a common set of ideas and of guidelines about prayer. These include the following:[18]

- Define prayer as "using our own words to talk with and listen to God at any time, at any place, and about any thing."
- Given the strong tendency of children during this age to use anthropomorphic images of God, encourage them to think of prayer primarily as a personal conversation with someone who loves them deeply and wants to be their friend.
- Encourage children to use their own words in prayer instead of always relying on set prayers.
- Teach children that God can answer prayers in a variety of ways, sometimes saying "Yes," sometimes "No," sometimes "Wait awhile," and sometimes "I have a better way."
- Encourage parents and church teachers to talk about their own experiences of prayer.
- Teach at least one extended unit on prayer in the church school.

4. During the latter part of the primary phase of the curriculum, children should study the Lord's Prayer in church school or preconfirmation classes. This unit of study should focus on both the meaning of this model prayer and how children might structure their own prayer life around the basic petitions of this prayer.

5. During the secondary phase of the curriculum, youth should be given the opportunity to explore a range of prayer practices that take advantage of the deeper subjectivity they are developing during this period. This might include:

- apprenticing youth in various disciplines of prayer such as praying the Psalms, meditative prayer, keeping a prayer journal, or praying through guided imagery;
- teaching at least one unit on the theology of prayer in the church school during this phase of the curriculum;
- introducing youth to new ways of praying, such as the *lectio divina* in small groups;
- using mission trips and/or service projects as opportunities to model prayer for the needs of others; and
- encouraging the leaders of youth to learn the skills of small group and individual spiritual direction.

6. Teaching prayer to adults should remain a priority and should be supported in a wide variety of educational venues such as the adult church school, retreats, officer training, the training of small group leaders, and mission/service groups. We should not assume that adults do not need support in learning how to pray and in deepening their understanding of prayer. Nor should we underestimate the importance of having adults in the congregation with maturity in this practice. In learning how to pray, children look to their parents, youth to older peers and adult leaders, and adult members to leaders or designated guides.

CONCLUDING REFLECTIONS

Discernment is an area that needs greater attention in the teaching ministry of most mainline Protestant congregations today. In your artistry as a teacher and leader, you would do well to spend time considering how you might make practices of discernment a more important part of the life of your congregation. In a very real sense, this calls for discernment on your part. The pace and scope of change in our world and the shifting nature of individuals' needs over the course of the life cycle make it especially important that you help the members of your congregation acquire facility in these practices. The Christian tradition has a wealth of resources on which you might draw. Your task in the artist's studio is to use these resources to create a plan of action that is suitable to your own particular congregation.

Epilogue

In this epilogue, I return to methodological issues treated briefly in the discussion of practical theology offered in the introduction of this book. At that point, I offered a definition of practical theology that focused on four core tasks: (1) the descriptive-empirical, (2) the interpretive, (3) the normative, and (4) the pragmatic. It is helpful to conceptualize the mutually influential relationship of these four tasks along the lines of a hermeneutical circle.

The Four Tasks of Practical Theology

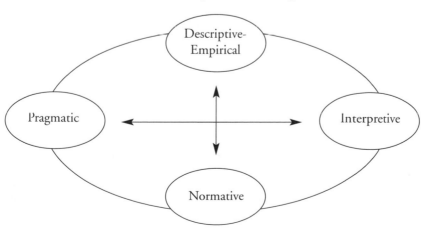

Hermeneutics is the art and science of interpretation. It focused originally on the interpretation of ancient texts. Over the course of the twentieth century, however, hermeneutics was broadened to include the interpretive dimension of all disciplines, resulting in a revision of the older view of science as completely objective and neutral. Within this important and broad-reaching discussion of hermeneutics, some philosophers and theologians have reworked the older concept of a hermeneutical circle to describe the different tasks involved in a comprehensive process of interpretation. It is helpful to view the tasks of practical theology along these lines.

The image of a circle calls attention to the mutually influential relationship of these four tasks. When practical theology carries out empirical research, for example, its findings are not self-interpreting; they only make sense when placed in an interpretive framework. This framework, moreover, commonly influences the way empirical research is carried out, but it also is sometimes revised in light of empirical findings. Likewise, the choice of what to investigate may be influenced by the perception of problems in contemporary praxis, often brought to the fore by the pragmatic task of practical theology or by issues raised in normative reflection on contemporary praxis.

The image of a hermeneutical circle, thus, portrays the distinct tasks of practical theology as interrelated. While distinguishable, they are not separable, for work on one task is apt to influence and be influenced by work on other tasks. It also makes it clear that there is no one starting point in the circle of practical theological reflection; a practical theologian may enter the circle at any point.

THE FOUR TASKS OF PRACTICAL THEOLOGY:
A RETROSPECTIVE

How have these four tasks been carried out in this book? Part 1 focused on the normative task of practical theology, identifying the tasks of catechesis, exhortation, and discernment through a close examination of Paul's letters. As a practical theologian, I entered into a dialogue with contemporary biblical scholars to understand Paul's letters in terms of their historical, rhetorical, social, and literary contexts. I did not claim to offer the one, true "biblical" perspective on the teaching ministry of congregations, but made the more modest claim that the normative perspective offered was the outcome of a situated rational conversation, shaped by the particular interpretive strategies and dialogue partners engaged.

This perspective informed my research on contemporary congregations reported in part 2, which focused primarily on the descriptive-empirical and interpretive tasks of practical theology. The empirical task was carried out through the qualitative research I conducted on three case study congregations, using the ethnographic methods of congregational studies: semi-structured interviews, videotaping, and participant observation. Broadly speaking, I used the data-gathering strategy of triangulation, using a combination of different research tools and perspectives to study each congregation.[1] Moreover, my approach to empirical research is more akin to interpretive social science than to grounded theory, at least as it is formulated by Barney Glaser.[2] I went to the field with certain concepts in hand, particularly the framework of catechesis, exhortation, and discernment. But as a result of my empirical work, I revised my understanding of this normative framework considerably, resulting in the four interdisciplinary frames developed in part 2. I also placed these frames in the broader interpretive frameworks of modernization theory and globalization theory. I did not develop these frameworks for the interpretive task of practical theology as fully as I would have liked, especially in light of the controversial status of globalization theory. But I said enough to indicate my own position and point the reader to other writings on this topic.

In short, the perspective developed in part 2 was the result of the interaction and mutual influence of the descriptive-empirical, interpretive, and normative tasks of practical theology. The final part of the book took up the normative task once again and then turned to the pragmatic task. In chapter 8, I entered into a conversation with the theologian Jürgen Moltmann, an interdisciplinary dialogue between dogmatic and practical theology. My concern at that point was not to carry out normative work along the lines of dogmatic theology, which articulates the beliefs of the church in doctrinal form and displays their inner coherence. Rather, it was to articulate a theory of divine and human action using patterns of theological construction that are appropriate to practical theology, viewed as a theological theory of action. I used concepts derived from Hans Urs von Balthasar's theology of Theo-drama to portray the substantive account of divine and human action derived from Moltmann. The result was a trinitarian perspective on creation, redemption, and glorification.

I attempted to carry forward the gains of this normative framework into the final chapters on catechesis, exhortation, and discernment. At that point, I offered action-guiding models of practice and rules of art, the focal points of the pragmatic task of practical theology. In the chapter on catechesis, I identified centers of interpretive activity; in the chapter on exhortation, I offered a three-fold covenant ethic; in the chapter on discernment, I offered a range of truth-seeking mechanisms and practices. Leaders and teachers were invited to consider how these models might inform the teaching ministries of their own congregations.

Throughout part 3, the normative and pragmatic tasks of practical theology interpenetrate. It is quite feasible and even desirable for other practical theologians to give greater prominence than I have here to the knowledge that emerges out of practice. I have argued that reflective practice is epistemic, that is, it yields knowledge that is different from that gained through empirical, interpretive, and normative work. This task of practical theology is underdeveloped in this book and stands in need of the insights of reflective practitioners who might test, refine, and alter the theory articulated in the final chapters. At a minimum, moreover, practitioners must rely on their own reflective judgments to implement the models developed in this book in their own local contexts.

METHODOLOGICAL REFLECTION AT A SECOND LEVEL

In this overview, I have attempted to clarify the way I carried out the core tasks of practical theology over the course of this book. In addition to these four tasks, practical theologians also make key decisions at a second level of methodological reflection, having to do with their understanding of (1) the theory-praxis relationship, (2) sources of justification, (3) models of cross-disciplinary work, and (4) theological rationale. Decisions made at this second level have a great deal to do with how a particular practical theologian carries out the descriptive-empirical, interpretive, normative, and pragmatic tasks in his or her work and how he or she sees these four tasks as related to one another.

Second Level of Methodological Reflection

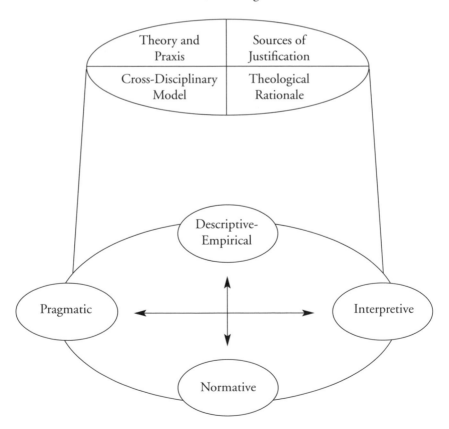

1. The *theory-praxis relationship* points to the crucial philosophical, sociological, and theological decisions a practical theologian makes about the nature of praxis and theory's relationship to it. In contemporary practical theology, a variety of understandings of the theory-praxis relationship are present. These range from the neo-Marxist perspective of critical social theory found in many feminist and liberation practical theologians to the neo-Aristotelian perspectives informing the proponents of the contemporary practices discussion to the neo-pragmatist perspective found in practical theologians such as Chris Hermans, Don Browning, and Marcel Viau.[3] Decisions about the theory-praxis relationship influence in fundamental ways the phenomena investigated in empirical work, the interpretive framework used to understand what is found, the norms offered to assess both church and society, and the models used to guide and reform present praxis.

2. *Sources of justification* refers to the way a particular practical theologian draws on the traditional sources of theological truth to underwrite her or his theological and ethical proposals: Scripture, tradition, experience, and reason. Here too, a wide variety of perspectives are present in contemporary practical theology. Working out of a Barthian perspective, for example, Deborah van Deusen Hunsinger grants primacy to Scripture as it gives witness to Christ, and to tradition as it helps the church make sense of Scripture's complex patterns.[4] The insights of reason and experience are interpreted in light of the knowledge gained from these sources. In contrast, Don Browning gives equal weight to all four sources of truth. For example, he constructs an ethic of equal regard through appeals to Scripture and tradition and, in equal measure, to the insights of contemporary experience and reason.

3. *Models of cross-disciplinary work* refers to the way a practical theologian engages other branches of theology and other fields of knowledge such as the social sciences, the arts, natural science, and so forth. I view cross-disciplinary work as quite complex and as including intradisciplinary, interdisciplinary, multidisciplinary, and metadisciplinary dimensions, which I have spelled out elsewhere.[5] It is easiest to illustrate the importance of methodological decisions about cross-disciplinary work by focusing on the interdisciplinary level. This has to do with the decisions a practical theologian makes about which fields are to be engaged and how their relationship to practical theology is conceptualized. Should she or he engage the therapeutic psychological disciplines, anthropology, sociology, or biology? Often the proposals of practical theologians differ because their interdisciplinary partners are quite different; one chooses to dialogue with cognitive psychology and another with sociology. Moreover, differences also emerge because various practical theologians conceptualize the relationship between practical theology and their interdisciplinary dialogue partner quite differently. In recent years, several distinct "families" of interdisciplinary work have emerged, composed of "family members" who resemble one another in certain ways.

The *correlational family* seeks to bring into a mutually influential conversation theology and other disciplines. It includes Paul Tillich's method of correlation, David Tracy's and Don Browning's revised correlational methods, and Rebecca Chopp's and Mathew Lamb's revised praxis correlational models.[6] The *transformational family* seeks to preserve theology's distinctive truth claims in interdisciplinary work, distinguishing or transforming other fields as they are appropriated within a practical theological perspective. It includes the Chalcedonian framework of James Loder and the ad hoc correlational approach of Hans Frei.[7] A relatively new "family" based on a transversal model of rationality has begun to emerge in the writings of Calvin Schrag and Wolfgang Welsch and developed in theology by Wentzel van Huyssteen.[8] I will describe this approach below, for it is the model used over the course of this book.

4. *Theological rationale* points to an account of the central theological convictions that explain why a practical theologian works in certain ways. It links substantive claims about God and the world in relation to God to other methodological decisions. For example, the theological rationale of James Loder and Deborah van Deusen Hunsinger affirms a strong Christocentrism, building on the arguments of Søren Kierkegaard and Karl Barth, respectively. This in turn is explicated in terms of the Chalcedonian paradigm, which provides key rules to guide thinking about the relationship between the human and divine. This theological rationale is linked to other methodological decisions, such as their interdisciplinary method and their understanding of the epistemological status of knowledge emerging out of praxis. In contrast, the theological rationale provided by many liberation and feminist practical theologians is based on an account of Christ as the liberator of the marginalized and oppressed, which informs their decision to adopt a neo-Marxist understanding of the theory-praxis relationship and a revised praxis correlational model of interdisciplinary work. The point to underscore is that methodological decisions in practical theology do not take place in a vacuum; they presuppose a substantive theological rationale that underwrites some of the most important methodological decisions a practical theologian makes.

TOWARD A POSTFOUNDATIONAL
MODEL OF PRACTICAL THEOLOGY

My own position on these methodological issues is best described in terms of a *postfoundational* model of practical theology. Postfoundationalism is a perspective articulated in the writings of philosopher Calvin Schrag and philosophical theologian Wentzel van Huyssteen. This perspective takes seriously the challenges of postmodern thinking to all totalizing, modernist attempts to secure true knowledge through foundationalist strategies. It acknowledges that knowledge is constructed on the basis of social practices, language, and values that are local and contextual. Even science is viewed as paradigm dependent and as carrying out research programs on the basis of widely diverse disciplinary commitments.

Yet postfoundationalism is unwilling to follow the most extreme forms of post-modern thinking down the path of cultural and moral relativism or a "many rationalities" approach. It may be helpful to sort out initially some of these differences with images.

Imagine a solid wooden house that is constructed on top of a durable and solid cement foundation. This is an image of foundationalism. It begins with Descartes' premise that we must doubt all things (especially the traditions and authorities of the past) and seek to build true knowledge on the foundation of beliefs that are indubitable, that is, beliefs derived through methods that are publicly available to all rational people and have the force of necessity and universality. Further knowledge constructed on the basis of this solid foundation of beliefs must pass the tests of logical consistency and coherence.

Typically, the formulation of a solid foundation of beliefs and the further construction of knowledge on the basis of them is pictured in terms of a determinant *set of rules* that constitute the inner core of reason or scientific method. Think of this as the rule book of edifice construction. While quite different structures may be built on a solid foundation, they will only be secure if they follow the basic procedures laid out in this rule book. Analogously, foundationalists believe that while different scientific disciplines carry out research on different phenomena (e.g., plants, animals, the human brain), they follow the same rational rules. Hence, the various branches of science and scholarship are differentiated in subject matter but unified in their rationality.

Postmodernism challenges this picture from a wide variety of directions. Philosophers and historians of science such as Thomas Kuhn have pointed out that science passes through paradigm shifts and uses different methods of research and warranting patterns to construct theories. Hermeneutical philosophers such as Martin Heidegger and Hans-Georg Gadamer have called attention to the ways all understanding is grounded in traditions of interpretation, which begin in the life worlds of everyday life but also include the prejudgments of research traditions. Argument theorists such as Stephen Toulmin have described the way various fields use different patterns of argumentation and rhetoric to establish their claims. Philosophers of language such as Ludwig Wittgenstein have pointed to the ways that meaning is determined by its concrete use in specific contexts, which can be conceptualized in terms of discrete language games. Poststructuralists such as Jean-François Lyotard, Jacques Derrida, and Michel Foucault have critiqued the idea that rationality is singular and innocent, calling attention to its narrativity, intertextuality, and regimes of power, respectively.

The postmodern challenge to modern foundationalism, thus, has taken a variety of forms. Sometimes this challenge is articulated as a commitment to non-foundationalism or antifoundationalism, which might be interpreted in a quite different image. Imagine rafts floating on the open sea.[9] Each raft is created out of different materials—bamboo, wooden logs, inflated tires, or air-filled plastic pontoons. Each raft has a unique shelter to protect its inhabitants from the elements: a small wooden hut, a plastic lean-to, or a simple cloth roof. Some rafts are navigated with sails; others, with long paddles; still others, with only a rudder. Occasionally, the rafts come together to form a precarious village on the open sea, allowing people to move from raft to raft. But this pieced-together village cannot last long, especially when the ocean grows rough. The rafts must drift apart in order to navigate the waves successfully.

There is no solid foundation in this image. The ocean is constantly shifting, and each raft must negotiate its unstable surface in ways appropriate to its own structure, navigational devices, and materials. So too, nonfoundationalism abandons any notion of a stable, objective world on which a firm foundation might be built. Natural and social "objects" are socially constructed, reflecting the language, interpretive patterns, and technologies that different cultures and disciplines bring to them. Just as each raft is discrete, so too, nonfoundationalism affirms the irreducible plurality of life—from different social roles, gender constructions, and regimes of power in social life to the diversity of perspectives found in and across different disciplines. While the rafts may temporarily mingle, they cannot be lashed together into a single, unified structure. Any such attempt at totalization in the form of a master narrative, universal model of rationality, or enforcement of a single moral code ultimately leads to the sinking of all. Each must remain free to navigate its own course and thereby make its contribution.

Imagine now a third image, whose topography is neither the solid ground nor the shifting sea. Picture riders floating above the earth in a large number of pods of different hues. The many sides of each pod are composed of porous, sticky membranes that are translucent. Some sides are denser, making it difficult to see out, and others transparent, making it possible to view the ground below, the sky above, or the sea in the distance. Each pod is equipped with a special window: Some are a magnifying device that brings distant objects close; others are an X-ray device that allows the viewer to see the internal structure of objects; still others provide thermal imaging, mapping the energy fields of different objects. When the wind shifts and the pods float into one another, their sticky membranes merge together, making it possible for the rider in each to gain the special vantage point afforded by the other. Sometimes a number of pods coalesce permanently, taking an entirely new shape and hue as their colors mingle together. Their riders are now able to see in many new directions, including the vantage points of several special windows. But often these mergers are temporary, and the pods soon drift apart.

This is my image of postfoundationalism. While it eschews the solid grounding of foundationalism—the pods float above the earth and are not tethered to the ground—there is an array of natural elements with which the pods interact. While it readily acknowledges the rich pluralism of postmodernism, expressed in the different hues, patterns of transparency, and special windows of each pod, postfoundationalism differs from nonfoundationalism in three key respects: (1) It points to the resources of rationality that are shared by the human species; (2) it develops an alternative to a rule-oriented model of rationality; and (3) it portrays the ability to move across cultures, domains, and disciplines in terms of transversal reason.

The Resources of Rationality

Postfoundationalism portrays human beings as sharing the resources of rationality, which have cognitive, evaluative, and pragmatic dimensions.[10] While human beings may use these resources in markedly differently ways, the fact that they are shared by the human species as a whole makes it possible to cross the boundaries of cultures, domains, and disciplines in search of greater understanding through rational conversation. The boundaries are not rigidly impermeable but are porous and can merge together, much like the membranes of our pods. Van Huyssteen portrays the shared resources of rationality as the outcome of humanity's evolutionary heritage.[11] Human consciousness, he notes, emerged gradually over six million years as a way of coping with and understanding the world. He traces advances in cognitive fluidity attending the emergence of the "modern mind" approximately 60,000 to 30,000 years ago and resulting in the ability to move effortlessly between different kinds of intelligence—just as our pods with their different transparencies and special windows were able to join together and expand the vision of their riders. By locating the resources of rationality in our common evolutionary heritage, van Huyssteen is able to acknowledge the diverse ways human intelligence is developed in different cultures, domains, and disciplines while, simultaneously, pointing to the shared grounds of human intelligence in all its different forms.

Rationality as Judgment, Articulation, and Disclosure, Not Rules

Surprisingly, a rules-based model of rationality is something foundationalism and nonfoundationalism both share, the difference being nonfoundationalism's belief that the "many rationalities" of different disciplines or cultures each have their own internal set of rules. In contrast, postfoundationalism develops a model of rationality that does not focus primarily on rules and includes (a) rational judgment: "the ability to assess evidence and then come to a responsible and reasonable decision without following any preset, modernist rules";[12] (b) articulation: the ability to the use appropriate forms of discourse to articulate good reasons for the position being put forward and the rationale for this position; (c) disclosure: a transactional view of experience in which human knowledge is shaped by its encounters with the natural and social world, which sometimes underwrites a "soft" form of critical realism.[13] While each of these dimensions warrants extended discussion, my comments will necessarily be brief.

The idea of *rational judgment* points to a constellation of factors that always are at play in human rationality, factors that are bracketed out when it is portrayed primarily as following a set of rules. These include personal and professional values, disciplinary perspective, acquired expertise, the ability to make sense of the particularities of a situation and evidence, openness to the feedback of competent peers, weighing the relative strength of one's claims, and awareness of competing perspectives. Arriving at a rational judgment, thus, involves far more than following standard rules that supposedly represent the core of all forms of rationality. Rules have a more limited role as a methodological statement of the procedures being followed in a particular project, position, or disciplinary paradigm. Moreover, the concept of rational judgment also breaks the close link that foundationalism posits between reason and necessity, universality, and consensus. It is quite possible for a person to render a rational judgment backed by good reasons that is not shared by competent peers in the same field who hold different values and disciplinary commitments.

Articulation takes account of the communicative turn in rationality. Breaking with the modernist philosophy of consciousness, it pictures reason as a special form of communicative praxis in which a particular community develops good reasons for its actions, values, and truth claims. Rational communication can take a wide variety of forms in different cultures, domains, and disciplines, ranging from the cooperative orientation of dialogue to the challenge/response patterns of argumentation.[14] Thus, articulation is inherently a rhetorical process in which good reasons are communicated on the basis of the genres and rhetorical strategies that are persuasive in a particular context.

Disclosure indicates postfoundationalism's commitment to a transactional view of human experience, which moves beyond objectivism and relativism. While all experience is interpreted—ruling out any notion of "pure" experience—human understanding is shaped by its interactions with the world. Such encounters may have the force of a disclosure that opens up new features of our social and natural worlds. This transactional view of experience is sometimes linked to a "soft" version of critical realism in which the frameworks we bring to our investigation of the world are modified by what we find.

Transversal Reason

Postfoundationalism develops the concept of transversal reason to highlight both the ability and obligation of human beings to move beyond their own cultural or disciplinary contexts to engage the perspectives of others. Wolfgang Welsch describes transversality as the ability to cross over to perspectives that are different from one's own—something I attempted to express in the image of pods with permeable membranes coming together and allowing the riders to take advantage of the different perspectives each pod affords. Others have borrowed an image from mathematics in which transversality denotes the intersection of a line with other lines or surfaces. Think of the ways surfaces both intersect and diverge when the sticks are thrown in a game of pick-up sticks. Analogously, in the pluralistic intellectual context of our postmodern world, the transversal play of reason explores the overlaps and divergences of different disciplines, domains, and cultures.

Van Huyssteen has developed this understanding of transversal reason into a new model of interdisciplinary work in theology. Unlike the correlational "family," which seeks to bring into a mutually influential relationship broad features of human experience (e.g., religion and culture, theology and science), a transversal model underscores the *concreteness* of interdisciplinary work, portraying it as a conversation between this particular scientist working in these specific ways with that particular theologian working in equally specific ways. Unlike the transformational "family," transversality underscores the permeable nature of cultural, religious, and disciplinary boundaries and the obligation to cross over to perspectives other than one's own in the form of interreligious, intercultural, and interdisciplinary dialogue.

This crossing over need not eliminate the specific truth claims and social practices of a given religious community as they are articulated by one of its theologians. But it does obligate the theologian not to determine in advance what might be learned when she or he enters the transversal play of reason. Sometimes crossing over to other perspectives may spark a recovery of certain dimensions of a theologian's own tradition that have been overlooked or neglected. This is how Paul Tillich portrayed his encounter with psychoanalysis and existentialism, which led him to recover a stronger doctrine of sin than found in liberal theology.[15] It also is the way Catherine Mowry Lacugna describes her encounter with contemporary feminism and object relations theory, which sparked her recovery of the image of the Trinity as "Persons-in-relation."[16] Sometimes a strong "No!" is the outcome of this dialogue, as Jürgen Moltmann was compelled to utter to modern science's compulsion to put nature on the rack.[17] And sometimes a dialogue with contemporary insights or movements leads theologians to revise considerably certain features of their own faith tradition, as seen in feminist theologians' critique of the patriarchy of Christianity. The important point to underscore is that a willingness to enter the transversal play of reason in interdisciplinary work rules out protectionist strategies that determine in advance what may or may not be learned in one's dialogue with other disciplines.

It remains for me to note some of the ways these three elements of postfoundationalism have informed this book, and I will take them up in order, beginning with the idea of the *shared resources of rationality*. At the most obvious level, I would not have been willing to bring practical theology into dialogue with other disciplines and to study congregations in cultures other than my own if I did not believe that rational conversation and understanding across boundaries is both possible and necessary. As noted above, I believe the most promising line of thinking about these issues in theology is found in van Huyssteen's effort to bring the perspectives of evolutionary epistemology and theological anthropology into dialogue, giving special attention to human uniqueness.[18]

My modest contribution to this line of thinking draws on the concept of the *community of creation* discussed in chapter 8 in which human beings are portrayed in terms of their discontinuity-within-continuity with other species of animals and the systems of the natural world. While the capacity to engage in the highest forms of reasoning may well be unique to *homo sapiens,* some of the resources making rationality possible—such as communication, information processing, and emotional assessment—are shared with other species of animals.[19] The theological concept of the community of creation encourages us to explore the overlaps and divergences between the human and animal worlds in our understanding of the shared resources of rationality—indeed, to expand our notion of transversality from human beings alone to other species. Moreover, viewing human beings as participants in the community of creation provides ethical guidance in thinking about the purpose and use of the unique human capacities for reasoning and for consciousness generally. Theologically, they represent both a gift and a calling, making possible the gift of covenant partnership with God and the calling to serve as good stewards of God's creation.

My commitment to a postfoundationalist model of rationality that features rational judgment, articulation, and disclosure informs this project in a variety of ways. Here I will focus on the model of practical theology presented initially in the introduction and revisited in this epilogue. This model identifies four tasks of practical theology on the basis of a "naturalized" view of rationality, that is, by paying attention to the ways prominent practical theologians have actually carried out their work since the 1960s. This model was not offered as the only way this field has or will carry out its work. Nor was it portrayed as offering a standard set of rules that all practical theologians must follow. Rather, this model is situated historically and viewed as responsive to a particular set of challenges. It offers a flexible and open definition of the field, which assumes that practical theologians will carry out the four tasks in quite different ways.

Moreover, I have attempted to clarify some of reasons for this pluralism in practical theology in this epilogue, pointing to methodological decisions that practical theologians make about the theory-praxis relationship, sources of justification, models of cross-disciplinary work, and theological rationale. Practical theologians will render rational judgments, articulate their positions, and grapple with the disclosures of new experience in markedly different ways. It is not to be expected that good reasons will take only one form or that consensus among one's colleagues is necessary to a well-established, rational position. What can be expected is that a practical theologian will offer reasons and a rationale for the way she or he has worked, a point to which I will return.

Finally, what are some of the ways *transversality* is found in this project? It is most readily apparent in the way I have engaged a wide variety of perspectives from other fields, especially in part 2 where theology was brought into conversation with the social sciences. At times I intentionally engaged several different dialogue partners in a single chapter, attempting to point out the concrete strengths and limits of each person's thinking. I did not, for example, engage in a dialogue with psychology in general in chapter 5 on the curriculum frame but did engage concretely the thinking of Howard Gardner and James Fowler. Moreover, I indicated points of overlap and divergence in the perspectives of multiple intelligence theory and faith development theory in order to build up a perspective on the curriculum that was richer than could be derived from either theory alone. This sort of marshalling of a variety of perspectives from other fields and indications of points of overlap and divergence along the lines of a transversal approach to interdisciplinary work has been a consistent feature of this book.

To this point, proponents of the emerging model of transversality in interdisciplinary work have been reticent about articulating the general rules that guide their conversation between theology and other fields. The reason for this reticence is their desire to distance themselves from a "rule" model of rationality, as noted above. I would like to end, however, with a brief outline of the rules that guide my thinking about interdisciplinary work at present, keeping in mind that such rules represent methodological guidelines followed in a particular project, position, or disciplinary paradigm—not a statement of the core features of a universal model of rationality. Even within a model of rationality and interdisciplinary work that is person- and perspective-specific—as the transversal model is—it is important to set forth the particular commitments that describe the ways a scholar carries out his or her interdisciplinary work. Drawing on the theological perspective developed over the course of this book, I can articulate two primary rules that have guided my interdisciplinary thinking: the Radical Monotheism Rule and the Trinitarian Rule, each of which is accompanied by several corollaries or principles.

The *Radical Monotheism Rule* harks back to H. Richard Niebuhr and beyond him to the Reformed tradition and to ancient Israel, especially the prophetic tradition. It states that God alone is divine and that an infinite qualitative distinction between God and creation must be recognized and maintained. No form of creation is to be confused with God; idolatry is prohibited; God alone is God. This distinction between creation and Creator guides our evaluation of the status of human creations in the form of culture, religion, theology, the arts, and the sciences. All have their appropriate place in human life, but they are not to be confused with God.

The Radical Monotheism Rule has two corollaries: the Critical Principle and the Pluralism Principle. The *Critical Principle* states that the quest for human understanding and intelligibility are inherently provisional, fallible, and subject to criticism. This underwrites the need for relentless criticism of self and others, especially when human projects begin to gather to themselves a status inappropriate to their creaturely provisionality and fallibility. The *Pluralism Principle* states that the provisional and fallible status of all human projects underwrites the need for openness to a multiplicity of perspectives. No one perspective is capable of capturing the fullness of truth, goodness, and beauty—hence both the epistemological need and the ethical obligation to transverse across a range of perspectives.

The Radical Monotheism Rule marks the distinction between creation and Creator, the human and divine, setting limits to what can be claimed for knowledge about God and the world in relation to God. The *Trinitarian Rule* describes what can appropriately be said about God on the basis of God's self-disclosure.

In terms of the social doctrine of the Trinity for which I have argued in this book, this self-disclosure is viewed as complex and differentiated, reflecting the differentiation of the three divine Persons revealed in the history of God's dealings with the world. The order of the divine Persons shifts as creation, redemption, and glorification come into view. Analogously, I believe it is appropriate to describe three somewhat different patterns of interdisciplinary work when dealing with matters related to creation, redemption, and glorification. I will describe these in terms of three corollaries or principles.

In matters having to do with our understanding of creation, interdisciplinary work is guided by the *Dialogical Principle,* in which we engage with critical openness the emergent realities of continuing creation. Hence, theology must be willing to revise its understanding of creation on the basis of its dialogue with the intellectual resources of the contemporary world. This is not an uncritical dialogue, for theology speaks back as an equal partner, but it is a dialogue undertaken in openness.

In matters having to do with our understanding of redemption, interdisciplinary work is guided by the *Dialectical Principle* in which priority is given to the pattern of redemption found in the life, death, and resurrection of Jesus Christ. Asymmetrical analogies to this pattern are discovered in other areas of human experience; the movement is *from* God's redemption of the world in Christ *to* analogies of this redemption found in the healing, liberation, and reconciliation of creation. This principle is dialectical in two senses. First and most importantly, it takes it bearings from the dialectic of cross and resurrection at the heart of Christ's redemption. God has entered fully into the suffering of nature and history in Jesus' messianic way of life, which culminated in his death on the cross. God offers the promise of the redemption of a suffering creation in the resurrection of Jesus. It is here and here alone that we learn the "hidden secret" of God's redemption. Second, given the priority of God's redemption in Christ, all other forms of healing, liberation, and reconciliation are to be engaged in interdisciplinary work as asymmetrical analogies to this pattern and, as such, are to be appropriated dialectically. This dialectical appropriation has been described succinctly by James Loder: Forms of human healing, liberation, and reconciliation are negated as forms of ultimate salvation, which is offered alone in Christ Jesus. This negation is, in turn, negated, and their status as analogies of God's redemption affirmed.

In matters having to do with glorification, interdisciplinary work is guided by the *Transformation Principle,* which focuses on the pattern of new creation in the Spirit in which the present is transformed to correspond more nearly to the eschatological beauty of God. This transformation has the character of a *novuum,* the qualitatively new and different, which breaks into and reorients the present and is not simply an outgrowth of prior processes and trends. New creation, moreover, is deeply particular and fragmentary, as expressions of beauty always must be; it also has the character of an anticipation, a preliminary but real participation in the glory and splendor of God's coming beauty. In short, all forms of transformation must be viewed in an eschatological framework—be they new forms of life articulated in radical politics or a social movement, new patterns of living of a utopian community, new beginnings of personal existence, or artistic creations disclosing alternative worlds in tension with our present world. Such forms of transformation may have very real political, social, and ethical implications but are viewed as signs of a fuller and more complete transformation yet to come. They do not usher in the kingdom but point ahead to the kingdom. Interdisciplinary work that is guided by the Transformation Principle, thus, uses patterns of interpretation that resemble those found in aesthetics. It interprets particular forms of transformation in their uniqueness, much as a particular work of art must be interpreted. It then moves back and forth between an interpretation of the eschatological symbols of the faith that disclose God's eschatological beauty and the ways this beauty is proleptically actualized in a concrete form of transformation in the present. This is not a simple dialogue, for it is a matter of disclosure. It is a work of the aesthetic imagination in which particular speaks to particular in ways that disclose alternatives to present existence, even as this also points ahead to God's promised future.

Obviously, I have barely skimmed the surface in my presentation of the "rules" guiding my thinking in this project. Some of these are more fully embodied in the present book than others, which will have to be fleshed out in future writing. The very incompleteness of my account of these guidelines is a fitting place to end this book, however. Jürgen Moltmann frequently described his theological writings as contributions to an ongoing conversation and not as finished parts of a closed, dogmatic system. This open-ended, dialogical image of theology is how I think of the contribution of this book. It would not have been possible without many conversations along the way, and is offered as a contribution to an ongoing conversation with others.

Notes

Introduction

1. See Friedrich Schleiermacher, *Brief Outline on the Study of Theology*, trans. Terrence Tice (Richmond, VA: John Knox Press, 1966).
2. See, e.g., Gerben Heitink, *Practical Theology: History, Theory, and Action Domains*, Studies in Practical Theology (Grand Rapids: Wm. B. Eerdmans, 1999); Johannes van der Ven, *Practical Theology: An Empirical Approach* (Kampen, the Netherlands: Kok Pharos, 1993); Don Browning, *A Fundamental Practical Theology: Descriptive and Strategic Proposals* (Minneapolis: Fortress Press, 1991).
3. I am borrowing and altering considerably to suit my own purposes the concept of a "discrimen" from Robert Johnson, *Authority in Protestant Theology* (Philadelphia: Westminster Press, 1959); and David Kelsey, *The Uses of Scripture in Recent Theology* (Philadelphia: Fortress Press, 1975).
4. James Loder describes this as the "generative problematic" of practical theology in "Normativity and Context in Practical Theology," in *Practical Theology: International Perspectives,* ed. Friedrich Schweitzer and Johannes A. van der Ven (Berlin: Peter Lang, 1999), 359–81. In this same volume, James Fowler uses the concept of the praxis of God to make a similar point; see Fowler, "The Emerging New Shape of Practical Theology," 75–92.
5. This concept was first introduced into practical theology by Schleiermacher in his *Brief Outline,* para. 265ff. See also James Duke and Howard Stone, eds.,

Christian Caring: Selections from Practical Theology, trans. James Duke (Philadelphia: Fortress Press, 1988), 99ff.

Introduction to Part 1

1. See Charles Cousar, *The Letters Paul Wrote* (Nashville: Abingdon Press, 1996), chap. 1.
2. See Carolyn Miller, "Genre as Social Action" *Quarterly Journal of Speech* 70 (1984): 151–67; Karlyn Kohrs Campbell and Kathleen Hall Jamieson, eds., *Form and Genre: Shaping Rhetorical Action* (Falls Church, VA: Speech Communication Association, 1987); Charles Bazerman, *Shaping Written Knowledge: The Genre and Activity of the Experimental Article in Science* (Madison: University of Wisconsin Press, 1988); and Carol Berkenkotter and Thomas Huckin, *Genre Knowledge in Disciplinary Communication: Cognition/Culture/Power* (Hillsdale, NJ: Lawrence Erlbaum Associates, 1995). For a more general discussion, see M. M. Bakhtin, *Speech Genres and Other Late Essays*, trans. V. McGee (Austin: University of Texas Press, 1986).
3. Much of the recent interest in rhetoric has been sparked by the following: George Kennedy, *Classical Rhetoric and Its Christian and Secular Tradition from Ancient to Modern Times* (Chapel Hill, NC: University of North Carolina Press, 1980); Amos Wilder, *Early Christian Rhetoric: The Language of the Gospel* (Cambridge, MA: Harvard University Press, 1964); Hans Deiter Betz, *Der Apostel Paulus und die sokratische Tradition: Eine exegetische Untersuchung zu seiner 'Apologie' 2 Kor 10–13* (Tübingen: Mohr Siebeck, 1972); and Vernon Robbins, *Jesus the Teacher: A Socio-Rhetorical Interpretation of Mark* (Philadelphia: Fortress Press, 1984). For an excellent recent example of this approach, see Margaret Mitchell, *Paul and the Rhetoric of Reconciliation: An Exegetical Investigation of the Language and Composition of 1 Corinthians* (Louisville, KY: Westminster/John Knox Press, 1991).
4. If Paul was born in Tarsus, as is portrayed in Acts 21:39 (cf. 9:11), then he grew up in a city well-known for an excellent liberal arts education that culminated in the teaching of rhetoric. Strabo compared the education of Tarsus favorably to that of Alexandria and Athens, noting that it included "the whole round of learning in general," an obvious reference to the liberal arts curriculum of classical education. See M. J. Mellink, "Tarsus," in *The Interpreter's Dictionary of the Bible,* vol. 4 (Nashville: Abingdon Press, 1962), 518–19. For a discussion of the place of rhetoric in classical education, see Henri Marrou, *History of Education in Antiquity,* trans. George Lamb (Madison: University of Wisconsin Press, 1956).
5. See Thomas Farrell, *Norms of Rhetorical Culture* (New Haven, CT: Yale University Press, 1993).
6. Stanley Stowers, *Letter Writing in Greco-Roman Antiquity* (Philadelphia: Westminster Press, 1986), 37. See also Abraham Malherbe, *Paul and the Popular Moral Philosophers* (Minneapolis: Fortress Press, 1989).
7. Stowers, *Letter Writing in Greco-Roman Antiquity,* 92.
8. See Donald Juel, *Messianic Exegesis: Christological Interpretation of the Old Testament in Early Christianity* (Philadelphia: Fortress Press, 1988).
9. See Christopher Stanley, *Paul and the Language of Scripture: Citation Technique in the Pauline Epistles and Contemporary Literature* (Cambridge: Cambridge University Press, 1992).
10. Juel, *Messianic Exegesis,* 41.
11. See Richard Hays's discussion of Rom. 10:6–9 in *The Echoes of Scripture in the Letters of Paul* (New Haven, CT: Yale University Press, 1989), 81.

12. See J. Louis Martyn's insightful perspective in "From Paul to Flannery O'Connor with the Power of Grace" in *Theological Issues in the Letters of Paul* (Nashville: Abingdon Press, 1997).

Chapter 1: The Purpose of Paul's Teaching Ministry in Congregations

1. See Loyd Bitzer, "The Rhetorical Situation," *Philosophy and Rhetoric* 1 (1968): 1–14.
2. For a discussion of problems translating *dikaioun* into English, see J. Louis Martyn, "The Apocalytic Gospel in Galatians," *Interpretation* 34, no. 3 (July 2000): 246–66; and E. P. Sanders, *Paul* (Oxford: Oxford University Press, 1991), 44–49.
3. Brendan Bryne, SJ, *Romans*, Sacra Pagina (Collegeville, MN: Liturgical Press, 1996), 19.
4. See, e.g., J. Louis Martyn, *Galatians*, Anchor Bible (New York: Doubleday, 1997); and Charles Cousar, *Galatians* (Atlanta: John Knox Press, 1982).
5. Martyn, "Apocalytic Gospel in Galatians," 247.
6. See Jerome Murphy-O'Connor, *Paul: A Critical Life* (Oxford: Oxford University Press, 1997), 8–15.
7. Byrne, *Romans*, 16–18.
8. Ibid., 62–63.
9. See Stanley Stowers, *The Diatribe and Paul's Letter to the Romans,* SBL Dissertation Series 57 (Chico, CA: Scholars Press, 1981).
10. I am largely following Byrne, *Romans*, 26–28.
11. Rom. 4:25; 8:32; Gal. 1:20; 2:20 (cf. Eph. 5:2, 25). See Jürgen Moltmann, *The Trinity and the Kingdom* (San Francisco: Harper & Row, 1981), 80–83.
12. The idea of a paradigm was first popularized by Thomas Kuhn, *The Structure of Scientific Revolutions* (Chicago: University of Chicago Press, 1970).
13. James Dunn, *The Theology of Paul the Apostle* (Grand Rapids: Wm. B. Eerdmans, 1998), 403.
14. See Richard Hays, "The Conversion of the Imagination: Scripture and Eschatology in 1 Corinthians," *New Testament Studies* 45 (1999): 391–412.
15. See, e.g., C. K. Barrett, *A Commentary on the Epistle to the Romans* (New York: Harper & Row, 1957), 123.
16. C. E. B. Cranfield, *The Epistle to the Romans*, International Critical Commentary, vol. 1 (Edinburgh: T. & T. Clark, 1975), 305.
17. Otto Michel, "Oikos," *Theological Dictionary of the New Testament*, ed. G. Kittel and G. Friedrich, vol. 5 (Grand Rapids: Wm. B. Eerdmans, 1967), 119–59.
18. Jer. 1:10, which Paul echoes in 2 Cor. 10:8 and 13:10.
19. For this line of interpretation, see Richard Hays, *First Corinthians*, Interpretation (Louisville, KY: John Knox Press, 1997; Dale Martin, *The Corinthian Body* (New Haven, CT: Yale University Press, 1990).
20. See Gerd Theissen, *The Social Setting of Pauline Christianity: Essays on Corinth* (Philadelphia: Fortress Press, 1982); and Abraham Malherbe, *Social Aspects of Early Christianity* (Baton Rouge: Louisiana State University Press, 1975).
21. See Wayne Meeks, *The First Urban Christians: The Social World of the Apostle Paul* (New Haven, CT: Yale University Press, 1983), chap. 3; and Meeks, *The Moral World of the First Christians* (Philadelphia: Fortress Press, 1986), chap. 4.
22. References to individual households are found in Rom. 16: 5, 10–11, 14–16; 1 Cor. 1:11, 16; 16:10; and to larger gatherings in Rom. 16:23 and 1 Cor. 14:23.
23. Meeks, *First Urban Christians*, 22–23 and chap. 2.
24. Ibid., chap. 2.

25. Ibid., 55.
26. Hays, *First Corinthians*, 206–51.
27. Ibid., 206.
28. See Margaret Mitchell, *Paul and the Rhetoric of Reconciliation: An Exegetical Investigation of the Language and Composition of 1 Corinthians* (Louisville, KY: Westminster/John Knox Press, 1991).
29. Gordon Fee, *The First Epistle to the Corinthians* (Grand Rapids: Wm. B. Eerdmans, 1987), 627–52; and Hays, *First Corinthians*, 221–31.

Chapter 2: The Three Tasks of Paul's Teaching Ministry

1. *Katecheō* refers to teaching in 1 Cor. 14:18–19 and Gal. 6:6.
2. See Clifford Geertz, *The Interpretation of Cultures* (New York: Basic Books, 1973).
3. See Hays, *Echoes of Scripture in the Letters of Paul*.
4. See Brian Rosner, *Paul, Scripture, and Ethics: A Study of 1 Corinthians 5–7* (Leiden: E. J. Brill, 1994), 183. Cf. Hays, "Conversion of the Imagination," 391–412.
5. See James Dunn's thorough and balanced treatment in *Theology of Paul*, 174–77.
6. Ibid., 174–77.
7. See. e.g., Leander Keck, *Paul and His Letters,* 2nd ed. (Philadelphia: Fortress Press, 1988), 40–43; and Victor Furnish, *Jesus according to Paul* (Cambridge: Cambridge University Press, 1993).
8. Dunn, *Theology of Paul*, chap. 8.
9. Keck, *Paul and His Letters*, 31.
10. Hays, *Echoes of Scripture*, 105ff.
11. Walter Bauer, *A Greek-English Lexicon of the New Testament and Other Early Christian Literature*, trans. and ed. William Arndt and Wilbur Gingrich, 2nd ed. (Chicago: University of Chicago Press, 1979), 614–15.
12. Hays, *First Corinthians*, 192–97.
13. Martin, *Corinthian Body*, chap. 5.
14. James Dunn, *Jesus and the Spirit: A Study of the Religious and Charismatic Experience of Jesus and the First Christians as Reflected in the New Testament* (Philadelphia: Westminster Press, 1975), 282–84.
15. Martyn detects catechists trained by Paul. See *Galatians*, 14, 544, 551–52.
16. See, e.g., C. H. Dodd, *Gospel and Law: The Relation of Faith and Ethics in Early Christianity* (New York: Columbia University Press, 1951). Cf. the critical overview of Victor Furnish, *Theology and Ethics in Paul* (Nashville: Abingdon Press, 1968), 269–79.
17. See Willis De Boer, *The Imitation of Paul: An Exegetical Study* (Kampen: J. H. Kok, 1962); J. Brant, "The Place of *Memēsis* in Paul's Thought," *Studies in Religion* 22 (1993), 285–300; D. Stanley, "Imitation in Paul's Letters: Its Significance for His Relationship to Jesus and to His Own Christian Foundations," in *From Jesus to Paul: Studies in Honor of Francis Wright Beare*, ed. P. Richardson and J. C. Hurd (Waterloo, Ontario: Wilfrid Laurier University Press, 1984), 127–44.
18. Beverly Roberts Gaventa, *First and Second Thessalonians,* Interpretation (Louisville, KY: John Knox Press, 1998), 2.
19. Ibid., 3. Cf. Ernest Best, *The First and Second Epistles to the Thessalonians*, Black New Testament Commentaries (London: Adam & Charles Black, 1972), 4–7.
20. Abraham Malherbe, *Paul and the Thessalonians: The Philosophic Tradition of Pastoral Care* (Philadelphia: Fortress Press, 1987), chap. 1.

21. Thomas Olbricht, "An Aristotelian Rhetorical Analysis of 1 Thessalonians," in *Greeks, Romans, and Christians: Essays in Honor of Abraham J. Malherbe*, ed. David L. Balch et al. (Minneapolis: Fortress Press, 1990), 226–27. Cf. Gaventa, *First and Second Thessalonians*, 5–7.

22. Meeks, *Moral World of the First Christians*, 125–30; Malherbe, *Paul and the Thessalonians*, chap. 2.

23. Frank Matera, *New Testament Ethics: The Legacies of Jesus and Paul* (Louisville, KY: Westminster John Knox Press, 1999), 123–25.

24. My treatment of this triad is indebted to Gaventa, *First and Second Thessalonians*.

25. Beyond Thessalonians, see Rom. 5:1–5; 1 Cor. 13:13; and Gal. 5:5–6. Cf. Eph. 4:2–5; Col. 1:4–5; Titus 2:2; Heb. 6:10–12; 10:22–24; and 1 Pet. 1:3–8. See A. M. Hunter, *Paul and His Predecessors* (London: SCM Press, 1961).

26. Gaventa, *First and Second Thessalonians*, 18.

27. Ibid., 45.

28. Ibid., 26–28, 31–34. See also Beverly Roberts Gaventa, "Our Mother St. Paul: Toward the Recovery of a Neglected Theme," *Princeton Seminary Bulletin* 17 (1996): 29–44.

29. Malherbe, *Paul and the Thessalonians*, 57; see also 56–60 and chap. 3.

30. The following discussion draws on Malherbe, *Paul and the Thessalonians*, 97–106.

31. Gaventa, *First and Second Thessalonians*, 63. Cf. Best, *First and Second Epistles to the Thessalonians*, 180–86.

32. See Best, *First and Second Epistles to the Thessalonians*, 187.

33. See Matt. 24:43/Luke 12:39. See Dunn, *Theology of Paul*, 300–305.

34. Gaventa, *First and Second Thessalonians*, 71–72.

35. Malherbe, *Paul and the Thessalonians*, 81.

36. Ibid., 88.

37. Gaventa, *First and Second Thessalonians*, 84.

38. Furnish, *Theology and Ethics in Paul*, 224–27; Michael Parsons, "Being Precedes Act: Indicative and Imperative in Paul's Writing," in *Understanding Paul's Ethics: Twentieth-Century Approaches*, ed. B. Rosner (Grand Rapids: Wm. B. Eerdmans, 1995), 217–47; William Dennison: "Indicative and Imperative: The Basic Structure of Pauline Ethics," *Calvin Theological Journal* 1 (1979), 55–78.

39. See Matera's helpful summary in *New Testament Ethics*, 154–59.

40. Beverly Gaventa, "Galatians 1 and 2: Autobiography as Paradigm," *Novum Testamentum* 28, no. 4 (1986): 309–26.

41. For a typology that describes some of the positions taken today, see Richard Longenecker, *New Testament Social Ethics for Today* (Grand Rapids: Wm. B. Eerdmans, 1984).

42. See Jim Wallis, *Agenda for Biblical People* (New York: Harper & Row, 1976); and Clark Pinnock, *Unbounded Love: A Good News Theology for the 21st Century* (Downers Grove, IL: InterVarsity Press, 1994).

43. This is close to the position of Richard Hays, *The Moral Vision of the New Testament* (San Francisco: HarperSanFrancisco, 1996); and Rosner, *Paul, Scripture, and Ethics*.

44. See Joseph Allen, *Love and Conflict: A Covenantal Model of Christian Ethics* (Nashville: Abingdon Press, 1984); and Gene Outka, *Agape: An Ethical Analysis* (New Haven, CT: Yale University Press, 1972).

45. See Oscar Cullmann, *Christ and Time: The Primitive Conception of Time and History* (Philadelphia: Westminster Press, 1950). J. Louis Martyn also seems to fit here. See his *Theological Issues in the Letters of Paul* (Nashville: Abingdon Press, 1997), chap. 15.

46. See Allen Verhey, *Remembering Jesus: Christian Community, Scripture, and the Moral Life* (Grand Rapids: Wm. B. Eerdmans, 2002); and James Gustafson, *Ethics from a Theocentric Perspective*, vols. 1, 2 (Chicago: University of Chicago Press, 1981–1984). Furnish's description of Paul's teachings as concrete, relevant, inclusive, and persuasive, as well as his accent on human insight is close to this position. See Furnish, *Theology and Ethics.*

47. Martyn, *Theological Issues*, 62–65, 69, 280–84. See also Ernst Käsemann, "Worship in Everyday Life: A Note on Romans 12," *New Testament Questions of Today* (Philadelphia: Fortress Press, 1969), chap. 9.

48. Martyn, *Theological Issues*, 284.

49. Ibid., 62–64.

50. See Richard West, "The Interlace Structure of *The Lord of the Rings*," and David Miller, "Narrative Pattern in *The Fellowship of the Ring*," in *A Tolkien Compass*, ed. Jared Lobdell (Chicago: Open Court, 1975), 75–91 and 93–103.

51. Hays, *First Corinthians*, 7–8.

52. Hays, "Conversion of the Imagination," 396.

53. For a cumulative argument, see the commentaries of Hays and Fee, cited above.

54. Fee, *First Epistle to the Corinthians*, 15–16.

55. Theissen, *Social Setting of Pauline Christianity*, chap. 4.

56. Hays, *First Corinthians*, 192–97.

57. Fee, *First Epistle to the Corinthians*, 531–69.

58. Ibid., 561.

59. Hays, *First Corinthians*, 241.

60. Rosner, *Paul, Scripture, and Ethics*, chap. 2.

61. Ibid., chap. 3.

62. Bruce Winter, "Civil Litigation in Secular Corinth and the Church: The Forensic Background to 1 Corinthians 6:1–8," in *Understanding Paul's Ethics: Twentieth-Century Approaches*, ed. B. Rosner (Grand Rapids: Wm. B. Eerdmans, 1995), 85–103. See also Alan Mitchell, "Rich and Poor in the Courts of Corinth," *New Testament Studies* 39 (1993): 562–86.

63. Hays, *First Corinthians*, 93–94.

64. Ibid., 102.

65. See Rosner, *Paul, Scripture, and Ethics*, chap. 5.

66. My interpretation draws on the commentaries of Fee and Hays, as well as Meeks, *Moral World of the First Christians*, 132–36; and Verhey, *Remembering Jesus*, 29–33.

67. Meeks, *Moral World of the First Christians*, 133.

Introduction to Part Two

1. For an overview of this subject, see Wentzel van Huyssteen, *The Shaping of Rationality: Toward Interdisciplinarity in Theology and Science* (Grand Rapids: Wm. B. Eerdmans, 1999). See also Richard Osmer, "A New Clue for Religious Education? Cross-disciplinary Thinking in the Quest for Integrity and Intelligibility," *Toward a New Religious Education in the Next Millennium*, ed. James Michael Lee (Birmingham, AL: Religious Education Press, 2000).

2. See Howard Gardner, *Frames of Mind: The Theory of Multiple Intelligences* (New York: Basic Books, 1983).

3. See Donald Capps, *Reframing: A New Approach to Pastoral Care* (Minneapolis: Fortress Press, 1990); Donald Schön and Martin Rain, *Frame Reflection: Toward the Resolution of Intractable Policy Controversies* (New York: Basic Books, 1994); and Lee Bolman and Terrence Deal, *Reframing Organizations: Artistry, Choice, and Leadership,* 2nd ed. (San Francisco: Jossey-Bass, 1997).

4. See Stephen Kline, *Conceptual Foundations for Multidisciplinary Thinking* (Stanford, CA: Stanford University Press, 1995).
5. See Richard Osmer and Friedrich Schweitzer, *Religious Education between Modernization and Globalization: New Perspectives on the United States and Germany* (Grand Rapids: Wm. B. Eerdmans, 2003). See also Mary Boys, *Educating in Faith: Maps and Visions* (Kansas City, MO: Sheed & Ward, 1989).
6. See Johnson, *Authority in Protestant Theology;* and Kelsey, *Uses of Scripture.*
7. Johannes A. van der Ven, *Ecclesiology in Context* (Grand Rapid: Wm. B. Eerdmans, 1996).
8. See my essay "The Teaching Ministry in a Multicultural World," in *God and Globalization: Theological Ethics and the Spheres of Life*, vol. 2, *The Spirit and the Modern Authorities*, ed. Max Stackhouse and Don Browning (Harrisburg, PA: Trinity Press International, 2002); chap. 1 and, with Friedrich Schweitzer, "Globalization, Global Reflexivity, and Faith Development Theory: The Continuing Contribution of Fowler's Research," in *Developing a Public Faith: New Directions in Practical Theology—Essays in Honor of James W. Fowler*, ed. R. Osmer and F. Schweitzer (St. Louis: Chalice Press, 2003). See also Osmer and Schweitzer, *Religious Education between Modernization and Globalization,* chap. 2.
9. See the following introductory texts: Malcolm Waters, *Globalization* (New York: Routledge, 1995); Roland Robertson, *Globalization: Social Theory and Global Culture* (Thousand Oaks, CA: Sage Publications, 1992); David Held et al., *Global Transformations: Politics, Economics, and Culture* (Stanford, CA: Stanford University Press, 1999); and Anthony Giddens, *Runaway World: How Globalization Is Reshaping Our Lives* (New York: Routledge, 1999).
10. Held et al., *Global Transformations*, 14–27.
11. Ibid., 15.
12. See David Held, *Democracy and the Global Order: From the Modern State to Cosmopolitan Governance* (Cambridge: Polity Press, 1995); John Thompson and David Held, eds., *Habermas: Critical Debates* (Cambridge, MA: MIT Press, 1982); David Held and Anthony McGrew, eds., *Governing Globalization: Power, Authority and Global Governance* (Cambridge: Polity Books, 2002). See also David Korten, *When Corporations Rule the World* (West Hartford, CT: Kumarian Press, 1995).

Chapter 3: Introduction to Case Study Congregations

1. Copies of the interview format can be obtained by writing me at Richard.Osmer@ptsem.edu.
2. My account of the history of the church draws on Joseph Kwak, *Principles of Church Growth for the Ministry of a New Generation: A Case Study of the Ministry Principles of the Somang Church* (Seoul: Kyemongmoonwha Publishing Co., 2001); and Yoon Tek Yim, *Stories of Somang (Hope) Church* (Cerritos, CA: Peters House, 2001), translated by one of my former doctoral students, Shin-geun Jang. I also draw on my interviews of long-time members.
3. See Robert Wuthnow, *The Restructuring of American Religion: Society and Faith since World War II* (Princeton, NJ: Princeton University Press), 153–64.
4. See Jose Cassanova, *Public Religions in the Modern World* (Chicago: University of Chicago Press, 1994) for a summary and critique.
5. Throughout this section, I draw esp. on Bruce Cumings, *Korea's Place in the Sun: A Modern History* (New York: W. W. Norton & Co., 1977).
6. See Won Kyu Lee, *The Reality and Prospect of the Korean Church* (Seoul: Bible Study Publication Co., 1994).

7. This incident and these statistics are reported in Cumings, *Korea's Place in the Sun*, 155.

8. Ibid., 177.

9. Joon Kwan Un, "After Church Growth in Korea: Search for an Alternative Ecclesial Model," *International Journal of Practical Theology*, vol. 1, no.1 (1997): 164.

10. See Young Shin Park, "Christianity and Social Change of Modern Korea," in *The Korean Church and Society*, ed. Won Kyu Lee (Seoul: Nathan Publishing Co., 1989).

11. Leonard Thompson, *A History of South Africa*, rev. ed. (New Haven, CT: Yale University Press, 1995), 36–39. Cf. Robert Shell, *Children of Bondage: A Social History of the Slave Society at the Cape of Good Hope, 1652–1838* (Hanover, NH: Wesleyan University Press, 1994).

12. Throughout this section, I draw on Thompson, *History of South Africa;* Robert Ross, *A Concise History of South Africa* (Cambridge: Cambridge University Press, 1999); Dirk Smit, "Südafrika," *Theologische Realenzyklopädie,* Band XXXII (Berlin: Walter de Gruyter, 2000), 322–32; and John de Gruchy, *The Church Struggle in South Africa* (Grand Rapids: Wm. B. Eerdmans, 1979).

13. See de Gruchy, *Church Struggle;* Nelson Mandela, *Long Walk to Freedom* (New York: Little, Brown & Co., 1994); and Desmond Tutu, *Crying in the Wilderness: The Struggle for Justice in South Africa* (London: Mowbray, 1990).

14. A helpful overview of the process and firsthand account of some of its proceedings are found at http://www.doj.gov.az/trc. See also Alex Boraine, *A Country Unmasked: Inside South Africa's Truth and Reconciliation Commission,* (New York: Oxford University Press, 2000); and James Cochrane, John de Gruchy, and Steve Martin, eds., *Facing the Truth: South African Faith Communities and the Truth and Reconciliation Commission* (Cape Town: David Philip, 1999)

15. Smit, "Südafrika," 327–28.

16. See de Gruchy, *Church Struggle,* and Peter Walshe, *Church versus State in South Africa: The Case of the Christian Institute* (Maryknoll, NY: Orbis Books, 1983). See also Eberhard Bethge, "A Confessing Church in South Africa?" in *Bonhoeffer: Exile and Martyr* (New York: Seabury Press, 1975), 167–78.

17. See John de Gruchy and Charles Villa-Vicencio, eds., *Apartheid Is a Heresy* (Grand Rapids: Wm. B. Eerdmans, 1983).

18. 175–82. Cf. G. Cloete and Dirk Smit, eds., *A Moment of Truth: The Confession of the Dutch Reformed Mission Church* (Grand Rapids: Wm. B. Eerdmans, 1984).

19. See Arthur Link, ed., *The First Presbyterian Church of Princeton: Two Centuries of History* (Princeton, NJ: Princeton University Press, 1967). Cf. William Schenck, *An Historical Account of the First Presbyterian Church of Princeton, N.J.* (Princeton: John T. Robinson, 1850).

20. See Wuthnow, *Restructuring of American Religion*. Wade Clark Roof and William McKinney, *American Mainline Religion* (New Brunswick, NJ: Rutgers University Press, 1987).

21. Quoted in Link, *First Presbyterian Church of Princeton*, 29.

22. See Richard Osmer, *Confirmation: Presbyterian Practices in Ecumenical Perspective* (Louisville, KY: Geneva Press, 1996), chaps. 4–6.

23. See Robert Lynn and Elliott Wright, *The Little Big School: 200 Years of the Sunday School* (Nashville: Abingdon Press, 1971); and Jack Seymour, *From Sunday School to Church School: Continuities in Protestant Church Education in the United States, 1860–1929* (Washington, DC: University Press of America, 1982).

24. Lewis J. Sherrill, *Presbyterian Parochial Schools, 1846–1870* (New Haven, CT: Yale University Press, 1932), 95–96.

25. Link, *First Presbyterian Church of Princeton*, 52.

26. Ibid., 39.

27. Ibid., 41.
28. The one possible exception is Maitland Bartlett, for we have no historical record of his education.
29. Link, *First Presbyterian Church of Princeton*, 65.
30. See Osmer, *Confirmation*, 133–60.
31. See Daniel Bell, *The Coming of Post-Industrial Society* (New York: Basic Books, 1976); and Malcolm Waters, *Globalization* (London: Routledge, 1995).
32. See Stephen Tipton, *Getting Saved from the Sixties* (Berkeley: University of California Press, 1982).
33. The statistics cited come from Roof and McKinney, *American Mainline Religion*, 16.
34. Wuthnow, *Restructuring of American Religion*, 91–95.
35. Roof and McKinney, *American Mainline Religion*, chap. 2.
36. Wuthnow, *Restructuring of American Religion*, chap. 6.
37. See Nancy Tatom Ammerman, *Congregation and Community* (New Brunswick, NJ: Rutgers University Press, 1997); Penny Edgell Becker, *Congregations in Conflict: Cultural Models of Local Religious Life* (New York: Cambridge University Press, 1999); and Stephen Warner, *New Wine in Old Wineskins: Evangelicals and Liberals in a Small-Town Church* (Berkeley: University of California Press, 1988).

Chapter 4: Somang Presbyterian Church

1. "The Sociology of Charismatic Authority," *From Max Weber: Essays in Sociology*, trans. and ed. H. H. Gerth and C. Wright Mills (New York: Oxford University Press, 1946), chap. 9.
2. Kwak, *Principles of Church Growth*, 69. Joseph Kwak is the son of Sun Hee Kwak, and this book reflects his father's philosophy of ministry as practiced over the past twenty-four years at Somang. He generously provided me a copy of the manuscript prior to its publication.
3. This is one of several questions I borrowed from the interview designed by Becker in *Congregations in Conflict*.
4. Sun Hee Kwak, *Eschatology and Christian Mission* (Seoul: Data World, 2000).
5. Ibid., 282–329.
6. Alasdair MacIntyre, *After Virtue: A Study in Moral Theory* (Notre Dame, IN: University of Notre Dame Press, 1981); and Stanley Hauerwas, *A Community of Character: Toward a Constructive Christian Social Ethic* (Notre Dame, IN: University of Notre Dame Press, 1981). For a helpful introduction to this perspective, see Dorothy Bass, ed., *Practicing Our Faith: A Way of Life for a Searching People* (San Francisco: Jossey-Bass, 1997).
7. Reinhard Hütter, *Suffering Divine Things: Theology as Church Practice* (Grand Rapids: Wm. B. Eerdmans, 1997), 36–37.
8. Niklas Luhmann, *Social Systems* (Stanford, CA: Stanford University Press, 1995). Cf. Ammerman, *Congregation and Community*.
9. Friedrich Schleiermacher portrayed it as the "feeling of absolute dependence" in *The Christian Faith* (Edinburgh: T. & T. Clark, 1986), 12ff.; Paul Tillich as "ultimate concern" in *Systematic Theology*, vol. 1 (Chicago: University of Chicago Press, 1951), 12–14; and David Tracy as the "limit-dimension" in *Blessed Rage for Order: The New Pluralism in Theology* (New York: Crossroad, 1975), 92–93.
10. See James Fowler, *To See the Kingdom: The Theological Vision of H. Richard Niebuhr* (Nashville: Abingdon Press, 1974).
11. H. Richard Niebuhr, *The Meaning of Revelation* (New York: Macmillan, 1941), chap. 2.

12. These summaries are based on Hütter, *Suffering Divine Things*, 29–37.
13. These summaries are based on ibid., 95–145.
14. Hütter derives these from Luther's "On the Councils and the Church," ibid., 128–33.
15. The phrase, "auxiliary practices" is from personal conversations at the Center for Theological Inquiry.
16. See John Howard Yoder, *Body Politics: Five Practices of the Christian Community before the Watching World* (Nashville: Discipleship Resources, 1992).
17. See Richard Foster, *Celebration of Discipline: The Path to Spiritual Growth* (San Francisco: Harper & Row, 1978).
18. Thanks to my colleague at Princeton Theological Seminary, Gordon Mikoski, for this term.
19. Howard Gardner has written extensively across several decades. The books most helpful to the perspective developed here are *Frames of Mind: The Theory of Multiple Intelligences* (New York: Basic Books, 1983); *The Unschooled Mind: How Children Think and How Schools Should Teach* (New York: Basic Books, 1991); *Multiple Intelligences: The Theory in Practice—A Reader* (New York: Basic Books, 1993); *The Disciplined Mind: What All Students Should Understand* (New York: Simon & Schuster, 1999); *Intelligence Reframed: Multiple Intelligences for the 21st Century* (New York: Basic Books, 1999).
20. Gardner, *Frames of Mind*, x.
21. David Feldman, *Beyond Universals in Cognitive Development* (Norwood, NJ: Ablex, 1980). Feldman and Gardner collaborated on Project Spectrum during the 1980s. For a discussion of Project Spectrum, see Jie-Qi Chen et al., *Building on Children's Strengths: The Experience of Project Spectrum* (New York: Teachers College Press, 1998). See David Feldman's contribution to this volume, "How Spectrum Began," chap. 1.
22. See Kwak, *Principles of Church Growth*, 72–81.
23. John Calvin, *Institutes of the Christian Religion*, Library of Christian Classics, vol. 20, ed. John McNeill, trans. Ford Lewis Battles (Philadelphia: Westminster Press, 1960), 86.
24. Kwak, *Principles of Church Growth*, 78. The second point emerges from my observation of age-level worship services.
25. Young-Gi Cho et al., *Studies on the Korean Preachers*, vol. 1 (Seoul: Korea Academy of Church History, 2000), has three articles on Rev. Kwak's preaching style. One of my former doctoral students, Shin-Geun Jang, was helpful in summarizing these for me.
26. Dr. Thomas Hastings at Tokyo Union Theological Seminary pointed this contrast out to me.
27. Kwak, *Principles of Church Growth*, 86–88.
28. Ibid., 133.
29. Kwak used this terminology in an early draft of *Principles of Church Growth*, but subsequently changed it to "dethroning." See 113–21.
30. Ibid., 116.
31. Ibid., 116–19.
32. Ibid., 94–102.
33. Ibid., 96.
34. Ibid., 97.
35. See Don Browning et al., *From Cultural Wars to Common Ground: Religion and the American Family Debate* (Louisville, KY: Westminster John Knox Press, 2000).
36. See Robert Wuthnow, *Christianity and Civil Society: The Current Debate* (Valley Forge, PA: Trinity Press International, 1996); Martin Marty, *The Public Church:*

Mainline-Evangelical-Catholic (New York: Crossroad, 1981); James Fowler, *Faithful Change: The Personal and Public Challenges of Postmodern Life* (Nashville: Abingdon Press, 1996); and J. L. Seymour, R. T. O'Gorman, and C. R. Foster, *The Church in the Education of the Public: Refocusing the Task of Religious Education* (Nashville: Abingdon Press, 1984).

37. Kwak, *Principles of Church Growth*, 121–28.
38. Yim, *Stories of Somang (Hope) Church*, 151.

Chapter 5: Nassau Presbyterian Church

1. Nassau keeps audiotapes of sermons, making it possible for me to listen to the original sermon.
2. James W. Alexander to John Hall, Nov. 17, 1837, in *Forty Years' Familiar Letters of James W. Alexander, D.D.*, ed. John Hall (New York, 1860), 1: 260.
3. Frank Burch Brown, *Good Taste, Bad Taste, and Christian Taste: Aesthetics in Religious Life* (Oxford: Oxford University Press, 2000), 23.
4. Within Becker's typology, Nassau is a *leader* congregation.
5. See C. Ellis Nelson, *Where Faith Begins* (Atlanta: John Knox Press, 1967); John Westerhoff, *Will Our Children Have Faith?* (New York: Seabury Press, 1976); Thomas Groome, *Christian Religious Education: Sharing Our Story and Vision* (San Francisco: Harper & Row, 1980); and James Loder, *The Transforming Moment: Understanding Convictional Experiences* (San Francisco: Harper & Row, 1981).
6. For bibliographical references, see part 2 of my *Confirmation*.
7. See Richard Baxter, *Chapters from a Christian Directory; or a Summ of Practical Theology and Cases of Conscience* (London: G. Bell & Sons, 1925).
8. G. H. Bantock, *Studies in the History of Educational Theory*, vol. 1, *Artifice and Nature* (London: Allen & Unwin, 1980), chap. 1.
9. See Howard Gardner, *To Open Minds* (New York: Basic Books, 1989).
10. Gardner, *Frames of Mind*, 26.
11. See Patricia King and Karen Kitchener, *Developing Reflective Judgment: Understanding and Promoting Intellectual Growth and Critical Thinking in Adolescents and Adults* (San Francisco: Jossey-Bass, 1994).
12. See Daniel Goleman, *Emotional Intelligence: Why It Can Matter More than IQ* (New York: Bantam Books, 1995).
13. See Thomas Armstrong, *Multiple Intelligences in the Classroom* (Alexandria, VA: Association for Supervision and Curriculum Development, 1994). Cf. Gardner, *Intelligence Reframed*, 174.
14. My discussion of the first two phases draws on Gardner's *Unschooled Mind* and the third on his *Disciplined Mind*.
15. See Gardner, *Unschooled Mind*, chap. 5.
16. See esp. C. A. Bowers, *Critical Essays on Education, Modernity, and the Recovery of the Ecological Imperative* (New York: Teachers College Press, 1993).
17. See Veronica Boix Mansilla and Howard Gardner, "What Are the Qualities of Understanding?" in *Teaching for Understanding: Linking Research with Practice*, ed. Martha Stone Wiske (San Francisco: Jossey-Bass, 1998), chap. 6; and Gardner, *Disciplined Mind*.
18. Gardner, *Teaching for Understanding*, chap. 6.
19. See Craig Dykstra and Sharon Parks, eds., *Faith Development and Fowler* (Birmingham, AL: Religious Education Press, 1986); and Richard Osmer and Friedrich Schweitzer, eds., *Developing a Public Faith: New Directions in Practical Theology—Essays in Honor of James Fowler* (St. Louis: Chalice Press, 2003).

20. See James Fowler, "Faith and the Structuring of Meaning," in *Toward Moral and Religious Maturity* (Morristown, NJ: Silver Burdett Co., 1980), 51–85.

21. See, e.g., Antonio Damasio, *The Feeling of What Happens: Body and Emotion in the Making of Consciousness* (New York: Harcourt Brace & Co., 1999).

22. For an overview of postconventionality, see Hyun-Sook Kim, *Christian Education for Postconventionality: Modernization, Trinitarian Ethics, and Christian Identity* (Seoul: Kangnam Publishers, 2002).

23. See Osmer and Schweitzer, *Religious Education between Modernization and Globalization*, 47–60.

24. James Fowler, *Stages of Faith: The Psychology of Human Development and the Quest for Meaning* (San Francisco: Harper & Row, 1981), 187–88.

Chapter 6: URC Stellenbosch

1. Throughout this section, my discussion draws on G. D. Cloete and D. J. Smit, eds., *A Moment of Truth: The Confession of the Dutch Reformed Mission Church* (Grand Rapids: Wm. B. Eerdmans, 1984); and Nico Koopman, "Christian Ethics in Postapartheid South Africa—A Reformed Perspective," unpublished manuscript.

2. See David Bosch, *Transforming Mission: Paradigm Shifts in the Theology of Mission* (Maryknoll, NY: Orbis Books, 1991); and Lesslie Newbigin, *The Open Secret: Sketches for a Missionary Theology* (Grand Rapids: Wm. B. Eerdmans, 1981).

3. Dietrich Bonhoeffer, "The Nature of the Church," in *A Testament to Freedom: The Essential Writings of Dietrich Bonhoeffer*, ed. G. Kelly and R. Nelson (San Francisco: HarperCollins, 1990), 89.

4. Hans Küng, *The Church* (New York: Sheed & Ward, 1967), 14.

5. For an overview, see Bolman and Deal, *Reframing Organizations*, 24–28.

6. See Peter Senge, *The Fifth Discipline: The Art and Practice of the Learning Organization* (New York: Doubleday, 1990).

7. See Chris Argyris and Donald Schon, *Organizational Learning: A Theory of Action Perspective* (Reading, MA: Addison-Wesley, 1978); and Argyris, *On Organizational Learning* (Oxford: Blackwell, 1992).

8. See Edgar Schein, *Organizational Culture and Leadership*, 2nd ed. (San Francisco: Jossey-Bass, 1992).

9. See Shari Tishman, David Perkins, and Eileen Jay, *The Thinking Classroom: Learning and Teaching in a Culture of Thinking* (Boston: Allyn & Bacon, 1995).

10. See James MacGregor Burns, *Leadership* (New York: HarperCollins, 1978); and Ronald Heifetz, *Leadership without Easy Answers* (Cambridge, MA: Belknap Press, 1994).

11. Heifetz, *Leadership without Easy Answers*, 22–27.

12. Ibid., 31.

13. See Charles Olsen and Ellen Morseth, *Selecting Church Leaders: A Practice in Spiritual Discernment* (Nashville: Upper Room, 2002); Suzanne Farnham et al., *Grounded in God: Listening Hearts Discernment for Group Deliberations* (Harrisburg, PA: Morehouse Publishing Co., 1999); and Thomas Green, SJ, *Weeds among the Wheat: Discernment, Where Prayer and Action Meet* (Notre Dame, IN: Ave Maria Press, 1984).

Chapter 7: The Pilgrimage Frame

1. While a doctoral student, I had the good fortune of working with John Carr at Candler School of Theology on a research project known as the Pilgrimage

Project, and with Charles Gerkin while he was writing *The Living Human Document: Re-visioning Pastoral Counseling in a Hermeneutical Mode* (Nashville: Abingdon Press, 1984), which develops the theme of pilgrimage in chap. 3.

2. See Sharon Daloz Parks, "Home and Pilgrimage: Companion Metaphors for Personal and Social Transformation," *Soundings: An Interdisciplinary Journal* 72, nos. 2–3 (Summer-Fall, 1989); and Parks, "To Venture and to Abide: The Tidal Rhythm of Our Becoming," in Osmer and Schweitzer, *Developing a Public Faith*, 56–73.

3. See Robert Kegan, *The Evolving Self: Problem and Process in Human Development* (Cambridge, MA: Harvard University Press, 1982).

4. See Miroslav Volf's discussion of Luther in *Work in the Spirit: Toward a Theology of Work* (Oxford: Oxford University Press, 1991), esp. 105–9. For a broader discussion of vocation, see Gordon Preece, *The Viability of the Vocation Tradition in Trinitarian, Credal, and Reformed Perspective: The Threefold Call* (Lewiston, NY: Edwin Mellon Press, 1998).

5. Particularly helpful are James Fowler, *Becoming Adult, Becoming Christian* (San Francisco: Harper & Row, 1984), chaps. 4–5; Fowler, *Weaving the New Creation: Stages of Faith and the Public Church* (San Francisco: Harper & Row, 1991), chap. 5; and Max Stackhouse, "Introduction: Foundation and Purposes," in *On Moral Business: Classical and Contemporary Resources for Ethics in Economic Life*, ed. M. Stackhouse, D. McCann, S. Roels (Grand Rapids: Wm. B. Eerdmans, 1995), 10–34.

6. See Jürgen Moltmann, *God in Creation: A New Theology of Creation and the Spirit of God*, trans. M. Kohl (Minneapolis: Fortress Press, 1985), chap. 4.

7. Moltmann discusses vocation throughout his writing. See, for example, *The Spirit of Life: A Universal Affirmation,* trans. M. Kohl (Minneapolis: Fortress Press, 1992), chap. 9.

8. Volf is critical of the vocational tradition, viewing it as beyond rehabilitation. As Preece notes in *The Viability of the Vocation Tradition,* however, it is possible to build on his insights and critically reconstruct this tradition. The references here come from Volf, *Work in the Spirit*, 112–13, 130–31.

9. Volf, *Work in the Spirit*, 111. He is quoting here from F. F. Bruce's commentary on Galatians.

10. See Fowler, *Becoming Adult, Becoming Christian*, 95.

11. See Osmer and Schweitzer, *Religious Education between Modernization and Globalization*, 34–47.

12. See Peter Berger, *The Heretical Imperative: Contemporary Possibilities of Religious Affirmation* (Garden City, NY: Anchor Press, 1979).

13. See Mara Krechevsky, *Project Spectrum: Preschool Assessment Handbook* (New York: Teachers College Press, 1998).

14. See, e.g., Friedrich Schweitzer, *The Postmodern Life Cycle* (St. Louis: Chalice Press, 2003).

15. See Erik Erikson, *Childhood and Society* (New York: W. W. Norton & Co., 1950), chap. 7; Daniel Levinson, *The Seasons of a Man's Life* (New York: Ballantine, 1978); and Levinson, *The Seasons of a Woman's Life* (New York: Alfred A. Knopf, 1996).

16. Jean Baker Miller, *Toward a New Psychology of Women* (Boston: Beacon Press, 1976); Carol Gilligan, *In a Different Voice: Psychological Theory and Women's Development* (Cambridge, MA: Harvard University Press, 1982).

17. See Judith Jordan, et al., *Women's Growth in Connection: Writings from the Stone Center* (New York: Guilford Press, 1991).

18. See, e.g., Carol Gilligan and Lyn Mikel Brown, *Meeting at the Crossroads: Women's Psychology and Girl's Development* (Cambridge, MA: Harvard University Press, 1992).

19. See, e.g., Mary Belenky et al., *Women's Ways of Knowing* (New York: Basic Books, 1986).

20. See Ruth Smith, "Moral Transcendence and Moral Space in the Historical Experiences of Women," *Journal of Feminist Studies in Religion* 4 (1988): 21–37; and Joan Tronto, "Beyond Gender Difference to a Theory of Care," *Signs* 12 (1987): 644–63.

21. See Deborah Tannen, *Gender and Discourse* (New York: Oxford University Press, 1994); and Nancy Chodorow, *The Reproduction of Mothering: Psychoanalysis and the Sociology of Gender* (Berkeley, CA: University of California Press, 1979), which influenced Gilligan. See also Chodorow, *Femininities, Masculinities, Sexualities : Freud and Beyond* (Lexington, KY: University Press of Kentucky, 1994); and David Buss, *The Evolution of Desire: Strategies of Human Mating* (New York: Basic Books, 1994).

22. See Barry Hewlett, ed., *Father-Child Relations: Cultural and Biosocial Contexts* (Hawthorne, NY: Aldine De Gruyter, 1992); and John Snarey, *How Fathers Care for the Next Generation* (Cambridge, MA: Harvard University Press, 1993).

23. I have adopted the language of "life chances" to describe this perspective from Held, *Democracy and the Global Order*.

24. For analysis of the impact of race, see Beverly Daniel Tatum, *"Why Are All the Black Kids Sitting Together in the Cafeteria?" And Other Conversations about Race* (New York: Basic Books, 1997).

25. Held, *Democracy and the Global Order*, 177.

26. See Paul Ricoeur, *Time and Narrative*, vols. 1–3 (Chicago: University of Chicago Press, 1984–88); Calvin Schrag, *The Self after Postmodernity* (New Haven, CT: Yale University Press, 1997); and Theodore Sarbin, ed., *Narrative Psychology: The Storied Nature of Human Conduct* (New York: Praeger, 1986).

Introduction to Part 3

1. See James Fowler, *Weaving the New Creation: Stages of Faith and the Public Church* (San Francisco: HarperSanFrancisco, 1991), chaps. 2–3; and *Faithful Change: The Personal and Public Challenges of Postmodern Life* (Nashville: Abingdon Press, 1996), chap. 12.

2. See James Loder and Jim Neidhardt, *The Knight's Move* (Colorado Springs: Helmers & Howard, 1992); and James Loder, *The Logic of the Spirit: Human Development in Theological Perspective* (San Francisco: Jossey-Bass, 1998).

3. Browning, *Fundamental Practical Theology*, 142–48.

4. For various references to Luther's use of this metaphorical complex see Hans Urs von Balthasar, *Theo-Drama: Theological Dramatic Theory*, vol.1 (San Francisco: Ignatius Press, 1988), 159–60.

5. See Reinhold Niebuhr, *The Self and the Dramas of History* (New York: Charles Scribner's Sons, 1955).

6. Balthasar, *Theo-Drama*, 1:10–13.

7. See Christopher Steck, *The Ethical Thought of Hans Urs von Balthasar* (New York: Herder & Herder, 2001), 21–22. See also Aidan Nichols, *No Bloodless Myth: A Guide through Balthasar's Dramatics* (Washington, DC: Catholic University of America Press, 2000).

8. Throughout this section, I am drawing on Moltmann's autobiographical reflections in "My Theological Career," in *History and the Triune God: Contributions to Trinitarian Theology* (New York: Crossroads, 1992), 165–82. See further Richard Bauckham, *The Theology of Jürgen Moltmann* (Edinburgh: T. & T. Clark, 1995); and Douglas Meeks, *Origins of the Theology of Hope* (Philadelphia: Fortress Press, 1974).

Chapter 8: Theo-Drama

1. Jürgen Moltmann, *The Coming of God: Christian Eschatology* (Minneapolis: Fortress Press, 1996), xiv.
2. Throughout this book, I have used feminine pronouns to refer to the Holy Spirit. For a discussion of the names of the triune God that shares this usage, see Moltmann, *History and the Triune God*, chaps. 1, 2, and 6.
3. Moltmann discusses *perichoresis* in a variety of places. See esp. *Trinity and the Kingdom*, 174–76, and *God in Creation*, 16–17.
4. See esp. Moltmann, *Trinity and the Kingdom*, 178–90; and Moltmann, *The Spirit of Life: A Universal Affirmation* (Minneapolis: Fortress Press, 1992), 72ff. As Bauckham points out, Moltmann offers different accounts of these patterns. See Bauckham, *Theology of Jürgen Moltmann*, 156–57.
5. Moltmann, *God in Creation*, 9.
6. Moltmann adds a doxological Trinity in *History and the Triune God*, 66–69.
7. Moltmann, *God in Creation*, 192.
8. Ibid., 38.
9. Keith Ward, *God, Chance, and Necessity* (Oxford: Oneworld Publications, 1996), 15.
10. For a fuller description of this process, see ibid., 105, 116, 118, 127, 135–36.
11. See Ian Tattersall, *Becoming Human: Evolution and Human Uniqueness* (New York: Harcourt Brace, 1998); Merlin Donald, *Origins of the Modern Mind: Three Stages in the Evolution of Culture and Cognition* (Cambridge, MA: Harvard University Press, 1991); and Steven Mithen, *The Prehistory of the Mind: The Cognitive Origins of Art, Religion and Science* (London: Thames & Hudson, 1996).
12. One of many places Moltmann offers this epigram is *God in Creation*, 17 (cf. his comments on p. 98).
13. Moltmann typically draws on Jewish mystical theology to describe the withdrawal of the immanent Trinity to make room for the time and space of a created other. See, for example, *God in Creation*, 87ff.
14. Bauckham, *Theology of Jürgen Moltmann*, 15–17.
15. See Ian Barbour's helpful introduction to this topic in *When Science Meets Religion: Enemies, Strangers, or Partners?* (San Francisco: HarperSanFrancisco, 2000), chap. 3.
16. Moltmann, *God in Creation*, 205–6.
17. See, for example, the Westminster Confession of Faith, which affirms, "After God had made all other creatures, he created man, male and female, with reasonable and immortal souls" (IV, 2).
18. The idea of the community of creation is central to all of Moltmann's *God in Creation*, but see esp. 69–71.
19. Ibid., 221–22.
20. Ibid., 77.
21. Ibid., 258–59. Cf. Moltmann's use of the analogy of the Spirit's indwelling (xv).
22. See Edward Wilson, *The Future of Life* (New York: Alfred A. Knopf, 2003).
23. Adrian Thomas, *Górecki* (Oxford: Clarendon Press 1997), 82.
24. Luke Howard, "A Reluctant Requiem: The History and Reception of Henryk M. Gorecki's Symphony No. 3 in Britain and the United States" Dissertation for the Doctor of Philosophy in Musicology, (University of Michigan, 1997), 44. See also "Lament of Our Lady at the Foot of the Cross," in Bogdana Carpenter, *Monumenta Polonica: The First Four Centuries of Polish Poetry* (Ann Arbor, MI: Michigan Slavic Publications, 1989), 15–19.

25. Foreword, "A Reluctant Requiem," 39–40. This song was published in 1954 as part of a collection, *Folksongs from Silesian Opole,* put together by Adolf Dygacz.

26. The scene of baby turtles comes from the accounts of naturalists, but was first "fictionalized" in Tennessee Williams's play *Suddenly Last Summer* (New York: New Directions, 1958). See Daniel Migilore's thoughtful reflections on this scene in *Faith Seeking Understanding: An Introduction to Christian Theology* (Grand Rapids: Wm. B. Eerdmans, 1991), 102. The wasp and the caterpillar is drawn from Stephen Gould, *Rocks of Ages: Science and Religion in the Fullness of Life* (New York: Ballantine, 1999), 183. The final accounts are my own fictionalized versions of actual events described in the proceedings of the Truth and Reconciliation Commission of South Africa at http://www.doj.gov.za/trc/hrvtrans.

27. Jürgen Moltmann, *The Way of Jesus Christ: Christology in Messianic Dimensions* (Minneapolis: Fortress Press, 1990), 294.

28. Ibid., 296.

29. Jürgen Moltmann, *Theology of Hope: On the Ground and the Implications of a Christian Eschatology* (New York: Harper & Row, 1967); *The Crucified God: The Cross of Christ as the Foundation and Criticism of Christian Theology* (New York: Harper & Row, 1974).

30. Bauckham, *Theology of Jürgen Moltmann*, 4.

31. This is one way Moltmann frequently summarizes the hope of Christian eschatology. See Richard Bauckham, *God Will Be All in All: The Eschatology of Jürgen Moltmann* (Minneapolis: Fortress Press, 1999).

32. See Moltmann, *Crucified God*, chap. 4.

33. See Moltmann's response to Trevor Hart's essay "Imagination for the Kingdom of God?" in Moltmann, "Hope and Reality: Contradiction and Correspondence," in Bauckham, *God Will Be All in All,* 77 86.

34. Moltmann, *Way of Jesus Christ,* 94–116.

35. Ibid., 253. For continuity with the categories of *The Crucified God,* see pp. 152, 165–69.

36. Ibid., 220, 241.

37. Ibid., 122.

38. While *The Church in the Power of the Spirit* precedes Moltmann's second, more systematic series of dogmatic theology, I believe certain continuities can be discerned with his brief descriptions of the church in *The Way of Jesus Christ.* There are differences to be sure, but these are differences in accent. From the beginning to the end of his theology, Moltmann develops what might be called a transformational public church ecclesiology. He is deeply committed to the church's participation in all spheres of life and as seeing itself as a small part of the larger whole of continuing creation. In *The Church in the Power of the Spirit,* greater emphasis is placed on the church's openness to the world, accenting themes such as the congregation's dialogue with its partners in history. In *The Way of Jesus Christ,* the image of a contrast society is more prominent, accentuating the distinctiveness of the congregation as a community that holds before the world an alternative to its systems of injustice and violence.

39. Moltmann, *Church in the Power of the Spirit,* 109.

40. C. S. Lewis, *The Last Battle* (New York: Collier Books, 1956), 171.

41. An overview of the diverse uses of the theme of glory in Scripture is found in Arthur Ramsey, *The Glory of the Lord and the Transfiguration of Christ* (London: Longmans, Green & Co., 1949).

42. Moltmann uses it in this comprehensive fashion in *Trinity and the Kingdom,* 122–28, and *Spirit of Life,* 298–301. Cf. *History and the Triune God,* chap. 6.

43. See Jürgen Moltmann, *Theology and Joy* (London: SCM Press, 1973), 58–62; *Church in the Power of the Spirit*, 108–14; and *Coming of God*, chap. 5.
44. For a fuller discussion, see Osmer and Schweitzer, *Religious Education*, part 2.
45. Moltmann, *Spirit of Life*, 3.
46. Ibid., 31.
47. Ibid., 29.
48. See John Dewey, *Democracy and Education: An Introduction to the Philosophy of Education* (New York: Free Press, 1916).
49. Moltmann, *Spirit of Life*, 27–28. In his very brief discussion of the religious dimension of experience, Moltmann draws on both Martin Luther and Paul Tillich.
50. Ibid., 35.
51. Ibid., 73–76.
52. Jürgen Moltmann, *The Coming of God: Christian Eschatology* (Minneapolis: Fortress Press, 1996), 267–79.
53. See Moltmann, *Spirit of Life*, part 2.
54. Ibid., 82.
55. See ibid., chap. 5.
56. See ibid., chap. 6.
57. Ibid., 161.
58. Ibid., 171.

Chapter 9: Catechesis

1. See Stephen E. Fowl, *Engaging Scripture: A Model for Theological Interpretation* (Oxford: Blackwell, 1998), chap. 7.
2. George Gallup, *Surveying the Religious Landscape: Trends in U.S. Beliefs* (Harrisburg, PA: Morehouse Publishing Co., 1999), 51.
3. Richard Hays, *The Moral Vision of the New Testament: A Contemporary Introduction to New Testament Ethics* (San Francisco: HarperSanFrancisco, 1996), 298.
4. See particularly Paul Ricoeur, *Interpretation Theory* (Fort Worth, TX: Texas Christian University, 1976), chap. 3; *The Rule of Metaphor: Multi-disciplinary Studies of the Creation of Meaning in Language* (Toronto: University of Toronto Press, 1977), chaps. 6–8; and *Time and Narrative*, vol. 1 (Chicago: University of Chicago Press, 1984), 52–87.
5. In biblical studies, this is explicated in helpful ways by Hays, *Moral Vision of the New Testament*, 5–7, 296–306; and Steven Kraftchick, "A Necessary Detour: Paul's Metaphorical Understanding of the Philippian Hymn," *Horizons in Biblical Theology* 15, no. 1 (1993): 1–37.
6. Luke Timothy Johnson, *Scripture and Discernment: Decision Making in the Church* (Nashville: Abingdon Press, 1983), 89ff.
7. Ibid., 105.
8. Hays, *Echoes of Scripture in the Letters of Paul*, 108.
9. Ibid.
10. Fowl, *Engaging Scripture*, 114.
11. See Wesley Kort, *Take, Read: Scripture, Textuality, and Cultural Practice* (University Park, PA: Pennsylvania State University Press, 1996); and Brian Blount, *Cultural Interpretation: Reorienting New Testament Criticism* (Minneapolis: Fortress Press, 1995).
12. See Suzanne Braden, *The First Year: Incorporating New Members* (Nashville: Discipleship Resources, 1987); and Roy Oswald and Speed Leas, *The Inviting Church: A Study of New Member Assimilation* (Washington, DC: Alban Institute, 1987).
13. See Jane Carew, *Making Disciples: A Comprehensive Catechesis for the RCIA Cat-*

echumenate (Huntington, IN: Our Sunday Visitor, 1997). For a description of the catechumenal approach in the Evangelical Lutheran Church of America, see *Welcome to Christ: A Lutheran Introduction to the Catechumenate*; *Welcome to Christ: A Lutheran Catechetical Guide*; *Welcome to Christ: Rites for the Catechumenate*. All of these resources were published by Augsburg Fortress Press in 1997.

14. See Thomas Luckman, *The Invisible Religion: The Problem of Religion in Modern Society* (New York: Macmillan, 1967); and Phillip Hammond, *Religion and Personal Autonomy: The Third Disestablishment in America* (Columbia, SC: University of South Carolina Press, 1992).

Chapter 10: Exhortation

1. See Paul Ricoeur, *Oneself as Another* (Chicago: University of Chicago Press, 1992). For an especially helpful interpretation of Ricoeur's model, see Johannes van der Ven, *Formation of the Moral Self* (Grand Rapids: Wm. B. Eerdmans, 1998); and Don Browning, "The Family and Moral and Spiritual Development," in *Developing a Public Faith* (St. Louis: Chalice Press, 2003).

2. See Lawrence Kohlberg, *The Philosophy of Moral Development: Moral Stages and the Idea of Justice* (San Francisco: Harper & Row, 1981); and Jürgen Habermas, *Moral Consciousness and Communicative Action* (Cambridge, MA: MIT Press, 1990).

3. William Damon, *The Moral Child* (New York: Free Press, 1988), 14.

4. See Fowler, *Faithful Change*, part 2.

5. See Kohlberg, *Philosophy of Moral Development*; Habermas, *Moral Consciousness and Communicative Action*; James Rest et al., *Postconventional Moral Thinking: A Neo-Kohlbergian Approach* (Mahwah, NJ: L. Erlbaum Associates, 1999); and Robert Selman, *The Growth of Interpersonal Understanding: Developmental and Clinical Analyses* (New York: Academic Press, 1980).

6. See, e.g., George Lakoff, *Women, Fire, and Dangerous Things: What Categories Reveal about the Mind* (Chicago: University of Chicago Press, 1987); Mark Johnson, *The Body in the Mind: The Bodily Basis of Meaning, Imagination, and Reason* (Chicago: University of Chicago Press, 1987); and George Lakoff and Mark Johnson, *Metaphors We Live By* (Chicago: University of Chicago Press, 1980).

7. Mark Johnson, *Moral Imagination: Implications of Cognitive Science for Ethics* (Chicago: University of Chicago Press, 1993).

8. Ibid., 8, 78–79, and 189–92.

9. Ibid., 9, 192.

10. Ibid., chap. 7.

11. Ibid., 105–6.

12. Van der Ven, *Formation of the Moral Self*, 52.

13. James Wilson, *The Moral Sense* (New York: Free Press, 1993), 79.

14. See David Farrington et al., "Long-term Criminal Outcomes of Hyperactivity-Impulsivity-Attention Deficit and Conduct Problems in Childhood," in *Straight and Devious Pathways from Childhood to Adulthood*, ed. Lee Robins and Michael Rutter (Cambridge: Cambridge University Press, 1990), 62–81.

15. Van der Ven, *Formation of the Moral Self*, 56–62.

16. Ibid., 48–52.

17. This Kantian strategy takes a variety of forms. See Ronald Green, *Religious Reason* (New York: Oxford University Press, 1978); Max Stackhouse, "Reflections on 'Universal Absolutes,'" *Journal of Law and Religion* 14, no. 1 (1999–2000): 97–112; Kohlberg, *Philosophy of Moral Development*; and Habermas, *Moral Consciousness and Communicative Action*.

18. This compatibility extends to Johnson's description of the cognitive function of rules and principles and the derivation of inclusive moral ideals from the historical experience and moral traditions. I do not, however, follow Johnson's justification of his position in terms of philosophical pragmatism.

19. See Wilson, *Moral Sense*.

20. See Daniel Elazar, *Covenant and Polity in Biblical Israel: Biblical Foundations and Jewish Expressions* (New Brunswick, NJ: Transactions Press, 1995); *Covenant and Commonwealth* (New Brunswick, NJ: Transactions Press, 1996); *Covenant and Constitutionalism* (New Brunswick, NJ: Transactions Press, 1998); and *Covenant and Civil Society* (New Brunswick, NJ: Transactions Press, 1998).

21. See Jon Levenson, *Sinai and Zion: An Entry into the Jewish Bible* (San Francisco: Harper & Row, 1985).

22. See, e.g., Joseph Allen, *Love and Conflict: A Covenantal Model of Christian Ethics* (Lanham, MD: University Press of America, 1995), 18–32.

23. See Max Stackhouse, "Religion, Society, and the Independent Sector: Key Elements of a General Theory," in *Religion, the Independent Sector, and American Culture*, ed. Conrad Cherry and R. A. Sherrill (Atlanta: Scholars Press, 1992), 11–30.

24. See Allen, *Love and Conflict*, chap. 2.

25. Browning, *Fundamental Practical Theology*, 158–60, 187–90; Louis Janssens, "Norms and Priorities in a Love Ethics," *Louvain Studies* 6 (1977): 207–38; Gene Outka, *Agape: An Ethical Analysis* (New Haven, CT: Yale University Press, 1972).

26. See Thomas Lickona, *Raising Good Children* (New York: Bantam Books, 1985).

27. See Andrew Purves, *The Search for Compassion: Spirituality and Ministry* (Louisville, KY: Westminster/John Knox Press, 1989). Purves distinguishes sympathy (and other terms) from compassion more sharply than I do here.

28. For an excellent discussion of these issues, see Eugene Roehlkepartain et al., *Growing Up Generous: Engaging Youth in Giving and Serving* (Washington, DC: Alban Institute, 2000).

29. John de Gruchy, *Reconciliation: Restoring Justice* (Minneapolis: Fortress Press, 2002), 26–27.

30. Comprehensive theories of peacemaking often work with three interrelated concepts of peace. *Positive peace* indicates a state of social harmony associated with justice; *negative peace* indicates the absence of these conditions, leading to distrust, tension, conflict, and war; *authentic peace* is a utopian image of a world of perfect peace and social harmony. See Kenneth Boulding, *Stable Peace* (Beverly Hills, CA: Sage, 1978); and Betty Reardon, *Comprehensive Peace Education: Educating for Global Responsibility* (New York: Teachers College Press, 1988), esp. chap. 2.

31. See Glen Stassen, *Just Peacemaking: Transforming Initiatives for Justice and Peace* (Louisville, KY: Westminster/John Knox Press, 1992); and Stassen, ed., *Just Peacemaking: Ten Practices for Abolishing War* (Cleveland: Pilgrim Press, 1998).

32. Duane Fiesen et al., "Just Peacemaking as a New Ethic," in Stassen, *Just Peacemaking: Ten Practices*, 9–10.

33. See, e.g., Edie Luther, ed., *Doing Peacemaking: Implementing the Commitment to Peacemaking in Your Congregation* (Louisville, KY: Presbyterian Peacemaking Program, 1998).

34. See David Steele et al., "Use Cooperative Conflict Resolution," in Stassen, *Just Peacemaking: Ten Practices*, 53–76. See also D. Sandole and H. Van der Merwe, eds., *Conflict Resolution Theory and Practice* (Manchester: Manchester University Press, 1993); and Richard Cohen, *Students Resolving Conflicts: Peer Mediation in Schools* (Glenview, IL: Scott Foresman, 1995).

35. Matt. 5:44; Luke 6:28; Rom. 12:12, 14.
36. Glen Stassen, "Take Independent Initiatives to Reduce Threat," in *Just Peacemaking*, ed. Stassen, chap. 2.
37. See Gregory Jones, *Embodying Forgiveness: A Theological Analysis* (Grand Rapids: Wm. B. Eerdmans, 1995).
38. De Gruchy, *Reconciliation*, 193–94.
39. Ibid., 108–12.
40. Ibid., chap. 1.
41. My thinking about these matters is influenced by Brown, *Good Taste, Bad Taste*; John W. de Gruchy, *Christianity, Art, and Transformation: Theological Aesthetics in the Struggle for Justice* (Cambridge: Cambridge University Press, 2001); and Moltmann, *Theology and Joy*.
42. Brown, *Good Taste, Bad Taste*, 24.
43. See de Gruchy, *Christianity, Art, and Transformation*, chap. 3.
44. Christine Pohl, *Making Room: Recovering Hospitality as a Christian Tradition* (Grand Rapids: Wm. B. Eerdmans, 1999), 19.
45. Ibid.; see chap. 4.
46. The background of my understanding of hope is Moltmann's *Theology of Hope* and *Coming of God*. Also important is Richard Bauckham and Trevor Hart, *Hope against Hope: Christian Eschatology at the Turn of the Millennium* (Grand Rapids: Wm. B. Eerdmans, 1999). This initial definition of hope draws on their comments on p. 52.
47. Bauckham and Hart, *Hope against Hope*, 86.
48. See Thomas Lickona, *Educating for Character: How Schools Can Teach Respect and Responsibility* (New York: Bantam, 1992), chaps. 7–8.
49. See Colin Manlove, *The Fantasy Literature of England* (New York: Palgrave, 1999), chap. 3.
50. See Don Browning, *The Moral Context of Pastoral Care* (Philadelphia: Fortress Press, 1976), chaps. 2–3.
51. See Robert Browning and Roy Reed, *Models of Confirmation and Baptismal Affirmation* (Birmingham, AL: Religious Education Press, 1995).

Chapter 11: Discernment

1. Among the many books in which John Dewey treats this topic, see *How We Think* (Boston: D. C. Heath, 1910).
2. See Damasio, *Feeling of What Happens*.
3. See Walter Brueggemann, *The Prophetic Imagination* (Philadelphia: Fortress Press, 1978).
4. Paul Wadell, *Becoming Friends: Worship, Justice, and the Practice of Friendship* (Grand Rapids: Brazos Press, 2002), 45–46.
5. See Janet Eyler and Dwight Giles, *Where's the Learning in Service-Learning?* (San Francisco: Jossey-Bass, 1999).
6. See Roberta Hestenes, *Using the Bible in Groups* (Philadelphia: Westminster Press, 1983); David Johnson and Frank Johnson, *Joining Together: Group Theory and Group Skills* (Englewood Cliffs, NJ: Prentice-Hall, 1982); and Gareth Icenogle, *Biblical Foundations for Small Group Ministry: An Integrational Approach* (Downers Grove, IL: InterVarsity Press, 1994).
7. See, e.g., George Parsons and Speed Leas, *Understanding Your Congregation as a System* (Washington, DC: Alban Institute, 1993).
8. See Nancey Murphy's overview in *Theology in an Age of Scientific Reasoning* (Ithaca, NY: Cornell University Press, 1990), 154–57.

9. Charles Olsen, *Transforming Church Board into Communities of Spiritual Leaders* (Washington, DC: Alban Institute, 1995).

10. For the sake of clarity, it is probably important to point out that Olsen uses the term *discernment* in a more restricted sense than I do.

11. The literature is vast. Here is a sampling, in addition to those works cited in subsequent notes: Henry Nouwen, *Reaching Out: The Three Movements of the Spiritual Life* (Garden City, NY: Doubleday, 1975); Elizabeth O'Connor, *Journey Inward, Journey Outward* (New York: Harper & Row, 1968); Parker Palmer, *The Active Life: A Spirituality of Work, Creativity, and Caring* (San Francisco: Jossey-Bass, 1999); Suzanne Farnham, *Listening Hearts: Discerning Call in Community* (Harrisburg, PA: Morehouse Publishing Co., 1991); Margaret Guenther, *The Practice of Prayer* (Cambridge, MA: Cowley Publications, 1998); Kent Groff, *Active Spirituality: A Guide for Seekers and Ministers* (Bethesda, MD: Alban Institute, 1993).

12. Marjorie Thompson, *Soul Feast: An Invitation to the Christian Spiritual Life* (Louisville, KY: Westminster John Knox Press, 1995), 6.

13. Ibid., 8.

14. Rose Mary Dougherty, *Group Spiritual Direction: Community for Discernment* (New York: Paulist Press, 1995), 2. Cf. Novene Vest, *Gathered in the Word: Praying the Scripture in Small Groups* (Nashville: Upper Room, 1996).

15. Ibid., 24.

16. Ibid., 25–26.

17. Kenneth Leech, *Soul Friend: An Invitation to Spiritual Direction* (New York: HarperCollins, 1980), 190–91.

18. Betty Shannon Cloyd, *Children and Prayer: A Shared Pilgrimage* (Nashville: Upper Room, 1997). These guidelines are taken from her excellent and helpful book.

Epilogue

1. See Norman Denizin, *The Research Act,* 2nd ed. (Englewood Cliffs, NJ: Prentice-Hall, 1989), 237–41; Uwe Flick, "Triangulation Revisited: Strategy of or Alternative to Validation of Qualitative Data," *Journal for the Theory of Social Behavior* 22 (1992): 175–97; and Flick, *An Introduction to Qualitative Research,* 2nd ed. (Thousand Oaks, CA: Sage Publications, 2002), 226–27.

2. See the appendix in Don Browning et al., *From Culture Wars to Common Ground: Religion and the American Family Debate* (Louisville, KY: Westminster John Knox Press, 1997), for a good introduction to interpretive social science. Barney Glaser especially emphasizes the emergent nature of theory out of empirical research in his account of grounded theory. See Glaser, *Basics of Grounded Theory Analysis: Emergence vs Forcing* (Mill Valley, CA: Sociology Press, 1992). From the perspective of interpretive social science, Glaser's approach seems hermeneutically naive.

3. See Chris Hermans, *Participatory Learning: Religious Education in a Globalizing Society* (Boston: Brill, 2003). Don Browning, *Pluralism and Personality: William James and Some Contemporary Cultures of Psychology* (Lewisburg, PA: Bucknell University Press, 1980); Browning, *Fundamental Practical Theology;* and Marcel Viau, *Practical Theology: A New Approach* (Boston: Brill, 1999).

4. See Deborah van Deusen Hunsinger, *Theology and Pastoral Counseling: A New Interdisciplinary Approach* (Grand Rapids: Wm. B. Eerdmans, 1995).

5. Osmer, "New Clue for Religious Education?"

6. See Paul Tillich, *Systematic Theology*, vol. 1 (Chicago: University of Chicago Press, 1951); Tracy, *Blessed Rage for Order;* Browning, *Fundamental Practical The-*

ology; Rebecca Chopp, *The Power to Speak: Feminism, Language, God* (New York: Crossroad, 1989); and Mathew Lamb, *Solidarity with Victims: Toward a Theology of Social Transformation* (New York: Crossroad, 1982).

7. See James Loder, *The Logic of the Spirit: Human Development in Theological Perspective* (San Francisco: Jossey-Bass, 1998); Deborah van Deusen Hunsinger, *Theology and Pastoral Counseling*; and Hans Frei, *Types of Christian Theology*, ed. George Hunsinger and William Placher (New Haven, CT: Yale University Press, 1992).

8. See Calvin Schrag, *The Resources of Rationality: A Response to the Postmodern Challenge* (Bloomington, IN: Indiana University Press, 1992); Wentzel van Huyssteen, *The Shaping of Rationality: Toward Interdisciplinarity in Theology and Science* (Grand Rapids: Wm. B. Eerdmans, 1999); Wolfgang Welsch, *Vernunft: Die zeitgenössische Vernunftkritik und das Konzept der transversalen Vernunft* (Frankfurt: Suhrkamp, 1995). A number of Welsch's articles are now available in English online at http://www2.uni-jena.de/welsch/start.html. See particularly, "Reason and Transition: On the Concept of Transversal Reason."

9. This image was prompted (with much creative license on my part) by Ursula LeGuin's *The Farthest Shore* (New York: Bantam Books, 1972), the third volume of her Earthsea Trilogy (to which she later added two more books and a volume of short stories). See the chapter "The Children of the Open Sea."

10. See Schrag, *Resources of Rationality*; and van Huyssteen, *Shaping of Rationality*. The idea that rationality includes cognitive, evaluative, and pragmatic dimensions is developed in Nicholas Rescher, *Rationality: A Philosophical Inquiry into the Nature and the Rationale of Reason* (Oxford: Clarendon Press, 1988).

11. Van Huyssteen, *Shaping of Rationality*, 116. See also his discussion of evolutionary epistemology in van Huyssteen, *Duet or Duel? Theology and Science in a Postmodern World* (London: SCM Press, 1998).

12. Van Huyssteen, *Shaping of Rationality*, 143. In forming this concept of rational judgment, van Huyssteen is especially in dialogue with Harold Brown, *Rationality* (London: Routledge, 1990).

13. The final two elements, articulation and disclosure, are found in Schrag, *Resources of Rationality*.

14. For a discussion of the different orientations of dialogue and argumentation, see William Isaacs, *Dialogue and the Art of Thinking Together* (New York: Currency Books, 1999); and Stephen Toulmin, *The Uses of Argument* (Cambridge: Cambridge University Press, 1964).

15. Paul Tillich, *Theology of Culture* (New York: Oxford University Press, 1959). See particularly his chapter on psychoanalysis and existentialism.

16. See Catherine Mowry Lacugna, *God for Us: The Trinity and Christian Life* (San Francisco: HarperSanFrancisco, 1991).

17. See my discussion of Moltmann in chapter 9.

18. Wentzel van Huyssteen, *Are We Alone?* (Grand Rapids: Wm. B. Eerdmans, forthcoming). This is the working title of his Gifford lectures.

19. For an extended treatment of chimpanzees, see Mithen, *Prehistory of the Mind*, and of dolphins, Alasdair MacIntyre, *Rational Dependent Animals: Why Human Beings Need the Virtues* (Chicago: Open Court, 1999).

Name Index

Subject Index